Refugees:
A World Report

Refugees:
A World Report

Edited by Lester A. Sobel

Contributing editors: Doug Grant, Christopher Hunt,
Hal Kosut, Chris Larson, Melinda Maidens,
John Minor

Indexer: Grace M. Ferrara

Facts On File
119 West 57th Street, New York, N.Y. 10019

Refugees: A World Report

Library of Congress Cataloging in Publication Data

Main entry under title:

Refugees, a world report

    Includes index.
    1. Refugees. 2. Refugees, Political.
I. Sobel, Lester A.   II. Grant, Alexander,
HV640.R43   361.5'3   79-16981
ISBN 0-87196-296-9

9 8 7 6 5 4 3 2 1
PRINTED IN
THE UNITED STATES OF AMERICA

Contents

Page

INTRODUCTION 1

The Century of Refugees 1

INDOCHINA 6

War & Aftermath Create Millions of Refugees 6
War's End Increases Refugee Swarms 11
U.S. Aids Refugee Resettlement 19
Refugee Flow Continues 23

AFRICA 31

Continent of Refugees 31
Biafran Secession 32
Angola 37
Mozambique 41
Burundi 42
Horn of Africa 45
Rhodesia/Zimbabwe 50
South Africa & Namibia 61
Uganda 64
Zairian Exiles Invade Shaba 70
Other Developments 74

THE PALESTINIAN REFUGEES 76

Origin & Growth of the Palestinian Refugee Problem 76
Tensions Mount in 1970s 82
'Black September': Jordanian Forces Break
    Commando Challenge 86
Widespread Violence 94
Refugee/Guerrilla Organization 102
The U.N. & the Palestinians 104
War in Lebanon 107
Terrorism Continues, Attitudes Remain Unchanged 113

COMMUNIST WORLD 116

Soviet Union 116
Bulgaria 116
China 134
Czechoslovakia 135
East Germany 138
Hungary 141
Poland 141
Rumania 142
Yugoslavia 143

LATIN AMERICA 146

Argentina 146
Bolivia 148
Chile 149
Cuba 154
Ecuador 156
Haiti 157
Mexico 159
Nicaragua 159
Paraguay 161
Peru 161
Uruguay 164
Venezuela 162

OTHER REFUGEES 165

    Burma 165
    Cyprus 165
    Netherlands 166
    India, Pakistan & Bangladesh 168
    Taiwan 170

INDEX 171

Introduction

'The Century of Refugees . . .'

THE GERMAN NOVELIST HEINRICH BOLL described the Twentieth Century as "the century of refugees and prisoners." Imprisonment, of course, is not a distinctly Twentieth Century phenomenon. Neither is flight to escape persecution, oppression or danger. The world has indeed seen much of both during this century, especially since the victory of communism in Russia and the rise of fascism and Nazism in Italy and Germany. But refugees have been fleeing their tormentors since the earliest days of civilization.

History records many aspects of the tragic story of the refugee. Spain created thousands of refugees by expelling Jews and Moors in 1492. Ironically, perhaps fittingly, this took place in the very year in which Columbus, acting on behalf of Spain, discovered a New World—a world that was to provide asylum for thousands of religious and political refugees of the Old World during the next five centuries.

For sheer numbers, however, the Twentieth Century does take first place in the problem of refugees. The Twentieth Century has had its full share of war and revolution, which are ideal circumstances for driving frightened people into flight. About a million and a half Russians became refugees after the Bolshevik revolution of 1917. Thousands of Armenians and Greeks fled Turkish atrocities in the 1920s. Jews and anti-Nazis fled in the 1930s after Adolf Hitler and his Nazi followers came into power in Germany and Austria. Benito Mussolini's rise in Italy resulted in similar flight by anti-fascist Italians. Francisco Franco's victory in Spain in 1939 also produced a stream of refugees. World War II finally turned the various streams into a flood of refugees and displaced persons. It is estimated that in Europe alone some 70 million people were driven from their homes by the two world wars.

Following World War I and the creation of the League of Nations, Fridtjof Nansen had been named by the league in 1921 as its high commissioner for refugee work. His International Office for Refugees and the International Labor Organization spent years on the problem, and Nansen passports enabled stateless wanderers to cross national boundaries in search of asylum. More than a decade later, after Nazi and fascist persecutions sent fresh thousands into flight, a conference of 32 nations was held on the problem in France in 1938, and a permanent international committee was formed later in London. Following World War II, the United Nations Relief & Rehabilitation Administration (UNRRA) was created to care for about eight million Europeans displaced from their homes.

The eventual resettlement of most refugees of World War II did not end the Twentieth Century's refugee problems. The partition of India in 1947 created a massive new refugee situation. Many Jewish refugees who survived the European Holocaust found their way to Palestine, where the Arab-Israeli war of 1948-49 produced several hundred thousand Palestinian Arab refugees. A high birth rate and the 1967 Arab-Israeli war increased the number of Palestinian refugees to perhaps two million (authorities agree on no number).

The Communist victory in China sent a stream of Chinese refugees from the mainland to Taiwan, Hong Kong, Singapore and other places of asylum. Refugees from East Germany flocked into West Germany until the East German government blocked such departures by turning the borders into no-man's-lands of fences, barbed wire, mines and quick-on-the-trigger guards where death could be the price of an attempted flight. Similar precautions were taken to prevent refugees from leaving other Communist countries of East Europe. The fighting in Korea put perhaps nine million refugees to flight. Some 700,000 refugees left Cuba after Fidel Castro and his Communist regime took power in 1959. About ten million people became refugees, at least temporarily, in 1971 as a result of the India-Pakistan fighting. The long war in Indochina turned more millions into refugees, and the problem of these refugees still troubles the world. Meanwhile, in Africa, where war, revolution and unrest are a legacy of colonialism, the number of refugees and displaced persons at times approaches four million.

After the UNRRA ended, the United Nations created an International Refugee Organization to continue what had become an unending task. Then, in 1951, the Office of the United Nations High Commissioner for Refugees (UNHCR) was established to protect and aid refugees throughout the world. The statute creating the Office of the UNHCR defined refugees qualifying for UNHCR assistance as persons who are outside of their country of nationality or habitual residence and are unwilling to return to such country because of well-founded fear of persecution on the grounds of political, religious, racial, nationality or social identity or ties. Since 1957, the U.N. General Assembly has passed a series of resolutions authorizing the High Commissioner to use his good offices on behalf of refugees outside the UNHCR mandate.

The general objectives of the UNHCR are to provide legal protection for refugees, to find permanent solutions to refugee problems and to supply interim care in emergency situations. In the early years of the organization, the program of assistance concentrated on the problem in Western Europe, where there were large numbers of refugees. In more recent years, refugee problems in Africa and Latin America required a shift in emphasis. In 1975 the events in Indochina created a large new group of refugees that required the attention and resources of the UNHCR. The U.N. High Commissioner in the following years devoted much attention to the legal protection function of his office. The dramatic problem of Indochinese refugees fleeing from the Indochina peninsula in often unseaworthy boats was a subject of the UNHCR's particular concern.

The number of refugees and displaced persons increased in Africa during 1976-78. The UNHCR estimated in his 1978 report that there were at least 3.7 million refugees and displaced persons on the continent by the end of 1977. It was said a year later that one out of every 80 Africans was a refugee. In Asia, the UNHCR was aiding 3.9 million refugees and displaced persons by the end of 1977; the caseload continued to rise in 1978-79 as refugees fled from Cambodia to Thailand and Vietnam and as refugee "boat people" sought asylum in frequently inhospitable countries. According to the UNHCR's 1978 report, the refugee population in Latin America had declined from 112,000 at the end of 1976 to approximately 108,000 at the end of 1977; those of Latin American origin numbered only about 29,000, the rest being almost entirely European. There were still about 546,000 refugees in Europe.

One major group of refugees for whom the UNHCR has no responsibility is the Arab Palestinians, most of whom had fled to Jordan, Lebanon, other Arab states and the Gaza Strip. The task of aiding this group was given by the United Nations to the U.N. Relief & Works Agency for Palestine Refugees in the Near East (UNRWA), which was established Dec. 8, 1949. The resolution creating the UNRWA directed it to carry out a program of direct relief and works in collaboration with local governments for refugees of the 1948-49 Arab-Israeli conflict. The Fifth U.N. General Assembly Dec. 2, 1950 assigned to the UNRWA the further responsibility of seeking the reintegration of the refugees into the economic life of the Near East either by repatriation or resettlement. The Assembly has periodically extended the UNRWA's mandate. Responding to the situation resulting from the Arab-Israeli conflict of June 1967, the U.N. General Assembly, at its Fifth Emergency Special Session, approved July 4, 1967 a resolution that "endorsed" the efforts of the UNRWA to provide "humanitarian assistance, as far as practicable, on an emergency basis and as a temporary measure," to other persons in the area who were displaced and in serious need of immediate assistance as a result of the hostilities. The Assembly has repeatedly reaffirmed this resolution.

As the decade of the 1970s reached its closing year, Sen. Edward M. Kennedy (D, Mass.) observed in the March 4, 1979 issue of *Newsweek* that "refugees have become a worldwide phenomenon—of countless men, women and children forced to leave their homes for as many reasons as there are behind the violence and conflict among people and nations. Yet today this drama is of greater and more pressing dimension than at anytime in recent years. . . . There are now more refugees needing homes in new countries than since the worst days after World War II."

Kennedy's concern over the problem of refugees is not a new one for him. Nine years earlier (May 28, 1970) he had told the Senate that "the troubles of our time are taking a growing toll in the flight of people from conflict and oppression. All over the world people are on the move." In this statement, made as the decade of the 1970s was beginning, Kennedy referred to a report of the U.S. Committee for Refugees (USCR).

"Since 1945," it was noted in the USCR report, ". . . there have been 75 wars. . . . [T]here remain today 17,318,320 refugees who are, in very large part, the casualties of a world in conflict. Of course, many millions of refugees have been resettled and are no longer refugees, but, from the wars' awful toll, others have been forced to take their places in this grim roster of human suffering. In the last six years since 1964, the total refugee population of the world has grown from 7,910,309. . . . We believe that there is a relationship between our warring and the number of refugees in the world. In any event, the shocking number of refugees on every continent is tragic evidence of man's inability to manage himself, his religion, his politics and his hungers with due concern for his fellow man. . . ."

This book is intended as a record of developments in the worldwide refugee problem during the 1970s. The material that follows consists principally of the account compiled by FACTS ON FILE in its ongoing examination of world affairs. Although much of this information is controversial, a conscientious effort was made to keep this volume free of bias and to produce a balanced and accurate reference tool.

LESTER A. SOBEL

New York, N.Y.
April, 1979

Indochina

War & Aftermath Create Millions of Refugees

Some four decades of war have turned many of the people of Vietnam, Cambodia and Laos into refugees. No estimate of the number can be regarded as accurate, but it is certain that the total over these years must amount to several million.

Many Indochinese have become refugees twice or even more often as the fortunes of war or politics have on occasion frightened them into flight, lulled them into efforts at peaceful return to their homes or persuaded them to attempt resettlement elsewhere. During the decade of the 1970s, it is estimated, most years have had at least a half million Indochinese living as refugees or displaced persons.

The departure of the U.S.' forces from Indochina, in 1973, and the victory of the North Vietnamese Communists, in 1975, did not end either fighting or the uprooting of people there. During the years that followed the U.S. departure and the defeat of the South Vietnamese regime, the killing and the displacement of Indochinese continued.

Vietnamese massacred in Cambodia. Bodies of hundreds of Vietnamese civilian residents of Cambodia, suspected victims of a mass killing, floated down the Mekong River in the southeastern part of the country April 11–17, 1970. Another 100 Vietnamese civilians were reported slain in a Cambodian government compound in Takeo April 16. The deaths resulted in a move to shift more than 50,000 Vietnamese as displaced persons from Cambodia to Vietnam.

The first bodies were sighted on the Mekong April 11 at a ferry landing at Neak Leung, 36 miles southeast of Pnompenh. A police official at Neak Leung reported counting 400 bodies April 15. Other sources said as many as 1,000 bodies had been seen in the river. Most of the victims were men. Many had their hands tied behind their backs.

A Reuters dispatch April 17 quoted witnesses as saying that the Vietnamese had been shot to death on Tachhor, a small island in the Mekong four miles upstream from Neak Leung. According to the witnesses, farmers and fishermen nearby, the shootings had started on the island April 10 after the arrival from the direction of Pnompenh of a passenger boat containing about 100 Cambodians and Vietnamese escorted by Cambodian soldiers. The disembarkation from boats followed by the shooting of the civilians continued for five successive nights, the reports said.

The Cambodian Information Ministry said April 14 that the killings were "not the result of collective assassination perpetrated by Cambodian armed forces." The ministry said the civilians had been caught inside their detention camp "between the firing of the Viet Cong invaders and the Cambodian forces defending" the village of Prasot. The statement noted that the Viet Cong had frequently "used Vietnamese residents of Cambodia as auxiliaries of their aggression."

Information Minister Trinh Heanh reiterated April 16 that the corpses sighted in the Mekong River "were victims of a battle" between the Viet Cong and Cambodian troops. He said the dead included Cambodians and Vietnamese civilians who had been thrown into the river by the Viet Cong after the fighting.

The Pnopmpenh government reportedly had been fomenting a campaign against both the Vietnamese residents of Cambodia and the Vietnamese Communist invaders since the ouster of Prince Norodom Sihanouk March 18. The Cambodians and the Annamese of Vietnam had been traditional enemies. Government planes April 11 had dropped leaflets on Pnompenh recalling a historic massacre "when the Khmers [Cambodians] once rose up and killed all Annamites on Cambodian territory in one night."

A Cambodian government statement April 19 denied a campaign was in progress against Vietnamese civilians in the country. It said the drive was directed only at Viet Cong and North Vietnamese invaders and not "against the peaceful Vietnamese . . . as long as they do not seek to trouble public order."

In an earlier mass slaying of Vietnamese in Prasot, previously reported April 10, the Associated Press said April 15 that available evidence showed the killings had been perpetrated by Cambodian troops.

In the incident at Takeo, about 150 Vietnamese civilians, herded under detention in a school building April 13, came under fire by Cambodian soldiers April 16. About 100, including perhaps 30 children, were killed. The account of the slaughter was related to foreign newsmen who visited the scene April 17 by some of the 50 survivors. The survivors said they had given no provocation and did not know why the shootings took place. Soldiers on guard at the school, who did not contradict the account of the slayings, indicated that the killings were in reprisal for a Viet Cong attack on Takeo April 15.

South Vietnamese Foreign Minister Tran Van Lam told a news conference April 17 that his government was asking Pnompenh to receive an official mission to arrange for the repatriation of 50,000 Vietnamese. Lam said 1,467 Vietnamese refugees had been registered by South Vietnamese border officials since March 18. He said several times that number had probably crossed into South Vietnam without authorization.

More than 200 refugees arrived in Saigon April 27 at the start of an airlift. Another group of refugees had flown to Saigon April 26 aboard a plane carrying a five-man South Vietnamese delegation that had discussed the repatriation plan that day with Cambodian officials in Pnompenh.

Some 30 U.S. river gunboats and 110 South Vietnamese vessels combined a military operation on the Mekong River in May with the rescue of Vietnamese refugees. Forty-seven of the boats arrived in the heart of Pnompenh May 11. The remaining fleet had returned to South Vietnam with several thousand Vietnamese refugees picked up along the banks of the Mekong since the convoy had started upstream earlier in the week.

The military and humanitarian aspects of the Mekong operation had been hastily combined after South Vietnamese Foreign Minister Tran Van Lam had inadvertently announced publicly May 7 that a fleet would be sailing up the river to rescue Vietnamese refugees. Lam was said to have been unaware that a military operation also was planned for this area.

Refugee pullout halted—South Vietnam May 22 announced a halt in the repatriation of Vietnamese refugees in Cambodia. About 50,000–80,000 already had been removed to South Vietnam since the start of evacuation efforts May 10. About 70,000 remained stranded in assembly camps in Cambodia.

Saigon halted the refugee withdrawal because measures adopted by the Pnompenh government provided greater security for the Vietnamese residents in Cambodia, according to Pham Huy Ty, the head of South Vietnam's permanent liaison mission in Pnompenh. The second phase of the program, to be tested for 10 days, would remove Vietnamese from refugee camps to their homes in Cambodia where they would try to resume their normal routine, Ty said.

Lt. Gen. Do Cao Tri, commander of South Vietnamese troops in Cambodia, warned May 22 that "if the Cambodians should continue to mistreat our compatriots, then our army will have an appropriate action." South Vietnamese State Minister Pham Quang Dan, chairman of a committee to aid Vietnamese repatriates, said Saigon's policy "is to transfer Vietnamese from dangerous to safe areas in Cambodia. Repatriation to Vietnam will be the exception from now on."

South Vietnamese Vice President Nguyen Cao Ky conferred with Cambodian officials in Pnompenh June 4–6 on various issues. Returning to Saigon June 6, Ky said under an agreement reached with Cambodia, Saigon would accept those Vietnamese refugees who wished to return to South Vietnam. Those who decided to remain, would receive "all kinds of assurances and protection" from the Cambodian government, Ky said.

But South Vietnamese Welfare Minister Tran Ngoc Phieu announced June 8 that the repatriation of Vietnamese from Cambodia was to be resumed. Phieu, who had been chief negotiator with Cambodia on the refugee problem, said Ky's visit had paved the way for resumption of the refugee evacuation. The decision to stop the flow of the ethnic Vietnamese, Phieu said, had been prompted by political opposition in Saigon against adding to the already large refugee population in South Vietnam. Phieu said 92,000

Vietnamese had been brought out of Cambodia since April.

Refugee data scored. A U.S. General Accounting Office report Dec. 5, 1970 disputed official statistics on the war refugee relief program in South Vietnam. The report, prepared for the Senate Subcommittee on Refugees and Escapees, headed by Sen. Edward M. Kennedy (D, Mass.), labeled as "misleading" official data issued in 1969 by the Nixon Administration and the Saigon government that there had been a "dramatic" reduction in the number of refugees—a decrease from 1.4 million in February 1969 to 268,000 by December 1969.

In addition to the official refugee number, the GAO said, there were 572,000 orphans, war widows and disabled persons "in need of assistance."

The GAO's assessment of the 1970 refugee relief and social relief programs in Vietnam was that "they have not indicated encouraging results with respect to war victims and community developments." The programs, currently dealing with some 600,000 persons, handled feeding, resettlement, payment of allowances and construction of schools.

In releasing the report, Kennedy said the conclusions reflected a "warped sense of reality and progress which pervades so much of our country's activities throughout Indochina."

Kennedy released a GAO report to his panel Dec. 12 citing shortages of skilled medical help, deficient facilities and a lack of reliable statistics concerning the South Vietnamese civilian health and war-related casualty programs. It said official figures on civilian casualties, a total of 245,700 since 1967, reflected only admissions to South Vietnamese Health Ministry and U.S. military hospitals and omitted any helped elsewhere or dead of wounds before treatment. The subcommittee estimated the total of civilian casualties since 1965 at more than a million, including at least 300,000 dead.

Kennedy said the data made "a mockery of our government's claim about conditions among Vietnamese civilians, and about the progress of the Saigon government" in dealing with the problem.

(A Quaker antiwar demonstrator outside the White House Dec. 24 said reports from field workers in Vietnam indicated that "the list of refugees is growing all the time." The comment came from Bronson P. Clark, executive secretary of the American Friends Service Committee, which was staging a Christmas Eve vigil to dramatize its report condemning the Administration's Vietnamization program and U.S. policies on the war.)

Vietnamese refugees increase. The start of new allied operations in Indochina in late 1970 had resulted in a sharp increase in the number of war refugees in South Vietnam, according to U.S. Congressional sources quoted by the New York Times March 12, 1971.

The report said the U.S. mission in Saigon had informed a number of senators that the monthly number of new refugees between October 1970 and February 1971 had increased more than five times. More than 500,000 refugees were estimated to have been in camps or on relief prior to that period. The greatest upsurge was recorded between November 1970 with the advent of the dry season and February as the allies began preparing the current drives into Cambodia and Laos. The rate was estimated at 27,000 a month.

The new refugees either had been forcibly relocated to other villages by South Vietnamese troops clearing the area for impending military operations or they had been forced to abandon their homes because of U.S. bombings or ground fighting. In one instance, U.S. B-52 bombing raids and South Vietnamese troop operations in the U Minh Forest of the Mekong Delta had resulted in evacuation of about 38,000 new refugees from the area between mid-December 1970 and the last week of February 1971.

The U.S.-run Civil Operations and Rural Development Support Organization had reported that as of May 1970, there were nearly 230,000 refugees in camps in Military Region I in the north and that "most of them do not have adequate opportunities for self-support."

American officials in Saigon reported March 11 that the South Vietnamese government had abandoned plans to shift refugees from the northern to the southern part of the country because the overwhelming majority opposed being moved. Instead, the refugees were to be resettled in safer districts within their provinces. U.S. experts estimated that the number of civilians involved in the proposed move totaled hundreds of thousands.

U.S. and Saigon authorities considered the northernmost section of the country to be hardest hit by the refugee problem. Because of the devastation wrought by the severe fighting in that sector, about one million Vietnamese were said to be living in a state of deprivation.

1970 civilian death toll. At least 25,000 civilians had been killed in the war in South Vietnam in 1970 and 100,000 wounded, according to a report made public March 14, 1971 by Sen. Robert F. Kennedy, chairman of the Senate Subcommittee on Refugees & Escapees.

The Senate panel also estimated that civilian casualties in Laos were now exceeding 30,000 a year, including more than 10,000 dead.

Laos refugee aid diverted. Sen. Edward M. Kennedy charged Feb. 6, 1971 that American assistance for war refugees in Laos was being supplied to guerrilla forces directed by the Central Intelligence Agency. "Until recent times," he said, "the U.S. AID [Agency for International Development] refugee program was simply a euphemism to cover American assistance to persons who agreed to take up arms against the [Communist] Pathet Lao."

"A very significant measure of this assistance apparently continues," Kennedy said. Such activity had been disclosed in 1970.

The information was based on reports from the General Accounting Office which were released by Kennedy's Senate Refugees and Escapees Subcommittee. The reports said "substantial amounts" of medical supplies were being furnished "Lao military" by AID.

U.S. hearings on refugees. Sen. Edward M. Kennedy and his Senate Subcommittee on Refugees & Escapees began hearings in Washington, D.C. April 21, 1971 on the Indochina refugee situation.

In opening his hearing, Kennedy said the U.S. military activity, especially the air war, was contributing to a "blood-bath" and "agony" among "a rapidly growing number of civilians in Vietnam, Laos and Cambodia." He said the war operations, and largely the U.S.-supported operations, had spawned 150,000 refugees since November 1970. His view contrasted with testimony by William E. Colby, who was in charge of the pacification program in South Vietnam, that the refugee problem had decreased "enormously" in the last two or three years.

Opening testimony before the Kennedy panel was given April 21 by Rep. Paul N. McCloskey (R, Calif.), who recently returned from an eight-day trip to Indochina, including Laos. He charged that the State Department had deliberately concealed the extent of American bombing of villages in northern Laos since 1968 and that bombing was "the most compelling reason" for the refugee movement in Laos.

Kennedy April 22 accused witnesses representing the State Department of having no plan to help war refugees in Cambodia. One of them, William H. Sullivan, deputy assistant secretary of state for East Asian and Pacific affairs, denied that U.S. bombing was the major cause of the refugee movement in Laos, attributing the abandonment of homes to North Vietnamese offensives.

Many refugees injured—At Boston hearings held Oct. 7, 1971 by the Veterans Against the War, Sen. Kennedy said the number of civilian war victims treated in South Vietnam hospitals in the first half of 1971 had been as high as in any previous year.

Kennedy also reported that 75%–80% of refugees recently treated had fled allied bombing in Laos.

2 million Cambodians homeless. The U.S. General Accounting Office reported Feb. 5, 1972 that the Cambodian Public Health Ministry estimated that more than 2 million Cambodians had been left homeless by the fighting in that country since 1970. The GAO report quoted refugees as saying that Viet Cong and South Vietnamese forces had "looted property, destroyed what they could not carry, burned villages, and raped, beat and murdered the villagers."

Refugees flee South. In May 1972 thousands of South Vietnamese civilians fled to Danang in the wake of the North Vietnamese capture of Quangtri Province and the subsequent threat to Hue. Refugees began leaving Hue for Danang May 4 and by May 6 city authorities reported that more than 300,000 persons had poured into Danang from the northern front. The influx swelled Danang's population to more than 700,000. A U.S. official who flew over Hue May 6 estimated that 80% of the city's 200,000 residents had fled.

South Vietnamese civilians also were streaming north into Danang from Quangtin and Quangngai Provinces to the south. There had been no significant fighting there, but U.S. officials believed those refugees had also been prompted by fear.

A U.S. Administration official said in Washington May 8 that 700,000 South Vietnamese civilians had fled their homes since the start of the Communist offensive March 30. The statement was made by Robert H. Nooter of the Agency for International Development in testimony before a hearing of the Senate subcommittee on refugees.

The subcommittee reported May 24 that the civilian toll from the North Vietnamese drive exceeded the previous high—North Vietnam's 1968 Tet offensive.

The panel estimated that the enemy offensive begun in March resulted in 40,000–50,000 civilian casualties, including about 15,000 dead, by the first week in May. The number of refugees on Saigon government rolls rose during the current drive by about one million to a total of 1.5 million homeless or displaced persons.

Subcommittee Chairman Edward M. Kennedy (D, Mass.) said the "people problems in Vietnam" were greater today than at any time during the war. He called the refugee total "an appalling commentary on the Administration's policy of continuing the war."

Kennedy said June 15 that the Agency for International Development had told him that the number of new refugees created by the fighting in South Vietnam had risen by 100,000 since May 8 and that the subcommittee estimated "up to 1.2 million new refugees since April 1."

(The U.S. State Department charged Aug. 7 that North Vietnamese forces had deliberately shelled refugees fleeing Quangtri Province April 29-30, killing 1,000–2,000 of the civilians. The attacks occurred on Route 1, just north Quangtri city, the department said. The department also confirmed a report that the Communists had executed civilians in Bindinh Province.)

More refugees in Indochina. The truce agreement of 1973 and the departure of U.S. forces did not end the fighting or the flight of civilians in Vietnam. The number of new refugees resulting from the continued fighting in South Vietnam since the 1973 truce agreement totaled 1.4 million, the U.S. Senate Judiciary Committee's Subcommittee on Refugees & Escapees said in a report Jan. 25, 1975. There were 594,000 new refugees in 1974 and 43,000 civilians hospitalized because of war-related injuries, the subcommittee said.

The subcommittee estimated that at the end of 1974 there were 3.3 million refugees in Cambodia, more than half the country's population, while the continued fighting forced another 60,000 to leave their homes during the first three weeks of January.

War's End Increases Refugee Swarms

Communists win Vietnam war, U.S. aids fleeing refugees. The war in Vietnam ended April 30, 1975 as the South Vietnamese government surrendered. Hours before Viet Cong and North Vietnamese troops entered Saigon, South Vietnam's capital, the U.S. completed an emergency airlift from the city. Under orders of U.S. President Gerald R. Ford, U.S. planes removed almost all Americans remaining in Vietnam as well as thousands of Vietnamese who had reason to fear the Communist victors.

The refugee situation had begun to deteriorate the previous month as Communist gains accelerated and an ultimate Communist victory became virtually certain.

Many flee Red advance—South Vietnamese forces had begun to abandon the provinces of Kontum, Pleiku, Dar Lac and Phu Bon and the northernmost provinces of Quang Tri and Thua Thien in the wake of a mounting North Vietnamese offensive for the past two weeks, it was reported March 18 and 20. The troop pullout was followed by an exodus of hundreds of thousands of civilians who were fleeing to the safety of the coastal areas still in government hands. Residents of Hue in Thua Thien were being evacuated to Danang, just to the south, while others in the highlands, including many soldiers, were streaming from Pleiku on Route 19, the only open road leading to the coast.

The areas being given up by the government totaled about 40% of the nation's 66,000 square miles.

The New York Times reported that military sources had said March 20 that North Vietnamese forces had aided a company of South Vietnamese soldiers in the evacuation of the citadel in Quang Tri city. There were increasing reports, however, of fleeing civilian and military refugees being attacked by Communist troops. Persons arriving March 20 in the coastal town of Tuy Hoa from Pleiku city, 135 miles to the west, told of North Vietnamese shelling of refugees to thwart their exodus.

The North Vietnamese troops March 25 forced South Vietnamese government troops to abandon the former imperial captial of Hue, giving Hanoi's soldiers complete control of Thau Thien Province.

Thousands of refugees from Hue and other abandoned areas fled to Danang, 50 miles to the south, capital of Quang Nam Province. But preparations were under way to remove the escapees further south by plane and ship as the Communists cut off Danang by land on all sides and threatened its capture.

About one-third of Hue's 200,000 persons were said to have fled, while most of those remaining had opted to stay under Communist rule.

Hue had become isolated from the rest of the country March 22, when the Communists cut Route 1 leading to Danang. The city then came under shelling, preventing air evacuation except for helicopter flights into the old part of Hue.

Danang's isolation was sealed by the North Vietnamese capture March 24 of the coastal cities of Tam Ky and Quang Ngai city, capitals of Quang Tin and Quang Ngai provinces, which came under virtual total Communist control. Refugees from the two cities had been moving north into Danang for the past few days.

Hanoi March 21 accused Saigon of "conducting extermination bombings of many of the district towns and provincial capitals abandoned in recent days by Saigon troops." According to the statement, refugees were being forced "to follow the retreating army" and were being "rushed into disguised concentration camps built with U.S. aid."

Communist forces continued their sweep down the South Vietnamese coast March 30–April 3, capturing the major cities of Danang, Chu Lai, Quang Ngai, Qui Nhon, and Tuy Hoa, while encountering little or no resistance from the disintegrating South Vietnamese forces. Tens of thousands of refugees were fleeing in panic as the U.S. prepared a major sealift to rescue civilians trapped by the war.

North Vietnamese troops March 30 pushed into Danang, South Vietnam's second largest city, and met meager opposition from demoralized government soldiers.

The loss of the city of 500,000 was attributed to a collapse in the army ranks, an influx of as many as 1.5 million refugees to the area and to chaotic conditions in the streets. There were reports of looting and mass desertions among government forces as refugees jammed docks and bridges to board barges for ships waiting in the South China Sea.

The Danang evacuation was later suspended because the Communists fired rockets at the barges and tugboats that were taking refugees to ships offshore, U.S. military sources reported April 1. As of April 1, 30,000–50,000 refugees managed to escape the city by sea and 2,000–4,000 fled by air before the North Vietnamese moved in, according to American estimates.

On the last flight out of Danang March 29—before a refugee airlift was halted because of mobs crowding the airport and runways—some 300 armed South Vietnamese soldiers forced their way onto the Boeing 727, one kicking an old woman in the face to deny her entry. Other refugees trying to get out tried to cling to the plane outside. Stranded South Vietnamese soldiers shot at the plane taking off. At least one person was said to have dropped into the sea during the flight. The body of a soldier was found in a wheel well on arrival in Saigon. The troops aboard were arrested.

Qui Nhon, the country's third largest city, was abandoned by government troops April 2. As in Danang, there was scant fighting, with thousands of civilians and army deserters fleeing.

Ford spurs refugee evacuation—U.S. President Ford announced March 28 he had ordered U.S. Navy transports and "contract vessels" to assist in the evacuation of refugees in the South Vietnamese coastal cities fleeing the North Vietnamese offensive. He called upon "all nations and corporations that have ships in the vicinity" to assist in the effort, which would be to move the refugees "to safety in the south."

Ford said he had directed that U.S. government resources "be made available to meet immediate humanitarian needs." He appointed Daniel Parker, administrator of the Agency for International Development (AID), as special coordinator for disaster relief. AID was paying the "contract vessels," which were private merchant ships under contract to the Navy.

White House press secretary Ron Nessen said March 30 "our vessels will not enter the combat areas or participate in any hostilities." "This humanitarian effort is not designed to become involved in hostilities," he said. The ships were to be kept well out from the Vietnamese coast, taking on refugees ferried out to them.

The Defense Department announced April 1 that 700 marines had been sent to assist four Navy amphibious and cargo vessels assigned to possible refugee evacuation. The units involved were four rifle companies and a headquarters company. They "will not depart the ships," the announcement said, and were to be used for individual ship security and shipboard evacuation control. The ships were said to be standing by in international waters off the central coast of South Vietnam.

As of April 1, the evacuation by sea was conducted wholly by the contract vessels, with no refugees having been picked up by U.S. Navy ships. There was a question of the legality of the use of U.S. military ships to evacuate the refugees, especially since the mobs at the threatened coastal cities included members of the South Vietnamese army also trying to flee the enemy. Congress had proscribed the involvement of U.S. military forces "in hostilities" without consulting Congress. Nessen emphasized in his remarks March 30 the humanitarian aspect of the U.S. effort and the care to be exercised to avoid "involvement in hostilities."

The U.S. ships, including four of the U.S. Navy, were stationed off Phan Rang, 160 miles north of Saigon, bringing civilians and troops out of the town. More than 1,400 were evacuated April 3 and taken to camps in the Mekong Delta to the south.

One American civilian contract ship carrying mutinous South Vietnamese troops from Vungtau, 40 miles southeast of Saigon, to a prison on Phu Quoc island

off the southern coast was seized by the soldiers April 4 and was forced to sail back to Vungtau. The troops were among many South Vietnamese soldiers being disciplined for looting and causing the deaths of many civilians in their panicky retreat from central Vietnam and coastal cities.

The South Vietnamese government announced April 4 that no more refugees would be permitted to enter Saigon because many Communist commandos had mixed with the flood of civilians streaming into the capital. Checkpoints had been established on all highways into Saigon to enforce the ban. Thousands of civilians and soldiers had forced their way into Saigon April 3 after fleeing from three U.S. ships carrying about 25,000 refugees to Phu Quoc island from Vungtau.

U.S. airlifts orphans, jet crashes. The start of a major American airlift of South Vietnamese orphans to the U.S. April 4 resulted in disaster as an Air Force C-5A cargo jet crashed shortly after takeoff from Saigon, killing over 200 persons, including more than 100 children. The aircraft carried at least 319 passengers, including 243 children.

The pilot, who survived, said he lost control of the plane after the rear door blew out; he attempted to return to Saigon when the jet crashed.

Plans to inaugurate the airlift had been announced in Washington April 2 by the U.S. Agency for International Development. The AID said about 2,000 of South Vietnam's 25,000 orphans would be taken to the U.S. for adoption by American families. Many of them were children of Americans who had served in South Vietnam, and all had already been adopted by families in the U.S., according to the agency.

The airlift continued April 5, despite the previous day's crash, as four American planes flew nearly 900 children to the U.S. An additional 263 orphans were flown that day to Canada and Australia. Australia had received more than 200 orphans from Saigon April 4.

Communists, others score airlift—The Viet Cong April 4 denounced the airlift of children as a U.S. pretext to continue interfering in the affairs of South Vietnam. The evacuation was being used by the U.S. to drag its allies into a last-minute effort to save the weakening Saigon government, the statement said.

North Vietnamese Premier Pham Van Dong charged April 6 that the airlift was "unhealthy and abominable" and that "our people will never tolerate such criminal action."

The North Vietnamese Communist Party newspaper Nhan Dan said the object of the evacuation was to "try to make people throughout the world believe that many Vietnamese are anti-Communist to provide a pretext for perpetuating [U.S.] action in our country."

South Vietnamese Deputy Premier Phan Quang Dan April 7 denied opposition charges that the U.S. had arranged for removal of the orphans to achieve a propaganda and political effect. Dan said: "We did not create the orphans, and we are not making propaganda." He was referring to a letter he had written April 2 to Tran Thien Khiem, then premier, requesting quick authorization of the emigration of 1,400 Vietnamese children to the U.S. in order to "create deep emotions all over the world, especially in the United States, which would be most helpful" to South Vietnam. The letter came into possession of an opposition group, which made it public April 6 along with an accompanying statement demanding that the airlift be halted immediately as "an unworthy attempt by the American and South Vietnamese governments to use orphans and war victims for propaganda purposes."

The opposition group also made public another letter, written by Dan to U.S. Ambassador Graham A. Martin, stating that the evacuation of the children "will help create a shift in American public opinion in favor" of South Vietnam. The U.S. embassy reported that Martin, who had met with Dan the previous week to discuss the problem of the orphans, agreed with the deputy premier's views. But the embassy insisted that Martin had brought up the matter because his "concern was simply the welfare of the children."

Vietnam orphan airlift ends. A U.S. Army spokesman in San Francisco announced April 14 the termination of the American airlift of homeless children to the U.S. from South Vietnam. In the last flight, 329 Vietnamese and Cambodian war orphans had arrived in Los Angeles April 12. The Cambodian children, numbering 53, were the first group of 200 that World Vision, an American relief agency, was planning to bring to the U.S.

Since the start of the Vietnamese airlift April 4, about 1,400 children had been flown to the U.S. for adoption, far short of the announced goal of 2,000.

Exodus under way. All flights departing from Saigon were full at the beginning of April. Private carriers were refusing freight by April 17 and terminating flights by April 22.

A round-the-clock evacuation of Americans and South Vietnamese, conducted by the U.S. Air Force, was under way April 22 when some 4,000 evacuees arrived at Clark Air Base, a U.S. facility, in the Philippines. It brought the total evacuation from Saigon since April 1 to 7,500, most of them Americans. Transshipment to the U.S. also was under way.

When the number of refugees at Clark field reached about 7,000 and was overflowing barracks, trailers and a tent city hastily arranged for accommodations, the airlift destination was transferred, April 23, to Guam, a U.S.-administered territory. Guam officials said the island could accept as many as 25,000 refugees on a permanent basis. The shift to Guam was effected also to avoid friction with the Philippine government, which was reassessing its policy toward the U.S. in the wake of the Vietnamese situation. On the refugee operation itself, the Philippine government remained aloof, neither agreeing to receive the refugees nor rejecting them.

The first planeload of refugees flown from the Philippines landed at Travis Air Force Base, Calif. April 20. Of three planeloads arriving within 48 hours, 190 of the 472 passengers were Vietnamese. They were processed through immigration and customs and most departed for other destinations within the U.S. Dependents unaccompanied by Americans were directed to report to immigration authorities at their final destination. Of 559 refugees arriving April 23, most were wives or fiancees of American civilians accompanying them. Only 135 Vietnamese without papers were detained by immigration. Another 19 were released to a church relief agency.

California Secretary of State Mario Obledo expressed concern to the State Department in Washington April 23 about the relocation problem posed by the Vietnamese refugees. San Francisco health director Francis Curry cautioned about the possible health problems from unscreened refugees.

Waldheim limits U.N. role. U.N. Secretary General Waldheim said April 2 the fate of Vietnamese refugees in areas occupied by Communist forces was "a very controversial political problem" and "it is not in the interest of the United Nations to get involved." He said the Communist authorities in Vietnam were seeking international help for the effort but they insisted it was exclusively their responsibility to take care of the refugees.

He had received assurances from North Vietnam and the Vietcong, he said, of their intention to "do everything" to feed and aid displaced people in areas under their control. But they pointed out that many of the people trying to evacuate were soldiers, Waldheim said, and "Hanoi and the Provisional Revolutionary Government are not ready to let those people go."

Waldheim made the comments in an interview in Rome with the New York Times in which he explained his rejection April 1 of a U.S. request that he appeal to the Communists not to interfere with the evacuation of refugees. "There is a war going on and one side has occupied a part of the territory and does not want to cooperate and this creates a political problem," he said.

The U.S. request came after Waldheim had issued a statement March 31 appealing "to the governing authorities concerned on all sides of the fighting" to make "effective efforts to limit the suffering of innocent people, especially women and children." The appeal urged humanitarian assistance for the civilian population of Indochina to be channeled through U.N. children and refugee aid programs on "both sides of the conflict."

U.S. Ambassador John Scali called on Waldheim at the United Nations in New York April 1 to urge Waldheim to go beyond his general appeal for a bid to all parties to avoid interference in a mass evacuation of innocent civilians desiring to leave danger areas.

Other countries assisting in the immediate evacuation of refugees included Australia, Great Britain and the Philippines. Medical supplies also were supplied by Scandinavian countries.

The National Council of Churches urged the U.N. April 2 to seek an immediate cease-fire in Indochina and assurances of safety for refugees.

Australian aid—Australian Prime Minister Gough William announced April 2, 1975 that his government had donated $A1 million for the relief of Indochinese refugees through the United Nations High Commissioner for Refugees. The funds were in addition to the $A200,000 announced March 28 for the Indochina Operational Group of the International Committee of the Red Cross. The contributions brought to $A2,350,000 the amount Australia had earmarked for Indochina relief during the current fiscal year.

Whitlam launched a nationwide appeal April 3 to raise another $A5 million for the refugees and said the government would start the campaign with a contribution of $A50,000.

Australian air force planes were flying in relief supplies for refugees in areas of South Vietnam still under government control, it was reported April 1. The aircraft were operating from Bangkok, Singapore and Tokyo.

U.S. troop use for evacuation barred. Preliminary legislation authorizing emergency evacuation and humanitarian relief to South Vietnam was approved by both houses of Congress by April 24. The legislation carried authority for the use of U.S.

troops to protect the evacuation of Americans and some endangered South Vietnamese from Saigon. But the House May 1 killed the measure in order to bar the use of U.S. troops in the evacuation of the city.

With the Communist forces encircling Saigon, poised for assault, Congress focused almost entirely on the evacuation issue. The Senate Foreign Relations Committee approved April 18 a bill authorizing $200 million in emergency relief for humanitarian and evacuation programs. The vote was 14–3. Half the authorization was for humanitarian relief in South Vietnam and Cambodia to be administered by international relief agencies. And the committee did not act on the bill until it received from the State Department a plan for accelerated evacuation of Americans in South Vietnam.

The Justice Department, which had the power to allow refugees to enter the country in emergency situations, announced April 22 a plan to waive immigration restrictions so that up to 132,000 refugees from Indochina could be admitted into the U.S.* The figure was to include 50,000 "high-risk" Vietnamese, such as employes of the U.S. or Saigon government and political figures and their families; 10,000 to 75,000 Vietnamese who were close relatives of American citizens; 1,000 Vietnamese already evacuated to the Philippines; 1,000 Cambodians employed by the U.S. who had been evacuated to Thailand; 5,000 Cambodian diplomats and their families around the world.

Meanwhile, U.S. sea forces were congregating off the coast of South Vietnam in the South China Sea for any evacuation need. About 5,000 Marines were aboard, and F-4 fighter-bombers were being readied in Thailand for air cover if necessary.

In the Senate April 23, the humanitarian aid authorization was raised $50 million and the Senate approved by a 75–

17 vote a bill for a $100 million "contingency fund" to be used by the President for evacuation efforts and a separate $150 million for humanitarian relief administered through international agencies.

The bill authorized the President to use armed forces if necessary in the evacuation of Americans and those endangered South Vietnamese incidental to the American rescue effort. The use of troops was restricted as to number, length of stay and geographic scope of operation and could be stopped by a Senate-House resolution.

There was concern expressed in debate about the possible escalation of the use of troops to evacuate South Vietnamese into another major commitment. But a proposal to kill the troop-use authority for non-Americans was rejected 80–12.

In the House, a companion measure for $327 million measure was debated into the evening with troop use the major issue. Arguing for use of troops to help evacuate South Vietnamese, Rep. Donald Fraser (D, Minn.), a longtime opponent of U.S. involvement in Indochina, said: "We owe it to a sense of decency and humanity to help get them out. I understand the distrust of the executive branch which runs so deep in this chamber, because I have shared it. But if the President should go beyond the authority granted by the bill he would be subject to impeachment."

At 2:40 a.m. April 24, the House passed by a 230–137 vote a bill to authorize $327 million for evacuation and humanitarian aid—$177 million that the President could use at his discretion for evacuation or humanitarian purposes, $150 million for humanitarian assistance. The bill would permit U.S. troops to be used in the evacuation effort for Americans and endangered South Vietnamese.

In the voting, Democratic leader Thomas P. O'Neill Jr. (Mass.) joined a dovish bloc of freshmen members in opposing passage. "I am opposed to the intervention of U.S. troops for the evacuation of South Vietnamese," O'Neill said.

After a joint Senate-House committee had approved a compromise version of the measure April 25 and the Senate had accepted the compromise by 46–17 vote the same day, the House May 1 voted 246–162 to kill the legislation.

---

*The attorney general had authority under the 1952 Immigration and Nationality Act to "parole" aliens into the U.S. "temporarily under such conditions as he may prescribe" for emergency or "public interest" reasons. The authority was in common use; 33,000 persons, 11,600 of them Cubans, were admitted under parole in 1974.

Emergency U.S. helicopter lift. With Saigon on the verge of falling to the Communists, President Ford April 29 ordered the airlifting of Americans and South Vietnamese from the capital. A sealift operation to rescue fleeing Vietnamese also was undertaken.

In a 19-hour operation extending into April 30, a fleet of 81 helicopters at Saigon's Tan Son Nhut airport evacuated 4,475 South Vietnamese and 395 Americans, bringing them to U.S. warships waiting offshore, while 1,120 South Vietnamese and 978 Americans were helicoptered from the roof of the U.S. embassy to the ships.

Ford's evacuation order was triggered by a Communist rocket and artillery attack earlier April 29 on Tan Son Nhut, in which two U.S. Marine guards were killed and a U.S. Air Force C-130 cargo plane was destroyed.

The evacuation was completed when the last 11 of the 800 Marines on guard were flown by helicopter from the embassy roof. U.S. Ambassador Graham Martin was one of the last civilians flown out in the final regular lift of 19 helicopters. Former Premier Nguyen Cao Ky was among the first group of evacuees to fly out of Saigon April 29.

The U.S. embassy April 29 was the scene of pandemonium as thousands of other Vietnamese sought to join the helicopter lift to escape the approaching Communist troops. Many tried to push through the gate, while others attempting to scale the compound walls were dislodged by U.S. Marines and civilians striking out with pistols and rifle butts. At the airport, Vietnamese guards fired in the air and in the direction of the evacuation buses, shouting, "We want to go too."

Vietnamese planes flee to Thailand—At least 74 South Vietnamese air force planes carrying about 2,000 refugees, including the pilots, flew out of the country April 29 and made an unauthorized landing at U Taphao air base in southern Thailand. The escapees requested asylum.

Refugee figure mounts. Secretary of State Henry A. Kissinger April 29 estimated the number of South Vietnamese refugees evacuated from the country at 55,000–56,000. But he revised this next day to as many as 70,000 after 22,000 South Vietnamese had fled by small boat into the South China Sea and been picked up by U.S. Navy ships, which the Defense Department said were stationed in international waters outside the three-mile territorial limit claimed by the former South Vietnamese government.

The fleet of 40 ships involved in the evacuation operation was reported by the Navy later April 30 to have moved out to a new holding area about 50 miles off the coast.

The sea evacuation figure rose May 1 to 32,000 as the Vietnamese continued to stream to U.S. ships by fishing boat and sampan.

An order "to terminate all refugee operations" was announced May 1 by the Defense Department and a Presidential statement later said "the evacuation is complete."

U.S. cares for Viet evacuees—At a news conference April 29, Adm. Noel A.M. Gayler, commander of the evacuation and commander in chief of America's Pacific forces, said the refugees had been airlifted to the carriers "without a scratch."

A total of 39,000 South Vietnamese had been evacuated as of the morning of April 28, according to the State Department, which said that 954 Americans were still in South Vietnam as of April 27.

Most of the refugees had been received on Guam, 33,858 as of 9 a.m. April 30.

Guam was receiving 5,000 refugees daily by April 24, and planes were soon landing every 18 minutes throughout the night and taking off unloaded within minutes for another trip.

The evacuation destination was shifted at noon April 26 to Wake Island to give Navy Seabees, working 12-hour shifts to erect 6,000 tents a day, time to construct a huge tent city for the refugees at Guam.

Wake, with a population of 225, soon was inundated with several thousand refugees, and 8,000 others arrived by air and sea from Saigon April 27–28 in the Philippines, at Subic Bay Naval Base and Clark Air Base, both American facilities. The Philippine government notified the U.S. it was permitting use of its country "in view of the emergency situation and for humanitarian reasons," but it attached some conditions: the U.S. should speed the transfer of evacuees to other sites, the maximum stay for an evacuee should be three days, no Vietnamese military personnel or political prisoners should be brought in.

The refugee airlift was resumed to Guam April 28, where 20,000 refugees already were lodged.

The Defense Department April 28 designated three military bases in three states as receiving centers for large numbers of the South Vietnamese refugees. The first shipment, including some Americans as well as Vietnamese, arrived at the Marine Corps' Camp Pendleton, Calif. next day. The other receiving centers were the Army's Ft. Chaffee, Ark. and Eglin Air Force Base, Fla.

Members of Congress representing the districts in which the bases were located voiced objections to the refugee operation. Sen. John L. McClellan (D, Ark.) objected to an "excessive" influx. He said next day, April 29, he had not been consulted about use of the base. Rep. Robert L.F. Sikes (D, Fla.) said April 29 there was no room at Eglin for the refugees.

Ambassador L. Dean Brown, the Ford Administration's coordinator for interagency relief effort, conceded April 24 that no resettlement plans had been formulated for the refugees because of the urgency of the evacuation effort. He said efforts were being made to "internationalize" the program, that appeals for assistance had been made to the United Nations and relief organizations and a number of countries approached about accepting some refugees.

Refugee flow continues—Twenty-six South Vietnamese naval vessels deposited 30,000 refugees at Subic U.S. Navy Base in the Philippines May 7. The Vietnamese vessels had been escorted across the South China sea by U.S. ships. The refugees immediately were transferred to civilian merchant ships chartered by the U.S. Military Sealift Command and destined for Guam. Before the ships entered Philippine waters, U.S. Navy officers boarded and took title to them to avoid infringing a Philippine demand that no South Vietnamese government ships or personnel enter its territory.

At Guam that day, the first shiploads of refugees arrived, the largest single daily influx, 20,000, for the island.

The captain of one of the ships reported that thousands of South Vietnamese had had to be left behind on the beaches of South Vietnam.

Ships bearing South Vietnamese refugees also turned up at Singapore and Hong Kong. They began arriving at Singapore May 2 and by May 4, 25 ships, none of them military, were anchored, and cordoned off, off Singapore, crammed with 3,000 South Vietnamese. After reprovisioning, the ships were planning to enter the refugee pipeline to the U.S. At Hong Kong, 4,500 South Vietnamese refugees arrived May 4 aboard a Danish freighter, after rescue from their sinking South Vietnamese ship two days before.

Refugees in Asia—Nearly a thousand refugees arrived in Pusan, South Korea May 13 after they fled Saigon aboard two South Korean naval vessels. In addition to the Vietnamese, the refugees included more than 300 South Koreans and 33 overseas Chinese. About 100 South Koreans remained in Saigon.

Saigon was reported May 11 to have sent notes to the Association of Southeast Asian Nations, advising them that the government would provide transportation home for the South Vietnamese who had taken refuge in their member countries—the Philippines, Malaysia, Thailand, Indonesia and Singapore.

About 2,000 persons demonstrated May 11 in Sakonnakhon, Thailand demanding the expulsion of all Vietnamese from the country. Vietnamese-owned shops were attacked. About 70,000 North Vietnamese had settled in Thailand after Vietnam was divided in 1954.

Vietnamese return to provinces. Saigon radio reported May 19 that thousands of Vietnamese refugees who had fled the central provinces during the previous month's fighting were returning to their homes as part of a resettlement program. The government had established a nationwide organization to deal with the refugees and other postwar problems.

In a previous action, about 30,000 of the more than 3 million residents of the Saigon area had been moved southward to the Mekong Delta, Saigon radio had announced May 12. Hanoi radio also reported that thousands of South Vietnamese who had attempted to flee the country during the Communist take-over, had been picked up and returned, many of them from the offshore islands of Son and Phu Quoc.

U.S. Aids Refugee Resettlement

As Vietnamese were still fleeing from South Vietnam in early May 1975, plans were getting under way in the U.S. to help resettle the refugees. President Ford proposed an initial program of $507 million, and Congress appropriated $405 within two weeks.

Ford asks $507 million refugee aid. President Ford asked Congress May 5 for $507 million for transportation and resettlement costs of the Vietnamese refugees over a 28-month period.

Ford then urged Americans at a televised evening news conference May 6 to welcome Vietnamese and Cambodian refugees seeking asylum in the U.S. He said he was upset at the opposition in the country to their resettlement here.

Ford was asked about his having used U.S. forces for Saigon's evacuation without Congress's "expressed concurrence." The prime objective, he responded, was to bring the Americans out. "In the process it did appear to be wise," he said, to take out a number of South Vietnamese who had been "very loyal" to the U.S. and "deserved an opportunity to live in freedom." Also, he said, "the possibility existed if we had not brought out some South Vietnamese that there could have been an anti-American attitude develop that would have complicated the evacuation of our American personnel."

"A maximum effort" was made to get every American out, he said, although "I'm sure there are some who were left."

A reporter questioned the role of U.S. Ambassador to Saigon Graham Martin. "There is some evidence," the reporter said, "that Mr. Martin's actions made it impossible for some Vietnamese to escape who were long-standing employes of the United States government. And others were evacuated on the basis of their ability to pay."

"Because of the ability of Ambassador Martin to handle a tough situation—and it was very difficult," Ford replied, "we got all Americans out" plus many Vietnamese. "I never had much faith in Monday morning quarterbacks, or grandstand quarterbacks," he said. "I would rather put faith in the man who carried out a very successful evacuation."

Ford was asked about reports that he was "damn mad" about the adverse reaction of American people to the Vietnam refugees. The reports emanated from a White House meeting earlier May 6 with Republican Congressional leaders. Ford said "I am primarily very upset" because the U.S. "has had a long tradition of opening its doors to immigrants from all countries. We're a country built by immigrants from all areas of the world, and we've always been a humanitarian nation, and when I read or heard some of the comments made a few days ago, I was disappointed and very upset."

Ford said he understood the attitude of some because "we have serious economic problems." But, he said, 60% of the refugees arriving were children and only 35,000 heads of family would be entering the job market. Referring to previous assimilation in the U.S. of refugees from Hungary and Cuba, who were "good citizens," Ford said "we ought to welcome these people in the same way." "I'm convinced that the vast majority of Americans today want these people to have another opportunity to escape the probability of death. And therefore, I applaud those who feel that way."

Kennedy scores evacuation mistakes— Sen. Edward M. Kennedy (D, Mass.) described the Ford Administration's evacuation operation May 13 as "ill-conceived, poorly implemented and undertaken with little command control in the field." Over half of the refugees fell "outside the categories targeted for evacuation," Kennedy said, and thousands designated for evacuation as "high risk" because of the U.S. association were left behind in the hasty last-minute evacuation from Saigon and thousands who should not have been evacuated were taken out.

Kennedy made the remarks in summarizing a staff report to his Senate Judiciary Subcommittee on Refugees and Escapees by two aides who visited refugee camps in the Pacific and the U.S. They reported that the unnecessary refugees included low-ranking soldiers, shopkeepers, Saigon bar girls and an entire fishing village.

Refugee reception in U.S. varies— Seventy South Vietnamese refugees, the first to arrive at Fort Chaffee, Ark., were welcomed by Gov. David Pryor May 2. "If you encounter some who are unfriendly," he told them, "remember that they are people like yourselves who have met unknown circumstances and are less than certain how to deal with them."

The refugees were flown directly from Wake Island; six transports carrying a total of 490 refugees arrived at Fort Chaffee May 2.

Refugee entry at Eglin Air Force Base, Fla., which began May 4, was attended by a high school band and mayors of nearby communities.

In California, where Camp Pendleton was the first U.S. entry point for refugees, the reception was cooler, due to fear of a refugee flood and resultant job competition at a time of high unemployment. Although California's two senators, Alan Cranston (D) and John V. Tunney (D), favored helping the refugees, their mail was running 10–1 against the refugees and Gov. Edmund G. Brown Jr. was protesting the influx "when we can't take care of the one million we have who are out of work." Brown's Administration proposed April 30 that Congress attach to the Vietnamese refugee aid bill under consideration a stipulation to provide "jobs for Americans first."

A Gallup Poll released at the same time reported 54% of those interviewed nationwide opposed resettlement in the U.S. for the evacuated South Vietnamese, while only 36% favored it.

Support for refugee assistance came May 6 from the AFL-CIO, whose executive council urged Congress to appropriate "without delay" sufficient funds to facilitate the resettlement of the refugees.

House Judiciary Committee Chairman Peter W. Rodino Jr. (D, N.J.) made a spe-

gration Subcommittee with the same message, not to forget the nation's "immigrant heritage" and to act quickly on the President's request.

The panel later May 7 approved a bill authorizing "such sums as may be necessary" for the evacuation and resettlement of Vietnamese and Cambodian refugees.

On May 8, the open-ended authorization was approved 30–4 by the full House Judiciary Committee, and a House Appropriations subcommittee voted out a $405 million refugee aid bill to provide for 115,000 refugees over a 14-month period.

In the Senate May 8, a resolution stating that "the Senate warmly welcomes the latest exiles to our shores" was passed 91–1.

Black Caucus urges domestic aid, too— The Congressional Black Caucus announced May 8 it would not support appropriations for foreign refugees unless President Ford gave some "commitments" to expand social aid to "domestic refugees"—the minorities, the poor and others made jobless by the recession. The Caucus deplored that in "a nation largely composed of refugees" the "issue of accommodating less than 150,000 is even raised." Members of the Caucus spoke of feeling "trapped" because the refugees were already in the country and pointed out that they would have opposed the evacuation if the issue had been raised with Congress.

Refugee flow to U.S. slowed— The flow of Vietnamese refugees to the continental U.S. was slowed May 10 by order of the Interagency Task Force because of "limited funding availabilities." At the time, more than 41,000 refugees were situated on Guam, the major transfer point, and more than 40,000 had already passed through Guam on their way to reception centers in the U.S.

The resettlement into U.S. society was being handled by voluntary agencies. These included the U.S. Catholic Conference, the American Lutheran Conference, the Mormon Church, the Church World Service of the National Council of Churches and the International Rescue Committee.

The government also had made ap-

Vietnamese refugees, with several, including African nations, agreeable to accepting small numbers.

Congress clears refugee aid bills. A bill appropriating $405 million for resettlement of Indochinese refugees was cleared by Congress May 16 and sent to the White House.

The final Congressional action was the Senate's acceptance, by a 79-2 vote, of an appropriations bill passed by the House May 14. The measure as adopted would provide $305 million for transportation and maintenance of the refugees and for grants to voluntary relief organizations for their resettlement operations. The remaining $100 million would go for medical aid, welfare, social service benefits and language and vocational training. The funds would cover the program through June 30, 1976.

A separate bill authorizing the refugee-aid program was approved May 16 by the Senate, by a 77-2 vote, but it differed slightly from the House version and was sent to conference with that chamber for preparation of a final bill. The Senate set a $405 million ceiling, the House $507 million. And the Senate bill had an amendment by Sen. George McGovern (D, S.D.) to permit the use of funds to return those refugees requiring it to Indochina.

In its May 14 action, the House had voted, 381–31, to approve the authorization and then, by voice vote, passed the companion bill to appropriate $405 million to fund the program. By a 353–54 vote, the House set a ceiling on the authorization of $507 million, the amount requested originally from Congress by President Ford.

Authorization passed—The authorization measure was cleared by voice votes of both houses and sent to the President May 21. As worked out by the conference committee, the ceiling was set at $455 million and the McGovern amendment was dropped, on the ground that the legislation already provided for the coverage specified. The final bill required a report from the Administration on the refugees requesting to return home, on arrangements for that and on the plan for re-

4th U.S. center opened—The Defense Department announced May 19 that a fourth refugee resettlement center was being activated, at Indiantown Gap, Pa., because of crowded conditions—45,000 refugees on hand—at the three other centers, Camp Pendleton, Calif., Fort Chaffee, Ark. and Eglin Air Force Base, Fla. In addition, there were 64,000 refugees at staging areas in the Pacific awaiting transfer to the United States. The number of refugees resettled to new homes was 17,-661.

1,000 refugees want to return home. Dean Brown, director of the Ford Administration's interagency task force on Indochina refugees, said May 22 that about 1,000 of the Vietnamese refugees desired to return to South Vietnam. The number was "smaller than we expected," Brown said in testimony before a House Judiciary subcommittee.

Among other data Brown reported to the House panel May 22: As of that morning, there were 130,425 Indochinese refugees under U.S. authority, of which 46,252 were in three restaging centers in the continental U.S.; 18,432 refugees had left the centers for resettlement; 1,800 refugees had expressed a desire to resettle in countries other than the U.S.; the government had compiled a list of 12,500 potential sponsors for refugee families; and an estimated 35,000 sponsors were needed.

Brown, on leave of absence from the Middle East Institute in Washington, of which he was president, finished his government assignment May 23 and was succeeded by Julia Vadala Taft, deputy assistant secretary for human development in the Health, Education and Welfare Department.

Kennedy scores program. The Ford Administration's program for resettling Indochina refugees was assailed by a Senate subcommittee June 8 as a "shambles" because of "failure of leadership." The charge was in a report issued by the Judiciary Subcommittee on Refugees and Escapees, the report written by the panel's counsel, Dale Stuart de Haan.

In a preface, subcommittee chairman Edward M. Kennedy (D, Mass.) described "little more than a holding operation" that was "without question, deficient," "a sloppy laissez-faire approach" to the problem.

Kennedy recommended that the Administration intensify efforts to repatriate the refugees to their homelands.

HEW assures states on welfare costs. Health, Education and Welfare Secretary Caspar W. Weinberger gave assurance June 11 that the federal government would underwrite the costs of welfare, medical and social services for the Vietnamese and Cambodian refugees during their resettlement.

Resettlement progress. Resettlement of the Indochina refugees was proceeding at a pace that could empty the relocation camps by fall, Julia Vadala Taft reported June 23, 1975. Taft, director of the Administration's Interagency Task Force on Indochina Refugees, said there were problems but "we can deal with them." One of the problems was a need for sponsors. Mrs. Taft met with reporters after the task force's first report was sent to Congress by President Ford.

Among the data: Of the 131,399 Vietnamese and Cambodian refugees, 40,655 had been resettled, including 3,962 to other countries; 27,072 were in camps in the Western Pacific; 61,320 were in relocation camps on the mainland U.S.

Taft also reported that 2,000 of the refugees had requested repatriation to Vietnam or Cambodia and that the refugees on Guam living in tents had been removed to fixed facilities as more adequate protection against typhoons.

Several preliminary sociological studies released by the task force June 26 showed that many of the refugees were educated and skilled workers. In one survey of 52,951 refugees, almost 90% of the 10,039 who listed themselves as heads of households had a high school, college or post-graduate education (33% reported having done college or post-graduate work). Also, of the heads of households, 31% had professional, technical or managerial skills, 13% clerical or sales experience, 12% were in service industries, 11% in farming or fishing industries.

U.S. to permit refugee return. The U.S.

about 1,600 South Vietnamese refugees on Guam to return to their homeland, but the Saigon government acted quickly to block the repatriation effort.

An official of the U.S. Interagency Task Force on Indochina Refugees, Robert V. Keeley, told newsmen on Guam Sept. 30 that the U.S. decision had been made at "the insistent request of the repatriates" but without concurrence of the South Vietnamese government.

South Vietnam called on the U.S. Oct. 4 to call off plans to send the refugees back, charging that Washington was attempting "to divert public attention, while at the same time continuing to carry out its plot against the Vietnamese people and violate Vietnamese authority." The statement insisted that "authorizing Vietnamese abroad to return to their country is a matter that falls within Vietnam sovereignty."

Resettlement program ends. The program to settle Vietnamese refugees in the U.S. ended Dec. 20, 1975 when the last of 140,000 refugees left Fort Chaffee, Ark. for absorption into U.S. society. Fort Chaffee, where 50,796 refugees had been processed since May 2, was the last of four processing centers established in the U.S. for the refugees.

Of the 140,000 refugees, of whom 5,000 were from Cambodia and the rest from South Vietnam, about 6,600 chose to resettle in countries other than the U.S. and 1,500 were returned to their home countries. Of the 130,000 resettling in the U.S., 27,000 chose California, 9,000 Texas, 7,000 Pennsylvania, 4,000 New York, 1,500 New Jersey and 1,200 Connecticut.

11,000 more in U.S. The U.S. State Department reported Aug. 16, 1976 that 11,000 additional refugees from Southeast Asia had begun arriving in the U.S. for resettlement. They were being admitted under special government order, raising to 145,000 the number of Southeast Asian refugees exempted from normal immigration quotas. Most of the new arrivals were Laotians who had fled to Thailand when the Laos government came under Communist control in 1975.

Refugee groups in U.S. split. Several

were at odds on adopting a common policy approach toward the Communist government in Saigon (reported Feb. 20, 1976).

A liberation front in exile, the Force of Renaissance for Vietnam, was said to be encountering strong resistance from the rival Vietnamese Alliance Association, which feared that the force's activities would provoke reprisals against relatives still living in South Vietnam.

A spokesman for the Force of Renaissance, Nguyen Van Nghi, said its aim was to counter "rampant and unchallenged Communist propaganda" being spread among the 132,000 refugees in the U.S., and to provide material aid to the 60,000 South Vietnamese troops that he contended were continuing guerrilla resistance in South Vietnam. It eventually planned to recruit an expeditionary force of Vietnamese volunteers in the U.S. and other countries who were "eager to return to their homeland to take up arms against the Communists," Nghi said.

The force, based in Southern California, was led by Pham Nam Sach, who claimed he had plotted the overthrow of President Nguyen Van Thieu with a group that included former Premier Nguyen Cao Ky just before Saigon's capture by the Viet Cong in April 1975.

The alliance had urged its followers and other Vietnamese to reject the Force of Renaissance and remain non-political. Three smaller groups, based in San Diego, Calif., supported the force. They were the Vietnamese Association for Culture Preservation, the Vietnamese Community Foundation and the Vietnamese Catholic Committee.

New wave of Viet refugees arrives. A Boeing 747 jet plane named *Clipper Plymouth Rock* landed in San Francisco Sept. 20, 1977 with 113 Indochinese refugees for resettlement in the U.S. They were the vanguard of a new immigration of 15,000 refugees from Southeast Asia authorized by Attorney General Griffin Bell Aug. 11.

The refugees would have parole status for two years and then would be eligible to apply for permanent resident alien status.

The first flight originated in Bangkok, Thailand. The relocation was being supervised by the Intergovernmental Committee for European Migration, an international group supported by 33 nations.

Resettlement in the U.S. was being handled by volunteer agencies. These included the United States Catholic Conference, the Lutheran Immigration and Refugee Service, the International Rescue Committee, the American Council for Nationalities Service and the American Fund for Czech Refugees.

Aid program extended. President Jimmy Carter Oct. 28, 1977 signed a bill that extended federal aid programs through Sept. 30, 1981 for refugees who had come to the U.S. following the 1975 communist takeover of Vietnam, Laos and Cambodia. The bill also opened the way for the refugees to apply for U.S. citizenship.

Currently, Indochinese refugees were classed as "parolees." The bill allowed them to apply for permanent resident alien status, the stepping-stone to naturalization as citizens.

The change in status was expected to help alleviate the employment problem among the refugees. Many states had laws barring persons who were not citizens or resident aliens from practicing certain professions.

The aid programs extended by the bill provided income assistance, medical aid and other social services. States with substantial refugee populations had lobbied vigorously for the extension. Otherwise the states themselves would have had to cover all the cost of the assistance. The bill provided over $100 million for fiscal 1978; the aid would taper off in subsequent years.

The bill had first passed the House of Representatives Sept. 27 by voice vote. The Senate passed it, with amendments, Oct. 10. The bill cleared Congress Oct. 18 when the House, by voice vote, agreed to the Senate amendments.

Refugee Flow Continues

Cambodia killings. Two U.S. news agencies quoted reports by Cambodian refugees of widespread killings of their countrymen by Cambodian soldiers in

June and July 1975. This tended to corroborate a claim made by Secretary of State Henry A. Kissinger June 23 that there had been "a rather heavy toll" among the Cambodians since the fall of the previous government.

According to an Associated Press dispatch from a Thai border town July 20, Cambodian soldiers had shot nearly 300 persons attempting to escape to Thailand from Cambodia. One account, given by about a dozen survivors at the frontier village of Aranyaprathet, told of three incidents in which men, women and children fleeing toward the Thai border were ambushed and shot down by Cambodian patrols near Battambang in northwestern Cambodia. One witness said the Cambodians were fleeing the harsh conditions imposed since the Khmer Rouge victory in April. About 7,000 Cambodians were said to have fled to Thailand since the Communist takeover, while others had taken refuge in South Vietnam.

Cambodian refugees returned. The Thai government Nov. 23, 1976 returned 26 Cambodian refugees to Cambodia on the ground that they were a threat to the national security. A government statement Nov. 25 said the Cambodians had entered Thailand to gather military intelligence. The 70,000 refugees in Thailand who escaped Communist rule in other Indochina states, including about 10,000 Cambodians, would not be permitted to stay, a government spokesman said.

Prince Sadruddin Aga Khan, the United Nations high commissioner for refugees, sent a note to the Thai government Dec. 3 protesting the forcible return of the Cambodians. The note recalled that Thailand had subscribed to a 1975 U.N. declaration on territorial asylum stipulating that anyone seeking refuge would not be returned to his country of origin.

Vietnamese orphans in Denmark. Premier Anker Jorgensen announced March 16, 1976 that 200 Vietnamese orphans who arrived in Denmark in April 1975 and were removed in February from the care of their guardian would be permitted to remain in Denmark.

Twenty-eight of the orphans March 19 fought a force of 40 policemen who came to relocate them from the cottage of their guardian, the West German journalist Henning Becker, to a government welfare center. Angered by the police action, 60 Vietnamese children March 21 went on a rampage in a Copenhagen schoolhouse, causing extensive damage. After they were subdued, the children were sent to different orphanages.

400 refugees in Australia. About 400 Laotian, Cambodian and Vietnamese refugees arrived in Australia March 19, 1976 from Thailand. Social Security Minister Sen. Margaret Guilfoyle March 22 said that the refugees would receive special social security payments immediately and would be entitled to other benefits after they moved from government to private accomodations.

3,000 foreigners out. The International Red Cross Sept. 14, 1976 ended its evacuation of foreigners from Vietnam who had remained behind when Communist forces conquered the South in 1975. A total of 215 were transported in the final planeload from Saigon to Bangkok. The Red Cross said it had removed more than 3,000 foreigners from the South since the start of the repatriation.

Flight by boat. The U.N. High Commissioner for Refugees March 25, 1977 reported a sharp increase in recent months in the number of persons fleeing southern Vietnam by sea. In February, the most recent month for which statistics were available, 706 persons had fled the country by boat, 521 more than in the first quarter of 1976, Commissioner Prince Sadruddin Aga Khan said. All had taken refuge in Thailand, Malaysia, Singapore and Japan.

The Vietnamese army newspaper Quan Doi Nhan later said that groups of Vietnamese had escaped from the South by boat in operations organized by the former South Vietnamese troops, who opened fire on Vietnamese security forces.

Other attempts to flee the country had been blocked, the newspaper said.

A prominent political defector had said May 3 that more than 1,000 refugees had been imprisoned in South Vietnam after they had decided to return to their homeland in 1975. The account was given by Nguyen Cong Hoan, a former member of the National Congress in Hanoi. He had arrived in Japan in April with 33 others.

Hoan said that after being evacuated to Guam, the refugees had decided to return to Vietnam, charging they had been deceived by U.S. authorities. They had sailed on a ship Oct. 16, 1975 and were imprisoned upon landing in Vietnam, he said

Israel welcomes Vietnamese—Sixty-six Vietnamese arrived in Israel June 26 and were granted asylum. They were given the status of temporary residents with permission to work and remain indefinitely.

The refugees, who had escaped in several vessels, were rescued June 8 by an Israeli freighter 30 miles off the Vietnamese coast. The Israeli government had sought without success to have the Vietnamese accepted in the ship's ports of call at Hong Kong, Taiwan and Japan. The refugees were then flown to Israel from Taiwan.

Postwar Indochina report. A report on conditions in Vietnam, Cambodia and Laos two years after Communist military victories in those countries was published by the New York Times May 1–3, 1977.

Many refugees from Cambodia who had made their way to Thailand told of crop failure, spreading hunger and disease among the harsh conditions plaguing the country.

Cambodian relations with Vietnam and the U.S. remained strained. There were continuing clashes along the Vietnamese-Cambodian border and large numbers of refugees had fled to Vietnam.

Since the Communists had won control of the country in 1975, more than 100,000 persons had fled Laos, including most of the professional and commercial elite. The exodus was continuing, with about 1,000 people a month making their way into Thailand.

The number of people fleeing Indochina was increasing, with the refugees finding it more difficult to receive haven in nearby Asian countries, the New York Times

reported in dispatches from the region June 12 and 19.

A boatload of 249 refugees, mainly Laotians, had been anchored off Singapore since February, it was reported June 12. The vessel had been chartered in January by the World Conference on Religion in Peace to cruise the sea lanes south of Vietnam to pick up as many as possible of the refugees who had fled in smaller boats; however, instead of moving into the sea lanes, the boat was loaded up with refugees already in Thailand. The vessel's destination was Australia, where it was planned that the passengers would run ashore to dramatize the plight of the Indochinese escapees.

The United Nations High Commission for Refugees reported June 16 that Australia had agreed to take "up to 50" of the refugees on the stranded ship; Switzerland, France, Britain and Austria also would accept some of the passengers. However, between 90 and 100 would be left aboard the vessel.

According to the June 19 account, many Vietnamese refugees landing in boats along the east coast of Malaysia daily were being turned back by Malaysian authorities. Thirty-three refugees had drowned a few days earlier off the Malaysian state of Sabah when their Philippines-bound boat struck a rock; four survived.

Malaysia had given shelter to 600 refugees in May, the report said. Haven usually was provided, at least temporarily, after refugees scuttled their boats.

Malaysia eases entry ban—Malaysia was easing its ban on accepting refugees from Vietnam, Cambodia and Laos, the New York Times reported Aug. 31. The action was spurred by President Carter's decision in July to admit more than 15,000 Indochinese refugees into the U.S. The Malaysia decision also was spurred by offers by other Western nations to take in the refugees, diplomats in Bangkok reported. Among these countries were Australia (1,500-2,000 a year), Canada (450), New Zealand (420), Belgium (150) and Denmark (50). France was taking in 1,000 a month.

About 3,000 persons who had fled their countries by boat were now in Malaysia. According to the Times, they were among 8,000 who had been in transit camps from Japan to Indonesia. Many of the 3,000 had been sent away several times until they scuttled their craft and had to be taken in by the Malaysians.

Malaysia and Thailand were characterized by the Times as the two Asian nations that had given temporary haven to the largest number of refugees. Thailand bore the brunt with 70,000 Laotians, 14,000 Cambodians and 3,000 Vietnamese.

A previous New York Times report from Tokyo Aug. 25 said Japan was considering appeals from the U.S. and the United Nations on the refugees. Many Vietnamese who had fled their country had arrived in Japanese ports after having been picked up at sea by ships bound for Japan. According to a Japanese official, the U.S. had asked Japan in July to be more liberal in granting temporary permits to the refugees, to reconsider its decision to impose a ban on permanent asylum and to increase its contributions to the Office of the U.N. High Commissioner for Refugees.

The Japanese official also said that the U.N. had assured Japan that if it granted temporary asylum to the refugees they eventually would be permanently resettled elsewhere.

'Boat people' flights increase. The number of Vietnamese fleeing by boat increased during the final months of 1977.

A Vietnamese freighter was hijacked in Saigon harbor Nov. 7 and arrived in Darwin, Australia Nov. 29 with 157 refugees aboard. The vessel also carried a crew of 21 and three Vietnamese military guards who had been overpowered by a group of armed refugees.

Seven Vietnamese boats with nearly 300 refugees had arrived in Australia in the previous three days, it was reported Nov. 23. This brought to 12 the number of such boats to arrive in the country in the past month. A total of 23 boats carrying 655 Vietnamese refugees had landed in Australia since the end of the Vietnam war in April 1975.

Thailand, which bore the brunt of the refugee influx, was taking a more hostile attitude toward the Vietnamese escapees, the New York Times reported from Thailand Nov. 25. The Bangkok government was said to have started to deny landing permits to boats in mid-September.

In one action, U.N. officials were reported to have intervened Nov. 14 when Thai police boats were about to escort back to Vietnam 120 refugees in the Lamsing camp who had arrived on four boats earlier in the month.

According to U.N. reports quoted by the Times, four other boats carrying 225 Vietnamese refugees had been sent back to sea from Thailand earlier in November. In another case, a boatload of 19 Vietnamese at first was denied permission to land at the Lamsing camp. The refugees were accepted after they scuttled their boat.

Government bans escapes. The Vietnamese government had launched a drive to block attempts by its citizens to escape the country, according to a New York Times dispatch from Thailand Dec. 25, 1977.

The report said 32 Vietnamese who had reached Thailand by boat Dec. 23 had told of government announcements on posters and in broadcasts warning of severe punishment for those trying to flee. The refugees, who had fled Dec. 16, said penalties ranged from three- to five-year prison terms for anyone caught escaping to five- to 15-year terms or death for boat owners who aided in the escapes.

Thais force refugees back to Laos. A Thai official said Feb. 16, 1978 that his country was forcing Laotian refugees who crossed into Thailand back across the border into Laos. Ubon Province Gov. Pramoon Chanchamnong said this forced repatriation had been going on for the past three months.

The new Thai policy made a distinction between political and economic refugees from Laos, as well as from Cambodia and Vietnam. Those who were regarded as having escaped for political reasons were eventually housed in refugee camps under the supervision of the United Nations High Commissioner for Refugees. The others were judged to be illegal entrants.

Australia admits refugees. Australian Immigration & Ethnic Affairs Minister Michael Mackellar said March 15, 1978 2,000 Indochinese refugees would be allowed to enter the country by June. The new admissions would bring to 9,000 the total number of Indochinese refugees admitted since the fall of the South Vietnamese government in 1975.

The immigrants would be selected from refugee camps in Malaysia and Thailand.

Australia was the only country in the Pacific area that had adopted a policy of accepting the refugees from the Communist nations of Indochina. Most of the other nations in the area did not want to anger the new Communist nations by accepting those who had escaped, or they simply lacked the economic resources to absorb the refugees.

Australia was the objective of many of the "boat people" who had sailed in often flimsy craft away from Indochina.

Mackellar announced May 17 that Australia had agreed to permit the entry of 9,000 Indochinese refugees over a 12-month period beginning in July.

The announcement stressed that the action was intended to curb the unauthorized influx of refugees into Australia by boat. The government hoped that the refugees would be content to wait in the camps if the prospect of legal immigration were offered them.

Australia already had accepted about

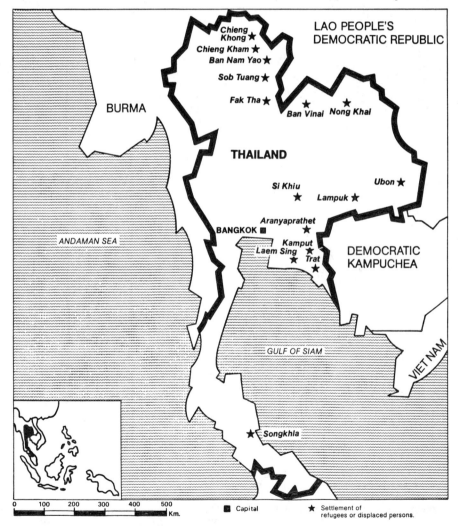

Map from U.N. High Commissioner of Refugees, August 1978

10,000 Indochinese refugees, including about 1,500 "boat people" who had made the perilous 2,000-mile voyage from the Asian mainland in open boats. About 41 boats had succeeded in making the voyage.

51 temporarily in Kenya. Fifty-one Vietnamese refugees arrived in Mombasa, Kenya April 17, 1978 on a Greek vessel that had rescued them from their foundering craft in the China Sea. Kenya said it would allow the refugees to stay for three months if another government would promise to accept them eventually. This was the first boatload of Vietnamese refugees to have reached Africa.

Chinese Flee Vietnam. Hundreds of ethnic Chinese had fled southern Vietnam since a government announcement in March 1978 that private businesses in Saigon were to be nationalized, it was reported May 1. Many of the businesses were owned by Chinese.

The head of the newly established Overseas Chinese Affairs Office in Peking, Liao Cheng-chih, May 1 said his country was concerned about the departure of the Chinese from Vietnam and that it was "closely following developments." He disclosed that "large numbers" of them had "in recent days hastily returned to China."

The Chinese news agency Hsinhua charged Sept. 11 that Vietnamese authorities had forced 518 ethnic Chinese across the Peilun River into China Sept. 2 and 5.

Refugee Flow Increases. The United Nations High Commissioner for Refugees said about 7,300 persons had fled Vietnam by boat in September 1978, a record monthly figure, it was reported Oct. 11.

The number of Vietnamese escaping by sea, according to the commissioner, had risen steadily since January, reaching a nine-month total of almost 40,000. At least 500,000 Vietnamese had left their country since the communist takeover of South Vietnam in April 1975. Thousands who departed in leaking or unseaworthy boats were believed to have drowned.

The number of refugees from Vietnam, as well as from Cambodia and Laos, escaping overland was estimated at about 9,000 a month.

The U.N. commissioner said Nov. 10 that a record monthly total of 12,186 such refugees had reached South China Sea ports and other sites in October. This brought to 51,090 the number of such arrivals between January and October, compared with 15,667 for all of 1977.

A total of 71,379 Vietnamese had escaped their homeland by sea since 1975, the High Commissioner's office said. Of these, 37,176 had settled permanently in other countries, while the remainder received temporary asylum elsewhere.

Figures released by the U.S. State Department Nov. 14 placed the number of people who had fled Vietnam in the previous six weeks at more than 20,000, about 75% of them ethnic Chinese. Many of them paid as much as $2,000 in gold to arrange their exits, the department said.

A freighter crammed with more than 2,500 Vietnamese, most of them ethnic Chinese, was anchored off the coast of Malaysia and barred by Malaysian authorities from landing its passengers. The Malaysians claimed that the passengers did not qualify as refugees because they reportedly had paid an average of $2,000 each to the Vietnamese authorities, who had permitted them to leave and arranged for the ship. The refugees reportedly had been picked up from smaller vessels Oct. 24 off the southern Vietnamese coast.

At the urging of the U.S. and the U.N. High Commissioner for Refugees, Malaysian authorities Nov. 14 permitted food and water to be taken to the ship.

U.N. Conference on Refugees. The United Nations High Commissioner for Refugees presided over a conference in Geneva Dec. 11–12, 1978 on the plight of refugees from Vietnam, Laos and Cambodia. The 34 nations participating ended the two days of talks without reaching a solution on finding asylum for the estimated 200,000 Indochinese who had fled their countries.

Vo Van Sung, the Vietnamese delegate to the conference, called the Vietnamese refugees a small minority who had been used to "unproductive consumption" and could not be integrated into the communist regime.

At the opening of the conference, the U.S. announced that it would accept 50,000 Indochinese refugees through April

1979, a doubling of the original number. An estimated 200,000 already had been admitted to the U.S.

U.S. Undersecretary of State David Newsom told the conference Dec. 12 that "the international community and not just a few nations must respond with greatly increased offers of permanent resettlement" for the refugees.

Malaysia and Thailand, where most of the refugees found temporary asylum, also called upon the other nations to aid the refugees.

Many Drown, Malaysia Lifts Ban. Malaysia decided Dec. 4, 1978 to lift its ban, admitting Vietnamese refugees stranded on boats off the Malaysian coast. At least 600 such refugees from four boats were permitted to land that day.

The government reversed its policy after more than 300 Vietnamese had drowned in several ships that capsized off the Malaysian and Thai coasts. In the worst incident, about 200 escapees from Vietnam died Nov. 22 when their fishing boat tipped over after it was towed away from the Malaysian shore by police at Kuala Trengganu, the capital of Trengganu state, where most refugees landed.

The accident, which occurred about 150 yards offshore, was witnessed by a large crowd of villagers, many of whom were said to have expressed their hostility toward the Vietnamese by throwing stones at their ship.

In another disaster, as many as 143 Vietnamese lost their lives Dec. 2 when their boat sank in rough waters of the South China Sea after having been denied permission to land in Malaysia. Police said 148 other refugees were rescued. The boat went down off the Malaysian village of Pasir Puteh.

A refugee boat heading for Malaysia Dec. 3 sank in heavy seas with the loss of at least eight lives; 46 others were rescued.

Another 48 Vietnamese drowned Dec. 3 after their refugee boat sank near the port of Narathiwat, Thailand. More than 300 other passengers, mostly ethnic Chinese, swam ashore to safety. Thai officials had refused the refugees permission to come ashore Dec. 2 pending investigation of reports that the Vietnamese had deliberately sunk their boat to avoid sailing any further.

A group of 34 Vietnamese refugees originally headed for Malaysia were taken off one of the Spratly Islands in the South China Sea Dec. 4 by a Taiwanese fishing boat and brought to Taipei. They had spent 54 days on the island, where 56 of their companions died for lack of food or water. The survivors said passing British and Japanese freighters had ignored their appeals for rescue.

Vietnamese refugees aboard the freighter *Hai Hong,* which had been anchored off Port Klang, Malaysia since Nov. 9, had begun to leave the vessel after being accepted by other countries. Canada Nov. 26 took in 159 of the 2,500 refugees, and it accepted 161 more Nov. 29. Another 222 arrived in France Nov 20 and 150 left for West Germany Dec. 2.

Malaysia announced Dec. 2 that the remaining passengers aboard the *Hai Hong* would be permitted to leave the ship and move temporarily into camps in Malaysia. The government's decision was based on a U.S. pledge to accept those refugees who could not find homes elsewhere.

The Carter Administration had announced Nov. 17 that it would permit an additional 2,500 boat people stranded in Malaysia to enter the U.S. while Washington tried to persuade Malaysia to grant safe haven to the same number of refugees aboard the *Hai Hong.* The 2,500 would be above the quota of 25,000 Vietnamese refugees set for admission to the U.S. for the 12-month period ending April 30, 1979.

U.S. To Admit 'Boat People'—U.S. Attorney General Griffin B. Bell told Congress Nov. 28 he was planning to admit 21,875 more Indochinese refugees— Vietnamese and Cambodians—in addition to the existing allowance of 25,000 per year.

About three-quarters of the increased allowance would be for the "boat people," such as on the Hai Hong.

Malaysia Restores Ban—Malaysian Prime Minister Hussein bin Dato Onn said Jan. 5, 1979 that Malaysia would no longer permit Vietnamese refugees to land. He said that more than 53,000 Vietnamese "illegal immigrants" were already in Malaysia.

Manila Aids Boat People. The Philippines Jan. 8, 1979 began to remove the first of 2,300 Vietnamese refugees stranded aboard a cargo ship in Manila Bay since Dec. 27, 1978.

The Vietnamese were to remain in the Philippines until they were accepted by other countries. The U.S., France, Israel and West Germany agreed to take in some of these Vietnamese from the boat or others already housed in a transit camp in Manila.

The Israeli Cabinet had announced Jan. 7 that it would fly a plane to Manila to bring back 100 refugees from the ship. The group arrived in Israel Jan. 24.

The Philippine government had threatened Feb. 2 to tow the ship, the *Tung An,* out of Philippine waters unless the refugees were given asylum elsewhere. At the same time, the government blockaded the bay to prevent the entry of more ships carrying Vietnamese refugees.

Three nations agreed Feb. 12 to admit most of the refugees.

The U.S. agreed to accept 600 refugees from the *Tung An* and 604 refugees who had been placed by Philippine authorities on an island 350 miles southwest of Manila. Canada said it would admit between 300 and 350 Vietnamese from the *Tung An,* and Australia said it would take 200.

Hong Kong Accepts Boat People. Hong Kong authorities Jan. 19 decided to admit temporarily 3,383 Vietnamese refugees aboard a boat offshore. All the passengers on the Taiwanese-owned freighter, the *Huey Fong,* left the vessel Jan. 20–23.

The ship, anchored in Hong Kong harbor since Dec. 23, 1978, had been barred from landing its passengers because its listed port of call was Koahsiung, Taiwan, not Hong Kong.

The officials of the British crown colony decided to lift the ban because of worsening weather and Taiwan's refusal to accept the refugees. They also had become concerned about the crowded conditions of the ship after it was discovered that the vessel carried about 1,000 more persons than originally estimated.

Many of the refugees would be eligible for admission to countries in which their relatives already resided, after they were processed, an official of the United Nations High Commissioner for Refugees indicated Jan. 22.

Another refugee freighter, the *Sun Luck,* anchored in Hong Kong harbor Feb. 7. It carried about 3,000 refugees and had slipped into the harbor during the night. Also during the night of Feb. 6–7, a fishing boat had left 223 Vietnamese on a deserted beach in Hong Kong.

U.N.-Hanoi Agreement. Vietnam and the United Nations High Commissioner for Refugees had agreed on a plan to permit the legal emigration of Vietnamese to nations ready to accept them, it was announced March 6, 1979. The accord, to end the dangerous plight of Vietnamese fleeing in flimsy boats, was announced by Deputy High Commissioner Dale S. de Haan after a week's visit to Vietnam.

Under the plan, the U.N. High Commissioner would act as an intermediary between Vietnam and the governments of countries to which the would-be-emigrant would wish to go. The emphasis would be on reuniting Vietnamese with other family members who already had fled to other countries.

In his negotiations with the Vietnamese, de Haan said they had dropped their previous demand that people of military age be barred from leaving. While common criminals would not be allowed to emigrate, people detained or imprisoned in reeducation camps for political reasons would not be included in the category of criminals and would be eligible to leave.

Refugee Bribe Racket Charged—U.S. Rep. Elizabeth Holtzman (D, N.Y.) charged Feb. 26 that Vietnamese officials had forced refugees to pay an estimated $30 million in bribes to leave the country. Holtzman made the statement in Hong Kong following a tour of four Southeast Asian nations the previous week, including a trip to Hanoi.

Holtzman said the Vietnamese officials with whom she had conferred denied any collusion in what she called an organized "racket in human beings." They admitted, however, that some local officials who had arranged for the departure of the refugees had been involved in corruption, including the acceptance of kickbacks, she said. Holtzman said Deputy Foreign Minister Pham Hien had assured her that the government was planning to correct the abuse by insuring a more orderly handling of the refugee problem.

Africa

Continent of Refugees

"This continent [Africa] has one of the worst, and least known, refugee problems in the entire world," reported John Worrall in U.S. News & World Report (Nov. 8, 1976). It was estimated that there were more than 1,500,000 refugees in 12 African countries by the end of 1978, and an even greater number of displaced Africans were said to have fled their homes although they were still in their own countries.

African refugees have run from war, coups d'etat, guerrilla fighting and tribal massacres in the Sudan, Uganda, Equatorial Guinea, Zaire, Angola, Burundi, Rwanda, Rhodesia (Zimbabwe), South Africa and South-West Africa (Namibia).

According to the U.N. High Commissioner for Refugees, in mid-1978 there were about 530,000 refugees in Zaire (from Angola, Burundi and Rwanda), 500,000 in Somalia (from Ethiopia), 250,000 in Angola (from Zaire and South-West Africa), 167,000 in Tanzania (from Burundi, Rwanda and Uganda), 160,000 in the Sudan (from Ethiopia and Zaire), 112,000 in Uganda (from Rwanda and Zaire), 70,000 in Mozambique (from Rhodesia), 65,000 in Zambia (from Rhodesia, Angola, South Africa and South-West Africa), 60,000 in Gabon (from Equatorial Guinea), 50,000 in Burundi (from Rwanda), 20,000 in Djibouti (from Ethiopia), 11,000 in Ethiopia (from the Sudan), 11,000 in Botswana (from Rhodesia, Angola, South Africa and South-West Africa), 7,500 in Rwanda (from Burundi), 6,000 in Kenya (from Uganda) and an unknown number in Cameroon (from Equatorial Guinea).

In addition, the U.N. High Commissioner's Office listed some 52,000 refugees in Algeria (from various parts of Africa and Latin America), 5,000 in Senegal (from different parts of Africa), and 4,500 in Egypt (from Africa, Europe and Asia).

African Refugee Total. More than 2.5 million Africans were refugees in African countries other than their own at the beginning of 1979, according to a report Feb. 22 by the U.S. Agency for International Development. An AID official said the figures were a conservative estimate and the true number could be three million. The majority of the refugees had fled from fighting in Rhodesia, Ethiopia, Angola and Zaire.

'Black tyranny' charged—Leo Cherne, chairman of the International Rescue Committee, had asserted in the July–

31

August issue of News American that, while white-ruled South Africa and Rhodesia were guilty of "indefensible policies of racism and apartheid . . . , the blunt fact remains that more than 97% of the [African] victims of cruel violations of human rights who are in flight have fled black tyranny!" He continued:

There are some 2,600 who are identified as having fled from South Africa. There are two estimates of the numbers who have fled Rhodesia or Zimbabwe. I'll take the higher one, 72,000. These stand in contrast to the more than 150,000 who have been compelled to flee Burundi; 145,000 from Equatorial Guinea; nearly a million who have fled Ethiopia; almost 200,000 who have fled Rwanda [and that's more than half of the total population of that country].

There are 260,000 who have fled Zaire. Angola alone has produced more than one million black refugees. Last spring Angola's President Neto said quite flatly, "We aren't a bourgeois democracy; from now on the dictatorship will be a little more strong." I heard no protest. Several months later Mozambique's President Machel was more frank: "The experiences of the Chinese people are regarded by us as sources of knowledge on how to liquidate the abrasive forces in the service of imperialism." I heard no protest.

Biafran Secession

The most pressing African refugee problem as the decade of the 1970s began was that created by the secession of Nigeria's Eastern Region, which had declared its independence in 1967 as the Republic of Biafra. Between July 1967 and January 1970, when the Biafran army was defeated and the Biafran republic extinguished, some two to three million people died of the effects of war and starvation, and an unknown greater number lived for long periods as refugees or displaced persons.

The secession was prompted by animosities among the dominant tribes—the Hausa of the North, Yoruba of the West and Ibo of the South, the latter being the most advanced. Two massacres of Ibos in the North in 1966 had led to the flight of 600,000 Ibo refugees from the North to the Ibo-dominated East and served as a prelude to the secession, which followed further massacres. War began in July 1967, and the civilian suffering followed.

Refugees flee. The refugee problem developed and grew in the early months of 1968 as Nigerian forces made headway against Biafra. In May, as the Nigerians captured towns on the periphery of the Biafran heartland, Ibo tribesmen, Biafra's predominant group, fled to the heavily-populated Ibo areas and thus added to the growing number of refugees. An estimated 200,000 Ibo refugees were reported in some 300 camps throughout Biafra.

Port Harcourt Taken. The Nigerian government announced May 19 that its army had captured Port Harcourt, the main port of Biafra, the secessionist former Eastern Region of Nigeria. According to most reports, the Biafran army and most of the 360,000 civilians in Port Harcourt had abandoned the city by May 16, and the Nigerian army met little resistance when they actually entered the city.

Famine Grows. Reports from Biafra, beginning in May 1968 and continuing through June and July, indicated that thousands of Ibo refugees were dying for lack of food and that 2 million might die by the end of August and 6 million in 6 months if massive food relief was not sent. The work of international relief organizations operating in Biafra, was being hampered by the failure of the Nigerian and Biafran governments to agree to a method of getting food to millions of persons in Biafran-held territory. The situation was growing worse as Ibo tribesmen, the majority group in Biafra, were driven into a shrinking area to escape from territory occupied by federal forces.

The Biafran government reported July 20 that an estimated "4 to 5 persons out of every 100 die weekly. Out of this number at least 3 die from starvation and related causes, and at least 2 out of every 3 who die thus are children." If the 3% starvation figure was applied to the 12 million persons that the Biafran government said were still living in Biafran-controlled territory, the number of deaths would be 360,000 a week; applied to the 4.6 million refugees claimed by Biafra, the deaths would total 138,000 a week. (Dr. Herman Middlekoop, representative of the World Council of Churches in Biafra, had estimated the number of deaths from starvation at 6,000 a day, or 42,000 per week.) The government report said that 750,000 of the 4.6 million refugees lived in some 650 registered camps, the rest in towns and villages. Deaths in camps "recently freed from Nigerian troops" were said to be as high as 10%-12%. According to the report, 3,000 tons of supplies a day would be necessary to feed all the refugees.

Leslie Kirkley, director of Oxfam (the Oxford Committee for Famine Relief), had said in London July 3, after a visit to Biafra, that about 400 Biafran children were dying daily in refugee camps and villages. He estimated that 400,000 Biafran children under the age of 10 were suffering from severe malnutrition.

Representatives of relief organizations in Biafra estimated that 200-400 more tons of food was needed daily to halt mass starvation. Super Constellations, chartered from private companies, had been flying in about 20-40 tons a night. Most of the flights came from Lisbon, with stops on the Spanish and Portuguese islands off the coast of Biafra. The landings were said to take place on crude airstrips in Biafran-held territory. The flights were arranged by the International Committee of the Red Cross, Oxfam, the World Council of Churches and Caritas, the international Catholic relief organization.

Caritas officials reported July 15 that their organization had flown 30 planeloads of food and medicine—about 315 tons—to Biafra since March. The officials said in Rome that the airlift would probably continue despite any future land convoys because the Biafrans would not eat food passing through Nigeria for fear it might be poisoned. (Such poisoning had been reported.) Pope Paul VI confirmed July 21 that the Vatican, through Caritas, was sending food and medicine to Biafra. Addressing pilgrims in Vatican City, the pope spoke of the serious suffering being caused by war.

He added: "We speak of Biafra especially." "Through our charitable agencies close to the International Red Cross and other beneficial initiatives, we have sent aid in food and medicine. We have hired planes, and we have tried to do what we could with difficulty, risks and much expense."

The International Committee of the Red Cross had appealed May 14 to all national Red Cross societies for emergency aid for victims of the Nigerian civil war. The appeal said that "famine and its sequels are decimating refugees." By mid-June, only 19 national societies had responded to the appeal. The British Red Cross donated $2,350; the U.S. Red Cross had not responded.

The 4th assembly of the World Council of Churches, meeting in Uppsala, Sweden, voted unanimously July 15 to raise an additional $3 million for relief activities in Nigeria and Biafra. The council, which, since March, had raised $3 million for relief supplies and $800,000 for transportation, also called on governments and other international relief agencies to make increased efforts to open up airlift and land routes for getting food to starving persons on both sides of the war. Dr. Eugene Carson Blake, the council's general secretary, had said July 14 that Swedish, Danish and U.S. church agencies were seeking to arrange charter flights to get food directly to Biafra. Blake added that the council had a base to which the supplies could be flown.

Relief Efforts Stalled. The International Committee of the Red Cross (ICRC) announced Aug. 14, 1968 in Geneva a plan to fly food to starving refugees in Biafra by means of a neutral airstrip under ICRC control.

The Nigerian Federal Military Government, however, rejected the plan Aug. 15. It was "unacceptable" that "any portion of Nigeria should be internationalized and handed over to a foreign agency," the federal government said.

The ICRC had cancelled its relief flights to Biafra July 29 because of technical difficulties in arranging for landings. The organization, which had flown charter planes from the nearby Spanish island of Fernando Po, had made 16 flights since the start of its Biafran operations in April. The flights were resumed Aug. 5 after August Lindt, ICRC commissioner for Nigerian refugees, had visited Biafra and Nigeria. But the flights were again suspended Aug. 10 after the Nigerians had fired on an ICRC-chartered DC-6 plane Aug. 8-9.

The relief flights were started again Aug. 13 when Count Carl-Gustav von Rosen, 59, flying for the Swedish charter airline Transair, piloted 10 tons of Caritas food and medicine to Biafra.

An airlift of starving Biafran children to São Tomé was initiated Sept. 4 by Caritas. The plan called for the evacuation of 50 children to hospital facilities on the island. An airlift of Biafran children to the Schweitzer hospital at Lambaréné, Gabon was announced Oct. 31 in New York by Mrs. Rhena Eckert-Schweitzer, daughter of the late Dr. Albert Schweitzer. Mrs. Schweitzer said that Biafran children had been arriving nightly in Gabon on returning relief planes and that 1,500 were currently being cared for by charitable organizations in Gabon.

The UN announced Nov. 13 that an agreement had been reached with the Nigerian government for the supply of additional food to war victims through the World Food Program.

U.S. Response to Aid Effort. The State Department announced Aug. 26 that the U.S. would contribute another 10,000 tons of food, valued at $2.2 million, for Nigerian and Biafran relief. An additional pledge of $2½ million, announced Nov. 8, brought total U.S. government contributions to $3.6 million, plus $9 million worth of food. The government had stipulated that food distribution be handled by the ICRC, the only organization acceptable to both the Nigerian and Biafran regimes. Private U.S. contributions to the relief effort totalled about $4 million.

The U.S. government Nov. 14 offered $500,000 to 3 religious agencies to help them charter a Hercules C-130 transport plane to fly relief supplies into Biafra. The offer was made to 3 U.S. groups —Catholic Relief Services, Church World Services (Protestant) and the American Jewish Committee—on condi-

tion that they coordinate their airlift with the ICRC.

Sen. Edward M. Kennedy (D., Mass.) told the U.S. Senate Sept. 23 that casualties in the Nigerian civil war were 10 times as great as in the Vietnamese war and that people were "dying of starvation at a rate which has grown from 300 a day in early summer to well over 6,000 a day at the present time." In his first Senate speech since the assassination of his brother, Robert F. Kennedy, Kennedy criticized international complacency towards the war, "one of the greatest nightmares of modern times." "I strongly believe," he said, "our own actions were belated and, like so much of our moral and humanitarian leadership in recent years, without a sense of urgency, creativity and deep compassion for those in dire need." Kennedy urged the U.S. to initiate UN action for a relief program and for a "mercy agreement" between Nigeria and Biafra. Kennedy Nov. 16 called on Pres. Lyndon B. Johnson and Pres.-elect Richard M. Nixon to press for a ceasefire in Nigeria and for action to send emergency supplies to Biafra. He appealed to both men to appoint a Presidential representative to "help mobilize public and private sectors in an international humanitarian alliance" on behalf of Biafra.

Pres. Johnson sent a message Sept. 13 to the Organization of African Unity (OAU), meeting in Algiers, asking the African leaders to break the "paralyzing deadlock" that had prevented adequate relief supplies from reaching "the helpless victims of the Nigerian civil war [who] have been denied succor too long." Mr. Johnson appealed to the OAU, "the highest voice and conscience of Africa," to "set aside partisan considerations and allow a prompt, effective solution to this agonizing problem."

The U.S. government announced Dec. 27 that it was contributing 8 C-97G Stratofreighter cargo planes to carry food relief to Biafra. The planes, each capable of carrying an 18-ton load, were to be turned over to the ICRC and to a joint religious relief operation for flights from Fernando Po, part of Equatorial Guinea, and from the Portuguese island of São Tomé. Following a Nigerian protest Dec. 30 over the U.S. donation of the planes, the State Department assured Nigeria that the action did not "reflect, either directly or indirectly, United States government political support of the rebellion, nor does it portend such support."

Aid Efforts Stymied. Relief shipments to Biafra vitually came to a halt in June and July 1969. Efforts to renew them bogged down in stalemated discussions between the International Committee of the Red Cross (ICRC), the federal Nigerian government and the breakaway Biafran state.

The ICRC suspended its relief flights to Biafra after one of its planes was shot down by federal jets June 5 with the loss of all four crew members. Pilots at Cotonou (Dahomey) refused to fly without safety guarantees and flights from the island of Fernando Po were grounded. Joint Church Aid relief operations in Sao Tome were able to make only a few flights in the face of stepped-up activity by the Nigerian air force.

Death Rate Rising. Biafran officials and relief personnel said in August 1969 that more than 1,000 children were dying each day in Biafra and that the death rate had risen 50% since the International Committee of the Red Cross (ICRC) had been compelled to stop its air lift operation.

Joint Church Aid, the French Red Cross and the Dublin-based Africa Concern had continued to fly food and medical supplies into the secessionist state at night, but the nightly average had dropped to about 150 tons of supplies. An estimated 500 tons nightly were reported necessary to prevent famine.

Biafra capitulates, millions reported to be refugees. The secessionist Republic of Biafra capitulated to the federal Nigerian government Jan. 12, 1970. The end of the civil war left millions of persons, most of them Ibo tribesmen, homeless and facing possible starvation.

Maj. Gen. Philip Effiong, 45, who had taken over Biafra's leadership Jan. 10 after Gen. Odumegwu Ojukwu fled to an unknown destination, announced the surrender over Biafra Radio. Maj. Gen. Yakubu Gowon, the federal Nigerian

leader, accepted the surrender and declared a general amnesty "for all those misled into attempting to disintegrate the country." Governments throughout the world responded to the end of hostilities with preparations for massive relief efforts aimed at refugees wandering in the Biafran war zone.

Reports from the scene estimated that nearly a million refugees were clogging the roads of Biafra in search of food and shelter. The thousands of Biafrans who had assembled near Uli in hopes of leaving the country by plane reportedly suffered heavy casualties in the final strafings of the airstrip. Other thousands were said to be cut off behind the lines of advancing Nigerian troops. Some relief officials predicted that a million persons would die of famine within a few days, according to Jan. 11 reports, and aid workers described scenes of horror and mass starvation along the refugee routes.

Foreign nations offer relief. The reaction of most world capitals to the Biafran events emphasized the need for massive relief efforts.

President Richard M. Nixon Jan. 11 ordered eight U.S. Air Force C-130 cargo aircraft and four helicopters on ready alert to help distribute food and supplies "as soon as the military situation permits." The President authorized an additional $10 million in food and medicine for Biafran relief. Other aid offers poured in from Canada, France, and smaller nations around the globe.

The first international group of newsmen authorized to visit former Biafran territory left for Port Harcourt Jan. 18. A report Jan. 20 said some newsmen reported the situation in the conquered areas was "more serious" than had been supposed, citing examples of gross mistreatment of civilians as well as of mass starvation.

The authorized press tour took newsmen from Aba on the southeast tip of the former enclave through Owerri, its provisional capital, to Orlu, headquarters for Radio Biafra, and back to Port Harcourt through Ihiala and Uli. The tour did not include the rural areas, where some reports said the situation was more extreme. Reporters said they were unable to obtain reliable information of the medical effects and gravity of the widespread hunger.

But reports filed Jan. 21 in major world newspapers carried similar descriptions of tragedy and incidents of brutality.

Reports said thousands of refugees were trapped in Owerri without food, medicine, transport or negotiable currency. Transport was seen as the major problem, and although foodstocks were adequate in quantity, protein nourishment—most needed by the starving population—was scarce.

Nigerian government officials continued to insist that relief was a Nigerian problem. The government announced Jan. 22 that the Red Cross would return all financial and material aid it had received from countries and organizations that had helped Biafra during the war.

The White House announced Jan. 22 that President Nixon had received an urgent request from the Nigerian government for refugee aid. Nixon ordered an immediate response and directed that all aid efforts should be put on an emergency basis. A U.S. jet transport carrying jeeps and portable hospital sections, flown by crews of the International Red Cross, left Jan. 22 for Lagos. The U.S. government also announced plans for sending supplies and high-protein food stocks for "as long as it is needed." A State Department spokesman said Jan. 22 that reports showed a "problem of greater magnitude than earlier . . . indicated."

A United Nations observer reported Jan. 26 that the relief program was inadequate. Prince Sadruddin Aga Khan said "the question of malnutrition, poverty and death will remain a cause of alarm for many months, and will need a major effort by all the voluntary and governmental agencies."

Foreign newspaper correspondents were barred from the war zone, and Nigerian officials were refusing to grant interviews in Lagos, according to Jan. 30 reports, but available information indicated that red tape was hampering distribution of food and medical supplies.

The International Committee of the Red Cross announced Feb. 6 that it would not undertake any further relief

work in Nigeria. The committee conceded that the decision was partially based on the refusal of the Lagos government to accept ICRC offers of aid.

Relief aid improves. The federal government's relief program had begun to achieve its aim of providing substantial relief to hard-pressed Biafran refugees, according to a New York Times report Feb. 14, 1970.

Nigerian Red Cross officials estimated they were feeding 2.8 million people and were distributing food—mostly dried milk and grain—at a rate of more than 2,000 tons a week.

The Times report said a steady stream of relief workers, doctors, nurses, nutritionists and technicians were moving between Lagos and the eastern zone.

Michael Ogon, state rehabilitation commissioner for the South-Eastern State, asserted Feb. 16 that refugees in his area were facing a "grave danger of starvation." Ogon said his commission was feeding one million people; but he charged that other states had received more than their fair share of relief supplies while the South-Eastern State had been neglected.

The Rehabilitation and Reconstruction Committee, with the help of the Nigerian army, had resettled more than 50,000 displaced persons in the Mid-West State, according to a radio report Jan. 29.

According to a report by the Associated Press Feb. 19, apparently the Nigerian Red Cross was distributing almost 3,000 tons of food a week to nearly three million refugees. Medical teams in former Biafran territory were reported caring for about 750,000 refugees, most of them suffering from malnutrition. More than 400 infirmaries were set up around the Orlu area.

Red Cross ends operations. The Nigerian Red Cross announced May 2, 1970 it would end its relief operation and turn responsibility over to the government by June 30. Red Cross President Sir Adetokunbo Ademola explained that "we feel that the emergency is over."

Ademola estimated that about 2.5 million people were being fed by the Red Cross in war-affected areas. That figure included 2 million children, who would continue to receive milk after the general distribution had ended, and 30,000 hospital patients suffering from malnutrition.

Angola

Angola achieved its independence from Portugal Nov. 11, 1975. Years of rebellion had caused the departure of thousands of Angolans as anti-government exiles and refugees before the Portuguese left. Continuing warfare between rival Angolan liberation movements after independence prevented an early solution to the refugee problem.

Pre-independence violence spurs flight. Many Angolans fled to neighboring countries in the years before independence to escape the warfare between rebels and Portuguese forces.

Agence France-Presse reported July 20 that over 128,000 refugees had left Angola for Zaire during the first six months of 1973.

Whites were abandoning their farms, and black farm laborers had been fleeing Duque de Braganca, Carmona and other towns amid reports of slaughters, the New York Times reported Oct. 20, 1974.

(The Gulf Oil Corp. evacuated 100 of its American staff dependents to South Africa Nov. 15 because of "the current worsening security situation" in the territory.)

About 300 whites tried to storm the government palace in Luanda June 13, 1975, demanding that the government provide them with military protection and act to expedite their departure from the territory. Several civilians were injured, but a serious confrontation with the Portuguese troops was averted.

The mass exodus of whites—80,000 already fled and 150,000 reportedly planning to leave—was reported to represent a depletion of more than a third of Angola's skilled and semiskilled work force and also entailed the loss of thousands of jobs held by blacks.

Although a lull in fighting had settled over the capital July 15, Luanda remained in a virtual state of siege. Thousands of white refugees from the suburbs flocked to the city in efforts to leave the tense colony as civil war threatened. Luanda airport, a July 15 report said, had become a squalid refugee camp as more than 1,000 whites left the capital daily. Officials of the Swiss airline Swissair said that day that it had begun an emergency airlift of thousands of Portuguese nationals from Angola to Lisbon, acting on a request from the Portuguese airline TAP, which was also to undertake emergency evacuations.

Other refugees had sought asylum at the governor's palace which, according to a July 14 report by United Press International, was ringed with armored cars to forestall a possible coup attempt by the Popular Movement for the Liberation of Angola (MPLA).

The Portuguese high commissioner, Brig. Gen. Antonio da Silva Cardoso, appealed July 16 to United Nations relief organs for food for 5,000 homeless white Angolans.

Refugees from the fighting throughout Angola were reported fleeing to cities in the south, which had until recently been considered safer than other regions, and crossing the border into South-West Africa as warfare intensified and conditions continued to deteriorate in the territory in July and August 1975.

Refugees began pouring into South-West Africa (Namibia) in late July at the rate of 100-200 a week, it was reported July 30 and several thousands had crossed the border by Aug. 11. South-West African authorities established a tent village in Ovamboland, near the town of Oshakati, Aug. 4 to house 2,000 refugees. Officials there confiscated weapons from the fleeing settlers. South Africa, which administered South-West Africa, said Aug. 4 it would follow a flexible approach to the refugee problem and stated that it regarded the Angolans as transients en route to other destinations.

Nova Lisboa, like Luanda, had become a mecca for fleeing settlers seeking to leave the territory, with more than 22,000 refugees housed in unsanitary facilities, according to an Aug. 5 report.

Other cities beset with growing refugee problems included Lobito, to which 2,000 evacuees from Porto Amboim and Novo Redondo had been brought by Portuguese troops July 31, and Benguela, which, according to an Aug. 9 report, was housing 6,000 refugees.

Portuguese authorities Aug. 8 appealed to the United Nations for food for 25,000 refugees and residents in Nova Lisboa and officials Aug. 10 stated there was a threat of starvation in Luanda.

U.N. sources in Geneva said Aug. 8 that 10 tons of food were being airlifted daily to Luanda on planes being used in the refugee evacuation operation.

Famine was also reported in the northern Angolan provinces of Uige and Zaire, to which some 3,000 black Angolans had recently returned, having years earlier fled across the border to neighboring Zaire, according to a Washington Post report Aug. 4. The Post report also noted a measles epidemic and outbreak of pneumonia in the north.

Two thousand whites demonstrated in Luanda Aug. 4 to demand protection and evacuation from Angola. Another 2,000 white settlers who had managed to flee the territory and return to Portugal, demonstrated in Lisbon Aug. 9, accusing the government of "betrayal" and demanding jobs or unemployment assistance, as well as indemnities for themselves, the repatriation of Portuguese remaining in Angola, and the return to the territory of High Commissioner Brig. Gen. Antonio da Silva Cardoso who had left Luanda Aug. 2.

According to an Aug. 2 report in the Washington Post, the government suspected many of the returning colonists of activities hostile to Portugal's ruling Armed Forces Movement.

Portugal Aug. 2 announced plans for an airlift operation to evacuate all 250,000–300,000 Portuguese refugees from warracked Angola before the territory acceded to independence Nov. 11. Airlift flights from Luanda to Lisbon began Aug. 4 and flights from Nova Lisboa, Angola's second largest city, began Aug. 10.

Lt. Col. Fernando Cardoso Amaral, head of Portugal's newly created relief agency, said Aug. 11 that Lisbon "can't abandon the Portuguese in Angola. It's our duty to get them out quickly."

Lack of fuel in Luanda and intense military operations in Nova Lisboa had interrupted the airlifts during their first week, but evacuations were proceeding, with 30,000 refugees flown from the territory by Aug. 11.

(According to an Aug. 10 report, approximately one-third of the 450,000 white Portuguese settlers in Angola had already fled the territory by commercial airline flights or by land or sea, before the airlift began. The Washington Post reported Aug. 4 that, since 1961, as many as 1.5 million blacks had fled Angola as well.)

Evacuations of refugees continued, with six planes leaving daily from Luanda and five from Nova Lisboa, it was reported Aug. 17. Some 2,000 of the refugees crowded in Luanda demonstrated Aug. 17 for immediate evacuation. Over 30,000 refugees were awaiting evacuation in Nova Lisboa, according to an Aug. 13 report.

The U.S. consul in Luanda advised all Americans, Britons and Canadians to leave Angola promptly Aug. 19 because their safety could not be assured.

Some 15,000 refugees from Angola had arrived in South-West Africa during the recent fighting, it was reported Aug. 19. More than 8,500 had crossed the border in an automobile convoy Aug. 18–19.

Refugees arriving at Oshakati Aug. 15 said that Portuguese troops had refused to escort a convoy of 2,000 vehicles from Sa da Bandeira, 150 miles from the border, southward to the South African-administered territory, the Financial Times of London reported.

According to an Aug. 24 report some 3,000 refugees were arriving in Lisbon daily on the evacuation flights. Squalid and deteriorating conditions prevailed, however, in the major refugee centers of Luanda and Nova Lisboa.

United Press International reported Aug. 28 that 40,000 refugees were being maintained in 23 camps in Nova Lisboa with inadequate sanitary and eating provisions. There was, according to a Sept. 9 report, a complete breakdown in the economic, social and administrative structures of the city.

Some 5,000 white settlers demonstrated in Luanda Aug. 24 to demand immediate evacuation.

U.S. authorities Sept. 2 proffered the use of two chartered planes to assist in the evacuation of refugees from Angola following an "urgent appeal" Aug. 27 from Portuguese President Francisco da Costa Gomes. The flights began Sept. 7.

The $5 million cost of chartering the civilian aircraft by the Military Aircraft Command was paid for from disaster relief funds and was provided without conditions, a department spokesman said.

France and Great Britain Aug. 28 had offered to provide one plane each to assist in the evacuation program. Switzerland continued to participate in the airlift.

Post-independence fighting heightens refugee problem. The civil war that followed independence produced additional thousands of refugees on into 1976.

According to a Jan. 13 report in the Financial Times of London, the southern coastal cities of Benguela and Lobito were under MPLA attack, as was the town of Lobango (formerly Sa da Bandeira), 180 miles north of the South-West African (Namibian) border. South Africa, the report said, had refused to accept some 2,-500 refugees who had fled the port cities aboard a freighter and 22 smaller ships which were presently anchored in South-West Africa's Walvis Bay.

In another development Jan. 22, Portugal resumed its airlift to evacuate refugees from Angola. The refugees included thousands who had escaped to Zaire and South-West Africa, and several thousand more who were stranded at Sa da Bandeira in southern Angola, according to officials in Lisbon.

Meanwhile, the head of Portugal's refugee agency, Maj. Fernando Cardoso Amaral, said the nation could not absorb the 350,000 refugees already in Portugal unless their relatives and friends helped out. There were 20,000 refugees in Portuguese hotels or boarding houses who had no relatives or friends or who had been "put out in the street," Cardoso Amaral said. Authorities planned to transfer them to unspecified "group lodgings" to free the hotels and boarding houses for the spring tourist season, he added.

Portuguese refugees from northern Angola said in Kinshasa, Zaire that retreating forces of the pro-Western National Front for the Liberation of Angola (FNLA) and its ally, Zaire, were pillaging and looting towns throughout the region as the Communist-supported Popular Movement for the Liberation of Angola advanced northward, according to a Jan. 29 report in the New York Times.

According to the fleeing settlers, who were to be repatriated to Portugal, Zaire army units had been the most active element in the looting, ransacking the principal northern town of Uige (formerly Carmona) before abandoning it earlier in the month without a fight.

Portugal Feb. 22 recognized the government established in its former colony by the Communist-supported MPLA. The action was taken during an all-night cabinet meeting called after the Luanda regime Feb. 21 suspended the visas of those Angolans who had gone to Portugal and now wanted to return to Angola. The MPLA's action was seen as an expression of impatience with Lisbon over the delay in extending recognition.

South Africans & refugees leave. South Africa, which had sent a buffer force of troops across the South-West African (Namibian) border into southern Angola during the communal fighting, withdrew its last remaining troops from Angola in late March 1976. The South Africans had aided Angolan refugees in the area, and they left after a large number of the refugees had found refuge elsewhere.

South African Defense Minister Pieter Botha said March 25, in announcing the scheduled withdrawal, that Pretoria had decided to leave Angola after receiving clarifications from United Nations Secretary General Kurt Waldheim of assurances previously conveyed to South Africa through British intermediaries. The government of the People's Republic of Angola, Botha said, had guaranteed that it would not damage a hydroelectric project being built by South Africa at Calueque in Angola at the Ruacana Falls on the Angola-South-West Africa border. The project would provide water and elec-

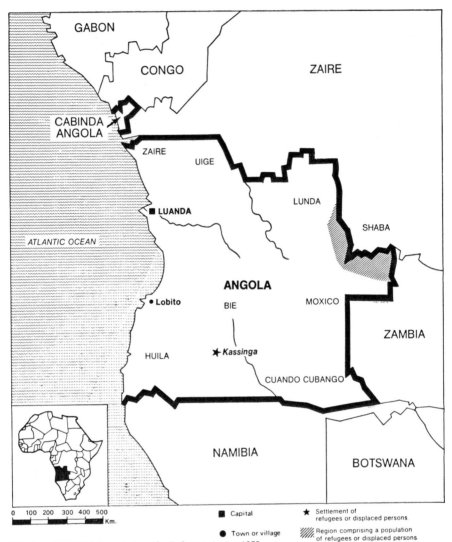

Map from U.N. High Commissioner for Refugees, August 1978

tricity to northern Ovamboland in South-West Africa (Namibia).

London March 21 confirmed its mediatory role in the development. It was reported March 25 in the Washington Post that the Soviet Union had approached Britain to relay to South Africa the position of the ruling Popular Movement for the Liberation of Angola (MPLA).

South African troops entrenched in the 30–50 mile buffer zone had conducted a preliminary withdrawal March 12 from Pereira d'Eca, site of a large refugee camp, about 30 miles within Angola. The withdrawal from the camp was made after all eligible refugees—those selected by Portuguese officials—had left Angola for Portugal. (According to a March 1 United Press International report, 400,000 refugees had fled Angola since fighting had intensified in the summer of 1975.)

Despite the closing of the Pereira d'Eca camp, there remained thousands of refugees, most of them black, in other camps at, notably, Cuangar and Calai near the South-West African border. Reports said most feared for their lives because of marauding bands of disaffected members of the defeated liberation movements, the National Union for the Total Independence of Angola (Unita) and the National Front for the Liberation of Angola (FNLA). The refugees had been cared for by South Africa, which discontinued its aid upon the completion of its troop withdrawal March 27, and the International Red Cross, which refused to continue to assist the refugees beyond that date unless asked to do so by the Luanda government.

(The United Nations had refused to aid the refugees because, a March 25 report said, it did not want to imply recognition of South Africa's presence in Angola. South Africa Feb. 12 had deplored the refusal of the U.N. High Commission for Refugees to respond positively to Pretoria's appeal for aid for the Angolan refugees, on whom South Africa had already spent $5 million.)

The Washington Post reported March 27 that 1,600 Angolan refugees had accompanied the South African troops who withdrew into South-West Africa. A spokesman for the Kavango Homeland in northern Namibia said March 29 that more than 4,000 Angolan refugees had crossed the border from Angola and would be allowed to stay for about a month. They would return to Angola "when the situation has cleared up," he said.

■ The United Nations High Commissioner for Refugees was put in charge of an $80-million international-aid program for Angola, the Aug. 6 London Times reported.

Namibia halts refugees. Authorities in South-West Africa (Namibia) Jan. 12, 1977 ordered a halt to the movement of Angolan refugees into Namibia because of fears of guerrilla infiltration. Cornelius Njoba, chief of the Ovambos, the largest Namibian tribe, had requested the action because "enemy infiltrators . . . disguised as refugees" had moved freely in both directions across the border and had taken information to guerrillas of the South-West African People's Organization, a group seeking to overthrow South African

administration of the territory. (It was estimated that 20,000 refugees had crossed the border since the Angolan civil war began in 1974.)

A South African official reported April 13 that about 700 Angolans had fled into Namibia since March to escape fighting in Angola.

Following fresh fighting in 1978, South African officials reported April 4 that more than 700 additional civilian Angolans refugees had sought asylum in northern Namibia since March.

Angolan Refugees Begin to Return. Angolan refugees living in Portugal had begun to return to Angola, according to a Financial Times (London) report Aug. 10, 1978. The report said that the return of the refugees was one of the agreements reached by Angolan President Agostinho Neto and Portuguese President Antonio Ramalho Eanes during their summit meeting in June.

According to the report, 2,347 Angolan refugees in Portugal had applied to return to Angola, and about 260 Angolans already had flown back to Angola. The Portuguese government was willing to help all refugees who wished to return to Angola because the estimated one million refugees in Portugal created a severe employment and welfare problem.

Mozambique

Mozambique achieved its independence from Portugal June 25, 1975 after a 10-year guerrilla campaign by black African nationalists. White Portuguese colonists had begun to flee the colony long before the independence agreement.

Whites flee during independence talks. It was reported June 26, 1974 that 20,-000–30,000 Europeans had left Mozambique since Portugal held talks June 5–6 with the Front for the Liberation of Mozambique (FRELIMO).

Because of increasing FRELIMO attacks, several Portuguese families living near the Rhodesian border had abandoned their farms and moved into Rhodesia, according to a Washington Post report Jan. 29.

Portuguese nationals expelled. About 2,-000 holders of Portuguese passports had been ordered to leave Mozambique by May 16, 1977 (reported June 1). The order had been issued in March and affected Mozambique residents who had chosen Portuguese citizenship voluntarily after independence had been declared in 1975.

According to the report, the ruling Front for the Liberation of Mozambique (Frelimo) had permitted all citizens to choose Mozambique or Portuguese citizenship within a 90-day period after Frelimo had assumed power. (Portugal, however, had said it would continue to accept applications for Portuguese citizenship for up to two years.) Later, Frelimo had barred Mozambique citizens from sending money abroad, and many Mozambicans had changed their citizenship in order to circumvent the ban. As a result, President Samora Machel had ordered all Portuguese citizens whose parents had been born in Mozambique to leave by May 16 or face detention in "reeducation camps." The deadline later had been extended at the urging of Portugal because of the delay in flying out the refugees.

Portugal seeks to bar refugees' entry— Refugees from Portugal's former African colonies, principally Mozambique, continued to arrive in Lisbon despite the Portuguese government's two-month-old ban on further immigration, it was reported Nov. 6.

More than 200 recent arrivals from Mozambique were squatting in the Lisbon airport, where a steady stream of refugees had been landing since May, when the Mozambican government began expelling citizens who chose Portuguese citizenship over Mozambican citizenship.

The Portuguese government had given food and lodging to more than one million refugees from its former colonies since the colonies won their independence in 1975. Recently it had ended this practice, evicting refugees from hotels and pensions where they had been lodged, but refugees kept streaming in from Africa.

The refugees, most of whom were of Goan-Indian and Mozambican origin, complained that in Mozambique they had suffered racism, indiscriminate arrests, food shortages and lack of medical care since a black government took control of the country upon independence.

U.S. gives food to aid refugees. The U.S. and Mozambique Dec. 2, 1977 signed an agreement under which the U.S. would provide Mozambique with food to compensate it for economic losses caused by Rhodesian attacks. Part of the food would go to 35,000 Rhodesian refugees in Mozambique. The agreement was in response to a United Nations Security Council call in June for aid to help Mozambique in the wake of new Rhodesian army raids.

The U.N. oversaw three refugee camps in Mozambique, which were run by Mozambique and contained an estimated 35,000 refugees from the Rhodesian war. According to a report Dec. 13 in the Washington Post, the U.N. provided about $2 million in aid for the refugees in 1977. About $1.4 million worth of additional aid in 1977 came from private organizations and other nations, notably Sweden, the report said.

Burundi

Refugee king seized & slain. Charles Ndizeye, the exiled King Mioame Ntare V of Burundi, was arrested by his country's regime March 30, 1972 in Bujumbura, the capital, after being taken there by Ugandan authorities who had apparently been promised that Ndizeye would not be harmed. Ndizeye had been deposed in 1966 by Col. Michel Micombero, who warned he would be treated "like a criminal" if he ever attempted to return to Burundi.

Ndizeye was executed within a month.

According to a statement released April 4 by the Uganda Ministry of Foreign Affairs, Ndizeye had arrived in Kampala March 21 from Europe and had obtained from President Idi Amin a promise to "use his good offices to secure an amnesty" from the Burundi government for the former king. After receiving a written promise March 30 from Col. Micombero that Ndizeye's "life and his security will be assured" if he were to return to Burundi, the Uganda authorities flew Ndizeye in a helicopter to Bujumbura. Burundi announced March 31 that the former ruler had been arrested while trying to invade the country with the help of foreign mercenaries.

The April 4 Uganda statement declared that "Uganda's action in returning the ex-king was made in good faith, prompted by the ex-king's willingness to return to Burundi as a private citizen and finally determined by the assurances given to the Uganda government . . . by the Burundi president that the ex-king would be granted an amnesty." The dispatch said Uganda was "bound to expect the Burundi government to honor its pledges and assurances" and it denied having returned Ndizeye either to have him "answer for any alleged crimes" or "to invade Burundi with the assistance of mercenaries."

The Burundi government asserted April 30 that Ndizeye had been killed in fighting the previous day when dissident forces tried to free him from house arrest. The government of Zaire announced May 3 it was sending troops to help Burundi "overcome agents of imperialism." Mandrandele Tanzi, director of the Political Bureau of the ruling People's Revolutionary Movement, said that approximately 4,000 refugees from Burundi were being sheltered in his country.

Micombero, in an interview published June 11 by Western newspapers, said that the fighting was in an uprising supported mainly by Bahutu tribesmen.

Micombero said the Hutu plotters had attempted to use the prestige of the former King Ntare V, under house arrest in Burundi at the time of the attack, by convincing him "that my regime was very unpopular and that it was now or never to make a comeback." The Burundi leader revealed that Ntare had been tried and executed April 29, the day the country was invaded by rebel forces.

Some of the refugees in Tanzania and Zaire said May 7 that in the southern part of Burundi massacres were being carried out by groups from the Bahutu tribe, which had long been subjugated by the Watutsi minority. Some versions claimed the Bahutu were supporting Micombero.

Micombero May 15 said the situation was "back to normal" in "almost every area of our republic" after two weeks of bloodshed that appeared to be caused both by efforts to settle tribal grievances and to overthrow the government. The number of dead was estimated at 10,000, with another 20,000 persons taking refuge in Tanzania and Zaire.

Reprisals add to refugees—The New York Times said June 25 that the Burundi government continued to carry out political executions of members of the Bahutu tribe in reprisal for the April invasion of the country.

The Times quoted a June 21 cablegram from U.S. diplomatic sources in Burundi which said: "Many Hutus are being buried while still alive. Leadership elements have been slaughtered. The rest are docile and obedient. They are digging graves for themselves and are thrown in afterward." The newspaper said the information had come from the office of Sen. Edward M. Kennedy (D, Mass.), chairman of the Judiciary subcommittee on refugees and escapees.

Kennedy's office also confirmed that some 25,000 Hutu refugees had fled to Tanzania, Zaire, Rwanda and the Central African Republic. The Burundi Red Cross and private organizations such as the U.S. Catholic Relief Services and Caritas International were at work but the government's relief program was "not uniformly administered." Male refugees were being "summarily" slaughtered despite government assurances to them of safe conduct back to their villages. (Lt. Col. Thomas Dabemeye, Burundi military commander in chief, June 17 had announced the end of operations against the rebels, according to a London Times report the following day.)

Kennedy charged in a July 28 statement that the Micombero government was continuing its reprisals against the Hutu. That day a U.N. team that had visited Burundi in June reported that half a million persons were in need of relief supplies.

Kennedy declared: "Reports from all sources say hundreds of people are still being killed each day." He said he had written U.S. Secretary of State William P. Rogers asking that the U.S. officially express its concern, adding: "Once again, massive human tragedy is apparently being swept under the rug in the councils of government—under the pretext that the death and displacement of tens of thousands of people is purely an internal affair of the Burundi government."

The U.N. mission, headed by Undersecretary General Issoufou Djermakoye, published an account of its visit July 28, noting that "the proportions of the human tragedy which the people of Burundi are experiencing is staggering." The report said the mission had been informed by the Burundi government "that 500,000 persons, including 50,000 widows and tens of thousands of orphans, are experiencing great suffering and are in need of humanitarian assistance." An estimated 40,000 persons had sought refuge outside the country.

A second U.N. technical mission was reported Aug. 3 in Burundi to study emergency aid requirements. However, the International Committee of the Red Cross announced that day it was withdrawing a relief team from the country because Burundi authorities had refused to allow Red Cross representatives to supervise distribution of relief supplies.

Planes kill refugees in Tanzania. The Tanzanian Foreign Ministry charged March 21, 1973 that three villages in the northwest part of the country were bombed March 15 by Burundi planes, killing 36 persons.

The statement said 20 of the victims had been Burundi refugees, of whom there were some 20,000 in Tanzania.

Dar es Salaam Radio said March 30 that Protas Mangoma, Burundi ambassador to Tanzania, had visited the site of the raid with a senior Tanzanian police official and that the fatality toll was now listed at 74. (The French newspaper Le Monde reported March 24 that Burundi Foreign Minister Artemon Simbananiye had accused Hutu "rebels" of recently attacking villages near the Tanzanian border and killing "many scores of persons." Simbananiye "categorically" denied that planes from his country's air force had bombed Tanzanian villages.)

A statement released April 3 by Tanzanian Foreign Minister John Malecela said Burundi had apologized for raiding the villages and had offered to pay compensation for the loss of life and property.

Refugees attack. Hutu refugees entered Burundi from Tanzania May 11, 1973 and from Rwanda May 13, precipitating fighting in which at least 50 persons were reported killed. An undetermined number of Hutus fled to refugee camps in Tanzania. The government issued a communique May 14 charging the Hutu government of Rwanda, in complicity with "Belgian interests," with "interference and provocation." Belgian sources said in Brussels May 16 that Rwanda had begun to arrest returning raiders.

At least 10,000 Hutus had been killed in Burundi since the May raid, according to a report cited by a U.S. State Department spokesman and published June 22.

Some of the 20,000 Hutus who fled to Tanzania in the latest fighting said the Tutsi were attempting to kill or expel all Hutus in southern Burundi near the border with Tanzania, where another 20,000 refugees had lived since 1972 fighting. Tanzania had moved about 16,000 refugees away from the border region. About 8,000 Hutu refugees were reported in Rwanda and another 50,000 in Zaire.

Tanzania's Roman Catholic bishops appealed to world opinion June 25 to curb what they said appeared to be "a war of extermination" in Burundi.

The U.S. was reported June 19 to have asked the Organization of African Unity (OAU) and United Nations Secretary General Kurt Waldheim to send observers to the area, to avoid a repetition of the 1972 events, in which about 100,000 Hutus, largely the educated elite, were reportedly massacred. U.N. officials said that reports from the area were still sketchy and contradictory, it was reported June 22. The Hutus had staged five revolts against the Tutsis since Burundi became independent in 1962.

Refugees flee to Zaire. A U.N. official in Zaire had reported that 11,000 Burundi refugees had fled to Zaire as a result of tribal warfare in Burundi, according to a report March 1, 1978.

Horn of Africa

Thousands of refugees were created in Horn of Africa countries by (a) unrest in Ethiopia that resulted in the overthrow of the late Emperor Haile Selassie in 1974, (b) violence in Ethiopia under the military regime that replaced the monarchy, (c) the continued Eritrian guerrilla secession movement and (d) warfare between Ethiopia and Somalia over Somalia's claim to Ethiopia's Ogadan area and its nomadic Somali inhabitants. Events of the 1970s included the transformation of the French Territory of the Afars & Issas into the independent Republic of Djibouti and the involvement of Soviet-supported Cuban troops in the fighting between Ethiopia and Somalia.

Refugees flee terror. Ethiopian refugees took flight in late 1970 following an upsurge of guerrilla war. The regime Dec. 16 declared a state of emergency in two-thirds of the northern province of Eritrea "in the face of infiltration by bandits supported by foreign governments." The affected area consisted of a six-mile belt along the coast and the boundary of Sudan.

A Dec. 17 report said a new wave of terrorism during November had resulted in a wave of refugee flights. About 17,000 refugees fled to the Sudan during the fighting, according to the report.

Flights to Sudan in '75. More than 30,000 refugees were reported to have crossed into the Sudan after the destruction of the Eritrean border town of Umm Hagar by Ethiopian troops, the London Times said April 3, 1975. A spokesman for the Eritrean Liberation Front (ELF) said in Beirut April 5 that an estimated 100,000 villagers had moved behind battle lines north of Asmara, capital of war-torn Eritrea Province. The spokesman said about 47 villages around Asmara had been destroyed by government bombing.

A Sudanese official said the number of Ethiopian refugees in the Sudan totalled 140,000, 40,000 of whom had crossed the border since the beginning of the year, Le Monde reported April 20.

Afars sultan flees to Djibouti after clashes. Sultan Ali Mirrah Hanfere, leader of the Afars tribe in Ethiopia, led his followers in heavy fighting against government troops in eastern Ethiopia during late May and early June, it was reported June 4, 1975. He then fled to Djibouti, capital of the French Territory of the Afars and Issas, June 2 where he was given refuge by the Afars-dominated government, the French high commissioner in the Territory said.

The fighting had reportedly waned by June 8, according to other Afar refugees who fled to Djibouti after the clashes.

The cause of the fighting was apparently Afars opposition to the government's land reform measures.

The sultan and his supporters had waged battles in the eastern Ethiopian region they inhabited, with heaviest fighting centered in the town of Aisaita, 30 miles west of the French Territory. Reports from the area said many persons had been killed or wounded when government aircraft strafed and bombed the town, which had been the sultan's headquarters.

The sultan's flight took place following the defeat of his forces in a battle on the desert road linking Addis Ababa with the Red Sea port of Assab, site of Ethiopia's only oil refinery. Three government soldiers and 15 Afar rebels were killed in the clash, during which the government sent in tanks and other heavy equipment.

The majority of the Afar people, which totaled about 200,000, lived in the lowlands of eastern Ethiopia; they constituted a large minority in the French territory, where they controlled the government.

Afars massacre denied—The provisional military government denied allegations by refugees who had fled to the French Territory of the Afars and Issas that Ethiopian troops had massacred 1,000 Afars villagers in the vicinity of Aisaita in June, it was reported Sept. 28.

The government countercharged that the slaughter had been carried out by followers of Sultan Ali Mirrah.

Mengistu in power, many defect abroad. Lt. Col. Mengistu Haile Marian, first vice chairman of the Dergue, Ethiopia's ruling military council, was named head of state Feb. 11, 1977. He became chairman of the Dergue to succeed Brig. Gen. Teferi Bante, who had been killed in factional fighting the week before. The Dergue made Mengistu chairman of its three governing

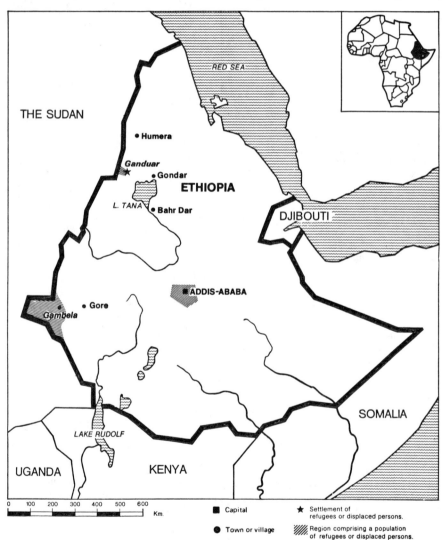

Map from U.N. High Commissioner for Refugees, August 1978

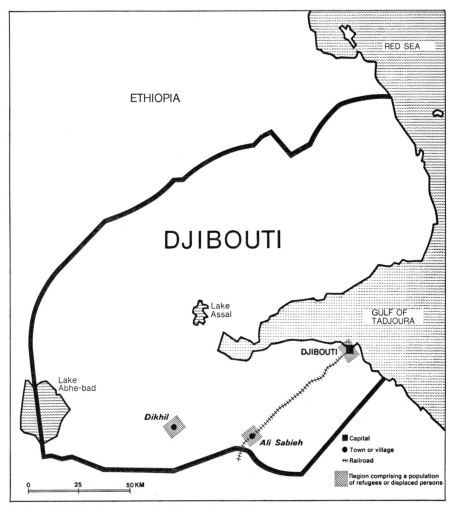

Map from U.N. High Commissioner for Refugees, August 1978

committees as well as chairman of the civilian Council of Ministers and the defense and security council, and commander of the armed forces.

A new Cabinet was named March 11, involving the replacement of seven ministers and a number of other major officials. Col. Feleke Gedle-Ghiorgis was named foreign minister to replace Ato Kefle Wodajo, who had not returned from a trip abroad. He was reportedly seeking a post at a university in Liberia.

Ato Kefle's defection was one in a series of defections of high ranking Foreign Ministry officials since the factional clash. The Ethiopian ambassador to Egypt, Getachew Mekasha, March 9 had announced he was seeking asylum in the U.S. because his country was "gripped by fear." Getachew had disputed official reports of a gun battle in Addis Ababa the day of Teferi's death, saying Teferi and his supporters had been ambushed by Mengistu and "arrested one by one and shot."

Fierce fighting had been continuing during the autumn, with Ethiopia reportedly gaining ground in September. According to Eritrean refugees in Khartoum, Sudan, the Ethiopian forces had help from Cuban troops. The refugees' assertions, reported Sept. 11 in the Times of London, appeared to refute Cuba's denials that its troops were engaged in fighting in Eritrea.

(Unlike Ogaden, which had been a part of the Ethiopian empire since the 19th century, Eritrea had been under Italian domination from the end of the 19th century until World War II. After its capture by Great Britain in 1941, Eritrea had been administered by Britain until 1952, when it became part of a U.N.-sponsored federation with Ethiopia. The Eritrean government voted in 1962 to end its

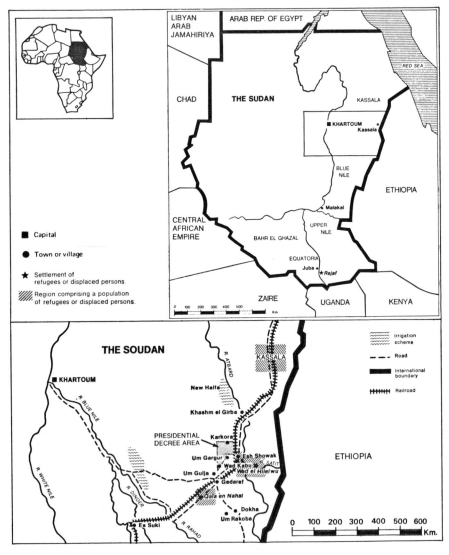

Map from U.N. High Commissioner for Refugees, August 1978

federated status and join Ethiopia. Rebels opposed to the union subsequently had embarked upon their campaign to make the province completely independent.)

Sudan's commissioner for refugees said about 200,000 persons, including 40,000 Eritreans, had fled to Sudan to escape "indiscriminate killings" by the government, according to a report Feb. 25.

Ethiopian royal family escapes. Ten members of the family of the late Ethiopian Emperor Haile Selassie had escaped from Addis Ababa and had reached Sweden, a Swedish official said Aug. 5, 1977. The group of four princes and six princesses, great-grandchildren of the emperor, had managed to escape house arrest in Ethiopia and had crossed into Kenya where they had asked for Swedish asylum. No details of their escape were released, and the official said they had requested anonymity.

Six of the great-grandchildren continued on to the U.S. Sept. 24. Reprisals against Selassie's family and political associates had reportedly been severe since his overthrow in 1974. The children's father remained in an Ethiopian jail where their mother had died in January.

U.S. food to Somalia for refugees. Richard Moose, U.S. assistant secretary of state for African affairs, held talks with Somali President Mohamed Siad Barre March 20–22, 1978 on the prospects of increased U.S. economic and military aid to Somalia. Moose and several other high-ranking U.S. officials were in Somalia March 18–23 in an effort to improve relations in the wake of Somalia's defeat in the war for Ethiopia's southeastern Ogaden region.

The Moose delegation signed an agreement March 19 to provide Somalia with $7 million worth of food relief over a period of six months. Payment for the supplies was to be stretched out over a period of 40 years. The U.S. already had furnished Somalia with $6 million in food relief since December to help ease the effects of drought and in anticipation of an influx of refugees from Ogaden.

The U.N. High Commissioner for Refugees reported that government estimates of the number of Ogaden refugees in Somalia fluctuated between 300,000 and 550,000 people.

Eritreans Flee to Mountains. A spokesman for one of the Eritrean secessionist groups said Dec. 11, 1978 that 100,000 Eritreans were fleeing into the mountains from an Ethiopian army advance. The secessionist guerrillas had been forced to retreat to the countryside following the recapture of Keren, the last rebel-held city, by Ethiopian government forces.

The Eritrean People's Liberation Front (EPLF), which had held Keren, reported at the beginning of December that 45,000 Ethiopian troops were advancing from the city. The EPLF spokesman added Dec. 11 that 5,000 refugees had been killed by Ethiopian air and artillery attacks. He said 250,000 Eritrean refugees had already fled to Sudan.

The spokesman added that rebel forces of the EPLF and its ally, the Eritrean Liberation Front (ELF), would continue their struggle in the rural areas. After they had won control of more than 90% of the coastal province, the separatists were pushed back during 1978 by a massive Ethiopian drive supported by Soviet and Cuban advisers.

The EPLF acknowledged for the first time Dec. 2 that the Soviets and Cubans had played a "decisive" role in the battle against the secessionists. Formerly, the guerrillas had referred to the Soviets as "supportive" of the Ethiopian troops. Both the ELF and the EPLF had received considerable support from the U.S.S.R. in the early years of their 17-year struggle and both movements considered themselves Marxist.

However, after the fall of Emperor Haile Selassie and the establishment of a self-styled Marxist military government in Ethiopia, Soviet support switched to the Ethiopian government. Soviet and Cuban experts helped Addis Ababa defeat Somali-backed rebels in the south, and immediately afterward turned their efforts toward fighting the Eritreans.

The Greek government March 10 had announced that it had granted asylum to

Kebede Gabre, the Ethiopian ambassador in Athens, and there were reports March 11 that the Ethiopian ambassadors in Bonn and Tokyo were seeking asylum in the U.S.

Rhodesia/Zimbabwe

Years of agitation for political equality for blacks in Rhodesia (or Zimbabwe, the name used by black nationalists) led to clashes with the (white) authorities and to the flight of thousands of black refugees from the country. By the beginning of the 1970s, the exiles had created strong guerrilla organizations in Zambia and Mozambique on Rhodesia's borders.

Guerrillas resume raids. African guerrillas in January 1970 carried out their first infiltration attacks in Rhodesia since mid-1968.

One guerrilla force crossed the Zambezi River from Zambia Jan. 3 and attacked a Rhodesian patrol launch, wounding a policeman.

Rhodesian officials reported that another nationalist band Jan. 16 raided the Victoria Falls airport and a detachment of South African police there. One infiltrator was killed and four South Africans were wounded.

The government announced Jan. 26 that an African member of the Rhodesian security forces and three nationalists were killed in another battle in the Zambezi Valley. The insurgents were said to include members of a banned South African party, the African National Congress.

Meanwhile, rival refugee groups frequently quarrelled among themselves, and the Zambian government May 6 issued an ultimatum to the Zimbabwe African People's Union (Zapu) to settle their quarrels within three days or face expulsion. President Kenneth Kaunda had met April 23 with leaders of the outlawed Rhodesian African movement to try to settle frictions which had erupted in fighting in Lusaka April 22.

ZAPU members kidnaped. Two senior officials and 19 other members of the Zimbabwe African Peoples Union (ZAPU) were reported kidnapped March 11, 1971 from the guerrilla organization's headquarters in Lusaka, Zambia.

Edward Ndhlovu, ZAPU's deputy national secretary, said the kidnapings had been carried out by a "group of ZAPU dissidents who have always refused to go to the front and have been masquerading [as guerrillas] in Lusaka for some time." Ndhlovu said the dissidents "have recently been holding a series of secret meetings in and near Lusaka aimed at frustrating the desire of the majority of ZAPU members in Zambia to hold a conference at which differences in the ZAPU leadership would be ironed out once and for all for the benefit of the armed struggle."

(It was reported Feb. 22 that the Liberation Committee of the Organization of African Unity [the OAU] had threatened to cut off aid to ZAPU unless the organization settled its leadership disputes.)

Rival groups merge. The two major Rhodesian rebel groups with offices in Lusaka, Zambia agreed to join forces under a single leadership Oct. 1, 1971. The merger was between the Zimbabwe African People's Union (ZAPU) and the Zimbabwe African National Union (ZANU) to form the Front for the Liberation of Zimbabwe (FROLIZI). Shelton Siwela, 29, a former guerrilla commander with ZAPU, was elected chairman of the new group's Revolutionary Command Council, which included former Vice President James Chikerema and former National Secretary George Nyandoro (from ZAPU) and former Foreign Affairs Secretary Nathan Shamuyarira (from ZANU).

Edward Ndhlovu, who had served as ZAPU's deputy national secretary, denounced the new group Oct. 1 because it "does not have either the blessings of the peoples of Zimbabwe or those of their leadership" and because it was short of "the necessary military power which all true revolutionary movements cannot do without."

ZAPU and ZANU announced in Dar es Salaam, Tanzania March 23, 1972 that they had formed a "joint military command" which would plan "revolutionary war" in Rhodesia.

Attacks from Mozambique. The March 1973 issue of Africa Report, published in New York by the African-American Institute, carried a dispatch in which journalist Peter Niesewand outlined the situation facing Rhodesian security forces along the country's northeastern border with Mozambique.

Niesewand contended the recent guerrilla incursions were carried out by ZANU (Zimbabwe African National Union) terrorists operating "in an extremely sophisticated manner" from Mozambique Liberation Front (FRELIMO) bases "so well equipped and entrenched that they even have cinema shows." The ZANU guerrillas had not entered Rhodesia from Zambia, Niesewand maintained, although ZAPU (Zimbabwe African People's Union) operatives regularly crossed from Zambia to plant land mines in Rhodesia.

Joint political unit. The two black Rhodesian rebel groups headquartered in Lusaka, Zambia announced the formation of a joint political council March 17, 1973 after four days of talks.

The council would be responsible for diplomatic activity and public relations. A joint military command, which had failed to promote unity between the two organizations, was to be revived.

The agreement was signed by Herbert Chitepo of the Zimbabwe African National Union (ZANU) and Jason Moyo of the Zimbabwe African People's Union (ZAPU). Each group was apparently to continue functioning on its own, while the united front made common policy.

Four black nationalist groups unite— Rhodesia's four black nationalist movements signed an agreement, the Zimbabwe Declaration of Unity, in Lusaka Dec. 9, 1974 to unite into a single body and to "struggle for the total liberation of Zimbabwe."

The purpose of the agreement was to unite the African National Council

(ANC), ZANU, ZAPU and Frolizi (Front for the Liberation of Zimbabwe), with ANC as an umbrella group under which groups would "merge their respective organs and structures." (Particular difficulty had been encountered at the Dec. 4-6 Lusaka talks in bridging the decade-long rift between ZAPU and ZANU, the latter being the more militant organization, responsible for maintaining the guerrilla warfare in northern Rhodesia.)

Children kidnapped. Several incidents were reported during 1973 of guerrillas kidnapping African children with the intention of training them to be guerrillas.

Guerrillas kidnapped 282 children, teachers and nurses in two raids on a Roman Catholic mission in northern Rhodesia July 6, avowedly to train the children as guerrillas outside Rhodesia. Rhodesian security forces rescued all but 20 of those kidnapped by the next day.

Guerrillas raiding from Mozambique kidnapped 93 more children and young villagers in September, but 62 were reported freed by security forces by Sept. 18.

Black nationalist leaders and Rhodesia's white minority government reached a tentative truce toward the end of 1974. Peace efforts foundered, however, over the inability of the two sides to agree on the basic issue—the demand that Ian Smith's white regime turn over power to the country's black majority.

ZANU leader killed in Zambia blast. Herbert Chitepo, a leader of the Zimbabwe African National Union, met his death in Lusaka, Zambia March 18, 1975

Home Affairs Minister Aaron Milner said March 28 that a number of Rhodesian black nationalists had been arrested in Lusaka in connection with the Zambian investigation of the murder.

Milner also announced that the Zambia offices of ZANU, the Zimbabwe African People's Union (ZAPU) and the Front for the Liberation of Zimbabwe (Frolizi) would be closed. Only the African National Council (ANC), into which the other three groups had agreed to merge, would be allowed to operate.

The bodies of 15 more Zanu members were found on the outskirts of Lu-saka, Zambia, in shallow graves, it was reported May 5. The body of another ZANU supporter, missing since February, had been found April 30. The bodies bore signs of torture.

An international commission named by Zambian President Kenneth Kaunda reported April 9, 1976 that ZANU's executive committee and military high command had "carried out" the murder. The commission also determined that the motive for the slaying was "the erroneous belief by the Karanga tribe elements that Mr. Chitepo and other Manyika tribe leaders in the [executive committee] had master-minded" a political imbroglio that resulted in many deaths in November–December 1974.

Members of the rebel group and Chitepo backers were killed in the plot, which was led by Thomas Nhari, a Chitepo opponent.

Another former ZANU guerrilla, Tyupo Shumba Chigowe, was sentenced to death by the Lusaka High Court April 14 for the murder of Edgar Madekurozwa, one of the Chitepo supporters slain in the aftermath of the Nhari rebellion.

Nkomo emerges as leader in ANC split. Joshua Nkomo, who was leader of the moderate Zimbabwe African People's Union (ZAPU), was elected president of the African National Council Sept. 28, 1975 in a controversial and disputed national congress held in Rhodesia. Nkomo's election signaled the split of the organization into two distinct factions.

The long-simmering feud within the ANC groups had begun escalating Sept. 3 when Nkomo denounced the Rev. Ndabaningi Sithole, leader of the militant Zimbabwe African National Union (ZANU), one of the ANC movements. Sithole earlier had announced the formation of the Zimbabwe Liberation Council (ZLC) as an external wing of the ANC, in Lusaka, Zambia. Neither Sithole nor James Chikerema, who was leader of the third black movement, the Front for the Liberation of Zimbabwe (Frolizi), were legally permitted to enter Rhodesia, where both were subject to immediate detention.

It was in his Sept. 3 statement denouncing the Sithole move that Nkomo called a national ANC congress to be held later in the month to elect a new president for the organization. The current ANC president, Bishop Abel Muzorewa, who had in the past been criticized by Nkomo, was on an extended fund-raising tour of Europe at the time.

Upon his return to Lusaka, Muzorewa Sept. 11 ordered the expulsion of Nkomo and several other persons from the ANC in order to "protect the integrity, unity and security of the ANC and the future of the people of Zimbabwe." In a Sept. 14 statement, acknowledging the organization's split, the Lusaka-based ANC denounced the Nkomo faction as a "breakaway" group, but said that two black political parties could simultaneously exist. Both groups, however, persisted in claiming to represent the ANC, the only legal black political organization in Rhodesia.

Smith & Nkomo agree to talks. Prime Minister Smith and Joshua Nkomo in Salisbury Dec. 1, 1975 signed a joint declaration of intent to hold talks in Rhodesia on a constitutional settlement.

It was the first indication of progress toward a settlement since the collapse in August of talks between Smith and a group of leaders of the black nationalist movement which had since split into two rival factions.

Despite an apparent government concession—the guarantee of full immunity from detention or restriction for any member of the ANC negotiating team and freedom to enter and leave Rhodesia as they wished (a crucial point which had contributed to previous failures to get talks under way)—the ANC exile faction, led from Zambia by Bishop Abel Muzorewa, repudiated the pact immediately. A prominent Muzorewa supporter, the Rev. Ndabaningi Sithole, asserted in Dar es Salaam, Tanzania Dec. 1 that "we intend shooting our way back into Zimbabwe until majority rule is eatablished in our country."

Smith-Nkomo talks collapse. Prime Minister Smith and Joshua Nkomo opened constitutional settlement talks in Salisbury Dec. 15, 1975, but the talks broke down March 19, 1976.

A joint statement issued in Salisbury declared the parties had "reached an impasse and are therefore breaking off the talks. This will provide an opportunity for consultation and consideration."

In separate statements following the announcement, Smith and Nkomo attributed the talks' collapse to the intransigency of the other and each called upon Great Britain to assist in the resolution of the dispute.

Casualties rise in guerrilla strikes. The intensified guerrilla campaign on the eastern frontier with Mozambique claimed the lives of 291 black nationalist insurgents and 39 Rhodesian troops, both blacks and whites, since Jan. 1, according to data released June 10, 1976 by Edward Sutton-Pryce, deputy minister in Rhodesian Prime Minister Ian Smith's office.

Zambia OKs guerrilla raids on Rhodesia. Zambian President Kenneth Kaunda said May 28, 1976 that his government would permit Zimbabwe guerrillas to use Zambia as a base for raids in Rhodesia.

Kaunda previously had supported continued efforts to secure a negotiated settlement in the Rhodesian conflict. In his May 28 statement, Kaunda said that guerrillas were already in training in Zambia for the opening of the front.

Rhodesia raids Mozambique. For the second time since June, Rhodesian forces entered Mozambique Aug. 8, 1976 in purported retaliation for attacks being launched against the Salisbury regime from there by Rhodesian black nationalists. An official announcement said that 300 guerrillas were killed in the raid as well as 30 regular Mozambique troops and 10 civilians.

The statement, released Aug. 10, said the raid had taken place two days earlier in retaliation for a mortar attack that day on a Rhodesian army base from a camp about three miles inside Mozambique and 20 miles south of Umtali.

Attack on refugee camp charged—An aide to the United Nations High Commissioner for Refugees (UNHCR) accused Rhodesia Aug. 20 of having destroyed a U.N. refugee camp in Mozambique Aug. 8, killing at least 675 civilians.

Hugo Idoyaga, a Uruguayan representative of the UNHCR in Mozambique, reported to UNHCR headquarters in Geneva Aug. 20 that he had found 10 mass graves of men, women and children in the Nyazonia camp Aug. 18. He also reported that on a May 28 visit to the camp he had seen no signs of guerrilla activity, as alleged by the Rhodesians.

In his report to the UNHCR, Idoyaga said that Rhodesian soldiers had disguised themselves as Mozambicans, using Mozambican uniforms and weapons and riding in vehicles marked with Mozambican registration numbers.

Edward Sutton-Pryce, a deputy minister to Prime Minister Ian Smith, held a televised news conference Aug. 28 and exhibited documents which he said represented proof that the camp had been a base for guerrilla activities. Among the papers shown were: a map of the camp, labelling some buildings "barracks"; information on recruits' backgrounds which gave their reasons for joining the guerrilla movement, and a list of names and personal information of over 2,000 Africans with "revolutionary" code names.

ANC rift. A meeting of five African heads of state Sept. 6–7, 1976 in Dar es Salaam, Tanzania failed to reconcile the opposing factions of the African National Council.

The conference had been called to determine a common strategy for dealing with the governments of Rhodesia and South Africa. Attending were Presidents Julius K. Nyerere of Tanzania, Kenneth D. Kaunda of Zambia, Samora M. Machel of Mozambique, Agostinho Neto of Angola and Seretse Khama of Botswana; Sam Nujoma, president of the South-West Africa People's Organization, and the leaders of the ANC factions. The presidents issued a joint statement Sept. 7 agreeing "to further intensify the armed struggle" in Rhodesia.

The main topic of the conference had been the widening ANC split between the moderate Zimbabwe African National Union (ZANU), led by Joshua Nkomo, and the more militant Zimbabwe African People's Union (ZAPU), led by Bishop Abel Muzorewa.

The two factions had split along ethnic lines, and their friction had been aggravated by Nkomo's decision to enter into negotiations with the Rhodesian government.

Muzorewa called for armed struggle as a "last resort" to achieve black majority rule. "We have been left with no choice but to take up arms," the Methodist minister said Aug. 19, before returning to his exile residence in Mozambique.

The ANC conflict had flared up June 6 when ZANU forces attacked a ZAPU military training camp in southern Tanzania, the Washington Post reported Aug. 23.

According to a ZAPU spokesman, Chinese military instructors had actively participated in the ZANU attack, which left 21 People's Union guerrillas dead and 28 others missing. (The ZAPU was backed by the Soviet Union, while the ZANU reportedly received Chinese assistance.)

The formation of a new black Rhodesian nationalist movement, the Zimbabwe Reformed African National Council, was announced Aug. 23 by a splinter group of the Muzorewa faction. Its leader, Robert Mugabe, in self-exile in Mozambique, said that the group would be willing to participate in talks with the Rhodesian government if other guerrilla leaders were invited to attend.

Sithole quits ANC. The Rev. Ndabaningi Sithole Sept. 9, 1976 announced his withdrawal from the African National Council. Sithole deplored the ANC's failure to unify its rival factions, the Zimbabwe African People's Union (ZAPU) and the Zimbabwe African National Union (ZANU).

Following his resignation, Sithole claimed sole leadership of ZANU, but it was unclear whether all or part of ZANU had withdrawn from the ANC.

Sithole's claim to ZANU leadership was challenged by Robert Mugabe, who had close ties with ANC guerrilla forces known as the Zimbabwe People's Army (ZIPA), it was reported Sept. 10. According to the report, ZIPA was almost completely under the control of the ZANU military leadership. ZIPA had been formed from the remnants of the Third Force, a guerrilla organization run by representatives of ZANU and ZAPU in an effort to unify the guerrilla command.

Mozambique camp attacked. Rhodesian forces Oct. 31, 1976 struck at guerrilla bases in Mozambique in apparent retaliation for Oct. 30 attacks that left four persons dead.

The Rhodesian forces spent two days in Mozambique territory and reportedly destroyed seven guerrilla camps before returning to Rhodesia Nov. 2. The troops had penetrated 50 miles into Mozambique at Tete Province in the north and Gaza in the south.

Mozambique charged Nov. 1 that Rhodesia had used tanks, aircraft and heavy artillery. Rhodesian officials called the charge "highly imaginative."

At a Nov. 3 press briefing, assistant police commissioner Mike Edden said that the raids had set back by two months plans for a major offensive of more than 1,000 guerrillas of the Zimbabwe African National Union. Edden said that the major military operations had taken place only in Tete Province and that the Gaza action had been in retaliation for earlier firing on a Rhodesian town. He did not release casualty figures, except to say that no Mozambican soldiers or civilians were killed.

British Foreign Secretary Anthony Crosland had announced Sept. 29, 1976 that Britain would convene an international conference "in southern Africa" to plan the creation of an interim Rhodesian government that would end white minority rule. After black African objections were expressed to southern Africa as a locale, the British shifted the site to Geneva, and the conference opened there in late October. But it adjourned in deadlock in December 1976 with Rhodesian Prime Minister Ian Smith charging that the British pandered to all black nationalist desires but disregarded white Rhodesian interests.

Talks open in Geneva. The Geneva conference on Rhodesian majority rule held its opening session in the Palais des Nations Oct. 28. Black and white delegations faced each other silently for 20 minutes while Ivor Richard, Britain's chief United Nations delegate who was chairman of the conference, read the opening statement.

The conference opening had been delayed more than two hours while Rhodesian nationalists threatened a boycott. Two African National Council (ANC) faction leaders, Robert Mugabe, leader of the Zimbabwe African National Union (ZANU), and Joshua Nkomo, leader of the Zimbabwe African People's Union (ZAPU), Oct. 27 had accused Britain of "collaboration with [Rhodesian Prime Minister] Ian Smith ... to wreck the conference." They demanded "a representative of ministerial rank with full powers to grant Zimbabwe its independence" to serve as the conference chairman. Nkomo and Mugabe agreed to attend after London promised to send a written explanation of its role at Geneva.

Smith leaves Geneva, talks adjourned. Ian Smith left the Geneva conference Dec. 12, 1976, asserting that he saw "virtually no change" in the deadlocked meeting.

He had said Dec. 10 that he had been "misled by the parties who arranged this conference" (a reference to Britain) into believing that a change in the strategy of the black nationalist delegates in Geneva was imminent.

The conference was adjourned Dec. 14.

Pressures on the Rhodesian government mounted during 1977 as the international community increased its demands for the transfer of rule to the black majority. As the year's end approached, there seemed to be evidence that the white minority regime, however reluctantly, was preparing to compromise if possible and to capitulate if necessary on the best terms it could negotiate. This development was accompanied by—and probably at least a partial result of—a heightening of the intensity of the fighting between black nationalist guerrilla and Rhodesian government forces.

4th guerrilla front, wide action. A fourth military front in the war in Rhodesia was reported Jan. 6, 1977 to have appeared in northwestern Rhodesia, near the Zambian border.

Previous fronts were established by guerrillas infiltrating from Mozambique in the east and north and from Botswana and Zambia in the west. The new guerrillas were reported by Rhodesian security forces to be members of the Zimbabwe African People's Union, the refugee faction headed by Joshua Nkomo. It was thought that Nkomo was mounting the offensive to compete for influence in the militant nationalist movement with Robert Mugabe's faction, the Zimbabwe African National Union.

Many abducted for refugee army. The Rhodesian military said Jan. 31 that 400 black students at a Lutheran mission school near the Botswana border had been taken from the school at gunpoint Jan. 30 by nationalist guerrillas and forced to march to Botswana. The statement said 230 male and 170 female students, aged 12–20, had been taken from the Manama Lutheran Mission secondary school 15 miles from Botswana. Five teachers, two nurses and a clerk were taken with the students.

The headmaster reported that the guerrillas had told the students they had to join Nkomo's ZAPU army. ZAPU had been reported undertaking a mass kidnap campaign to strengthen its guerrilla forces, which were smaller than Mugabe's Zimbabwe African National Union.

Five of the students and two teachers reportedly escaped from the group and returned to the mission school that night. The Botswana government Jan. 31 confirmed that the group had arrived in two border villages.

(One of the mission nuns Feb. 2 said 10 children and two teachers had escaped from Botswana Jan. 30. Two more children were reported to have left Botswana Feb. 5.)

Most of the students taken from the mission school chose to stay with nationalist guerrillas in Botswana, it was announced Feb. 6. After visiting with their parents that day only 51 students decided to return home.

The meeting with the parents was supervised by three International Red Cross officials, two Rhodesian Catholic priests, a British diplomat and a representative of Botswana President

Seretse Khama. Parents reported their children feared reprisals by nationalist guerrillas if they returned to Rhodesia. The two priests who had accompanied the group said Feb. 7 the children had been influenced to stay by "indoctrination, threats and promises."

More than 100 of the 331 children in Botswana left Feb. 8 for guerrilla training in Mozambique.

Earlier, ZAPU had been accused of a mass kidnap campaign in its efforts to gather recruits for its guerrilla army, the London Times reported Jan. 21. Africans who had been kidnapped to Botswana and had escaped said armed terrorists had invaded their village and forced 124 men to march at gunpoint over the border. Government officials estimated that about 1,000 Africans had been abducted since November 1976 from Matabeleland in the southwest, compared with 600 during the previous 15 months.

A report in the Johannesburg's Rand Daily Mail July 7 said black refugees in Botswana were being flown to Zambia for military training. The report said a regular air shuttle service for transporting recruits existed between the two countries. A Botswana government spokesman was reported to have confirmed that 600 refugees were flown to Zambia each week. Most of the refugees had come from Rhodesia, but a steady flow of blacks from South Africa also was reported.

Missionaries flee. A Catholic churchman said April 3, 1977 that at least 33 missionaries had left Rhodesia because they feared guerrilla attacks on their missions. Father Mel Hill said more would leave because "the Catholic Church goes along with the advocates of turning a blind eye" to guerrilla activities.

Rhodesia raids in Mozambique. Rhodesian troops were reported June 2, 1977 to be withdrawing from Mozambique territory after completing a five-day raid on guerrilla bases that had included the brief capture of Mapai, a village 60 miles inside the country. The raid was the third major Rhodesian incursion into Mozambique in a campaign to destroy guerrilla bases near the border.

According to a military communique, Rhodesian forces had crossed the border early May 29 from an outpost 300 miles south of Salisbury, destroying a guerrilla base and killing more than 20 guerrillas. Two more bases were reported destroyed the next day, with the loss of another 20 guerrillas, as the troops struck deeper into Mozambique. One of the bases reportedly was "the controlling center for all incursions into southeastern Rhodesia," according to a military communique.

Mapai was captured May 31, and Rhodesia announced it would hold the town until the area had been cleared of all guerrillas. Gen. Peter Walls, commander of the operation, acknowledged that day that the troops had found fewer guerrillas than intelligence reports had led them to expect. He said the refugee forces were members of the Zimbabwe African National Liberation Army, the military wing of Robert Mugabe's ZANU.

The Rhodesian government June 2 defended the incursion into Mozambique as "a necessary part of self-defense."

Foreign Minister Pieter van der Byl, replying to international criticism, denied that Rhodesia had invaded Mozambique, saying its forces "were led in there by the terrorists" and had taken "a great deal of trouble" to avoid contact with Mozambique soldiers.

Rhodesian troops were reported to have completed their withdrawal from Mozambique territory June 4.

A military communique June 10 said Rhodesian troops had staged a second raid into Mozambique earlier in the week. It said the objective had been a guerrilla base located through information obtained from the May 29 raid. The guerrillas had fled the camp, according to the report, but had left behind a large quantity of equipment and weapons including about 90,000 rounds of ammunition. The communique said one Rhodesian soldier had been killed in the attack.

Six refugees from Mozambique said the Rhodesian troops had been welcomed by the local population as liberators from the country's Marxist government. At a Salisbury news conference reported June 9 in the New York Times, the refugees said they had welcomed the rule of the

Front for the Liberation of Mozambique (Frelimo) in 1975 but subsequent repression and food shortages had forced them to flee to Rhodesia the previous week.

(Foreign journalists who had visited Mozambique had found general satisfaction with Frelimo, according to the Times. However, the newspaper noted that their visits had been closely escorted and they had not been able to make contact with dissidents.)

U.S. food for refugees in Mozambique—The U.S. and Mozambique Dec. 2, 1977 signed an agreement for the U.S. to provide Mozambique with food to compensate it for economic losses caused by Rhodesian attacks. Part of the food would go to 35,000 Rhodesian refugees in Mozambique. The agreement was in response to a United Nations Security Council call in June for aid to help Mozambique in the wake of the Rhodesian army raids.

The U.N. oversaw three refugee camps in Mozambique, which were run by Mozambique and contained an estimated 35,000 refugees from the guerrilla war.

Sithole returns to Rhodesia. Rev. Ndabaningi Sithole, one of the rivals for leadership of the Rhodesian nationalist movement, came back home July 10, 1977 after two years of self-imposed exile. Prime Minister Ian Smith reportedly had said Sithole would be permitted to return if he renounced terrorist tactics for achieving majority rule. On his arrival in Salisbury, Sithole endorsed the U.S.-British effort to find a peaceful solution to Rhodesian majority rule and denounced the decision of the Organization of African Unity to support the Patriotic Front. (Sithole had fled Rhodesia in 1975 while under detention.)

Members of the Zimbabwe African National Union living in London had announced Jan. 14 their shift of loyalties from ZANU leader Robert Mugabe to Rev. Sithole. A spokesman for the London group accused Mugabe of being paid by the U.S. Central Intelligence Agency.

Chikerema returns, backs Smith. James Chikerema, one of Rhodesia's first black nationalist leaders, returned to Salisbury Sept. 18 after 13 years of self-exile and announced the next day that he supported Prime Minister Ian Smith on two major points concerning majority rule. He asserted that the army and police forces should remain under white control during the transition period and that whites should have a measure of parliamentary power under the future black government.

Chikerema denied having made any deals with the Smith government for being allowed to return without facing arrest. He said he had not abandoned the guerrilla movement and warned that "the armed struggle will go on" until majority rule was achieved.

Rhodesia Offers Guerrillas Amnesty. The Rhodesian government announced Jan. 20, 1978 an offer to give amnesty to refugee nationalist guerrillas who "wished to return to Rhodesia in peace." The government said it had dropped thousands of leaflets concerning the amnesty in areas where guerrillas were known to operate. It added that a number of guerrillas already had surrendered.

According to a report Jan. 23, Salisbury had imposed news censorship on the guerrilla amnesty, apparently in reaction to news reports of white hostility to the amnesty program.

Rhodesian Army Raids Zambia. Rhodesian troops crossed into Zambia March 5–6, 1978 and reported killing 38 rebels at a camp near the borders of Rhodesia, Zambia and Mozambique. Salisbury reported the raid March 7, saying the guerrillas had been ZAPU members.

The U.N. Security Council March 17 unanimously condemned the raid.

The government claimed the raid was a "self-defense" operation designed to halt a planned ZAPU infiltration of Rhodesia.

It was the first time that the Rhodesian government officially had acknowledged a raid into Zambia. Rhodesia had mounted several raids on suspected guerrilla camps in Mozambique.

Lt. Gen. Peter Walls, commander in chief of Rhodesia's security forces, said March 12 that evidence from the raid pointed to Soviet and Cuban involvement with the guerrillas.

Abducted Students Choose to Return. ZAPU guerrillas March 29, 1978 abducted more than 400 students from a Rhodesian mission school near the Botswanan border in an attempt to force them to join the nationalist fighters. However, most of the students, aged 13–20, voluntarily returned to their homes March 31.

The refugee fighters had forced 420 students and 12 teachers at the Tegwani Mission School to walk 10 miles to the Botswanan border. The mass abduction was the biggest since January 1977, when more than 400 students were taken from another mission school.

Unlike the 1977 kidnapping, however, most of the Tegwani students returned to Rhodesia. The Botswanan government March 30 had said it would provide transportation for all but 48 of the kidnapped students and teachers. The 48 persons had chosen to stay in Botswana, according to officials.

Nkomo, Mugabe Parties Legalized. The Rhodesian interim regime May 2, 1978 lifted the 1962 ban on the Zimbabwe African People's Union (ZAPU), the political party headed by Joshua Nkomo, and the 1964 ban on the Zimbabwe African National Union (ZANU), the party headed by Robert Mugabe.

In a major policy statement, the government also promised unconditional amnesty to all guerrillas of the Patriotic Front, the ZAPU-ZANU coalition led by Nkomo and Mugabe, if the fighters agreed to lay down their arms.

Nkomo admits Cuban role. ZAPU leader Joshua Nkomo disclosed June 6, 1978 that Cubans were training his army in Zambia. In an interview with a Zambian newspaper, Nkomo said he accepted the Cuban help and arms from the Soviet Union in order to "scare away" the West from involvement in Rhodesia.

According to diplomatic sources, about 75 Cubans were training Nkomo's army, estimated at 6,000–8,000 men.

In a previous interview June 5, Nkomo rejected returning to Rhodesia and joining the multiracial government of whites and moderate blacks. He said he would only return "as a fighter" to remove what he termed the fascist government of Ian Smith and his black collaborators.

Mozambique Guerrilla Camps Raided. The Rhodesian military command said July 31 that security forces had raided 10 guerrilla training camps in Mozambique. The attacks, which had begun July 30, were described as "self-defense operations" in response to reports that 2,700 guerrillas were being trained to "disrupt a cease-fire" that had been reached in the guerrilla war.

A guerrilla spokesman in Mozambique reported July 31 that 12 people had been killed and 110 wounded in the raids. He said Rhodesian jets had attacked a school in one of the camps.

Rev. Ndabaningi Sithole, one of the leaders of Rhodesia's multiracial transitional government, Aug. 2 defended the raid. In a television interview, he said the raid had been necessary to protect the March agreement that established the transition to majority rule in the country. It was the first public defense of a Rhodesian raid into Mozambique by a black nationalist leader.

Church Group Aids Rebels. The World Council of Churches (WCC) announced Aug. 10, 1978 its grant of $85,000 to the Patriotic Front guerrilla forces fighting the Rhodesian interim multiracial government. The council said the grant, made under its program to combat racism, had been approved because "the illegal white minority regime" was still effectively in power in Rhodesia.

The council said the money was to be used for humanitarian purposes only, such as food, health care and educational training for the black Rhodesian refugees in neighboring countries. The WCC said the funds had come from gifts by member churches and individuals and from the

Swedish, Norwegian and Dutch governments.

The WCC decision provoked an immediate outcry from the group's members, which included Protestant, Anglican and Orthodox sects.

Opponents of the grant said the council was encouraging bloodshed.

The donation "pits black against black," in the words of Louis Miller, associate general secretary of the Methodists' world mission board, the Washington Post reported Aug. 18. The Salvation Army suspended its membership in the WCC as a protest against the grant, it was reported Aug. 22.

Smith, Nkomo Meet in Zambia. Rhodesian Prime Minister Ian Smith and guerrilla leader Joshua Nkomo met secretly in Zambia Aug. 14, 1978 to discuss a role for the Patriotic Front guerrilla coalition in the Rhodesian transitional government. Both men confirmed the meeting Sept. 2 after repeated denials since Aug. 31, when reports of the meeting were revealed.

Nkomo said Zambian President Kenneth Kaunda and Nigerian Foreign Minister Joseph Garba had attended the talks. He added that Smith had offered to transfer power in Rhodesia directly to the Patriotic Front.

Smith, however, denied having made such an offer and called the talks "exploratory and inconclusive." He said he had informed the other members of the Rhodesian transitional government's executive council in advance of his meeting with Nkomo. However, one member of the Council, Rev. Ndabaningi Sithole, Sept. 2 denied that he had known of Smith's visit.

The revelation of the Smith-Nkomo meeting brought to a halt U.S.-British efforts to convene a conference of the transitional government and the Patriotic Front.

Nkomo declared Sept. 11 that as a result of his meeting with Smith, all plans for a conference sponsored by the U.S. and Britain were "dead now and buried." However, a spokesman for Robert Mugabe, Nkomo's partner in the Patriotic Front, said the guerrilla coalition was still committed to negotiations.

The spokesman also charged that Nkomo's guerrilla forces were not assuming their fair share of the fighting in Rhodesia. The criticism was the first public airing of the dispute over which faction in the Patriotic Front was doing the most fighting. It was believed that most of Nkomo's forces remained in their bases in Zambia, while the bulk of the guerrilla attacks were carried out by Mugabe's forces. According to reports, observers believed that Nkomo was saving his forces to take power in Rhodesia once the guerrillas had won the war.

ZAPU Downs Civilian Aircraft. An Air Rhodesia commercial jet with 56 persons aboard crashed Sept. 3, 1978 on a flight from Kariba to Salisbury. ZAPU leader Nkomo Sept. 5 declared that his forces had been responsible for shooting down the plane.

Thirty-eight persons were killed in the crash. Ten of the survivors were subsequently massacred by guerrillas at the crash site. Nkomo denied that his men had been responsible for shooting the survivors.

Air Rhodesia authorities at first had discounted the possibility that the plane had been shot down. However, the government confirmed Sept. 7 that a heat-seeking missile had hit the plane. It was thought to be the first time that a regularly scheduled civilian aircraft had been shot down by a ground-to-air missile.

Nkomo charged that the plane was carrying military supplies, and in a later report ZAPU claimed South African army officers were aboard. Air Rhodesia officials and survivors of the crash denied the charge.

A second Air Rhodesia passenger flight was downed by rocket fire shortly after take-off from Kariba Feb. 12, 1979. All 59 passengers and crew members were killed. Nkomo confirmed Feb. 14 that ZAPU was responsible.

In a news conference in Lusaka, Zambia, Nkomo said the guerrillas had fired on the plane after receiving information that Lt. Gen. Peter Walls, Rhodesia's army commander, would be on board. Walls, however, was not on the plane.

Air attack in Zambia. Rhodesian planes Nov. 2, 1978 bombed a guerrilla camp six miles (10 kilometers) from Lusaka. It was the second Rhodesian attack in two weeks near the Zambian capital.

Lusaka at first charged that the camp was used to house children. However, later reports indicated that the area was only a storage depot for food, clothing and other supplies. Casualties were estimated at between 10 and 20 men killed and 50 injured.

The U.S. denounced the raid as a threat "to create an even more dangerous situation in southern Africa" and jeopardize chances for peace talks.

Refugee crisis mounts. U.S. Sen. Edward M. Kennedy (D, Mass.) Sept. 15, 1978 expressed his "growing concern [at] the mounting refugee crisis developing in Southern Africa—especially the plight of some 1.2 million refugees from the escalating conflict and violence in Zimbabwe (Rhodesia)." Kennedy continued in a statement in the Congressional Record:

I have been equally alarmed at the persistent failure of our Government to respond to the growing refugee crisis among Zimbabweans dislocated within their country. For over a year and a half, the administration has wrapped in redtape and bureaucratic indecision an urgent appeal for relief assistance from the International Committee of the Red Cross (ICRC)—one of the world's most respected humanitarian agencies, and the only international agency providing assistance within Zimbabwe.

Officials in the Agency for International Development (AID) have all but ignored for over a year a direct appeal from the ICRC for Zimbabwe. Despite a meeting in September 1977 with a senior official from the International Red Cross—and the outstanding appeal from the ICRC in June 1977, for $4 million in relief assistance—AID officials sat on any action for a full year. And then it was $1 million, none of which could go to refugees within Zimbabwe.

Yet, by every account, the refugee crisis in Zimbabwe was growing daily. Over one-sixth of all black Zimbabweans have been displaced by the war between Rhodesian forces and nationalist guerrillas. Some half million have been herded into what the government calls "protected villages," but which in reality are nothing more than fetid refugee camps. Another 100,000 have filed across the border into neighboring Botswana, Mozambique, and Zambia. Relief needs—especially food, shelter, and medicine—have grown steadily.

After receiving no response from the United States to its first appeal for Zimbabwe on refugees, the Red Cross issued on May 1, 1978, a second appeal for $12 million for Africa, including Zimbabwe, to meet relief needs for 6 months.

But, Mr. President, what has been the response of the United States?

To date, not one penny has been offered to the new appeal. We have pledged $1 million for a $16 million program to date—a shamefully modest response to a crucial humanitarian program in a crucial part of the world.

To date, no international disaster assistance funds have been made available by AID even though at least $3 million remain available until the fiscal year ends in just 2 weeks. Inadequate use has been made, of the special requirements fund for Southern Africa, which has no legal prohibition against assistance to refugees in Zimbabwe provided through international organizations.

When asked what the Department of State and AID are now doing to respond to the latest ICRC appeal for Zimbabwean refugees—the answer is that they are meeting about it. . . .

White exodus. The fighting and the imminence of black rule in Rhodesia spurred the departure of thousands of white citizens. A record total of 18,069 whites left in 1978, according to official figures released Jan. 25, 1979. Immigrants numbered 4,360, for a net loss of 13,709 whites. For December 1978 the figures were: 2,937 white emigrants and 166 white immigrants. Rhodesia's white population was estimated at less than 250,000 after emigration was taken into account.

The figure for the white population was approximate because the government statistics accounted only for those persons who had officially emigrated. Many Rhodesians simply left the country for vacations and did not return.

Camp in Angola. Rhodesian warplanes Feb. 26, 1979, for the first time, penetrated Angolan territory to hit a camp housing guerrillas of Joshua Nkomo's Zimbabwe African People's Union. The Angolan government reported Feb. 28 that 160 persons had been killed and more than 500 wounded.

A Rhodesian military communique said the camp was near the Angolan town of Luso, 180 miles (288 kilometers) inside the Angolan border. According to the Rhodesians, the camp was used as a training center for ZAPU guerrillas before they were transferred to Zambian guerrilla camps in preparation for infiltrating Rhodesia.

Meanwhile, Rhodesian planes continued to attack guerrilla camps in Zambia and Mozambique. Two Zambian camps were hit Feb. 23, resulting in 18 deaths and more than 100 wounded, according to Zambian figures. A guerrilla camp in Mozambique was bombed March 1.

Rhodesian authorities said the raids were intended to slow down guerrilla infiltration of Rhodesia. They said guerrilla activity had increased as part of a campaign to disrupt the April elections for a majority rule government.

South Africa & Namibia

The stern enforcement of South Africa's apartheid (racial segregation) laws has resulted in the departure from South Africa of many white as well as black foes of apartheid. Two major anti-apartheid organizations, the Pan-African Congress (PAC) and African National Congress (ANC) were outlawed in 1960 and are now virtually refugee groups operating in exile from Angola, Zambia, Mozambique, Tanzania and elsewhere with funds mainly from non-South African sources.

Many refugees were created by the dispute over South-West Africa (renamed Namibia by black nationalists and their supporters). South Africa had received a League of Nations mandate for the territory and has struggled against nationalist and United Nations demands that the area by given complete independence.

Refugee leaders slain. Abraham Tiro a black former student leader who had been dismissed from a South African teaching post after clashes with school officials over apartheid, was killed by a parcel bomb in Botswana, it was reported Feb. 6, 1974. The South African regime denied any involvement in the incident, despite charges by the Botswana government that "certain powerful circles in South Africa" may have instigated the assassination.

John Dube, an official of the African National Congress of South Africa, was killed and two others injured by an explosion in a Zambia building housing various southern Africa opposition groups, it was reported Feb. 12.

600 students flee abroad. More than 600 students were believed to have fled to Botswana and Swaziland in the wake of police roundups of students who had boycotted exams. Justice Minister James Kruger Nov. 15, 1976 gave the students until Nov. 22 to return without facing charges of illegal border crossing (most did not have passports) in an unsuccessful attempt to bring them back. Student activists in South Africa quoted in the Nov. 24 Washington Post appealed to the U.S. to aid the refugees and warned that if the West did not help, the students might accept offers from Communist guerrillas. The Post quoted black community leaders as saying that older South African exiles had already approached refugee students with offers of guerrilla training in Mozambique, Tanzania and the U.S.S.R.

South African gets Dutch asylum. The Netherlands gave a resident's permit to a South African conscientious objector seeking to avoid the South African draft, the London Times reported Nov. 12, 1976. Derek Paul Schmulew's two previous requests for political asylum had been denied. He agreed to accept so-called "B" status, which under Dutch law made him a resident on humanitarian grounds. In granting the status, the Ministry of Justice warned that the Netherlands would not become a haven for all South Africans seeking to avoid service, but would judge each case on its merits. (An estimated

6,000 South Africans a year left the country to avoid the draft, according to sources quoted by the Times.)

Botswana bars guerrillas. The Botswana regime said Dec. 7, 1976 that it would no longer harbor nationalist guerrillas fighting the South African and Rhodesian governments, although it had come under pressure from "front-line" African states (near or bordering Rhodesia and South Africa) to do so. Botswana's exports reached the ocean only via South African rail links and its economy was closely tied with South Africa's.

2 journalists escape. Eric Abraham, a journalist placed under a banning order in November 1976, arrived in Botswana Jan. 5, 1977 after having escaped from his Cape Town home. He had been denied an exit visa to Great Britain in December 1976. The banning order had restricted his movements to daylight hours and prevented him from being in groups of more than four persons.

Donald Woods, editor of the East London Daily Dispatch, reached Botswana Jan. 3, 1978 after escaping from South Africa, where he had been under a five-year banning order for his anti-apartheid activities. Woods had escaped from his East London home in disguise and crossed the border into Lesotho Dec. 30, 1977 before flying to Botswana.

Woods had been joined in Lesotho by his wife and their five children the day after his escape. He said he and his family would go to Great Britain where they had received permission to settle. He said he would not return to South Africa until "there is a change of government or a change of heart in the government."

Woods' banning order in October 1977 forbade him to publish, be quoted in the media or meet with more than one person (outside his family) at a time. Friends said Woods had made up his mind to leave after one of his daughters had been injured by a T-shirt that had been soaked in acid. The shirt had been mailed to the Woods home in November 1977, and a private investigator for Woods said two government officials were responsible for tampering with the shirt. Their names were not disclosed.

Ovambos flee Namibia to Angola. More than 500 persons had entered Angola from South-West Africa (Namibia) since mid-June 1974. They illegally crossed the sealed Ovamboland border, according to a July 9 report. Chief Philemon Elifas, chief minister of Ovamboland, issued an appeal June 24 for the exodus to cease. Many teachers and other skilled workers were leaving.

A number of leaders of the South-West Africa People's Organization (SWAPO) were also reported to have fled. According to the Africa Research Bulletin July 15, Jannie de Wet, commissioner-general for the Indigenious Peoples of South-West Africa, alleged that they had crossed the border into Angola for guerrilla training.

South Africa orders Angola buffer zone. South Africa May 19, 1976 announced plans for a 1,000-mile buffer zone along the Angolan-Namibian border to stem forays by South-West African guerrillas from refugee camps in Angola.

The Johannesburg decision followed an April pledge by Angola that it would attempt to guarantee the integrity of the border that was regularly crossed by members of SWAPO.

To create the half-mile-wide "no-man's land," the South African government also announced sweeping measures empowering authorities to evacuate villagers from "prohibited areas," conduct searches, restrict travel and arrest suspected terrorists.

Zambia arrests Namibians. The Zambian government announced May 4, 1976 that it was holding an undisclosed number of SWAPO members under "protective custody" in Lusaka to encourage "unity" within the organization. SWAPO sources said that about 40 members of a dissident faction of the group's external wing had been arrested because of fierce infighting. Zambia supported the external wing's leader, Sam Nujoma.

Two men who had fled a SWAPO camp in Namibia May 1, 1977 said that more than 1,000 Namibians were imprisoned in the camp for having criticized SWAPO policies. They added that 15 persons had been killed trying to escape.

Shipanga Released—Andreas Shipanga, former SWAPO secretary of information, was freed May 25, 1978 from a Tanzanian jail. He had been held in detention without trial in Zambia and Tanzania since April 1976.

Shipanga and 18 other SWAPO members had been jailed because of disagreements with SWAPO President Sam Nujoma. Shipanga reportedly favored a moderate political course for Namibia and was pro-West.

Shipanga and his followers were flown out of Tanzania. They said June 19 that they had formed a new political party, the SWAPO-Democrats, and would return to Namibia to work with the Namibian National Front, a group of moderates who favored the Western efforts to achieve a Namibian solution.

South African raid in Angola. South African troops in Namibia entered Angola May 4, 1978 and attacked SWAPO bases.

South African Defense Minister Pieter W. Botha, who announced the raid, said the "limited military action" had been mounted in response to a recent increase in guerrilla attacks in Namibia.

It was South Africa's largest military operation in Angola since its unsuccessful intervention on behalf of pro-Western forces in the Angolan civil war in 1975. South African troops also had staged "hot pursuit" raids, brief attacks across the border, in search of SWAPO guerrillas in the past.

Botha did not reveal the size of the invading South African force, but according to press reports it numbered between 300 and 700 men. Five soldiers were reported to have been killed in the 12-hour attack. Military officials said that the main headquarters of SWAPO at Cassinga, 150 miles (250 kilometers) north of the Angolan-Namibian border, and two smaller bases were destroyed.

The Angolan government charged May 6 that 504 Namibian refugees and 16 Angolan soldiers had been killed in the South

African attack. SWAPO sources May 7 gave the death toll as 1,000, including women and children. A South African military spokesman admitted May 6 that women and children were in the SWAPO camps but said many of the women were wearing military uniforms.

South African military authorities May 27 announced that they had released 63 of the prisoners they had captured in the raid on the Angolan camp. The announcement was the first official indication that South Africa had taken prisoners in the raid. Those released were trainees, according to the authorities, who indicated that other guerrillas were still in custody.

An estimated 3,000–5,000 SWAPO guerrillas and refugees were based in Angolan camps, according to reports. SWAPO attacks had increased during 1978, and large quantities of weapons and ammunition had been captured by South African soldiers during the fighting.

U.N. Condemns Attack—The United Nations Security Council May 6 unanimously condemned the raid into Angola as a "flagrant violation" of Angolan sovereignty.

South Africa was condemned for its "extreme barbarity" in the raid by the United Nations High Commissioner for Refugees and the World Health Organization, it was reported June 16. Representatives who examined the site of the attack said 600 refugees had been killed and more than 400 wounded.

(Meanwhile, South Africa denounced the U.S. May 12 for its warning against any further raids on Angola. Foreign Minister Roelof Botha condemned the U.S. for calling the timing of the raid "unfortunate" while ignoring guerrilla attacks by SWAPO.)

SWAPO Gets Church Grant. The World Council of Churches (WCC) had given a grant of $125,000 to the South-West Africa People's Organization (SWAPO), the guerrilla group fighting South Africa for control of Namibia, it was reported Sept. 26, 1978. This was the largest gift in 1978 from the WCC's fund to combat racism. The WCC in August had contributed $85,000 to guerrilla forces in Rhodesia from the same fund.

Pretoria Rejects Namibia Truce. The South African government rejected a U.N. plan March 5, 1979 for a cease-fire in Namibia. Next day South African forces in Namibia began a major raid against SWAPO guerrillas in Angola.

Uganda

Perhaps as many as 300,000 Ugandans were murdered by the regime of Idi Amin in the eight years that Amin ruled his land-locked country. The reign of terror started with the 1971 coup that put Amin into power and continued until a force of Ugandan refugees and Tanzanians unseated him in 1979. Streams of refugees sought foreign asylum from the Ugandan horrors throughout this period. One of the first refugees was Milton Obote, the president deposed by Amin's coup.

Coup overthrows Obote. President Milton Obote, attending a conference of Commonwealth leaders in Singapore, was deposed Jan. 25, 1971 in a coup led by Maj. Gen. Idi Amin.

As one of its first official acts Jan. 25, the new government ordered the release of all political prisoners, estimated to number nearly 100, and requested the return of political exiles. Many of those affected by the order were followers of Sir Edward Mutesa, whom Obote had ousted as president in 1966. Mutesa had been kabaka (king) of the Baganda tribe. He had died in exile in Britain in 1969.

General Amin charged Jan. 26 that Obote, a member of the Langi tribe, had sent messages from Singapore to Acholi and Langi tribesmen in the army ordering them to disarm and kill all other tribesmen. Amin declared, however, that Obote was welcome to return to Uganda as a private citizen and that his Uganda People's Congress would not be disbanded. (Amin himself was a Moslem and member of the Kakwa tribe from west of the Nile.)

Reward for Obote, others. The Ugandan government May 13, 1971 offered a reward of one million shillings ($139,200) for the return alive of former President Obote. Rewards of half million shillings each were offered for two of his support-

ers, Lt. Col. Oyite Ojok and Akena Adoko, head of Obote's disbanded secret police, the General Service Department.

The rewards were to be paid "either openly or secretly to anyone, anywhere, in any currency he wishes."

According to the London Times April 20, the Uganda government had protested to Sudan against the incursion from Sudanese territory of 500 Uganda refugees fighting for the restoration of Obote. The Amin regime accused the Tanzanian government April 20 of giving Obote facilities for guerrilla training. Tanzania denied the charge April 22.

Amin May 16, 1972 withdrew the reward offer. He said Obote and his aides were "free to return as citizens of Uganda and no harm will be done to them." He thanked Tanzanian President Julius K. Nyerere for having granted Obote political asylum.

Uganda massacres alleged. Western press sources Feb. 14, 1972 reported on the slaughter of 4,000–5,000 Langi and Acholi tribesmen of the Ugandan army, said to have been executed at intervals by the government of President Idi Amin since it took power in January 1971.

The account, written by a London Observer reporter and appearing in the Washington Post, was obtained in interviews with 19 Ugandan soldiers who had broken out of their country's prison at Mutukula Feb. 6 and were being held near the northern Tanzanian town of Tabora.

According to the men, they and hundreds of fellow tribesmen had been rounded up by Amin during the course of 1971 and taken to prisons throughout Uganda, where large numbers of them were killed. Those interviewed Feb. 14 said that on Dec. 28, 1971 they and some 500 others were transferred from Luzira to Mutukula prison and that by Feb. 4 all but 102 of the prisoners had been shot or beaten to death. During the Feb. 6 escape, 79 of those remaining were shot by guards, including Mohammed Hassan, former head of the army's Criminal Investigation Division, who reportedly had been too weak to attempt the break.

The men said they believed themselves to be the only survivors of the nearly

5,000 Langi and Acholi who had been in the army at the time of Amin's coup.

President Amin had said Feb. 6 that 15 escaped detainees had been returned by Tanzania, a gesture he described as "prompt and friendly action." In an official statement the following day, the Tanzanian government denied returning any of the detainees to Uganda.

Asians ordered out. President Amin declared Aug. 5, 1972 that Asians with British passports would be given three months to settle their affairs and leave Uganda. Britain expressed disapproval of the expulsion deadline Aug. 7 and several of the other countries involved indicated unwillingness to accept the Asians.

Amin said in a broadcast that there was "no room" for the Asians in the country because they were "sabotaging the economy" and did not have "the welfare of Uganda at heart." Most shops in the main towns, he said, were controlled by Asians, who engaged in such practices as hoarding, profiteering and currency frauds. "Why have Ugandans not taken over such businesses?" he asked.

Amin's insistence on the deadline for expulsion of Asians holding British passports was conveyed at an Aug. 15 meeting with Geoffrey Rippon, a minister without portfolio in the British government.

Rippon was quoted as saying that Britain would "demonstrate that we are prepared to accept our share of the responsibility. . . .But it is not in the interests of anybody that thousands of human beings should find themselves, as it were, in limbo, without their legal status defined or in camps. . . ."

Agence France-Presse reported Aug. 11 that Asians appealing to the Immigration Department in Kampala had become stateless when their certificates of Ugandan citizenship were canceled by officials there. British Home Secretary Robert Carr met with representatives of airlines and shipping companies in London Aug. 12 and emphasized that British passport holders from East Africa should not be embarked unless they had United Kingdom entry certificates.

Amin revealed Aug. 19 that all Asians, even citizens of Uganda, would be told to leave the country. The move would be "carried out as a second-phase operation after the present one involving the Asians holding British passports and nationals of India, Pakistan and Bangla Desh." Expulsion of Asian professionals, he said, had been decided "in light of sabotage and arson, which the Indians have now started to carry out in the country."

In an Oct. 25 directive, Amin extended his expulsion order against Asians to "any person of Indian, Pakistan or Bangla Desh origin, extraction or descent" from any country in the world.

Foreign reaction—Surendra Pal Singh, the Indian deputy foreign minister, said Aug. 11 that British Asians from Uganda would need visas to enter India.

A spokesman for the Indian government, cited in the London Times Aug. 7, said New Delhi would not accept the majority of Asians threatened with expulsion from Uganda. The Times described Indian policy as requiring that British passport-holders of Indian origin, who were admitted to India in small numbers, be allowed into the country only if British officials stamped their passports acknowledging them as a British responsibility.

In Nairobi, Vice President Daniel Arap Moi said Kenya would not become a "dumping ground for the citizens of other countries" and if necessary it would seal its border with Uganda and deploy "maximum border patrols."

Kenya's Deputy Home Affairs Minister Martin Shikuku warned Aug. 21 that non-citizens would be asked to leave the country "unless they stop sabotaging our economy." Shikuku said he approved of Amin's decision. President Jomo Kenyatta said Aug. 22 that foreigners must either support local aspirations or "pack their luggage and go back to their respective mother countries."

The government-owned newspaper Liberian Age commented Aug. 11 in Monrovia that Uganda's action was "a sign that the patience of Africans is running out." The expulsions would "serve as a warning to those who flock into a developing country, exploit its resources and ship the money out without reinvesting any penny there for the social growth of that country."

President Julius Nyerere of Tanzania

said Aug. 21 that the decision to expel Asians holding Ugandan citizenship was "racialism," adding: "Either the Asians are citizens or they are not and once they are, you are enjoined to accord them the same treatment that you accord all the others." Saidi Maswanya, the Tanzanian home affairs minister, had indicated Aug. 10 that his country would not allow Asians expelled from Uganda to settle there.

In a statement from Zambia, President dent Kenneth Kaunda said Sept. 6 that Amin's actions toward the Asians were "terrible, horrible, abominable and shameful," adding: "We can only hope that what happened in Uganda does not happen somewhere else."

Britain attacks ousters—British spokesmen continued to denounce the ouster of Asians but promised to aid the refugees.

In an Aug. 31 television broadcast, Foreign Secretary Sir Alec Douglas-Home called Amin's expulsion order "inhuman and unjust," saying he hoped the Ugandan leader "could be persuaded to change his mind and we are still working for this."

Douglas-Home emphasized that all foreign countries which "might take some of these unfortunate people have already been approached." He then detailed a process by which "successive British governments" had "accepted an obligation" to take in Asians with British passports "in the last resort if these people were ever expelled." It was also the case that under "international law a state has a duty to accept those of its nationals who have nowhere else to go." He said the government "fully realizes that additional burdens will be placed on local communities, many of which are already coping with considerable social problems. We will help them and we will make additional resources available to them."

(Edward Marston, an alderman of the city of Leicester, led a five-man delegation to the Foreign Office Aug. 31 and told officials that Leicester was "full up and all our social services are already overloaded." One of 12 members of the Community Relations Commission, Bernard Perkins, resigned Aug. 24, claiming that although it was "wrong

forcibly to expel tens of thousands of people from their homes" it was "equally wrong to expect the people of this country, whatever their color, to accept a further massive influx of immigrants.")

The first planeload of British Asian refugees from Uganda arrived in England Sept. 18 aboard a chartered jet.

The 189 passengers were met by Sir Charles Cunningham, head of the Uganda Resettlement Board, as well as other officials who interviewed the refugees about housing and job placement. They were advised not to settle in Birmingham, parts of London and other areas that had large Asian communities and would not welcome more Asians.

The London Times Oct. 3 said British officials working with the Uganda Resettlement Board had changed the emphasis of their policy in order to reduce the large number of Asians in refugee camps.

The New York Times said Nov. 5 that Britain had taken more than 22,000 Asians who had left Uganda holding British citizenship. The Times noted that about half the newly-arrived Asians were still living in camps.

Others accept refugees—Other countries also agreed to admit some of the Asian refugees expelled by Uganda.

Prime Minister Pierre Elliott Trudeau said Aug. 24 that Canada would accept a number of the Asians being expelled from Uganda. Although some reports indicated that as many as 5,000 might be admitted, Trudeau dismissed these estimates as "pure speculation."

In Canberra, Immigration Minister James Forbes said Aug. 22 that some Uganda Asians would be accepted by Australia if they had useful professional qualifications.

Lord Hailsham, the Lord Chancellor and principal legal adviser to the British government, announced Sept. 14 that more than a dozen countries including New Zealand and Sweden had offered to accept Asians expelled from Uganda.

Australian officials announced Sept. 29 that 101 Ugandan Asians had been approved for entry into the country.

It was also reported Sept. 21 that West Germany had agreed to accept about 1,000 Uganda Asians.

The U.S. State Department said Oct. 2 that the country planned to admit up to 1,000 stateless Asians from Uganda. Charles W. Bray 3rd, the department's spokesman, said Attorney General Richard G. Kleindienst had decided to use his authority to admit the Asians without going through normal visa procedures. They were to be chosen "with a careful eye to the professional capabilities of the applicants so as to insure that they will have means of self-support and would not affect the labor situation."

Refugee invaders defeated. A force of some 1,000 troops, believed to be a guerrilla army composed mainly of exiles loyal to former Uganda President Milton Obote, attacked Uganda from Tanzania Sept. 17, 1972. The invaders were repulsed by Sept. 20.

The attack began at dawn Sept. 17 when the guerrillas crossed into Tanzania at the border town of Mutukula. By nightfall, the nearby towns of Kyotera and Kalisizo had fallen and Masaka, an administrative center on the road to Kampala, was threatened. Battalion-size barracks at Mbarara were surrounded.

In answer to official Ugandan charges that the attackers had been Tanzanian troops, Maj. Gen. Sam Sarakikya, the Tanzanian army commander, said Sept. 17 that there were "absolutely no" Tanzanian soldiers involved. He explained: "It could be guerrillas or refugees or anybody. It is difficult for me to say."

Uganda military sources Sept. 18 reported that Mbarara had been cleared, Kyotera and Kalisizo had been recaptured and troops loyal to President Idi Amin were "pushing very hard toward Mutukula." Other sources said at least one group of up to 500 exiles had dug in between Masaka and the Tanzanian border and had been given a resupply of ammunition and equipment. Observers explained the apparent failure of the invasion by speculating that the guerrillas had counted on large-scale defections from the Uganda army, which never occurred, and by noting that they had

launched their attack through an area populated mostly by the Baganda, a tribe which had never supported Obote.

Uganda radio charged Sept. 18 that the attack had been carried out by regular Tanzanian troops and Uganda guerrillas supported by British and Israeli mercenaries. Among those it said had been killed in the fighting around Mbarara were "three Israelis." The radio claimed three former Uganda army officers loyal to Obote, including Lt. Col. David Oyite Ojok, had been killed.

Lugbaras flee. More than 300 Lugbara tribesmen reportedly fled Uganda by March 31, 1974 to seek refuge in Zaire and the Sudan following an unsuccessful coup attempt March 24.

The French newspaper Le Monde reported March 29 that 400 people had been executed in Kampala alone within six hours after President Amin reasserted control. Most of those killed were Christian Lugbaras believed involved in the abortive uprising.

Cabinet members flee. Finance Minister Emmanuel Wakhweya fled in 1975 to London where, in an interview published in the weekly newspaper The Observer Jan. 19, he said there was no longer a role for a finance minister in Uganda because Amin's policies were bringing the country to the brink of economic catastrophe.

Three Cabinet members defected abroad during 1977: Industry Minister Semei Nyanzi refused to return to Uganda from a foreign tour, the London Times reported Feb. 28. Health Minister Henry Kyemba defected just before the June 15 conference of Commonwealth nations. And the London Daily Mirror July 2 reported that Ugandan Justice Minister Godfrey Lule had defected to Great Britain with his family. Lule had told the newspaper that he had defected because he feared for his life in the wake of a false report that he had been plotting to assassinate President Idi Amin. He described Uganda as "an open prison ruled by terrorism and corruption." According to the Daily Mirror, Lule had arrived in Britain from Geneva where he had denied allegations by the International Commission of Jurists that more than 80,-000 people had been killed since Amin had come to power.

EAC employees refuse to return— Ugandan employes of the East African Community (EAC) had refused an order from President Idi Amin to return to Uganda from Tanzania, the Tanzanian regime's newspaper said Aug. 17, 1977. After the virtual breakup of the EAC, Amin July 30 had ordered all 700 Ugandan employes to return from EAC offices in Tanzania and Kenya, but the 200 Ugandans in Tanzania had refused.

*Pilot defects—*Charles Balidawa, a Ugandan pilot decorated by Amin for saving the lives of six British passengers in January, asked for asylum in Britain March 13, 1977. He had arrived in London one month before on a senior pilot's training course but had requested asylum after receiving word that his family had escaped to Kenya.

A report describing atrocities and torture in Uganda, written by Balidawa and broadcast by the British Broadcasting Corporation, appeared to have prompted Amin March 13 to warn all U.S. and British nationals of "pressure" if they reported "false information" about Uganda.

Refugees flee purge of Christians. In the early months of 1977 Ugandan refugees fled to Kenya and Tanzania to escape what they described as a massive campaign against Acholi and Lango tribesmen, the majority of whom were Christians, in a drive against suspected enemies of President Amin. Refugees in Kenya March 2 and in Tanzania Feb. 23 said thousands of tribesmen had been taken away by security forces and were feared dead. Kenyan church sources, cited Feb. 25 in the New York Times, said the purge against the Christian tribesmen had begun Jan. 25, the anniversary of the coup d'etat that had brought Amin to power in 1971. Educated Ugandans of all tribes, businessmen, former opponents, civil servants

and their relatives also were victims. Two government security units, the Bureau of State Research and the Public Safety Unit, were reported to the main organs of repression.

A high-ranking officer who deserted from the Ugandan army said "Amin personally gave the order that all Lango and Acholi soldiers should be killed," according to the Washington Post March 28. Lango tribesmen, who numbered about 400,000 out of a total Ugandan population of 10 million, and Acholis, who numbered about 500,000, had made up 50% of the 10,000-man armed forces in 1971, the year Amin seized power from former President Milton Obote. Obote was a Lango, and Amin reportedly suspected all Lango tribesmen of remaining loyal to the ousted president, who lived in exile in Tanzania. Amin was a member of the smaller Kakwa tribe; the officer quoted by the Post said most of the men in Amin's State Research Bureau were Kakwas or mercenaries from Sudan, Zaire, Rwanda and Burundi who had tribal affiliations with the Kakwas.

A refugee in Lusaka, Zambia, cited in the Post March 29, said his town of Lira had been sealed off Feb. 5 by the State Research Bureau. Several businessmen, former government officials and some of their relatives had been taken away from the town and were presumed dead, the refugee reported. Agents from Amin's secret forces were reported to be infiltrating Kenya to spy on Ugandan refugees, according to the Financial Times (London) March 9.

A Post report April 2 said soldiers who had escaped from the Ugandan army reported that Soviet advisers were working in the State Research Bureau and were training Ugandan troops in the use of tanks, missiles and artillery. The deserters added that Soviet and Palestinian pilots were flying MiG-21's given to Amin by Moscow. However, they said no Cuban military instructors were among the troops, contrary to previous reports.

The former soldiers also reported that more than 7,000 troops had been killed, dismissed or had fled from the army as the result of a purge that had begun in June 1976, after the failure of an assassination attempt against Amin.

Refugees reaching Kenya in June said there had been another attempt on Amin's life by a group of army officers led by an air force major. The attempted coup had failed because Amin had been informed of the plot in time, according to the Washington Post June 24. Refugees quoted in the report said Amin had escaped with minor injuries. (Since his successful coup in 1971, Amin reportedly had survived more than 12 assassination attempts.)

Refugees reaching Nairobi June 20–23 had reported new purges in the wake of the assassination attempt, the Post reported June 23. Sources cited in the report said the victims were members of the southern Baganda and Basoga tribes. Christians, civil servants and military personnel were also victims in the reprisal campaign after the assassination attempt, the refugees reported.

Amin foes unite. Ugandan exiles had gathered secretly in Zambia to form a united front to overthrow Ugandan President Amin, a Kenyan newspaper said Aug. 8, 1977. The Standard said that the Ugandan anti-Amin organizations were planning a merger and they had the tacit approval of the Zambian government.

Former President Milton Obote Jan. 12, 1979 issued a statement calling for Amin's overthrow. It was the first time Obote had publicly called for Amin's ouster.

Obote, living in exile in Tanzania, said "Uganda-wide rebellion" was the only answer to "the crime of genocide" Amin had perpetrated on the Ugandan people.

A newly formed refugee anti-government group claimed responsibility for bombing a power line and a fuel depot Feb. 3 in Kampala, the capital. Electricity and water supplies to the city were cut for two days. Foreign residents reported hearing sporadic gunfire Feb. 4.

A spokesman for the Save Uganda Movement, which was made up of Ugandan exiles, said in Nairobi, Kenya Feb. 5 that in addition to the bombings, the group had distributed leaflets in Kampala calling for Amin's overthrow.

Refugees join invasion force. Border fighting between Tanzania and Uganda turned into a full-scale invasion of Uganda by Tanzanian-backed forces determined to overthrow President Idi Amin, with the attackers said Feb. 28, 1979 to be moving on Kampala, the capital.

Amin reported Feb. 11 that Tanzanian troops had renewed their advance into his country. The Tanzanian forces were joined by guerrilla units composed of Ugandan exiles opposed to Amin.

According to reports, there were two separate anti-Amin groups in the fighting: 1,400 exiles loyal to former Ugandan President Milton Obote and 1,500 guerrillas of the Save Uganda Movement, which had carried out several acts of sabotage in Kampala.

(There were additional reports that the invasion had triggered mutinies in the Ugandan army and sabotage by rebels inside Uganda.)

Capital seized, Amin replaced. A force of 5,000 Tanzanian soldiers and 3,000 Ugandan exiles entered the capital of Kampala April 11 after six months of fighting. As Kampala residents cheered the victorious rebels, a group of Ugandan exiles in Dar es Salaam, Tanzania announced the formation of a provisional government to replace Amin's regime.

The invaders had advanced slowly through southern Uganda from Tanzania in early March. Their advance began with the capture of two important southern Ugandan towns, Mbarara and Masaka.

By March 25, the invading forces were reported to have captured Mpigi, a strategic town overlooking Kampala, 20 miles (33 kilometers) to the southwest. Mityana, 35 miles (56 kilometers) northwest of Kampala, was reported taken March 28. Kampala was virtually surrounded by enemy troops and within range of artillery fire.

The advance of the Tanzanians and exiles was halted March 31 by Libyan reinforcements. Early in March, Libya had airlifted tons of equipment to Uganda and sent 2,000 troops, according to reports. (Libya denied sending soldiers.)

The Libyans failed to halt the invasion force. By April 1 the Tanzanians and Ugandan exiles were reported to be on the advance again.

The Libyans suffered a defeat at Lubo-
wa, five miles (eight kilometers) from
Kampala. By April 4, the invaders were
within the outskirts of the capital city.
Entebbe fell April 4, and the Libyans were
reported to have abandoned Kampala.
According to reports, they were flown back
to Libya April 6–7.

Fresh Ugandan troops from the northwest were brought in April 8 to stem the
invaders' advance. But they too were
defeated, and under cover of heavy artillery fire the invasion force took control
of the capital.

The Tanzanians and exiles received a
triumphal welcome from residents of
Kampala.

(Stores were ransacked throughout
Kampala in the wake of the rebel victory.
Consumer goods were scarce in Uganda as
a result of pervasive corruption under
Amin's regime. Most of the shops had been
expropriated from Ugandan Asians by
Amin and turned over to his personal
friends.)

The provisional government formed to
take over Uganda was led by Yusufu K.
Lule, 67, a former official of Makerere
University in Kampala. He appointed a
14-member Cabinet April 11 in Dar es
Salaam and pledged to organize elections
in Uganda as soon as possible.

(Lule had been chosen to lead the provisional government at a meeting March
23-25 of Ugandan exile groups in the
northern Tanzanian town of Moshi.)

Zairian Exiles Invade Shaba

*Zairian refugees mounted two major
invasions of the Zairian province of Shaba
during 1977 and 1978. In each case, the
exile attackers were defeated after initial
successes.*

Province invaded from Angola. Zaire's
Shaba (formerly Katanga) Province was
invaded March 8, 1977 by forces striking
across the border from Angola, according to a government broadcast March
10. The invaders were reported to have
seized Kisengi, Kapanga and Dilolo, strategic towns in the mineral-rich southern
province.

The Congolese National Liberation
Front (FLNC) March 11 claimed
responsibility for the attack. In a communique issued in Paris, the group said the invasion was "a national uprising by the
Congolese people." (Before independence
in 1960, Zaire had been the Belgian
Congo. The FLNC had been organized in
1963 by Katanga secessionists who had
fled to Angola after the defeat of the
separatist movement led by the late Moise
Tshombe.)

Zaire March 11 charged that Angolan
troops were among the invaders, and the
next day it called Angola "a base for aggression against Zaire." Angola denied
the charges. (Angola had charged Zaire
with harboring guerrillas of the National
Front for the Liberation of Angola
[FNLA] who were continuing to fight the
Angolan government in the north. Zaire
had backed the FNLA during the Angolan
civil war.)

The Zaire army did little fighting, according to intelligence reports cited in the
Washington Post March 25. Official accounts of major bombing operations
March 23 were exaggerated, according to
the report, since most of Zaire's planes
were grounded for lack of spare parts.

The inhabitants of Shaba seemed to be
sympathetic to the invaders, according to
another Post report March 24. They were
members of the Lunda tribe, whose territory spread across Shaba, Angola and
Zambia, and they were said to be loyal to
Daniel Tshombe, brother of the late
Moise Tshombe, who had led an unsuccessful Katangan secessionist movement
in 1963. (The Lunda tribe was one of an
estimated 200 tribes that made up Zaire.)

A contingent of 1,500 Moroccan troops
was flown to Kinshasa April 9 to help the
Zairian forces against the invaders.

The troops were dispatched in response
to a request April 7 by Zaire President
Mobutu Sese Seko. They were immediately sent to Kolwezi, principal target
of the rebel advance. The insurgent forces
reportedly had pushed to within 50 miles
of Kolwezi after the fall of the Zaire army
command center of Mutshatsha.

The French government April 10 disclosed that it had sent a fleet of 11 military planes to Morocco to airlift the troops to Zaire in response to a request from Morocco and Zaire. The government announcement called Zaire "a victim of armed subversive activities . . . originating from abroad." The French Defense Ministry disclosed April 11 that a number of French military instructors were stationed in Zaire to train the army in the use of military equipment France had provided under a 1974 arms contract. The instructors had been in the country for several months, the ministry said.

French President Valery Giscard d'Estaing April 12 defended the French action, saying: "Subversion in Africa would have consequences for both France and Europe." He did not specify the source of the invaders' support, but he noted Soviet policy of "making its presence felt in troubled areas" of Africa.

The State Department April 12 announced the U.S. was sending $13 million in "non-lethal" military equipment to Zaire in addition to the $2 million in aid it had sent in March. The department said the aid consisted of a $9-million C-130 transport plane and $4 million worth of spare parts, fuel and communications equipment. The U.S. rejected an additional Zairian request for "emergency assistance." The department denied the U.S. had cooperated with other countries furnishing military aid to Zaire.

(U.S. government officials privately had expressed the opinion that U.S. caution on Zaire aid reflected the fear of a repeat of the U.S. experience in Vietnam, it was reported April 13. They added there was a growing belief the U.S. should avoid African conflicts where its vital interests were not affected. There was also a belief that the U.S. should remain uncommitted to avoid giving the Soviet Union an excuse to enter the conflict. The White House April 12 had said "we do not see the Zaire situation as an East-West confrontation.")

In an interview reported in the April 18 issue of Newsweek on sale April 11, President Mobutu said he was "bitterly disappointed by America's attitude" and charged the U.S. had "decided to surrender piecemeal to the Soviet-Cuban grand design in Africa...." At a rally April 9 in Kinshasa, Mobutu had said he was "ignoring" the role of Angola in the conflict because it was a puppet of the Soviet Union and Cuba. He charged that the two latter countries were behind the "invasion."

Besides Moroccan, French and U.S. help, Zaire had received expressions of support from several other countries. Sudanese Foreign Minister Mansour Khalid April 7 had said his country would aid Zaire in any way short of sending military assistance, because of the need to meet its own military threats. That day, the Zaire government had announced China had agreed to send 30 tons of equipment to Zaire. An Egyptian military team had visited Zaire to discuss possible military aid, Mobutu had said April 9. Belgian Premier Leo Tindemans April 12 had said there were about 80 Belgian military instructors in Zaire.

Angolan President Agostinho Neto April 11 said his government "condemns with the greatest vigor foreign meddling, be it African or other, in the domestic affairs of Zaire." He denied charges of Cuban and Soviet involvement in the invasion.

By late April, the refugee forces were on the run and had been virtually defeated. The Mutshatsha command center was retaken by Zairian troops April 25.

The recapture of the strategic village, on the railway along the southern border of Shaba (formerly Katanga), was achieved with little fighting since most of the FNLC forces and the civilian population had fled before the approaching troops.

Fighting had been at a standstill since the arrival of 1,500 Moroccan soldiers April 9, according to government reports and Western diplomatic sources. Major fighting resumed April 15 at Kazenze, a village midway between Mutshatsha and Kolwezi, the principal mining town in the copper-rich province. The Zairian troops apparently began the fighting at Kazenze and were followed by about 400 Moroccans the next day. In the days that followed, Zairian troops continued their offensive, moving forward from Kolwezi as the FNLC retreated to the border towns they initially had captured.

Most of the fighting reportedly was carried on by the Zairian troops, including a company of 150–200 pygmy bowmen with poisoned arrows. The Moroccan soliders apparently provided organizational and logistical support to improve the morale and effectiveness of Zaire's army, which had been described as disorganized and unprepared.

The government troops met with little resistance from the retreating Katangan seccessionist forces. A press tour of the war zone April 25 showed little evidence of fighting, and there were indications the rebels had not been equipped with advanced weapons as Mobutu had reported. Captured weapons displayed April 20 in Kinshasa, Zaire's capital, had included old automatic rifles and a box of four Soviet-made antitank mines.

Two prisoners of war displayed in the capital April 20 told reporters they had been trained in Angola by Cubans, who had escorted them to the Zaire border. However, according to a report April 26 in the Washington Post, when the prisoners had been captured they had said no Cuban troops had crossed into Shaba. They had said they had been given assistance by "whites" in Angola who were presumed by observers to be Portuguese.

May 1978 invasion. In the 1978 invasion, exile guerrillas moved into Shaba Province May 11 and quickly occupied Kolwezi and Mutshatsha. The attack was by the National Front for the Liberation of the Congo (FNLC), the same group that had invaded Shaba in March 1977.

Zaire radio reported the invasion May 14, charging that the rebels, who numbered 4,000, were receiving support from Angolan and Cuban forces.

The Zairian government May 15 charged that the rebels had thwarted the Zairian defenses by entering Shaba through Zambia. In contrast to its previous invasion, the FNLC attacked the two major Shaba towns directly.

French & Belgians rescue whites— French and Belgian paratroopers were dropped into the Zairian mining town of Kolwezi May 19 and 20 to rescue more than 2,500 Europeans caught in the fighting there.

About 1,750 Belgian troops and 1,000 members of the French Foreign Legion had been flown into Zaire May 18 in preparation for the rescue operation. The U.S. provided 18 transport planes and support personnel to unload equipment, and Great Britain supplied four transport planes. It was the first European rescue operation in Zaire since the evacuation of foreigners during the 1964 secession battle in Shaba Province, which was then known as Katanga.

The rescue operation had been carried out with the approval of Zairian President Mobutu Sese Seko. Two separate French airdrops brought a total of 600 troops into Kolwezi May 19. The Belgians followed May 20 with 700 troops flown in from the Zairian town of Kamina, 120 miles (200 kilometers) north of Kolwezi. The airlift of Europeans began May 20, as the two forces joined up and established control over the city.

The rescue mission was undertaken when reports of massacres of Europeans by rebels reached Europe. The official Zairian news agency May 19 reported that 44 Europeans had been found dead in the town. French Legionnaires later confirmed the report.

Estimates of the European death toll ran as high as 200 by the time the rescue operation had been completed, according to French officials May 23. A number of Europeans, as well as two Americans, were still unaccounted for and were presumed to have been taken hostage by the rebels as they retreated to Zambia.

The total death toll of blacks and whites in the city was estimated at 500, but it was doubted that an exact figure would ever be established. Refugees arriving in Belgium reported that rebels had gone on a rampage of looting and murder directed against whites during their eight-day occupation of Kolwezi. Some refugees reported that Zairian soldiers had taken part in the carnage.

The French said their military casualties were two killed and nine wounded. The Belgians said one of their men had been wounded.

The Belgian troops withdrew from Kolwezi May 22, leaving the city in the hands of the French forces. According to reports, the French had done most of the fighting to drive the rebels out of the city, while the Belgian troops had provided assistance to the Europeans who were evacuated.

French President Valery Giscard d'Estaing announced May 23 that the French troops would leave Kolwezi as soon as all French nationals had been rescued.

(Several hundred heavily armed rebels were reported moving through Zambia on their way to Angola. According to witnesses, the rebels drove trucks and cars seized in Kolwezi and were holding European hostages.)

French, Belgians Disagree—Belgium and France were reported to have disagreed sharply over the conduct of the Shaba rescue operation. The French military action was interpreted by Brussels as an attempt to supplant Belgian interests in Zaire, a former Belgian colony.

Belgian Premier Leo Tindemans May 19 charged that his government had not been consulted by the French over the plan to drop French troops into Kolwezi. He said he had been "informed" of the French action but was not asked for approval.

Tindemans said the Belgian intervention in Zaire was for humanitarian purposes only, implying that the French had other motives for their actions. According to Belgian officials, Belgium, which had $1-billion worth of investments in Zaire, was concerned that France was seeking to edge it out of the country.

The Belgians wanted to conduct their rescue operation in cooperation with international organizations and with the approval of other African nations besides Zaire. The Belgians reportedly had been forced to move into Kolwezi as a result of the French Legionnaires' moving into the city.

France denied that Belgium had been ignored in the planning for the military operation in Shaba. Foreign Minister Louis de Guiringaud said May 19 that the French paratroop drop had been decided upon with the approval of the Belgian government and after consultations with Great Britain and the U.S. He said the

only difference between France and Belgium was that France was ready to intervene in Shaba sooner.

De Guiringaud stressed that the operation had been mounted with the permission of the Zairian government. He added that France had decided to act quickly because of the reports reaching Paris about the threat to the European population.

Zairian President Mobutu criticized Belgium May 21 for its hesitation in coming to the rescue of the Zairian government. In addition, European refugees had asserted that if troops had arrived in Kolwezi sooner, many deaths could have been avoided.

Moscow Scores Western Action—The Soviet news agency Tass May 22 condemned what it called the Western invasion of Zaire. Tass said the rescue operation was an "overt act of aggression" that had provoked the bloodshed in Shaba.

Tass said the rescue of Europeans was a "fig-leaf to cover up an undisguised interference into the internal affairs" of Zaire. It asserted that the Europeans were "allegedly" in danger and that the real motive for the French-Belgian operation was to secure Shaba for Western business interests. It added that the charge of Soviet and Cuban aid to the Shaba rebels was merely an excuse for the Western intervention.

Zambians expelled, Lundas flee—Zambian government sources told newsmen June 21 that Zaire had driven out several hundred Zambians from Shaba. The Zambians, who worked in the mining industry, were ordered to leave because Zaire charged that Zambia had aided the Shaba rebels.

According to a report July 27 in the Washington Post, refugees reaching Zambia from Shaba included Zairians belonging to the Lunda tribe, the same tribe as the Shaba rebels. They were quoted as saying Zairian soldiers had killed and tortured several hundreds of Shaba civilians and had destroyed villages along the path of the Shaba invaders. Sources cited by the Post July 11 said 900 persons had been arrested in Shaba for allegedly sympathizing with the rebels.

Mobutu Sets Amnesty. President Mobutu Sese Seko announced an amnesty for all Zairian political exiles June 24, including those living in Europe as well as in other African countries. In a speech at a rally near Kinshasa, the capital, he said the return of the estimated 200,000 refugees would be overseen by the Organization of African Unity and the United Nations.

It was believed that Mobutu's announcement had been made in response to demands by Western nations that the president liberalize his regime and end political corruption in return for Western economic aid.

Opposition groups abroad rejected Mobutu's amnesty offer June 26 as a trap.

The amnesty was extended to prisoners inside Zaire, including former Foreign Minister Nguza Karl-I-Bond, whose death sentence in 1977 after the first invasion of Shaba had been commuted to life imprisonment. Nguza was released from prison July 14 along with a number of other prisoners who had been pardoned.

(According to the United Nations High Commissioner for Refugees, 140,000 Zairians had returned to Shaba Province as a result of Mobutu's amnesty.)

Other Developments

Chadian refugees vs. repression. The Democratic Movement for the Renovation of Chad, an opposition party formed in Paris in 1973, issued a communique Oct. 31, 1974 condemning President Francois Tombalbaye's regime for its "tribalistic and repressive policies."

The Chad ambassador to West Germany, Italy and Switzerland, Jules-Pierre Toura Gaba, resigned effective Jan. 1, and said he would settle in Belgium or France and work to oppose the "disastrous" policies of Tombalbaye.

Tombalbaye (who had changed his first name to Ngarta) was overthrown and slain in a military coup April 13, 1974.

Equatorial Guinea. Refugees from Equatorial Guinea charged in Madrid that

in the past five years 319 persons had been executed by order of President Francisco Macias Nguema, the London Times reported Dec. 23, 1974. Among those killed were members of the present and former governments, military officers, students, farmers and village chiefs.

Anti-Macias group says 100,000 in exile—The National Alliance of Democratic Restoration, which represented opponents of the Equatorial Guinean regime of President Francisco Macias Nguema, charged that one fourth of the population of Equatorial Guinea was presently living in exile, having fled the "terrible repression which reigns" throughout the country, it was reported Jan. 24, 1976. The Alliance, in a Geneva statement, said 60,000 Equatorial Guineans had taken refuge in Gabon, 30,000 in Cameroon, 5,000 in Nigeria, 6,000 in Spain and several thousand more in other European countries.

Executions—Refugees in Madrid July 11, 1977 reported the executions of 28 persons sentenced to death without trial by President Francisco Macias Nguema. They said the prisoners, who included the former head of the country's central bank, had been killed May 21 by government troops at a prison camp 11 miles outside the capital of the mainland province of Rio Muni.

Some refugees in neighboring states estimated that thousands of people had been killed in Equatorial Guinea since the country had gained its independence from Spain in 1968, according to an Associated Press report published in the Washington Post Jan. 25, 1978.

Gabon ousts Beninese workers. President Omar Bongo of Gabon July 23, 1978 announced the expulsion of all 10,000 Benin workers from the country. The action followed bloody street battles between Gabonese and the immigrant laborers from Benin.

Ghana coup ousts Busia. Ghanaian army officers led by Col. Ignatius Kutu Acheampong seized power in a bloodless coup in Accra Jan. 13, 1972. They overthrew the government of Prime Minister Kofi A. Busia, who was in London for treatment of an eye ailment. Indicting the Busia regime for "general mismanagement" of the country, the officers withdrew the constitution and dissolved parliament. They suppressed an attempted countercoup Jan. 15.

Nkrumah dies in exile—Kwame Nkrumah, 62, former president of Ghana and the first black man to lead an African colony to independence after World War II, died April 27, 1972 in Bucharest, Rumania, where he had been under treatment for cancer. Nkrumah had been living as a refugee in Guinea.

Amnesty—Amnesty for all exiled Ghanaians was given July 10, 1978 by Lt. Col. Fred Akuffo, Ghana's new military leader. He invited back those who had left for political reasons and promised that the military regime would hand over power to an elected civilian government by July 1979.

Jehovah's Witnesses flee Malawi. Reportedly because of attacks on them by members of the Malawi Congress party's youth wing, some 10,000 Jehovah's Witnesses had fled the country and were encamped in eastern Zambia, the New York Times Oct. 21, 1972.

Visitors to the camp, located 10 miles from the Malawi border at Sinda Misale, saw dozens of injured men who claimed to have been the victims of violence at the hands of the Young Pioneers after President Hastings Banda denounced the sect as "devil's" witnesses at a September convention of the Malawi Congress party.

Deacon Dulani Mwale, a leader of the refugees, said he was told at least 60 Jehovah's Witnesses had been killed in Malawi.

The London Times reported Oct. 24 that the U.N. High Commissioner for Refugees had provided the Zambian government with $40,000 to help feed and clothe the refugees.

The London Times reported Dec. 13 that the number of refugees had risen to 19,000 and that 265 of them had died in the camps. Samuel Kafumukacha, acting permanent secretary for the Eastern Province, attributed the deaths to "lack of good drinking water," according to The Times of Zambia Dec. 12.

The repatriation to Malawi of some 19,000 of the sect members from eaatern Zambia ended Dec. 21. The London Times Dec. 19 said the death toll of those in the camp had risen to 342.

Goan community expelled—The first contingent of a small Asian community being expelled from Malawi arrived in Britain May 16, 1976. The 75 refugees represented about one-fifth of Malawi's Goan community, a group of Portuguese Indian origin, many of whose members were born in British Africa and thus were entitled to British colonial passports. Fourteen of the refugees continued on to Portugal. The other 61 remained in Britain.

Saharan refugees. It was estimated that 105,000 nomads from the former Spanish Sahara were refugees in Algeria, the Paris Le Monde reported Jan. 21, 1977.

Sudan. President Gaafar el-Nimeiry signed an agreement April 12, 1978 with members of the National Front, a coalition of right-wing exiles that had staged several attempted coups d'etat against him. Under the terms of the agreement, the Front was to disband its guerrilla training camps abroad and turn over all weapons to the Sudanese army. Nimeiry in turn pledged that all National Front exiles could return home to Sudan with all political and civil rights. The pact completed Nimeiry's reconciliation moves with his political opponents led by Sadik al-Mahdi, who had returned to Sudan in September 1977, and paved the way for the return of Sharif Hussein al-Hindi, whom Nimeiry had pardoned in 1977.

The Palestinian Refugees

Origin & Growth of the Palestinian Refugee Problem

The problem of the Palestinian Arab refugees was created by the war of 1948–49, from which Israel emerged as an independent nation. Some 550,000 to 729,000 Palestinian Arabs (estimates are in dispute) left their homes in contested areas in advance of, during or after the fighting. Few of them were ever readmitted to the land that became Israel. (Israeli spokesmen say that at least as many Jews fled to Israel from Arab lands in which Jews had often suffered persecution.) Most of the Palestinian Arab refugees found asylum in the Gaza Strip, the West Bank (of the Jordan River) and various Arab countries, particularly Transjordan (later renamed Jordan), Lebanon and Syria.

A high birth rate and further flights as a result of the June 1967 war increased the number of Palestinian Arab refugees to 1,375,915 by the end of 1968, according to the U.N. Relief & Works Agency for Palestine Refugees in the Near East (UNRWA). An additional 250,000 Palestinian Arabs not carried on UNRWA rolls were also said to have been displaced.

Three wars have taken place between Israel and its Arab neighbors since the 1948–49 conflict. In addition, the Israeli state has been under almost unceasing attack by Palestinian refugees (and others) who are variously referred to as commandos, fedayeen (self-sacrificers), guerrillas and/or terrorists.

Palestinian Joint Command. The formation of a joint Arab military command comprising 8 Palestinian organizations aimed at stepping up raids on Israel had been announced in Cairo Jan. 20, 1968 after a 3-day closed-door meeting.

Announcing the action, a conference spokesman, Palestinian Dr. Isam Sartawi, said infiltrators would intensify their attacks to bring about the "liquidation of the Zionist state." Opposing a peaceful solution of the Middle East dispute, Sartawi said that "through our guns we are going to establish an independent Palestine." Sartawi disclosed that "for purposes of military expediency" the commando force would be divided into 3 corps: Al Asifah (Storm), Al Saiqah (Lightning) and Khaled Ibn Walid (a famous Arab commander of medieval days).

The Cairo meeting had been called by Al Fatah, the largest of the Palestinian guerrilla organizations. The other organizations participating were the Palestine Liberation Front, the Organization for Support Action, the Palestinian Revolution, the Palestinian Revolutionary Youth Movement, the Vanguard for Palestine Liberation, the Palestinian Revolutionaries Front, the Popular Front for the Liberation of Palestine and the Vanguard of the People's War of Liberation.

The Palestine Liberation Organization, recognized by Arab governments as representing all Palestinian Arabs, did not attend the Cairo conference.

Al Fatah, in a statement issued in Beirut Feb. 6, said that its commandos had established "many well-hidden, well-stocked bases" in Israel or in Israeli-occupied Arab territories and were "now operating daily." Al Fatah said its guerrilla actions were "in no way aimed at the Jewish people as such."

Palestinian Covenant Adopted. The 100-member Palestine National Council, including representatives of the Palestine Liberation Organization, Al Fatah and other Palestinian organizations from all parts of the Arab world, convened in Cairo July 10, 1968 for its first meeting. The council adopted the previously prepared (and revised) Palestinian National Covenant and mapped out plans for a co-ordinated strategy against Israel.

Covenant's contents—The major points of the Palestinian National Covenant:

Article 1. Palestine is the homeland of the Palestinian Arab people and an integral part of the great Arab homeland, and the people of Palestine is a part of the Arab nation.

Article 2. Palestine with its boundaries that existed at the time of the British Mandate is an integral regional unit.

Article 3. The Palestinian Arab people possesses the legal right to its homeland, and when the liberation of its homeland is completed, it will exercise self-determination solely according to its own will and choice.

Article 4. The Palestinian personality is an innate, persistent characteristic that does not disappear, and it is transferred from fathers to sons. The Zionist occupation, and the dispersal of the Palestinian Arab people as a result of the disasters which came over it, do not deprive it of its Palestinian personality and affiliation and do not nullify them.

Article 5. The Palestinians are the Arab citizens who were living permanently in Palestine until 1947, whether they were expelled from there or remained. Whoever is born to a Palestinian Arab father after this date, within Palestine or outside it, is a Palestinian.

Article 7. The Palestinian affiliation and the material, spiritual and historical tie with Palestine are permanent realities. The upbringing of the Palestinian individual in an Arab and revolutionary fashion, the undertaking of all means of forging consciousness and training the Palestinian, in order to acquaint him profoundly with his homeland, spiritually and materially, and preparing him for the conflict and the armed struggle, as well as for the sacrifice of his property and his life to restore his homeland, until the liberation—all this is a national duty.

Article 9. Armed struggle is the only way to liberate Palestine and is therefore a strategy and not tactics. The Palestinian Arab people affirms its absolute resolution and abiding determination to pursue the armed struggle and to march forward toward the armed popular revolution, to liberate its homeland and return to it, [to maintain] its right to a natural life in it, and to exercise its right of self-determination in it and sovereignty over it.

Article 10. Fedayeen action forms the nucleus of the popular Palestinian war of liberation. This demands its promotion, extension and protection, and the mobilization of all the mass and scientific capacities of the Palestinians, their organization and involvement in the armed Palestinian revolution, and cohesion in the national struggle among the various groups of the people of Palestine, and between them and the Arab masses, to guarantee the continuation of the revolution, its advancement and victory.

Article 13. Arab unity and the liberation of Palestine are two complementary aims. Each one paves the way for realization of the other. Arab unity leads to the liberation of Palestine, and the liberation of Palestine leads to Arab unity. Working for both goes hand in hand.

Article 14. The destiny of the Arab nation, indeed the very Arab existence, depends upon the destiny of the Palestine issue. The endeavor and effort of the Arab nation to liberate Palestine follows from this connection. The people of Palestine assumes its vanguard role in realizing this sacred national aim.

Article 15. The liberation of Palestine, from an Arab viewpoint, is a national duty to repulse the Zionist, imperialist invasion from the great Arab homeland and to purge the Zionist presence from Palestine. Its full responsibilities fall upon the Arab nation, peoples and governments, with the Palestinian Arab people at their head.

For this purpose, the Arab nation must mobilize all its military, human, material and spiritual capacities to participate actively with the people of Palestine in the liberation of Palestine. They must, especially in the present stage of armed Palestinian revolution, grant and offer the people of Palestine all possible help and every material and human support, and afford it every sure means and opportunity enabling it to continue to assume its vanguard role in pursuing its armed revolution until the liberation of its homeland.

Article 16. The liberation of Palestine, from a spiritual viewpoint, will prepare an atmosphere of tranquility and peace for the Holy Land, in the shade of which all the holy places will be safeguarded, and freedom of worship and visitation to all will be guaranteed, without distinction or discrimination of race, color, language or religion. For this reason, the people of Palestine looks to the support of all the spiritual forces in the world.

Article 17. The liberation of Palestine, from a human viewpoint, will restore to the Palestinian man his dignity, glory and freedom. For this, the Palestinian Arab people looks to the support of those in the world who believe in the dignity and freedom of man.

Article 19. The partitioning of Palestine in 1947 and the establishment of Israel are fundamentally null and void, whatever time has elapsed, because they were contrary to the wish of the people of Palestine and its natural right to its homeland, and contradict the principles embodied in the Charter of the United Nations, the first of which is the right of self-determination.

Article 20. The Balfour Declaration, the Mandate Document, and what has been based upon them are considered null and void. The claim of an historical or spiritual tie between Jews and Palestine does not tally with historical realities nor with the constituents or statehood in their true sense. Judaism, in its character as a religion of revelation, is not a nationality with an independent existence. Likewise, the Jews are not one people with an independent personality. They are rather citizens of the states to which they belong.

Article 21. The Palestinian Arab people, in expressing itself through the armed Palestinian revolution, rejects every solution that is a substitute for a complete liberation of Palestine, and rejects all plans that aim at the settlement of the Palestine issue or its internationalization.

Article 22. Zionism is a political movement organically related to world imperialism and hostile to all movements of liberation and progress in the world. It is a racist and fanatical movement in its formation; aggressive, expansionist and colonialist in its aims, and fascist and nazi in its means. Israel is the tool of the Zionist movement and a human and geographical base for world imperialism. It is a concentration and jumping-off point for imperialism in the heart of the Arab homeland, to strike at the hopes of the Arab nation for liberation, unity and progress.

Israel is a constant threat to peace in the Middle East and the entire world. Since the liberation of Palestine will liquidate the Zionist and imperialist presence and bring about the stabilization of peace in the Middle East, the people of Palestine looks to the support of all liberal men of the world and all the forces of good, progress and peace; and implores all of them, regardless of their different leanings and orientations, to offer all help and support to the people of Palestine in its just and legal struggle to liberate its homeland.

Article 26. The Palestine Liberation Organization, which represents the forces of the Palestine revolution, is responsible for the movement of the Palestinian Arab people in its struggle to restore its homeland, liberate it, return to it and exercise the right of self-determination in it. This responsibility extends to all military, political and financial matters, and all else that the Palestine issue requires in the Arab and international spheres.

Article 27. The Palestine Liberation Organization will cooperate with all Arab states, each according to its capacities, and will maintain neutrality in their mutual relations in the light of, and on the basis of, requirements of the battle of liberation, and will not interfere in the internal affairs of any Arab state.

Article 28. The Palestinian Arab people insists upon the originality and independence of its national revolution and rejects every manner of interference, guardianship and subordination.

Article 29. The Palestinian Arab people possess the prior and original right in liberating and restoring its homeland and will define its position with reference to all states and powers on the basis of their positions with reference to the issue [of Palestine] and the extent of their support for [the Palestinian Arab people] in its revolution to realize its aims.

Article 30. The fighters and bearers of arms in the battle of liberation are the nucleus of the popular army, which will be the protecting arm of the gains of the Palestinian Arab people.

Palestinians adopted a new tactic in 1968 in their campaign against Israel. They began a series of armed seizures of Israeli airliners in flight or of attacks on passenger-laden Israeli planes on the ground. Later, the attacks were directed against non-Israeli aircraft as well.

Plane Hijacked Over Italy. An Israeli commercial airliner, en route from Rome to Tel Aviv, was hijacked over Italy July 23, 1968 by three armed members of the Popular Front for the Liberation of Palestine (PFLP), an Arab guerrilla group active in attacks on Israel. The plane landed in Algiers.

The Algerian government immediately released 19 non-Israeli passengers, who were flown to Paris later July 23 in an Algerian plane. 10 Israelis—4 women passengers, 3 children and 3 of the plane's air hostesses—were released July 27 and were flown to Geneva before going on to Tel Aviv. The Algerian government temporarily held the plane —an El Al Boeing 707 jet—7 crew members and 5 Israeli male passengers.

A PFLP statement issued in Beirut July 23 claimed that members of its "specialized unit" had taken over the Israeli airliner without the advance knowledge of the Algerian government. The front urged Algeria to hold the plane and its Israeli passengers and crew but to release the non-Israelis. PFLP officials said July 24 that the organization had asked the International Red Cross to supervise the exchange of the Israeli crew and passengers in Algiers for captured Palestinian guerrillas imprisoned in Israel.

Algerian Foreign Min. Abdelaziz Bouteflika, arriving in Paris July 24 on a diplomatic visit, denied that his government was "involved, either directly or indirectly" in the hijacking.

Algeria Aug. 31 released the last passengers and crewmen of the airliner. The plane was released a few hours later and was flown to Rome by a French pilot. The Israelis were flown to Rome in an Italian jet and returned to Israel Sept. 1.

Israel informed the Red Cross Sept. 2 that it would free 16 convicted Arab infiltrators, captured prior to the June 1967 war, in exchange for the release of the hijacked plane.

Attack in Athens. Two armed Arabs attacked an Israeli passenger plane in Athens the day after Christmas 1968.

The Israeli jetliner, an El Al Boeing 707 carrying 41 passengers, was attacked at the Athens airport Dec. 26 as it was about to take off on a flight to New York from Tel Aviv. The 2 Arab assailants fired a submachinegun at the plane and its passengers and tossed incendiary grenades at one of the plane's engines, setting it ablaze. One passenger was shot to death and the plane's hostess was seriously injured when she jumped out of the plane with the passengers. Greek police arrested the 2 suspects, identified as Maher H. Suleiman, 19, of Tripoli, Lebanon and Mahmoud M. Mohammad,

25, a Palestinian Arab refugee. The 2 men had arrived at the Athens airport earlier Dec. 26 on an Air France flight from Beirut. They said they were members of the Syrian-based Popular Front for the Liberation of Palestine (PFLP) and were under orders of a PFLP official in Beirut "to destroy an Israeli plane and kill Jews."

The PFLP Dec. 26 claimed credit for the Athens airport attack. Charging that El Al was no longer "an airline undertaking innocent civilian transport," the statement said that El Al planes, "in secret flights under supervision of the Israeli Defense Ministry," had transferred "air force pilots trained in flying Phantom jets in preparation for a surprise attack and new aggression against the Arab states."

The 2 arrested Arabs were convicted and sentenced in Athens March 26, 1970.

Mahmoud Mohammad was sentenced to 17 years and five months, Maher Suleiman to 14 years and three months. Both were convicted of interfering with air traffic, arson and illegal use and possession of explosives. The original charge of premeditated murder against Mohammad, for shooting a machinegun that had killed an Israeli passenger, was revised to a lesser count of manslaughter by negligence.

Palestinian Arab extremists had also publicized their cause with terrorist strikes outside the Middle East.

Israeli centers hit in Europe. Arab youths Sept. 8, 1969 threw bombs at the El Al Airlines office in Brussels, Belgium and tossed hand grenades at the Israeli embassies in The Hague, Netherlands and in Bonn, West Germany.

A spokesman for the Popular Front for the Liberation of Palestine (PFLP) in Amman said the coordinated attacks were carried out by teen-age members of the "Young Tigers" of the "Ho Chi Minh Section" of the PFLP. Four persons were slightly injured in the Brussels incident— three El Al employes and a passerby. Police arrested two Arab youths. No one was injured in the embassy blasts. Two

hand grenades, thrown at the rear of the embassy in Bonn, exploded under the window of Ambassador Asher ben Nathan. One Arab youth was arrested.

A PFLP spokesman said Sept. 9 that its forces planned an all-out war against Israeli commercial interests around the world and warned travelers not to use Israeli planes or ships.

A bomb planted by Arab terrorists had injured two persons Aug. 25 at the London office of Zim, the Israeli shipping company. PFLP leader George Habbash warned in Amman Aug. 29 that other Jewish-owned firms in London faced similar assaults.

Two Jordanian members of a commando group tossed a hand grenade into Israel's El Al airline office in Athens Nov. 27, wounding 15 persons and causing heavy damage. One of the injured, a 2-year-old Greek boy, died Nov. 29.

Arafat Heads PLO. Yasser Arafat, leader of Al Fatah, was elected Feb. 3, 1969 as chairman of the newly formed 11-member executive committee of the Palestine Liberation Organization (PLO).

In a statement that he made after his election at a PLO meeting in Cairo, Arafat pledged to intensify the "armed revolution in all parts of our Palestinian territory to make of it a war of liberation." "We reject all political settlements," Arafat added.

Commandos Move to Jordan. Arafat then announced plans to transfer a large part of his Palestinian guerrilla force from Egypt and Syria to Jordan, the Cairo newspaper Al Ahram reported Feb. 6. The PLO's force was said to consist of three battalions: 3,800 men in Egypt, 3,000 in Syria and 1,200 attached to an Iraqi division in Jordan.

Arafat and the PLO's executive committee conferred in Amman Feb. 16 with Jordanian King Hussein. It was believed to be the first meeting between Hussein and a PLO executive chairman.

Iraq Curbs Commandos. The Lebanese Communist newspaper Al Nida reported

April 17, 1969 that the Iraqi regime had curbed the activities of Arab commandos stationed in Iraq.

In a note dated March 31, the secretary of Iraq's ruling Revolutionary Command Council, Chafic al-Daraji, had ordered one of the principal guerrilla groups, the Palestine Liberation Organization (PLO), to work through a newly established Iraqi-controlled "Arab Liberation Front." The note complained that PLO members had ignored Baghdad's orders to keep Iraqi military intelligence authorities informed of "matters pertaining to their presence in Iraq." Specifically the PLO was accused of holding unauthorized rallies and fund drives and of establishing contacts with "certain Iraqi political organizations." The note suggested that the PLO establish training camps at Al Rutbah, close to the Jordanian border. It said the guerrillas must not operate outside the battle ground "and must concentrate in Jordan. There is no reason for them to be in Iraq."

Ibrahim Bakr, deputy chairman of the PLO's executive committee, said in Beirut April 18 that as a result of meetings he had held with Iraqi leaders in Baghdad, Iraq's restrictions against the commandos could be disregarded. Iraq, he said, had agreed to support increased guerrilla operations.

Lebanon Fights Commandos. Lebanese Premier Rashid Karami submitted his resignation April 24, 1969 following clashes between security forces and demonstrators demanding an end to government restrictions against guerrillas who sought to use Lebanon as a base for attacks on Israel.

The government reported that 12 persons, including two gendarmes, had been killed and about 90 injured in clashes April 23-24. The fighting, which also involved Palestinian refugees, took place in Beirut, Sidon, Tyre, Tripoli, Baalbek and Nabatiah, which were placed under curfew April 23; the restrictions were eased April 25.

The pro-commando demonstrations were called by the Progressive Socialist Party, the Arab Nationalist Movement,

the Baath party and the Communist Party. All were illegal except the Socialists.

Karami submitted his resignation after two ex-premiers, Abdullah Yaffi and Saab Salal, had charged in parliamentary debate April 24 that the government was unduly harsh in suppressing the demonstrators.

Alluding to fears of Israeli retaliation against Lebanon for guerrilla attacks, Karami told parliament: "There are two sides in Lebanon, one saying commando action should be carried out from Lebanon, whatever the circumstances," and another saying "the commandos represent a danger to Lebanon. . . . That is why no government can take either view without splitting the country."

(Karami continued in office despite his resignation.)

Palestinian commandos surrounded a Lebanese army post April 29, but Lebanese troops lifted the siege April 30. Several men were wounded. The operation was part of Lebanon's drive to prevent guerrilla attacks against Israel.

The attackers were members of Saiqah, the commandos of the Palestinian branch of the Syrian Baath party, which reportedly was controlled by the Damascus government. The Lebanese army post, situated between the villages of Merj Ayun and Hasbeya, six miles from the Israeli frontier and 11 miles from the Syrian border, was astride a commando infiltration route from Syria.

Anti-commando action mounts—A stepped-up Lebanese campaign to control activities of anti-Israeli Palestinian commando groups operating in Lebanon precipitated a major military confrontation between the government and the guerrillas. Scores were killed and wounded in fighting between both sides and in guerrilla-instigated riots and clashes in Beirut and Tripoli Oct. 18-25.

The clashes threatened an open break between Lebanon and Syria (which vowed strong support for the guerrillas), prompted the resignation of Lebanese Premier Rashid Karami Oct. 22 and further embroiled Israel, the Soviet Union and the

U.S. in the growing Middle East crisis. The crisis appeared to ease as a tacit cease-fire went into effect throughout Lebanon Oct. 27, while commando and government negotiators sought a compromise.

Karami offered his resignation again Oct. 22 and dissociated himself from government forces' attacks on the guerrillas.

Beirut-commando truce—The fighting was finally halted by a truce agreement reached by Lebanon and the Palestine guerrilla leadership in Cairo Nov. 3. A cease-fire had been announced by the negotiators at the start of the talks Nov. 2. The Lebanese and the Palestinians also agreed on an immediate suspension of restrictive and punitive actions taken by both parties since the outbreak of the fighting.

Participating were Al Fatah leader Yasser Arafat, Brig. Razik el Yahya, commander of the Palestine Liberation Army, Maj. Gen. Emile Bustani, commander of the Lebanese army, two other Lebanese officials and Egyptian Foreign Minister Mahmoud Riad and Gen. Mohammed Fawzi, Egyptian minister of war.

Fighting follows truce—Three Palestinian commandos were killed and six were wounded in a clash with Lebanese troops Nov. 20 at a government army camp at Nabatiyeh, 40 miles south of Beirut.

According to a Beirut communique: Four armed uniformed commandos complained to the Nabatiyeh telephone substation that service had been cut off to a nearby refugee camp housing 3,000 Palestinians. Army authorities then warned the commandos that "strong measures" would be taken if they continued to violate the ban against wearing uniforms and carrying weapons outside the camps. A force of 100 commandos later attacked the army post with machine guns and the government forces repelled the attackers with counterfire.

Government sources said the attack had been instigated by As Saiqah.

The U.N. Relief and Works Agency had reported Nov. 12 that the comman-

dos had taken control of 14 of the 15 U.N.-operated refugee camps in Lebanon since the October fighting. Lebanese authorities had been ousted from all but one camp, in the Beirut suburb of Mar Elias, which held 400 refugees.

Jordan Sentences Guerrillas. A state security court in Amman sentenced nine Palestinian guerrillas to death for instigating riots in the Jordanian capital Nov. 3, 1968 aimed at overthrowing King Hussein, it was reported Nov. 12, 1969.

Eight others, including Taher Dablan, leader of the group, were sentenced to 15 years at hard labor and six to five years. Four were acquitted.

Tensions Mount in 1970s

The tensions between the Palestinian Arab guerrillas and their Arab hosts appeared to grow during 1970. Lebanon and Jordan especially found the Palestinian commandos to be increasingly dangerous guests as fedayeen attacks on Israel from these two countries made them subject to almost certain military retaliation by Israel's defense forces.

Lebanon-commando dispute. A fresh dispute broke out between Lebanon and the Palestinian commandos operating against Israel from Lebanese territory. The controversy concerned implementation of the Nov. 3, 1969 Cairo agreement that ended bloody clashes between the forces of both sides and sought to curb the guerrillas to prevent retaliatory attacks by Israel against Lebanon.

In a new attempt to settle their differences, Interior Minister Kamal Jumblatt conferred Jan. 8 with a delegation of the Amman-based Armed Struggle Command of the various Palestinian commando groups. Jumblatt announced after the talks that the guerrillas had promised to refrain from shooting across the border into Israel, that he had asked the commandos not to establish their military camps closer than 500-1,000 yards from Lebanese villages, and that the guerrillas had agreed to stop military training of other Palestinians in civilian refugee camps in Lebanon.

A charge that Lebanon was violating the Nov. 3 Cairo agreement was contained in a statement issued Jan. 10 by representatives of two major commando groups—the Palestine Liberation Organization, headed by Yasser Arafat, and the Popular Front for the Liberation of Palestine. The statement asserted that the government had restricted the movement of some commando groups the previous week while not interfering with others. It did not identify the groups.

Jumblatt Jan. 15 ordered the closing of two Palestinian commando offices in the southern towns of Hasbeya and Nabatiye after Lebanese demonstrators protested their presence near village schools. The inhabitants feared students there would be endangered by possible Israeli reprisals.

Following meetings with Arafat Jan. 19, Jumblatt said the commandos had agreed that "responsibility for law and order" in the 15 refugee camps in Lebanon would rest. with Lebanese authorities. Lebanese forces had policed the camps until an outbreak of commando-government clashes in October 1969.

Commando-Phalangist clashes—At least 30 persons were killed and more than 80 were wounded March 24-27 in clashes in Lebanon between Palestinian commandos and armed civilian followers of the Christian Phalangist Party, which was opposed to the presence of the Arab guerrillas in the country.

The most serious outbreak occurred March 25 when Phalangists killed eight commandos and wounded at least 13 in two clashes at Kahhala, about 10 miles east of Beirut. The fighting was precipitated by the movement of a commando convoy through the village accompanying the body of a guerrilla officer to the Syrian border. (The officer was one of the three guerrillas slain the previous day in a clash with cigarette and hashish smugglers in a Beirut suburb.) Interior

Minister Kamal Jumblatt went to Kahhala and arranged a truce. But the cease-fire was shattered when the convoy returned to Kahhala later in the day and was fired on by the villagers. All six commandos in a jeep were killed.

Lebanon seeks commando curbs. The Lebanese government decided May 27 to enforce its curbs on Palestinian commandos in the wake of Israeli raids in reprisal for a guerrilla attack on an Israeli school bus May 22, 1970.

Interior Minister Kamal Jumblatt, who later conferred with commando leaders, announced that starting June 15, the army would arrest any guerrillas firing rockets into Israel from Lebanon or placing explosives near the border. He said that the army would enforce regulations against carrying of arms in public by unauthorized persons and that Palestinians violating Lebanese law would be prosecuted in Lebanese courts.

The National Assembly May 26 had allocated about $10 million for the relief of about 17,000 refugees who had fled southern Lebanon to escape the violence along the Israeli frontier.

Jordan-commando clashes. At least 30 persons were killed or wounded in clashes between Jordanian troops and Palestinian commandos in and around Amman Feb. 10-12, 1970.

The fighting was precipitated by the violation of a government decree, issued Feb. 10, restricting commando activities in order to prevent a possible challenge to King Hussein's rule. The directive, which also applied to the general populace, barred commandos from openly carrying arms in towns, gave them two weeks to turn in caches of weapons and explosives and to obtain license plates for their vehicles, required all citizens to carry identity cards, banned demonstrations and unauthorized publications and outlawed all political party activity.

Al Fatah, speaking for all 10 Palestinian guerrilla groups in Jordan, declared in a broadcast Feb. 10 that the decree was a U.S.-supported attempt to disarm the Palestinians in preparation for a settlement with Israel. Al Fatah reported Feb. 11 that all the commando units had agreed to be represented by a Unified Command to insure unity in their dealings with Hussein.

The clashes were ended by a suspension of the government decree agreed to in talks between Hussein and commando representatives Feb. 11–12.

Hussein asserted at a news conference Feb. 14 that the government's confrontation with the commandos was the result of a "misunderstanding." He said the Feb. 10 decree had been drawn up without consulting the commandos in advance because they were only a reaffirmation of existing laws and were not expected to provoke the violent reaction they did.

A further government-commando accord reached Feb. 22 said that both sides were in "full understanding on strengthening national unity and on mobilization of the masses in Jordan so they may stand united with the gallant Jordanian forces and the struggling resistance organizations."

Maj. Gen. Mohammed Rassoul Kilani, who reportedly advocated a tough policy against the commandos, was removed as Jordanian interior minister Feb. 23.

Jordan troops battle commandos. About 200 persons were killed and 500 were wounded in clashes between Jordanian army troops and Palestinian guerrillas in and around Amman June 6–10, 1970. Ninety percent of the victims were civilians. The casualty report was issued by the Palestinian Red Crescent, equivalent of the Red Cross. The fighting was halted when King Hussein yielded to commando demands to oust two top Jordanian army officers accused by the commandos of plotting with the U.S. against the Palestinian cause.

The underlying cause of the violence remained commando opposition to Jordanian government attempts to restrain their operations against Israel.

The brunt of the fighting for the commandos was believed conducted by the Popular Front for the Liberation of Palestine (PFLP), the most extreme of the guerrilla groups.

King Hussein was the target of an assassination attempt June 9. A government broadcast said his motorcade came under "criminal attack" near Suweilih, a small town west of Amman, where the king had a summer villa. Hussein was reported returning to his palace in Amman to deal with the crisis at the time. An Amman broadcast June 11 said Hussein disclosed that his bodyguard was killed and five other persons were wounded in the attack.

The fighting was finally halted June 10 by implementation of the truce agreement, but the clashes that day were reported the fiercest since the outbreak of fighting June 6. In one incident, Jordanian forces shelled a refugee camp at Wahdat, which housed about 15,000 Palestinians and where some of the commando groups had their headquarters.

The truce pact was reached in negotiations between Hussein and Yasser Arafat, leader of Al Fatah. It called for the return of all guerrilla forces to their barracks, the establishment of joint controls and checkpoints, the release of prisoners and the formation of two committees to investigate the cause of the clashes and to prevent their recurrence.

The PFLP rejected the truce agreement and demanded instead the abolition of what it called the government's anti-commando organizations and the dismissal of officials believed to be hostile to the commandos.

Following further talks with Arafat June 11, Hussein yielded to PFLP demands and dismissed his uncle, Maj. Gen. Nasser Ben Jamil, as commander in chief and Maj. Gen. Zaid Ben-Shaker as commander of the Third Armored Division, which surrounded Amman.

Arab commandos reorganize. A new 27-man Central Committee of the 10 Palestinian commando organizations was formed at an emergency meeting of all the guerrilla groups in the Palestine Armed Struggle Command in Jordan June 9, 1970. Yasser Arafat was elected commander-in-chief of Palestinian forces and president of his Palestine Liberation Organization's Supreme Military Council.

The decision to reorganize the commando leadership had been made at a meeting of the Palestine National Council May 29–June 4 in Cairo. The council consisted of 112 members, representing the commandos, students, workers and individual leaders of the Palestinian community in various Arab countries.

The Supreme Military Council, composed of the 10 commando groups, divided Jordan into several military zones and appointed a separate command for guerrillas operating from each zone. Each Palestinian refugee camp in Jordan would be represented by a political officer who would act as liaison between the Military Council and the refugees.

The Central Committee constituted the highest political authority for the commandos. The committee was an expansion of the 11-man executive committee of the Palestine Liberation Organization.

The 10 commando groups in the Central Committee were: Al Fatah, the largest of the groups; As Saiqah, the second largest group, sponsored by the ruling Baath party of Syria; the Popular Front for the Liberation of Palestine; the Popular Democratic Front for the Liberation of Palestine; the Popular Front for the Liberation of Palestine (General Command); and the Palestine Arab Organization (The last three had broken away from the PFLP); the Action Group for the Liberation of Palestine, an offshoot of Al Fatah; the Arab Liberation Front, sponsored by the Iraqi Baath party; the Popular Liberation Forces, the military branch of the PLO; and the Popular Struggle Front.

Only four of the 10 groups were represented on the PLO executive committee. They were Al Fatah, As Saiqah, the Popular Democratic Front for the Liberation of Palestine and the Popular Liberation Forces.

The Palestine National Council also established a joint committee of commandos and leftist organizations in Jordan and Lebanon. The inclusion of the PFLP on the Central Committee was the first time that organization became involved in any overall commando group.

Jordan-commando accord. An agreement aimed at settling the long-standing dispute between Jordan and the Palestinian commandos was signed in Amman July 10, 1970.

The accord's principal points:

The commandos would remove their forces from Amman and other major towns, but a civilian militia would be permitted to remain under supervision of a joint government-commando committee.

The commandos would refrain from: carrying arms in public places, using unlicensed vehicles, military training with live ammunition, storing heavy weapons and explosives in populated centers and maintaining bases in towns.

The commandos would obey Jordanian statutes, hand over law violators and refuse to accept recruits liable for service in the Jordanian army.

The Amman government pledged to support the Palestinian guerrilla movement and to bar any government body from carrying out acts detrimental to the commandos.

Palestinians urge war. Arab guerrillas called for a continued military struggle against Israel at a meeting of the Palestinian National Council in Amman Aug. 27–28, 1970.

The council asserted that anyone opposed to the Palestinians' campaign to destroy Israel "is a traitor to his cause and the revolution and deserves severe punishment." Appealing for Jordanian support, the council said "our people reject imperialist and reactionary conspiracies to divide the country into a small Palestinian state and another Jordanian state."

'Black September': Jordanian Forces Break Commando Challenge

In a bloody and bitter struggle that Palestinian guerrillas later memorialized as their "Black September," King Hussein's armed forces broke the growing Arab commando challenge to his control of Jordan. The final, unsuccessful guerrilla campaign against the king was apparently signalled by an attempt to assassinate Hussein Sept. 1, 1970. Heavy fighting followed, with Iraq and Syria aiding the Palestinian commandos. Ultimately, Hussein's forces prevailed.

Iraq warns Jordan. As fresh fighting was reported Sept. 1, 1970 between Palestinian guerrillas and Jordanian troops, the Iraqi government warned Jordan that the 9,000–12,000 Iraqi soldiers in Jordan would act if the clashes between army troops and fedayeen continued. Two Iraqi leaders arrived in Amman Sept. 2 to strengthen ties between the commandos and the Iraqi units based in Jordan while the Hussein government replied sharply to the threat from Baghdad.

Hussein plea & Arab League peace efforts ineffective. In a radio broadcast Sept. 3, his first since the assassination attempt, Hussein appealed for peace between his troops and the commandos.

Secret contacts between the two sides Sept. 4 led to a first cease-fire agreement Sept. 5. The Amman government, bowing to guerrilla demands, announced it had ordered a pullback of military units around the capital. The commando Central Committee, spokesman for the 10 groups, said all commando units had been instructed "to stop all military demonstrations."

Representatives of the 14 states of the Arab League Council met in Cairo Sept. 5 in emergency session called by the PLO to work out a solution to the crisis in Jordan. The League announced Sept. 6 that it had decided to reactivate the four-power Arab mediation committee.

The announcement by the League came, however, amid reports from Jordan that new battles had broken out, with 35 commandos dead and wounded.

A new cease-fire agreement was concluded early Sept. 8 between guerrillas and government troops, but commando leaders called off the agreement a few hours later, charging that armored units had shelled their bases in the north. The seven-point pact called for a ban on all military activity in Amman. Army units were to be pulled back from the outskirts of the capital, and guerrillas were to remove their fighting men from the city streets and main access roads. The accord was signed by Premier Rifai and Yasser Arafat. However, the Marxist-led Popular Front for the Liberation of Palestine (PFLP) and the Popular Democratic Front for the Liberation of Palestine denounced the cease-fire agreement and called for a purge of anticommando elements within the Jordanian Army and administration.

A third cease-fire agreement was reached Sept. 10 following an emergency meeting of cabinet ministers and members of the Central Committee. Representatives of the PFLP attended the meeting. The new cease-fire carried the same provisions as the earlier accords. In addition, the Jordan government announced that King Hussein had given full military powers to Chief of Staff Maj. Gen. Mashur Haditha, said to be the only military leader trusted by the commandos.

Commando leaders Sept. 11 added new demands to the burdened peace accord with a call for a new "national authority" to govern Jordan. The demands were broadcast throughout the Arab world by the commando radio station in Baghdad. The guerrillas said the new "national authority" should pull Jordan's army out of the cities and redeploy it along the cease-fire line with Israel.

The fourth cease-fire agreement was negotiated by the Arab League mission and signed Sept. 15 by Rifai and Arafat. The 11-point document called for replacing army guards by police units throughout Amman, reductions in army strength near the capital and the evacuation of all new positions by both sides.

In addition, the commandos were to remove roadblocks and stop all interception, interrogation and arrest procedures. The army agreed not to intercept commandos.

The agreement, to go into effect Sept. 16, was presented by Rifai to King Hussein, who reportedly declared that he "had been betrayed." The king immediately dismissed the Rifai government.

Military regime installed. King Hussein announced the formation of a military cabinet Sept. 16 to deal with the mounting civil strife in Jordan.

The new government was headed by Brig. Mohammed Daoud as premier and minister of foreign affairs and justice and included five other generals, two colonels and three majors. However, Hussein simultaneously named Field Marshal Habes al-Majali to replace Maj. Gen. Mashur Haditha as commander in chief of the army and military governor of Jordan.

Commandos reject regime. The Central Committee of the joint commando Palestine Liberation Organization rejected the military government Sept. 16 as the product of "a fascist military coup." It ordered commandos to hold their positions and fortify them against attack by the army.

Central Committee statements broadcast that day by the commando radio stations in Baghdad and Damascus said that the Popular Front for the Liberation of Palestine had been readmitted to the committee and that all of the guerrilla units were now under the command of Yasser Arafat. The committee called for a general strike Sept. 17 to help it topple the government.

The Baghdad and Damascus broadcasts made it clear that the commandos had the backing of the Iraqi and Syrian governments.

Hussein's forces descend on Amman. Columns of tanks and troops under orders from Jordan's new military government entered Amman at dawn Sept. 17 and immediately engaged Palestinian guerrillas emplaced in buildings throughout the Jordanian capital. The fighting quickly spread to other parts of the country. In the north, fighting broke out in the guerrilla strongholds in Irbid and Zerqa.

The fiercest fighting was in the capital, where Jordanian tanks and infantry units surrounded and attacked the Al-Husseini and Wahdat refugee camps, sites of commando operational headquarters. According to Jordanian government broadcasts, Wahdat was almost totally destroyed by artillery shells.

Hussein's military government charged in a broadcast that the guerrillas began the fighting by firing on the army's general staff headquarters shortly before dawn. The commando radio denied the account, asserting that the army started the shooting by opening fire on the two Palestinian refugee camps.

By 5 p.m. the official Amman radio announced that the government troops were in command of the city except for scattered pockets of guerrilla resistance.

As the fighting ebbed in the capital at sunset, the clashes in the north increased in intensity. At Zerqa, 13 miles northeast of Amman, government forces overran a guerrilla redoubt that had once been the staging area for commando forays against Israel. Government troops also dislodged guerrilla units from the crossroads town of Suwaylih, 14 miles northwest of Amman.

Syrian tanks reportedly enter Jordan. A Jordan radio broadcast Sept. 20 said that a Syrian motorized brigade spearheaded by tanks had crossed the border into northwestern Jordan in an attempt to link up with Palestinian commandos holding a vital highway junction.

There were reports that the troops crossing the Jordanian border were not Syrian regulars, but members of the Damascus-sponsored As Saiqah commando group, an arm of the Palestinian Liberation Front. A Reuters newsman said in a Sept. 20 dispatch that the armored brigade bore the markings of the Palestinian Liberation Army, which maintained combat-ready units attached to Syria's armed forces.

Palestinian commandos, fighting from behind a column of Syrian tanks, Sept. 21 routed Hussein's forces in northern Jordan. The guerrilla radio reported that all the cities in the north, except Amman, had fallen to the commandos.

In Amman, where government forces were reported to have gained control over most of the city, Hussein declared a unilateral cease-fire. Shortly thereafter, however, the commando leadership said the fighting in the capital was continuing.

In the north, Syrian tanks linked up with commandos and the combined force lifted a government siege of Irbid, Jordan's second largest city. At the crossroads area of Ramtha and Mafraq, which controlled the highways into Syria and Iraq, Jordanian troops were pushed back 10 miles by the guerrillas.

In a radio communique, Jordanian commander Majali said that his forces controlled all of Amman and had succeeded in dislodging guerrilla units from Zerqa.

(In his broadcast, Majali offered a reward of 5,000 dinars [$11,000] to anyone delivering to the government Dr. George Habash, the leader of the Popular Front for the Liberation of Palestine. A similar award was also announced for the capture of Nayef Hawatmeh, head of the Popular Democratic Front for the Liberation of Palestine.)

Jordan gains upper hand. Jordanian tanks rolled across the desert Sept. 23, pushing back a large Palestinian guerrilla force that had driven a wedge between government forces in the north and south. A column of Syrian tanks, which had spearheaded the guerrilla advance, was chased back across the border into Syria after constant pounding by Jordanian jets.

Field Marshal Habes al-Majali, commander of the Jordanian forces, announced a cease-fire order in Amman to end the shooting. The order was ignored, however, as both sides continued to exchange small-arms fire throughout the city. King Hussein said Sept. 23 that most of the capital was under government control.

Hussein later noted an agreement between his government and four captured commando chiefs that he said amounted to capitulation by the guerrillas. The accord was repudiated in a broadcast from Damascus by Arafat.

The level of fighting ebbed Sept. 24 as Arafat announced shortly after midnight that he would meet with four envoys representing the Arab chiefs of state who were meeting in Cairo to seek an end to the war in Jordan.

Fighting ends in cease-fire accord— Peace returned to Jordan for the first time in 10 days Sept. 25 as King Hussein's government and the Arab commando leadership jointly ordered an immediate nationwide cease-fire.

The four Arab peace envoys, headed by President Mohammed Gaafar al-Nimeiry of the Sudan, were reported to have played a major role in arranging the cease-fire accord. According to Arab diplomats, Nimeiry and his group met with Arafat Sept. 25 and received from him a letter that "the Palestine revolution will adhere to this decision [the cease-fire] if the other side also adheres to it." The agreement was quickly endorsed by King Hussein over the Amman radio.

The pact called for the withdrawal of all guerrilla forces from "all cities and towns" and their redeployment along the Israeli cease-fire lines. The agreement also provided that all citizens, including the commandos, would be subject to Jordanian laws.

Hussein forms new government— King Hussein Sept. 26 appointed a new civilian-military government of "national reconciliation" to replace the all-military government he installed 11 days before on the eve of his drive to crush the Arab commando movement.

Despite Hussein's announcement that the cabinet would be headed by a Palestinian civilian, a commando spokesman in Damascus said the guerrillas would accept nothing less than the 34-year-old monarch's removal from power.

The new cabinet of seven civilians and six army officers was to be headed by Ahmed Toukan. Toukan had served as chief of the Jordanian Royal Court in Amman and as defense minister. The new premier was from Nablus, on the Israeli-occupied west bank.

The commandos assailed Hussein and his new cabinet through a spokesman in Damascus. The spokesman for the Central Committee said the appointment of the new cabinet "does not change our attitude in the least. Nor will it make any change in the situation, as long as the royal regime exists and the real criminals, first and foremost King Hussein, are in power."

Agreement ends fighting. King Hussein and Yasser Arafat conferred with Arab chiefs of state in Cairo Sept. 27 and joined them in signing an agreement to end the fighting.

The two key provisions in the 14-point agreement provided that (1) Hussein would continue in control but under the supervision of other Arab nations until the situation in Jordan could be normalized and (2) the guerrillas would have full support of the Arab world until "full liberation and victory over the aggressive Israeli enemy."

The Arab chiefs appointed Premier Bahi Ladgham of Tunisia as head of a three-man committee to restore order in Jordan and oversee military and civilian developments. The other two representatives would be a Jordanian selected by Hussein and a Palestinian picked by Arafat.

The Arab leaders instructed the committee to prepare an agreement between the Jordanian government and the Palestinians "insuring the continuation of the Palestinian resistance and respect

for the sovereignty of Jordan, with the exception of the needs of resistance activity."

In addition to Hussein and Arafat, the settlement was signed by King Faisal of Saudi Arabia, Sheik al-Sabah of Kuwait, Nasser, Premier Muammar el-Qaddafi of Libya, President Gaafar al-Nimeiry of the Sudan, President Suleiman Franjieh of Lebanon, Ahmed al-Shami of Yemen, and Premier Ladgham of Tunisia.

Jordan accepts only Al Fatah. Jordanian Information Minister Adnan Abuh Odeh said Oct. 1 that in the future his government would recognize only one of the 10 Arab guerrillas organizations—Al Fatah, headed by Yasser Arafat. Asserting that all other guerrilla groups were illegal, Odeh said "We are not going to suppress anyone, but we want to deal only with Fatah."

Commandos quit north Jordan. Palestinian commandos began withdrawing from towns in northern Jordan Oct. 6 in accordance with the Sept. 27 agreement. They moved to encampments in the countryside, and some reportedly went to Syria.

Both guerrillas and Jordanian troops had begun moving out of Amman Sept. 30 in implementation of the Cairo accord; the pullout was reported complete Oct. 4.

A truce pact to restore peace in northern Jordan, supplemental to the Sept. 27 Cairo agreement, had been signed Oct. 1 by Jordanian army officers and guerrilla representatives in Ramtha. Principal points of the agreement:

■ Both sides were to withdraw their armored units from the Ramtha-Irbid-Jerash triangle.

■ All unarmed units would be permitted to go south to Amman or other towns.

■ Cease-fire orders were to remain in effect in Irbid and Ramtha.

■ Guerrillas must keep their weapons at their bases or in their homes and must not carry them in the streets.

■ All prisoners were to be set free. (Jordan reported Oct. 6 that at least 10,400 guerrillas had been released from detention camps the previous day, bringing to a total of 18,882 the number of commandos freed since the Cairo agreement.)

The cease-fire continued to be punctuated by clashes.

The five principal Palestinian guerrilla groups in Jordan were reported Oct. 9 to have established a joint organization, called the Military Leadership Committee, to coordinate their military activities. The groups involved were Al Fatah, the Palestine Liberation Forces, the Popular Front for the Liberation of Palestine, the Popular Democratic Front and As Saiqa.

New Jordan-commando pact. An agreement signed by Jordan and the Palestinian commandos Oct. 13 designated Jordan as "the main base for the liberation of Palestine" while recognizing the sovereignty and unity of the kingdom. The accord was signed in Amman by King Hussein and Yasser Arafat. The pact had been drafted by the Arab mission headed by Tunisian Premier Bahi Ladgham.

The principal points of the agreement:

The commandos were permitted to operate and guard their offices anywhere in Jordan and to maintain an armed militia in any sector inhabited by Palestinians. They were granted the right to self-determination and their forces were authorized to try any commando arrested for violating Jordanian law. The commandos, however, were barred from appearing in the cities with their arms except to guard their offices and leaders or in traveling among their bases.

Arafat's Palestine Liberation Organization would be allowed to publish a newspaper and operate a censor-free radio station, a right afforded to none of the other commando groups.

Jordan government shift. The Jordanian government of Premier Ahmed Toukan was replaced Oct. 28 by a new cabinet headed by Wasfi Tell as premier. Tell held the additional post of defense minister. The new cabinet included seven Palestinians and three senior army officers.

King Hussein appointed the new cabinet with instructions to honor the government-Palestinian commando agreement of Oct. 13. Tell was known to oppose the presence of the Palestinian commandos in Jordan. During the civil war in September, the commandos had charged he was one of the planners of the Jordanian army sweep against their bases in Amman and other parts of the country.

Jordan-commando accord. The Jordanian government and the Palestinian commandos reached a new agreement Dec. 14 in an effort to halt the fighting between their forces. The accord, like the previous ones, was soon violated by a fresh outbreak of clashes.

The latest pact was announced Dec. 15 by Premier Wasfi Tell and the inter-Arab committee that was supervising the truce in the "Black September" war. It called for the Central Committee, which represented the 10 commando groups, to establish firmer control over its militia and to disarm the militiamen. The arms were to be stored and the Jordanian government would have no access to them. The commandos were to be rearmed only in case of national emergency or war with Israel.

In a move aimed at further unifying their forces, the commandos had announced establishment of a secretariat and an information office Dec. 8. It was also announced that the Central Committee had created a "central military command." Its function would be to direct the operations of full-time and part-time commandos and to oversee the regular forces of the Palestine Liberation Army.

Repeated clashes continued between Jordan and its Palestinian guerrilla guests during 1971. By mid-year, King

Hussein's forces appeared to have achieved the upper hand again. Many Palestinian guerrillas were reported moving to Lebanon, Syria and Iraq.

Jordan in anti-commando drive. Jordanian troops launched a major attack on Palestinian commando bases north of Amman Jan. 8, 1971. Heavy fighting continued in the area and in the capital itself until Jan. 13 when a truce was agreed to by both sides. An estimated 60 persons were killed or wounded in the fighting.

The fighting broke out Jan. 8 around the towns of Jarash, Salt and Ruseifa. The government said the clashes in the Jarash area followed the kidnaping Jan. 7 by commandos of two noncommissioned army officers and the killing of a Jordanian soldier. Guerrilla statements asserted that government forces had shelled commando bases and confiscated their arms. Al Fatah claimed that a hospital at El Rumman had been shelled and that the al-Baqaa refugee camp, a few miles west of Amman, had been bombed.

The commandos reported Jan. 10 that thousands of persons were leaving the al-Baqaa refugee camp after it had come under Jordanian fire. The refugees were heading for the Israeli-occupied west bank, according to the report. Amman denied the guerrilla version of the incident, saying that government army trucks had been sent to the camp to remove 384 Syrian and Iraqi guerrillas to return them to their respective countries.

Government and commando representatives, assisted by the inter-Arab truce officials, met Jan. 12 to negotiate a truce that was agreed to the following day. A 13-point agreement that went into effect Jan. 14 reportedly contained nothing new except a timetable to implement the unfulfilled pledges outlined in the pact that had ended the September 1970 fighting. The latest treaty called on the guerrillas to withdraw to bases outside the cities and towns and for both sides to release all prisoners by Jan. 20.

Other points of the agreement: The government was to return guerrilla weapons and provide for free commando movement. It also was required to return the office of the Palestine Armed Struggle Command at Ramtha seized during the September fighting. The commandos were to be permitted to reopen within a month their closed offices and bases specified under previous agreements.

The Jordanian and commando forces fought another round of clashes in and around Amman Feb. 11-15. No casualty figures were given, but the news agency Reuters reported a large number were killed and wounded in fighting Feb. 13.

The commandos April 2 blew up a branch pipeline at an oil refinery at Zerqa, 25 miles north of Amman, planted mines on roads leading to the Jordan Valley, where government troops were guarding the truce line with Israel, and shelled the northern town of Ramtha from positions inside Syria.

A guerrilla announcement April 2 declared that the fedayeen were fighting to force King Hussein to replace Wasfi Tell as premier and to oust the high-ranking officers whom they regarded as responsible for starting the latest round of fighting.

Yasser Arafat was reported April 5 to have said that his followers had no choice but to continue the armed struggle against King Hussein. He insisted that the guerrillas must have the use of Jordan as their main base of operations against Israel.

The commandos' military leadership, the General Command of the Forces of the Palestine Revolution, disclosed April 5 that the fedayeen had launched an offensive in "all parts of Jordan, especially along the Jordan-Syrian frontier."

Amman press reports April 5 told of a meeting of commando leaders in the border town of Dera, Syria April 1 in which they had decided on a "scorched earth" policy to force King Hussein to accede to their demands for freedom of action and movement in Jordan.

Combatants accept new truce—An agreement to end the latest fighting between Jordan and the Palestinian commandos was reached April 9.

The truce was arranged through the mediation of Syria and was announced by Maj. Gen. Mustafa Tlas, Syrian chief of staff. Tlas made the announcement after returning to Damascus following a 24-hour visit to Amman, where he had met separately with King Hussein and the commando leaders.

Under the accord, a six-member committee was to be established to supervise the original peace agreements, frequently violated, that had ended the September 1970 fighting in Jordan. The committee was to be composed of two men each from Jordan, Syria and the commandos.

Clashes resume in Jordan. Jordanian and Palestinian commando forces fought a battle for more than six hours near Jarash in northern Jordan May 29.

The government charged May 31 that the Palestinian forces were waging "a campaign of subversion, sabotage and terror" for the purpose of setting up "a Palestinian state governed by the guerrillas." A Jordanian spokesman said the fedayeen had attacked phosphate mines, burned private farms, mined roads and kidnaped civilians in several villages in the north after accusing them of collaborating with government authorities.

Kamal Adwan, an Al Fatah leader, said in Beirut June 1 that the commando bases in the northern areas of Jarash and Salt were under Jordanian army siege and had been shelled in the past three days with heavy losses. Adwan said that Israeli and Jordanian troops were cooperating with each other in firing on commandos entering or leaving the Israeli-occupied west bank.

Hussein orders commandos suppressed. King Hussein June 2, 1971 ordered a "final crackdown" against the Palestinian commandos, whom he again charged with attempting "to establish a separate Palestinian state and destroy the unity of the Jordanian and Palestinian people."

Hussein's directive, given to Premier Wasfi Tell, demanded "bold, decisive action against the handful of professional criminals and conspirators who use the commando movement to disguise their treasonable plots."

Seven commando groups June 5 called for the overthrow of King Hussein's government and the formation of a national union government. A joint statement broadcast by Baghdad radio said "this is the only way to prevent a unilateral peace agreement between Jordan and Israel." The statement was signed by Al Fatah, the Popular Front for the Liberation of Palestine, the Popular Democratic Front, the Popular Front-General Command, the Palestine Liberation Organization, the Arab Liberation Front and the Popular Struggle Liberation Front.

Jordan claims commandos crushed. Jordanian army forces launched an all-out attack against Palestinian commandos in northern Jordan July 13. After several days of heavy fighting, the government claimed the guerrillas had been crushed and that more than 2,000 of them were captives. Most of the seized commandos were later released.

The new outbreak of clashes caused a further deterioration in relations between Amman and Egypt, Syria and Iraq, which assailed the crackdown against the Palestinian guerrillas.

The government announced July 14 that it had launched the assault to oust the guerrillas from inhabited areas following attacks they had made on Jordanian troops in the Jarash area. The fighting was centered in the Ajlun-Jarash area, 25 miles north of Amman, stronghold of the commando movement. The main Palestinian resistance was reported quelled by July 15.

Palestinian sources reported July 18 that scores of commandos had fled across the Jordan River into Israeli-occupied territory to escape capture by the Jordanian forces. Israeli officials, confirming the unprecedented development, reported July 19 that 72 guerrillas had crossed into the occupied west bank July 17-19 and surrendered to Israeli authorities.

In a review of the latest fighting, Jordanian Premier Wasfi Tell told newsmen July 19 that the commandos had lost all their bases in Jordan. He said Jordan's troops had captured 2,300 fedayeen and that only about 200 others were at large, but were being rounded up by "routine patrols."

Tell indicated that the captured commandos were being divided into "good" and "bad" categories. The latter had sought the overthrow of King Hussein's government. They included men from the Popular Front for the Liberation of Palestine, the Popular Democratic Front for the Liberation of Palestine and the Arab Liberation Front. Tell said members of these groups would be thrown out of Jordan or jailed. The "good" commandos, of whom there "are not very many," would be permitted to operate against Israel from a specified area in Jordan, Tell said.

A government announcement July 21 said 2,000 captured Arab commandos had been released. An Amman spokesman said several hundred had left for Iraq and Syria the previous day. The spokesman said most of the others would remain in Jordan, having agreed to surrender their weapons and return to civilian life. Authorities July 20 had freed 831 guerrillas in Amman and in the northern city of Irbid. Another 500 were set free in Amman July 21.

Jordanian premier assassinated. Premier Wasfi Tell of Jordan was shot to death by three Palestinians while entering a hotel in Cairo Nov. 28, 1971. Jordanian Foreign Minister Abdullah Salah was slightly injured and an Egyptian policeman accompanying the two men was seriously wounded. At least 10 shots were fired. The three gunmen and another Palestinian were arrested. In Beirut, the Popular Front for the Liberation of Palestine took credit for the assassination.

The gunmen described themselves as members of a Palestinian commando faction called the Black September Organization, a name memorializing guerrillas slain in Jordan in September 1970.

The three assassins were identified as Monzer Suleiman Khalifa, 27; Gawad Khali Boghdadi, 23; and Ezzat Ahmad Rabah, 23. The fourth man was not identified.

(The four defendants, who admitted their roles in the assassination, were released by a Cairo court Feb. 29, 1972 on bail to be provided by the PLO. No trial date was set. A medical and ballistics report said the bullets that had killed Tell had not been fired from the guns the defendants had carried.)

Envoys attacked abroad. The Jordanian ambassadors to Britain and Switzerland were the targets of assassination attempts Dec. 15 and 16, 1971.

Ambassador Zaid al-Rifai was shot and wounded in the hand Dec. 15 when a gunman waiting in ambush near a London street intersection fired at his car.

In Geneva, two Swiss policemen were seriously injured Dec. 16 when a package left at Jordan's U.N. mission and addressed to Ambassador Ibrahim Zreikat exploded as they were opening it. The reception room of the mission was destroyed. Zreikat was in another room and escaped unhurt. Police and firemen had been called to examine the parcel by mission authorities.

The Black September Organization said it was responsible for the attempt on Rifai's life.

Jordan expels Palestinian guerrillas. The Palestinian news agency in Beirut reported Dec. 17, 1972 that Hussein had expelled the last unit of the Palestine Liberation Army from Jordan. The agency said the commandos' 4th Battalion had crossed into Syria that day.

Jordan thwarts commando plot. The Jordanian regime announced that it had arrested in Amman Feb. 15, 1973 a number of men "who infiltrated into the country to commit acts against the security of the state." It was subsequently disclosed that the Jordanians had seized 17 Palestinian commandos, including Abu Daoud, a member of Al Fatah's executive unit, the Revolutionary Council, thwarting a reported plan to assassinate King Hussein and overthrow his government.

Amman radio announced March 4 that the 17 men had been tried by a court-martial and were sentenced to be executed. Hussein March 6 offered to suspend the death sentences if the guerrilla groups agreed to "put an end once and for all to their plots against Jordan."

Hussein announced March 14 that he had commuted the death sentences.

Jordan grants amnesty to commandos. King Hussein Sept. 18, 1973 proclaimed an amnesty for about 1,500 political prisoners, including 754 Palestinian commandos imprisoned after fighting with Jordanian forces in 1970 and 1971.

A total of 347 guerrillas were let out of the Amman jail Sept. 19 and another 400 were released Sept. 20. Among those freed Sept. 19 was Abu Daoud.

Widespread Violence

Terrorism by Palestinian refugees ranged from aircraft hijackings in almost any country to bombings in Israel and Israeli-occupied territory. The incidents described here are only a sampling of those that took place during the 1970s.

Commandos hijack jets, finally free hostages in return for release of jailed terrorists. Members of the Popular Front for the Liberation of Palestine Sept. 6, 1970 hijacked three jet airliners bound for New York from Europe and diverted them to the Middle East. The attempted seizure of a fourth, an El Al plane bound from Amsterdam, was thwarted when security guards aboard the aircraft shot and killed one hijacker and wounded his companion. The plane then made an unscheduled landing in London and later flew on to New York. The wounded hijacker, held by British police, was identified as Leila Khaled, who had been involved in the hijacking of a TWA 707 to Syria in 1969 and who had been released by the Syrians.

The other planes seized were: a Swissair DC-8, bound from Zurich, with 155 passengers and crew; a TWA Boeing 707 from Frankfurt, with 151 passengers and crew; and a Pan American World Airways 747 jumbo jet, bound from Amsterdam with 152 passengers and a crew of 17. The Swissair and TWA planes were flown to what was described as a "revolution airport" in the desert at Zerqa, Jordan. The Pan Am plane was first flown to Beirut and after refueling, flew to Cairo, where the aircraft was blown up on the runway minutes after the passengers and crew were evacuated.

The PFLP held the occupants of the two planes in Jordan as hostages for imprisoned commandos in Israel, Great Britain, Switzerland and West Germany. The Popular Front warned that it would blow up the two planes with its passengers if the guerrillas, jailed for attacks involving planes, were not freed by 10 p.m. (New York Time) Sept. 9.

Switzerland and West Germany at first agreed to meet the commando demands to release six Arab guerrillas held in the two countries but reversed their decisions Sept. 8 in favor of joint international efforts to negotiate the passengers' release.

The guerrillas removed 127 passengers from the two planes in Jordan, mostly women and children, and housed them in two hotels in Amman. A commando spokesman said they were free to leave Amman. The remaining passengers on the two aircraft, all males, were of American, Israeli, British and West German nationality. The planes were surrounded by the commandos and by an outer ring of Jordanian army troops, including more than 50 tanks and armored cars.

Meanwhile, another plane, a British Overseas Airways Corp. (BOAC) VC-10 jet, was seized Sept. 9. It was hijacked after takeoff from Bahrein, a stop on its regular Bombay-London route. The VC-10, with 105 passengers and a crew of ten, was ordered to land at Beirut for fuel and to pick up a woman commando. Following orders relayed by commandos at the Beirut control tower radio, the plane circled southern Lebanon and was flown to the desert airstrip near Amman later Sept. 9.

The PFLP said Sept. 9 in Beirut that the VC-10 and those aboard would be hostages for the release of Leila Khaled, the commando woman jailed in London after her capture during the abortive hijacking attempt on the El Al 707 Sept. 6.

The TWA, Swissair and BOAC planes were blown up by the terrorists at the "revolution airport" in Jordan Sept. 12.

Despite the commandos' initial threats to blow up their captives with the planes, none was harmed and most of the passengers and crews were permitted to leave Jordan soon after the jets were destroyed. However, at least 54 passengers and crewmen remained in commando hands Sept. 15, hostages to the demands for the release of commandos held by Great Britain, West Germany, Switzerland and Israel.

The Palestine Liberation Organization's main coordinating body, the commando Central Committee, suspended the Marxist PFLP from membership Sept. 12 for its destruction of the aircraft. A statement broadcast by the committee said the PFLP had pledged to follow policy guidelines set by the Central Committee Sept. 10 on the release of the jets and passengers,* and that "the Central Committee was surprised by the PFLP's violation of the afore-mentioned decisions."

The remaining hostages were freed by the guerrillas in separate groups Sept. 25, 26 and 29 as part of a deal for the release of Arab terrorists held in Europe.

Gaza violence. Arab guerrillas carried out attacks against Israelis and Arab civilians in the Gaza Strip Jan. 2, 4 and 9, 1971.

In the first incident Jan. 2, a civilian car was attacked in Gaza town and two Israeli children were killed. The action prompted Israeli military authorities Jan.

---

*Commando radio broadcasts from Baghdad, recorded Sept. 11 by the BBC Monitoring Service, gave the following text of the Central Committee policy statement on the hijacked aircraft: "The committee has decided the following: (1) To transfer all the passengers to Amman. . . . (2) To release all passengers of various nationalities with the exception of Israelis of military capacity. These passengers will be released when an official statement is issued by the foreign countries concerned that they are ready to free the Palestinian girl and other fedayeen held . . . in Western Germany, Switzerland and Britain. (3) To release the three aircraft and their crews as soon as the fedayeen in question arrive in Jordan or in any other Arab country. . . . (4) To hold the Zionist passengers of military capacity in Amman until an agreement is reached in the current negotiations with the Red Cross on the release by the Zionist authorities occupying Palestine of a number of Palestinian men and women fedayeen imprisoned in enemy jails."

3 to dismiss Gaza Mayor Ragheb el-Alami and to clamp a curfew on parts of the strip, particularly in refugee camps said to harbor guerrillas.

Israeli military patrols came under three guerrilla assaults in the Gaza Strip Jan. 4. One guerrilla was killed.

An Israeli army patrol Jan. 9 killed three guerrillas in fighting off an attack by a unit of the Popular Front for the Liberation of Palestine. Later in the day, the guerrillas hurled grenades at Arab civilians, injuring 12. The attack was said to be aimed at intimidating Arab civilians into joining a general strike in the town of Gaza in tribute to the three dead guerrillas. The guerrillas succeeded in closing down the town's shops, schools and public transport Jan. 9–10.

According to Israeli authorities, guerrilla violence in the Gaza Strip had killed 100 persons in 1970; all but 12 were Arabs.

Palestinian commandos inflicted casualties on other Arabs in retaliation for suspected cooperation with Israeli authorities in a series of hand grenade attacks in the Gaza Strip June 6, 11 and 23. Two Arabs were shot to death following a grenade assault June 6.

Arab laborers waiting for Israeli buses to take them to work were the target of grenade attacks June 11. Two Arabs were killed and 81 injured. The incident occurred near the Muwazzi refugee camp in south Gaza.

In an operation aimed at facilitating the policing of suspected guerrilla hideouts, Israeli bulldozers July 30 had begun cutting security lanes in the Jabaliya refugee camp in Gaza city. About 400 huts were demolished and 1,200 refugees were transferred to new quarters, most of them to El Arish, in the northern Sinai south of the Gaza Strip. The bulldozer operations were resumed at the Jabaliya camp Aug. 2 and a similar undertaking was started in the Shatti camp. At the same time Israeli authorities distributed leaflets in both camps advising guerrillas to surrender. Gaza city Arabs July 28 had staged protests against the removal of refugees from the Jabaliya camp.

Israeli troops and police Aug. 14 used force to reopen stores shut by a general strike in the Gaza Strip protesting the Israeli action there. Leaflet appeals by two Palestinian commando groups urging the walkout resulted in a standstill of all commercial activity in Gaza city and in the refugee camps.

Several of the reopened shops were targets of Arab guerrilla grenades Aug. 16. Twenty-three Arabs were injured, none seriously, in two attacks—one in Gaza city and another at a refugee camp.

Maj. Gen. Shlomo Gazit, Israeli military coordinator for the occupied areas, said in an interview published Aug. 20 that 60,000–70,000 Arabs now in Gaza refugee camps would be moved into four new villages that would be built in the strip.

But Israel Aug. 30 announced the suspension of evacuations of Arabs from their camps in the Gaza Strip. The action followed protests from the Arab residents, Egypt and U.N. Secretary General U Thant.

An Israeli defense forces radio broadcast said the transfers had stopped earlier in the week after 13,366 persons had been removed from the camps. This figure represented about 6% of the refugees of the 1948 war. About 2,000 had been sent to El Arish in northern Sinai and about 300 others were moved to the west bank. The broadcast said the U.N. Relief and Works Agency (UNRWA), which built and operated the camps, as well as Arab property owners, had been compensated by the military government. The Israelis also reported that Arab commandos operating in the Gaza Strip had been wiped out by an anti-guerrilla operation and that violence there had virtually ceased.

Israeli troops killed six Palestinian commandos in the Gaza Strip Oct. 22. Two Arab girls were killed during the fighting by grenades thrown by the guerrillas. The fighting broke out when the Israelis encountered the guerrillas during a search of a refugee camp.

Twelve more commandos were killed in the Strip Nov. 29–Dec. 1. Six of the guerrillas were slain during a search of the Burej refugee camp Dec. 1.

Israelis raid Lebanon. An Israeli helicopter force Jan. 14, 1971 penetrated 28 miles into Lebanon to attack a Palestinian commando base at the coastal village of Sarafand.

Lebanese and Israeli communiques Jan. 15 provided conflicting versions of the incident. A Beirut report said Lebanese troops joined the guerrillas in repelling the invading force of 300 men, killing or wounding 15–20.

Discounting the Arab description of the raid, Israeli officials said Sarafand was attacked because it had served as a commando sea base to raid Israel. A Tel Aviv spokesman said six frogmen had penetrated Israel from Sarafand on a sabotage and kidnaping mission Jan. 2 and that five had been captured since then. In the strike at Sarafand, two houses and other guerrilla facilities were blown up and 10 guerrillas were killed, the spokesman said.

Israeli forces crossed into Lebanon June 28 to attack a guerrilla base at Blida. About 200 troops involved in the operation were said to have blown up three houses apparently used by the commandos for attacks on Israel.

Israeli troops four miles inside Lebanon Aug. 9 attacked two Palestinian bases near the villages of Hebbariye and Rashaya. The Israelis withdrew accross the border after the six-hour battle.

German airliner seized, then freed. A West German Lufthansa jumbo jet airliner enroute from New Delhi to Athens was hijacked by five Palestinians Feb. 21, 1972 and was diverted to Aden, Southern Yemen Feb. 22. All 172 passengers held hostage, including Joseph P. Kennedy 3rd, son of the late Sen. Robert F. Kennedy, were released later Feb. 22. The 16 crewmembers were freed Feb. 23, and the hijackers surrendered to Yemeni authorities.

The plane was commandeered one-half hour out of New Delhi when the guerrillas, armed with hand grenades, dynamite and pistols, broke into the cockpit. The pilot said the Arabs did not say they wanted to fly to any specific country, but submitted compass readings that would have brought the aircraft to the desert along the Red Sea on the coast of the Arabian Peninsula. He said the hijackers were persuaded to have the plane fly to Aden instead.

The Palestinians described themselves as members of the Organization for Victims of Zionist Occupation, based in a refugee camp in the Israeli-occupied Gaza Strip.

The Bonn government disclosed Feb. 25 that it had paid $5 million in ransom for the release of the Lufthansa jet airliner and its crew.

Transport Minister Georg Leber said the Palestinian commandos had demanded the money in a letter addressed to Lufthansa and mailed at Cologne Feb. 22. It had stipulated that the ransom be carried by messenger to a secret meeting place outside Beirut, Lebanon. The West German government, which was a majority shareholder in the airline, complied with the request.

Leber identified the hijackers as members of the Popular Front for the Liberation of Palestine.

The Middle East News Agency reported that the five hijackers were released by the Yemen authorities Feb. 27.

Tourists slain at Israeli airport. Three Japanese terrorists used by an Arab commando group attacked the Lod International Airport near Tel Aviv the night of May 30, 1972, killing 24 persons and wounding 76. The death toll was 28 by June 24. One attacker was slain by his own grenade, another was shot to death, apparently by bullets fired by his own companions, and the third was captured by an El Al airliner mechanic.

The captured attacker told Israeli authorities he was a member of "the Army of the Red Star" (also referred to as the United Red Army), a left-wing Japanese group recruited by the Arab guerrilla movement.

The three Japanese had debarked with 116 other passengers from an Air France flight from Rome. Entering the passenger lounge, the three men picked up two valises from a conveyor belt, unzipped them and whipped out machine-guns and grenades. Then they began firing and lobbing grenades indiscriminately at a crowd of about 300 in the waiting room. One of the terrorists fired at aircraft on the runway from an opening of the baggage conveyor, and the other, who

eventually was captured, raced out to the tarmac, shooting at anyone in sight.

The Japanese embassy in Israel identified the captured men as Daisuke Namba, 22, and the others as Ken Torio, 23, and Jiro Sugizaki, 23.

Tokyo police June 1 reported that Daisuke Namba's name actually was Kozo Okamoto. The two terrorists who died were correctly identified later as Rakeshi Okudeira and Yoshuyiki Yasuda.

Okamoto was convicted by an Israeli military court July 17 and given a sentence of life in prison.

Arab commandos claim credit—In a statement issued from its Beirut headquarters May 31, the Popular Front for the Liberation of Palestine said it was responsible for the Tel Aviv airport attack.

The PFLP "announces its complete responsibility for the brave operation launched by one of its special groups tonight in our occupied land," the statement said.

PFLP spokesman Bassam Zayid said in Beirut May 31 that the front had instructed the three Japanese gunmen not to fire on the Air France plane passengers but on those debarking from an El Al flight due to arrive 10 minutes later and those waiting for them. "We were sure that 90%–95% of the people in the airport at the time the operation was due to take place would be Israelis or people of direct loyalty to Israel," Zayid said. "Our purpose was to kill as many people as possible at the airport, Israelis, of course, but anyone else who was there."

11 Israelis slain at Olympics. Seventeen persons, among them 11 members of the Israeli Olympic team, were shot to death Sept. 5, 1972 in a 23-hour drama that began when Arab terrorists broke into the Israeli dormitory at the Olympic village in Munich, West Germany. Nine of the Israelis, seized by the Arabs as hostages, were killed along with five of their captors in an airport gun battle between the Arabs and West German police.

The Arabs and their hostages had been taken by helicopter to the airport 15 miles west of Munich where a jet was being made ready to fly them all to Cairo.

The other two Israelis were killed in the initial Arab attack on their living quarters. The 17th victim was a West German policeman. The three surving Arab terrorists were captured.

In Cairo, the organization called Black September claimed responsibility for the attack.

The bloody drama began at 4:30 a.m. Sept. 5, when the commandos scaled an eight-foot wire fence that surrounded the Olympic village compound.

At about 5:30 a.m. the commandos burst into the quarters where the Israeli athletes were staying. As they rushed in, they were intercepted by Moshe Weinberg, the Israeli wrestling coach, who held a door against the commandos while shouting for the Israeli athletes to flee. Seconds later the Arabs broke in, killing Weinberg, 33, and Joseph Romano, 33, a weight lifter.

Six of the fifteen Israelis managed to escape the building. The nine, who were trapped inside their quarters, were reported to have fought the attackers for a time with knives. The Arabs, however, overpowered the Israelis, seizing them as hostages.

Once in control of the Israeli quarters in Building 31, the Arabs made known their demand: they wanted the release of 200 Arab commandos imprisoned in Israel.

Throughout the late morning and afternoon, West German officials negotiated with the Arabs on the patio of the Israeli dormitory.

The stalemate was broken at about 9 p.m. when the West Germans succeeded in persuading the terrorists to move out of Building 31 with the hostages. As part of the bargain, the West Germans agreed to have three helicopters transport the Arabs and the nine Israelis to the military airport at Furstenfeldbruck.

When the convoy arrived at the airport, two of the terrorists walked from the helicopters to inspect a Boeing 707 jet that was to take them to Cairo. As they walked back to the helicopters, German riflemen reportedly opened fire. The Arabs, armed with automatic weapons, returned the fire.

Arabs force release of Munich slayers. Two Arab guerrillas of the Black September group hijacked a West German airliner over Turkey Oct. 29, forcing the Bonn government to release the three Arabs held for the Munich murders. The freed killers were flown to Libya.

The aircraft, a Lufthansa Boeing 727 with 13 passengers and seven crewmen, was commandeered by the two guerrillas after it left Beirut, Lebanon for Ankara, Turkey. Threatening to blow up the plane and its occupants unless their demands were met, the commandos forced the pilot to fly to Munich, with fuel stopovers at Nicosia, Cyprus and Zagreb, Yugoslavia. As the plane circled the heavily-guarded Munich airport, however, the hijackers ordered it flown back to Zagreb. It circled the airfield there for an hour and did not land until a smaller jet carrying the three guerrillas released by the West Germans arrived at the Yugoslav airport. The three freed prisoners then boarded the hijacked airliner, which flew to Tripoli, Libya.

Western diplomats slain in Saudi embassy in Sudan. Three diplomats—two U.S. and one Belgian—were murdered March 2, 1973 in Sudan by Black September terrorists who had seized the Saudi Arabian embassy the previous day during a reception for one of the men later slain.

The Arab terrorists took over the Saudi Arabian embassy in Khartoum March 1 and held six diplomats hostage, demanding the release of Arab prisoners in various countries. When the terrorist demands were refused during negotiations that followed, they murdered three of the hostages—U.S. Ambassador Cleo A. Noel, Jr.; George C. Moore, the departing U.S. charge d'affaires; and Guy Eid, the Egyptian-born charge at the Belgian embassy.

The terrorists ended their three-day occupation of the embassy at dawn March 4, surrendering to Sudanese authorities, who promised only that they would not be killed immediately.

The attack began about 7 p.m. March 1 when a Land Rover with diplomatic plates, later identified as belonging to Al Fatah, drove up to the gates of the embassy, where a party celebrating

Moore's departure was in progress. The eight invaders, led by Abu Salem, second-ranking official at the Fatah office in Khartoum, crashed the gate and entered the building firing machine-guns and revolvers. No police guards were on duty.

Several hours later the guerillas issued an ultimatum that they would kill the six hostages within 24 hours unless certain demands were met. They insisted on the release of Abu Daoud and other members of Fatah imprisoned in Jordan as well as of Maj. Rafeh Hindawi, a Jordanian officer under life sentence for plotting against the Amman government.

Telephone contact with the commandos was maintained by Sudanese Interior Minister Mohammed el Baghir who informed them early March 2 that the Jordanian government had refused demands for the release of Daoud, Hindawi and the others.

The three Western diplomats were killed March 2 at about 9:30 p.m., the Sudanese government announced the following day.

The commandos remained in the embassy throughout March 3, occasionally speaking through a bullhorn to Sudanese soldiers outside and refusing to hand over the bodies of the slain diplomats unless the government guaranteed the commandos safe conduct to an unspecified Arab capital. Baghir told the terrorists later in the day that an emergency Cabinet session had rejected their request for an airplane and that they would be given until dawn the following morning to surrender. The commandos surrendered on that schedule.

(According to the Washington Post March 6, Sudanese Information Minister Umar al-Hag Musa confirmed that a major role in the surrender of the commandos had been played by Yasir Arafat, leader of Al Fatah. The Post quoted Musa as having said: "He helped in the last part, when it became clear they had no way out.")

Baghir reported March 10 that a confession by one of the terrorists had revealed that the attack had been directed from the Beirut headquarters of Al Fatah and that the terrorists had maintained radio contact with Al Fatah.

The eight terrorists were convicted of murder and were given life sentences by a Khartoum court June 24, 1974, but Sudanese President Gaafar el-Nimeiry immediately commuted the sentences to seven-year terms and announced that the convicted men would be turned over to the Palestine Liberation Organization (PLO), headed by Arafat, who had been accused of complicity in the case. The eight men were released to the PLO June 25 and flown to Cairo.

Gaza Arabs score terror. Gaza Arabs Feb. 15, 1973 had protested a recent outbreak of Palestinian commando terrorism in the Israel-occupied area.

Six members of the Shatti refugee council resigned to protest the murder of the council chairman Feb. 11. Other Gazans were circulating a petition calling on Arab world leaders to persuade the commandos to halt their attacks in the Gaza Strip. The petition followed an unsuccessful attempt Feb. 13 to assassinate former Gaza Mayor Rashid Shawa.

Commando massacre at Rome airport. Five armed Palestinian commandos attacked a U.S. airliner at Rome's international airport Dec. 17, 1973, killing 29 persons aboard the plane. Two other persons, including an Italian policeman, were shot to death as the gunmen were hijacking a West German Lufthansa airliner nearby. The hijacked plane was flown to Kuwait Dec. 18 after short stopovers at Athens and Damascus. The guerrillas released 12 hostages and surrendered.

The Palestinians began shooting as they removed submachineguns from luggage in the lounge of the airport at Fiumicino, 15 miles from Rome. The men made their way to a Pan American Boeing 707 that was preparing to take off for Beirut and Teheran. They hurled incendiary bombs inside the aircraft, killing the 29 people aboard and heavily damaging the plane.

The guerrillas herded five Italian hostages into the Lufthansa plane and killed a sixth, the Italian customs policeman, as he tried to escape. The second man shot outside the plane died on the way to the hospital. The plane, carrying the guerrillas, the Italians and the crew, took off, and the pilot was ordered to head for Beirut. Lebanese authorities, however, refused landing permission, and the jet was flown to Athens, where it landed Dec. 18.

In negotiations by radio with Greek authorities in the Athens airport control tower, the guerrillas reportedly demanded the release of two Arab terrorists held since August for an attack on the Athens airport. The terrorists killed one of their Italian hostages and dumped his body from the plane before leaving Athens.

The plane then flew to Damascus, where Syrian authorities permitted the loading of food and fuel.

On landing in Kuwait later Dec. 18, the five guerrillas released their hostages in return for "free passage" to an unknown destination. But Kuwait announced Dec. 23 that they would be turned over to the Palestine Liberation Organization (PLO) for trial.

The PLO had said Dec. 17 that the assault was against the interests "of our people." A PLO official said Dec. 18 his group would "do everything in our power to stop such acts."

U.S. officials Dec. 26 identified the terrorists as members of the Popular Front for the Liberation of Palestine. They said Libya had provided and transported the weapons used.

18 slain in Kiryat Shmona. Three Arab guerrillas, apparently coming from Lebanon, crossed the border April 11, 1974 into the Israeli town of Kiryat Shmona, less than a mile away, stormed a four-story apartment building, forced their way into apartments and began shooting indiscriminately, killing 18 persons, including eight children and five women. Two of the dead were Israeli soldiers who had taken part in the assault on the terrorists after the commandos attacked a second building in the town. All three infiltrators were killed when explosive-laden knapsacks they were carrying ignited after being hit by Israeli fire, according to Israeli accounts.

Credit for the attack was claimed April 11 by the Lebanese-based Marxist Popular Front for the Liberation of Palestine-General Command (PFLP-GC).

The PFLP-GC issued three communiques, apparently while the attack was in progress. The first said the attack was being carried out by a "suicide squad based in Israel." It said hostages had been seized and warned their lives would be in danger if Israeli forces attempted to storm the buildings that were under siege. A second communique demanded the release of 100 prisoners from Israeli jails. (Israel denied that any hostages had been taken in the Kiryat Shmona attack.) A final communique said shortly after the guerrillas had died that "Our men carried out their instructions. They set off explosive belts they wore for the operation when the enemy stormed the building they were holding. They died along with their hostages."

A member of the PFLP-GC Politburo, identifying himself as Abdul Abbas, said in Beirut April 12 that "this operation was just the beginning of a campaign of revolutionary violence within Israel that is aimed at blocking an Arab-Israeli peace settlement."

Terrorists kill 25 in Maalot. Twenty-five Israelis, all but four of them teen-aged school children, died as a result of an attack by three Palestinian commandos May 15, 1974 on the Maalot village, five miles from the Lebanese border.

The Beirut-based Popular Democratic Front for the Liberation of Palestine, headed by Nayef Hawatmeh, took credit for the attack. The three guerrillas, who were said by Israel to have infiltrated from Lebanon, burst into a high school at Maalot, where about 90 students from other towns on an excursion were sleeping.

Israeli troops stormed the building after a breakdown in negotiations with the guerrillas, who were seeking the release of 20 commandos imprisoned in Israel in return for the lives of the youths. Sixteen children were killed immediately, and five of 70 injured students died later. Israel claimed the children were shot by the guerrillas, all of whom were slain themselves in the exchange of fire with the soldiers. One Israeli soldier was killed.

Before taking over the school, the commandos had burst into an apartment in Maalot and killed a family of three. Police said that prior to arriving in Maalot, the guerrillas had killed two Arab women and wounded several others after firing on a van carrying workers.

After the terrorists broke into the school, they began to herd the students into classrooms. Seventeen children and three accompanying adults escaped by jumping through windows. Later in the morning, the commandos freed a woman officer with the group and sent her out with their ultimatum demanding the release of the 20 Arab prisoners by 6 p.m. By that time the freed prisoners were to be in Damascus or Cyprus along with Francis Hure, French ambassador to Israel, and Red Cross representatives.

The commandos threatened to blow up the school with wired charges unless the deadline was met. Israeli officials said they agreed to the demands.

Defense Minister Moshe Dayan and Lt. Gen. Mordechai Gur, army chief of staff, arrived on the scene to take command of the rescue operations. The guerrillas asked that Ambassador Hure and Rumanian Ambassador Ion Covaci be brought to the school to act as mediators. The negotiators were to bring a code word to the terrorists signifying the arrival of the freed 20 prisoners in Damascus or Cyprus, at which time half of the hostages were to be released. The others, Covaci and the three terrorists would depart in another aircraft, with the release of the remaining youths contingent upon the arrival of the plane in an Arab capital, preferably Damascus. The code word never arrived, and after the terrorists refused an Israeli demand to extend their deadline, the Israelis decided to storm the building.

Arabs hijack British plane, surrender. Four Palestinian terrorists hijacked a British Airways passenger jet in Dubai Nov. 22, 1974, brought it to Tunis after refueling in Tripoli, Libya, killed a hostage Nov. 23 and finally surrendered Nov. 25.

The gunmen described themselves as members of the "Martyr Abou Mahmoud Squad," a splinter group named after a dissident guerrilla leader slain by PLO men in Beirut in September.

The British Airways VC-10 jet was seized by the gunment after it had landed in Dubai on a flight from London to the British protectorate of Brunei, in North Borneo. An Indian stewardess was shot in the back during a shootout on the plane. She was permitted to be taken to a Dubai hospital, where her wound was described as not serious.

The plane was forced to fly to Tunis with 22 passengers, 13 crew members and 12 ground service employes, who had been aboard the aircraft when it was seized. On landing at the Tunisian airfield later Nov. 22, the guerrillas threatened to kill their hostages unless Egypt freed 13 other Palestinian guerrillas imprisoned in Cairo. Eight had been convicted by Sudan for the slaying of three Western diplomats in Khartoum in March 1973 and five were awaiting trial by a PLO court for a December 1973 attack on the Rome airport.

The hijackers' demands were at first rejected Nov. 22 by Egypt and the PLO following a meeting between President Anwar Sadat and PLO representatives.

The hijackers released four passengers Nov. 22 and 13 others Nov. 23. The 13 were let go after the five terrorists involved in the Rome airport raid were freed by Egypt and flown to Tunis. Two other Palestinian guerrillas held by the Netherlands also were released on the hijackers' demand and were flown to Tunis. The seven released Palestinians then boarded the plane.

The hijackers later Nov. 23 shot and killed a West German hostage, Werner Gustav Kehl, 43, in public view from behind the open doorway of the jet.

The hijackers released the remaining passenger hostages Nov. 25 but threatened to blow up the plane with themselves, the seven released guerrillas and the jet's three crewmembers unless they were granted asylum in Tunisia. The Tunis government agreed to their demands, and the gunmen and the seven Palestinians surrendered to Tunisian authorities later Nov. 25. But immediately after they gave up, Tunisian Foreign Minister Habib Chatti denied any binding agreement. He said his government had only "verbally accepted" the hijackers' condition not to be turned over to the PLO, but that there was no written agreement to that effect. Chatti said the asylum offer was falsely given to avoid a slaughter aboard the plane.

The PLO said Nov. 27 that it had seized 26 people in Beirut and other Arab countries as allegedly involved in the hijacking.

PLO sets penal code. A Palestine Liberation Organization (PLO) penal code to punish Palestinians involved in the hijacking of airplanes, ships or trains was announced by the PLO in Damascus, Syria Jan. 29, 1975. Hijackers whose actions resulted in death would receive the death penalty.

A Palestine guerrilla official showed correspondents a "corrective camp" 15 miles southeast of Damascus for offenders against PLO regulations. The camp was said to contain about 70 prisoners serving terms for offenses ranging from drinking on duty to attempts to "sabotage" the guerrilla movement.

18 die in Tel Aviv attack. Eighteen persons were killed when eight Palestinian guerillas attacked a shorefront hotel in Tel Aviv March 5, 1975 after landing in small boats on a beach. Six hours after the seizure of the building, Israeli soldiers stormed the hotel and killed seven of the guerrillas. The eighth was captured during mop-up operations the following morning. Two soldiers and eight civilians were killed. A third Israeli soldier, who had been passing, was slain when the terrorists shot their way inside.

Credit for the attack was claimed by Al Fatah. The eight guerrillas, who were believed to have come from Lebanon, were dropped off from a 120-ton ship offshore. Its capture, along with six crewmen, was announced by an Israeli military spokesman March 6; it was described as a "Fatah ship."

A number of hotel guests escaped at the time of the guerrilla attack. But an estimated nine guests failed to get out and were held hostage. In their negotiations with Israeli authorities, the guerrillas at first demanded a plane to take them to Damascus and the release of 10 prisoners held by the Israelis, including Archbishop Hilarion Capucci.

A guerrilla statement issued in Beirut gave a different version of the incident. It said that the guerrillas had blown themselves up after the battle with Israeli forces started and that 50 Israeli soldiers had been killed or wounded, while 20 hotel guests had been killed and 30 others wounded.

Jerusalem blast kills 14. A Palestinian terrorist bomb exploded July 4, 1975 in Jerusalem's central Zion Square, killing 13 Israelis and wounding 78. A 14th victim died July 5. The incident was followed by an Israeli reprisal air, ground and sea attack July 7 against suspected Palestinian guerrilla bases in southern Lebanon.

Responsibility for the Jerusalem blast was attributed by the Palestine Liberation Organization's General Command of the Palestine Revolution to a group calling itself the Martyr Farid al Boublay Brigade, reportedly operating in Israel.

The blast resulted from an explosive charge concealed inside a refrigerator, which had been left in front of a store during the height of the morning rush hour in one of the city's busiest intersections.

The Jerusalem attack followed a disclosure July 3 by PLO leader Yasir Arafat that his guerrilla forces had stepped up their attacks on Israel.

Refugee/Guerrilla Organization

PLO opens more foreign offices. A decision by Britain to permit the Palestine Liberation Organization to open an office in London was assailed by Israel July 4, 1972. Foreign Minister Abba Eban told the Knesset the move would harm Israeli-British relations.

Allied officials in West Berlin reported Aug. 18, 1973 that Yasser Arafat and East German Communist Party Secretary Erich Honecker had reached an agreement for the PLO to open an office in East Berlin.

An East German statement said the purpose of the commandos' office would be "to further mutual understanding" between East Germans and Palestinians and "to increase solidarity in their joint struggle against imperialism and Zionism."

Paris authorizes PLO office—France authorized the Palestine Liberation Organization to open an official information and liaison office in Paris, the first in a Western capital, the Foreign Ministry announced Oct. 31, 1975. But the office would not be given diplomatic privileges or immunity. French officials said the move was aimed at "promoting a dialogue with the Palestinians" and "prompting the PLO to take a responsible and moderate stand."

Russians arm commandos. A New York Times dispatch from Geneva Sept. 17, 1972 said that the U.S.S.R. for the first time had begun sending arms directly to Al Fatah, the chief Palestinian guerrilla organization. Sources in the Swiss city said the first shipment had arrived within the last few weeks.

The Soviet arms shipment was confirmed by pro-commando sources in Beirut Sept. 21. Its destination, according to the sources, was Syria where Al Fatah maintained its military headquarters.

Arafat reelected PLO head. The Palestine National Council Jan. 12, 1973 reelected Yasser Arafat as chairman of the executive committee of the Palestine Liberation Organization (PLO). The council announced its action at the conclusion of a six-day conference in Cairo.

The Iraqi news agency reported April 21 that Arafat had taken over the complete leadership of the combined commando movement's political and governmental relations in the wake of the Israeli slaying of three Fatah leaders in Beirut April 10. Arafat replaced Abu Youssef, one of the slain men, as head of the political department of the Palestine Liberation Organization.

Arab leaders call PLO Palestinians' representative. Following the October 1973 war, the leaders of 15 Arab states and representatives of Palestinian refugees held a conference in Staoueli, Algeria Nov. 26–28.

The heads of the Arab states Nov. 27 officially recognized the Palestine Liberation Organization, headed by Yasser Arafat, who was in attendance, as the sole legitimate representative of the Palestinian people.

Palestinians discuss future state. The Central Council of the Palestine Liberation Organization (PLO) met in Damascus Feb. 16, 1974 to discuss the possible establishment of a Palestinian state in territories held by Israel and whether to attend the Geneva peace conference when it resumed.

A working paper drawn up at the conference called for the right of Palestinians to "establish a national authority on any lands that can be wrested from Zionist occupation." This was the first time the commando groups agreed to consider accepting control of any territory held by Israel. Previously they had insisted that all territories occupied by Israel, including Israel itself, be taken over by the Palestinians for establishment of a secular state of Moslems, Christians and Jews.

The working paper was drawn up by Al Fatah and was also endorsed by As Saiqah and the Marxist Popular Democratic Front for the Liberation of Palestine. Two other commando groups, the Popular Front for the Liberation of Palestine (PFLP) and the Arab Liberation Front, rejected the proposal.

The PFLP submitted its own working paper, which rejected the Middle East peace settlement, the Geneva conference and establishment of a Palestinian state in the West Bank and Gaza Strip.

PLO plans moves. The Palestinian National Council met in Cairo June 1–9, 1974 to press demands to be represented at the Geneva peace conference and to map plans for a future Palestinian state. The 150-member council served as the PLO's parliament.

Among the major actions taken by the council at the nine-day conference:
■ The Executive Committee (cabinet) was enlarged to 14 members by adding

four independent moderates recently expelled by the Israelis from the West Bank and by giving a seat to the extremist Popular Front for the Liberation of Palestine-General Command, which previously had been represented only on the council. Yasser Arafat was reelected Executive Committee chairman.

■ The Palestinian leadership was to seek representation at the Geneva conference but was instructed to obtain a change in terms of reference at the meeting so as to make "the national rights of the Palestinian people" a topic of discussion. "National rights" meant minimally the right of the Palestinians to establish a "national Palestinian authority" on any part of the West Bank or Gaza Strip that might be evacuated by Israel. The Palestinian radical wing regarded the phrase to mean the displacement of the state of Israel by a "secular democratic state" in all of Palestine in which Moslems and Jews would have equal rights.

■ The Palestinian leadership was barred from attending any conference based on U.N. Security Council resolution 242 of November 1967 which referred to the Palestinian "refugee problem" but not to the Palestinian nationalist movement.

■ The PLO was to increase its military operations "inside occupied lands," meaning Israel proper and the Arab territory occupied by Israel.

Militant group quits PLO. The militant Popular Front for the Liberation of Palestine (PFLP) announced its withdrawal Sept. 26 from the Executive Committee of the Palestine Liberation Organization (PLO).

In making the announcement in Beirut, Ahmed Yamani, PFLP representative in the Executive Committee, accused the PLO of "deviation from the revolutionary course" by joining in U.S.-sponsored moves for political settlement of the Arab-Israeli conflict. He said he had "accurate information" of PLO contacts with the U.S. through a third party.

Yamani disclosed that two other PLO factions supporting the PFLP's decision, the Popular Front for the Liberation of Palestine-General Command and the Iraqi-sponsored Arab Liberation Front, had also decided to withdraw from the Executive Committee.

Arab rulers back PLO role. A summit meeting of 20 Arab heads of state in Rabat, Morocco Oct. 26–28, 1974 unanimously approved a five-point resolution recognizing the Palestine Liberation Organization (PLO), headed by Yasser Arafat, as "the sole legitimate representative of the Palestinian people."

The deputy secretary general of the Arab League, Sayed Nofal, who read the text of the declaration to newsmen at the conclusion of the meeting, said King Hussein of Jordan, at odds with the PLO as to who would administer any West Bank territories relinquished by Israel, accepted the summit decision "without any reservations."

Arafat warned in a New York Times interview in Beirut Nov. 8 that there would be no peace in the Middle East until the U.S. recognized the right of the Palestinian people to statehood and stopped "the flow of arms to Israel and the economic, diplomatic and political" support for Israel's "expansive and aggressive ambitions."

He said a Palestinian government in exile would soon be formed as a step toward establishment of Palestinian sovereignty over the Israeli-occupied West Bank and Gaza Strip, which, he said, would serve as a "nucleus" of a future Palestinian state that would absorb Israel.

The U.N. & the Palestinians

PLO Chief Yasser Arafat addressed the U.N. General Assembly Nov. 13, 1974 on the world body's overwhelming invitation. His appearance before the U.N. was the culmination of a long series events in which the U.S.S.R. and Communist, Arab and Third World nations prevailed on various U.N. bodies to adopt "pro-Palestinian" and "anti-Israeli" statements and resolutions.

Among the first of these U.N. actions was a 50–20 vote of the U.N. General Assembly's Special Political Committee Dec. 6, 1969 to affirm the "inalienable rights of the people of Palestine." This was followed Dec. 10 by a 48–22 Assembly vote holding Israel responsible for the plight of Arab refugees and a 52–13 Assembly vote Dec. 11 to endorse a Nov. 20 resolution of its Social Committee calling on Israel to cease "reported repressive practices toward the civilian population" in Arab areas.

General Assembly accepts PLO. The General Assembly Oct. 14, 1974 recognized the Palestine Liberation Organization (PLO) as "the representative of the Palestinian people" and invited it to participate in the Assembly's debate on Palestine.

A resolution to this effect was approved by a vote of 105–4 with 20 abstentions. The U.S., Israel, the Dominican Republic and Bolivia voted against the measure, but many other nations in the Western bloc voted for it, including most members of the European Economic Community.

The resolution was introduced by Syria and sponsored by 71 nations, including all Arab states except Jordan.

John A. Scali, the chief U.S. delegate, said the U.S. vote against the resolution "in no way reflects a lack of understanding or sympathy for the very real concern and yearning for justice of the Palestinian people."

Arafat addresses Assembly. The U.N. General Assembly opened debate Nov. 13, 1974 on "the Question of Palestine." PLO leader Yasser Arafat delivered the opening address. He said his group's goal remained the creation of a Palestinian state that would include Moslems, Christians and Jews.

Israel's delegate Yosef Tekoah denounced Arafat's speech in rebuttal, asserting that his proposal would mean the destruction of Israel and its replacement by an Arab state.

In his speech, Arafat outlined the historical reasons for the Palestine problem, attributing it to a "Zionist scheme" to bring Jewish immigrants into the country as part of a wave of colonialism in Africa. The Israelis had launched four wars of aggression against the Arabs and were planning a fifth conflict, he said. Arafat warned that the "only alternative open before our Arab nations, chiefly Egypt and Syria, was to expend exhaustive efforts in preparing forcefully to resist this barbarous invasion, and this in order to liberate Arab lands and to restore the rights of the Palestinian people."

In calling for a secular state of Palestine, Arafat declared that "when we speak of our common hopes for the Palestine of tomorrow we include in our perspective all Jews now living in Palestine who choose to live with us there in peace and without discrimination."

Arafat appealed to the Assembly "to aid our people in its struggle to attain its right to self-determination." Concluding his address, the PLO chief said: "I have come bearing an olive branch and a freedom fighter's gun. Do not let the olive branch fall from my hand."

Resolution grants Palestinians sovereign right. The United Nations General Assembly concluded its debate on the Palestine question Nov. 22 by approving two resolutions declaring that the Palestinian people had the right to independence and sovereignty, and granting the PLO observer status at the U.N.

The resolution on rights was adopted by an 89–8 vote, with 37 abstentions. The negative ballots were cast by Israel, the U.S., Norway, Iceland, Bolivia, Chile, Costa Rica and Nicaragua. The resolution on PLO status was passed by a 95–17 vote, with 19 abstentions.

The resolution on sovereignty stated that the Palestinian people were entitled to self-determination without external interference and to national independence. It affirmed "the inalienable rights of the Palestinians to return to their homes and property from which they have been displaced and uprooted."

PLO delegate Nabil Shaath told a news conference that the U.N. decision meant "We are entitled to use political and diplomatic, as well as military means to continue our struggle."

PLO gets U.N. member status. The U.N. Security Council reopened debate on the Middle East Jan. 12, 1976 by voting to permit the Palestine Liberation Organization to participate in the discussions with the rights of a U.N. member nation. The vote was 11–1, with the U.S. voting against the proposal.

Immediately after the vote, the Palestinian delegation, led by Farouk Kaddoumi, head of the organization's political department, took its place at the Council table. In his address, Kaddoumi repeated the Palestinian position, calling for the establishment of a democratic and secular state in Palestine, which would mean the elimination of Israel, denouncing "imperialist, Zionist" action to deprive the Palestinians of their land and calling Israel a "racist entity."

U.S. vetoes Council's proposal—The United Nations Security Council's debate on the Middle East ended Jan. 26 with the defeat of a pro-Palestinian resolution by a U.S. veto. The vote was 9-1. Approval was registered by France, the Soviet Union, Japan and the resolution's six sponsors—Pakistan, Tanzania, Rumania, Panama, Guyana and Benin. Britain, Italy and Sweden abstained.

Asserting that "the question of Palestine is the core of the conflict in the Middle East," the resolution stated that: (a) the Palestinian people were entitled "to exercise its inalienable national right of self-determination, including the right to establish an independent state in Palestine"; (b) the Palestinian refugees had the right "to return to their homes and . . . those choosing not to return [had the right] to receive compensation for their property"; (c) "Israel should withdraw from all the Arab territories occupied since 1967"; and (d) all states in the region should be guaranteed their "sovereignty, territorial integrity and political independence . . . and their right to live in peace within secure and recognized boundaries."

Assembly asks Israel to stop Gaza moves. The U.N. General Assembly Nov. 23 approved, 118-2 (2 abstentions), a resolution calling on Israel to halt the transfer of Palestinian refugees in the Gaza Strip from their camps to new homes and to immediately return all of the refugees to their settlements. Israel and Costa Rica voted against and Malawi and Papua New Guinea abstained. The U.S. joined the majority.

The Israelis argued that the resettlement program was voluntary and emphasized that the new dwellings were replacing the hovels that had housed the Gaza refugees since the 1948 war.

The resolution was one of several endorsing the annual report of the United Nations Relief and Works Agency (UNRWA) that maintained camps for Palestinian refugees. U.N. officials in Gaza had charged that Israel was forcing the Arabs there to purchase the new homes in order to get rid of the camps so it could maintain that there was no longer a refugee problem in the area. Ronald Davidson, deputy director of UNRWA, argued that as long as the refugee camps existed, the Palestinians could lay claim to their original homeland. By moving the Arabs to new housing Israel "could claim the people are resettled in permanent homes," he said.

Davidson also complained that Israel required the razing of the camps, which were U.N. property, before families moved to their new projects even though the camps were needed for other refugees because of the growing population.

Palestinian state backed. The U.N. General Assembly Nov. 24, 1976 approved, 90-16 with 30 abstentions, a resolution calling for the right of the Palestinians to establish their own state and to reclaim their former homes and properties in what was now the state of Israel. The action was in support of recommendations by the 20-member U.N. Committee on the Exercise of the Inalienable Rights of the Palestinian People.

Citing the "legitimate and inalienable rights of the Palestinian people," the committee report declared that they had the right "to return to their homes and property and to achieve self-determination, national independence and sovereignty."

The resolution endorsed the committee's call for the refugees displaced by the 1967 war to reclaim their homes immediately. As for the Palestinians displaced between 1948, when Israel was established, and 1967, the assembly urged the U.N. to carry out "necessary arrangements" with the Palestine Liberation Organization and the states involved to allow for the return of those refugees. Those who chose not to go back "should be paid just and equitable compensation."

War in Lebanon

Many Palestinian Arabs displaced by the Arab-Israeli wars had proven to be uncomfortable guests in the Arab states in which they found asylum.

In the case of Lebanon, armed clashes between Palestinian commandos and Lebanese Christian forces mushroomed into virtual civil war by mid-1975. Other Arab nations tried to end the fighting, and Syria became an active participant in the struggle before the Lebanese war was brought to an end late in 1976.

Christians & Palestinians clash. Right-wing Christian Phalangist Party militiamen and Palestinian guerrillas fought in Beirut's streets April 13-16, 1975, leaving about 300 killed and many wounded. The clashes were halted by a truce arranged by Arab League Secretary General Mahmoud Riad, who had been sent to Beirut by Egyptian President Anwar Sadat. Violence also had broken out in other parts of Lebanon April 15; three persons were shot to death in Tripoli and two were reportedly killed outside a Palestinian refugee camp in Saida.

The fighting erupted April 13 when a Phalangist militia commander was shot to death in a dispute. Christians in a Moslem sector of the city retaliated by ambushing a bus carrying Palestinians from a rally, killing 27 passengers and wounding 19.

The Phalangists had long been opposed to the Palestinian presence in Lebanon, asserting that guerrilla raids against Israel invited Israeli retaliation against Lebanon and that Palestinian support of left-wing parties in Lebanon constituted an armed threat to the Phalangists and other right-wing groups.

Lebanon seeks to end civil strife. A resumption of fighting between Palestinian guerrillas and Lebanon's right-wing Christian Phalangist militia in Beirut May 19 left at least 130 dead and about 200 wounded through May 27 and spread to other groups, including Lebanese Moslems and left-wing military forces of various Moslem political leaders. The clashes were responsible for a government crisis marked by the formation of a military cabinet, which collapsed three days later.

President Suleiman Franjieh appointed the military cabinet May 23, the first since Lebanon's independence in 1943. The new government, which had only one civilian, was headed by a retired brigadier general, Nureddin Rifai, a Sunni Moslem who had served as commander of the internal security forces.

The military regime came under immediate criticism from all Moslem political and religious leaders, the Palestinians and other Arab governments. The left-wing Popular Front for the Liberation of Palestine charged that the purpose of the new cabinet was to provoke intervention by the Lebanese army against the Palestinians and thus "clear the way for a political capitulation by the Arab states to Israel." The Lebanese army officer corps was dominated by Christians.

The appointment of the military regime intensified military action by Lebanese Moslem groups and the Palestinians, who threw up barricades and sandbag positions. Faced with this mounting political and military pressure, Premier Rifai and his cabinet resigned May 26.

After two days of consultation with political leaders, President Franjieh appointed Rashid Karami as premier May 28.

New fighting in Beirut. Fighting broke out in Beirut June 23, 1975 between the militia of the right-wing Christian Phalangist Party and the left-wing Moslem Progressive Socialist supporters of the Palestinian guerrillas. A cease-fire was arranged July 1, at which time police sources reported 280 killed and more than 700 wounded.

A few hours before the truce was proclaimed July 1, a new cabinet headed by Premier Rashid Karami was formed and took office.

Palestinians blamed for civil war. Christian leaders met in Baabda near Beirut Dec. 31, 1975 to discuss the crisis. On emerging from the talks, Phalangist Party leader Pierre Gemayel said his side was opposed to dividing the country between

Christians and Moslems, "but for artificial and external reasons, it may be impossible for the present co-existence to continue and therefore partition may take place." Gemayel charged that the role played by the Palestinian guerrilla movement in the country was "a main reason for the tragedy Lebanon is facing now."

Palestinians & Christians fight. Christian Phalangist Party militiamen Jan. 4, 1976 blockaded the Palestinian refugee camps of Tell Zaatar and Jisr el Bacha in Beirut's eastern suburbs, precipitating violent clashes that spread to neighboring areas and continued through Jan. 7.

The Phalangists prevented the arrival of trucks carrying flour to the camps and nearby Moslem shantytowns, which had been without fresh food since Jan. 3.

Amin Gemayel, son of Phalangist Party leader Pierre Gemayel, called the blockade a "military, not a humanitarian question." He charged that the Palestinians were attempting to isolate the nearby Christian district of Ashrafiyeh. The Phalangists said the attack on the camps had been launched by Christians who had been forced to leave small settlements around the area. The Moslems charged that the Phalangist aim was to provoke the Palestinians into all-out warfare. The Phalangists, who had long opposed the presence of the Palestinians in Lebanon, were irritated by the location of the Tell Zaatar camp and other Moslem enclaves in the largely Christian area of the eastern Beirut suburbs.

Palestinian guerrillas' expanding involvement in the conflict alongside their Lebanese Moslem allies was underscored by Interior Minister Camille Chamoun's assertion Jan. 8 that the struggle now was "principally between Palestinians and Lebanese."

Phalangist militiamen laid siege Jan. 12 to a refugee camp housing 3,000 Palestinian Christians at Dbaiye, seven miles northeast of Beirut, and captured it Jan. 14. A Lebanese security official said more than 100 persons had been killed and 250 wounded, mostly Palestinians, in the battle for the camp.

Syria mediates agreement. A Syrian-negotiated truce and political agreement aimed at ending the factional warfare in Lebanon was announced by President Suleiman Franjieh Jan. 22, 1976.

The events leading up to the latest cease-fire, the 24th in several months, were marked by a Lebanese air force attack on Palestinian and Lebanese Moslem positions Jan. 16 and the resignation of Premier Rashid Karami Jan. 18 after a truce he had helped arrange the previous day collapsed. Fighting then escalated throughout the country, and it was accompanied by the entry into Lebanon from Syria of an undetermined number of Palestinian Liberation Army troops, the military wing of the Palestine Liberation Organization, who joined other Palestinian and Lebanese Moslem forces in an offensive that resulted in the capture of many-Christian-held areas.

Premier Karami withdrew his resignation after a meeting Jan. 24 with Moslem leaders and the head of the Syrian mediation team, Foreign Minister Abdel Halim Khaddam.

Lebanese civil war renewed. The Syrian-mediated truce that had ended the fighting between Lebanon's Moslems and Christians in January and Damascus' subsequent efforts to implement a political reform program collapsed in early March as Moslem soldiers of the Lebanese army rebelled, precipitating a renewal of civil strife that engulfed Beirut and other parts of the country.

The latest flare-up was presaged by a proclamation Jan. 21 of an army dissident force headed by Lt. Ahmed al-Khatib, known to have the support of the Palestinian Al Fatah guerrilla group. Numbering an estimated 1,400 deserters at the outset, the force called itself the Lebanese Arab Army and demanded political and economic changes in Lebanon to improve the positions of the Moslems. It first went into action March 8, seizing control of an army artillery position at Amun, and then taking over another army garrison at Rasheiya March 9, both in the southern part of the country near the Israeli border.

A new leader of the rebellion emerged March 11 with the commander of the Beirut military garrison, Brig. Gen. Abdel

Aziz al-Ahdab, 52, proclaiming himself military governor of Lebanon. Siding with Khatib's Lebanon Arab Army, Ahdab demanded the resignations of Karami and Franjieh within 24 hours.

Franjieh was forced to flee his presidential palace March 25 after it came under artillery attack. The president moved out of Beirut and set up new headquarters in the Christian stronghold port of Junieh, north of the capital.

As Saiqah involvement. A 10-day truce went into effect April 2 to allow time for the choice of a new president, but clashes and abductions continued.

The fighting took on a new complexion as Palestinian guerrillas of the Syrian-supported As Saiqah organization became increasingly involved in clashes with Lebanese Moslem leftists and Palestinian leftist groups.

Syrian troops move into Lebanon. Syrian troops began to move into Lebanon in small force April 9 in an apparent attempt to apply pressure to hasten a political resolution of the civil war.

The first report on the Damascus military thrust said 200–400 soldiers backed by tanks pushed three miles across the border into the Bekaa Valley and occupied a Lebanese customs point at Masnaa on the Beirut-Damascus road.

Syrian President Hafez al-Assad warned Lebanese and Palestinian leaders April 12 that Damascus had "total freedom of movement" and would take any step to prevent further bloodshed in Lebanon. He specifically directed his remarks to "our Palestinian brothers to understand and be alert to the seriousness of the plot" being carried out in Lebanon.

Several thousand Palestinian and Lebanese leftists staged protest marches in Tyre and Saida April 14 against the Syrian intrusion.

Egypt, PLO reconcile dispute. Egypt and the Palestine Liberation Organization reached a broad understanding for cooperation in Lebanon and elsewhere, a New York Times dispatch from Beirut said May 5, 1976. The report quoted sources

close to PLO chief Yasser Arafat as having said that the main purpose of the understanding was to strengthen Arafat's position against what they termed "a Syrian attempt to bring the Palestinian resistance movement under control of Damascus."

Saudi Arabia was said to have mediated the Egyptian-PLO dispute, which had arisen after Egypt had signed the Sinai disengagement agreement with Israel in 1975.

The Times reported the following terms of the Egyptian-PLO accord:
■ Cairo permitted more than 1,000 Egyptian-based Palestine Liberation Army (PLA) soldiers to leave for Lebanon to offset the presence of the Syrian-controlled As Saiqah and Syrian-based PLA units.
■ The PLO agreed to soften its public criticism of the Sinai agreement and to halt its personal attacks against Egyptian President Anwar Sadat.
■ Egypt pledged return of the Palestinian Cairo radio program, the Voice of Palestine, which it had seized in 1975.

Lebanon elects new president. The Lebanese parliament May 8 elected Elias Sarkis to replace President Suleiman Franjieh. Sarkis received 66 votes and three ballots were blank. The 29 other parliament members, all supporters of rival candidate Raymond Edde, boycotted the session to protest what they charged were open military and political intervention by Syria in favor of Sarkis.

PLO admits participation in war. In May 1976 the PLO admitted that it had taken part in some of the Lebanese fighting.

Farouk Kaddoumi, head of the PLO's Political Department, disclosed May 10 that Al Fatah forces had sided with Lebanese leftist and Moslem gunmen against Christian militiamen in a major battle that had raged the previous three days in the mountains in eastern Lebanon.

Kaddoumi said the Palestinians were forced to enter the fighting because Christian forces had launched an offensive that could change the military balance in violation of Syrian assurances to the contrary. This was the first public admission by a Palestinian official of the participation of Palestinian forces in the civil war.

Fresh Syrian troops committed. Syria sent several thousand troops into northern and eastern Lebanon May 31–June 1 in an apparent attempt to end the fighting.

An estimated 2,000 Syrian troops moved late May 31 into the Akkar Valley in northern Lebanon, where two Christian villages had been under heavy Moslem shelling for several days. Leaders of the villages, Qobayat and Andakit, had appealed for Syrian intervention "to prevent our annihilation."

More Syrian troops—estimates varied from 1,000 to 4,000—crossed Lebanon's eastern border June 1 and fanned out in the Bekaa Valley, disarming Moslem leftists and their Palestinian allies. The troops lifted the siege of the Christian city of Zahle, took the strategic Chtaura crossroads, occupied the Lebanese air force base at Rayak and entered a number of hamlets where Christians and Moslems had fought recently.

The Syrians took up strategic positions June 2 in the Akkar and Bekaa Valleys and above Saida, the key port for Palestinian supplies.

Increasing Syrian military pressure prompted eight Lebanese leftist and Palestinian fighting forces to agree to operate jointly under a Central Military Command, it was reported June 5. The command consisted of Kamal Jumblat's Moslem militia, the renegade Lebanese Arab Army and six Palestinian groups: Al Fatah, the Popular Front for the Liberation of Palestine (PFLP), the PFLP-General Command, the Democratic Front for the Liberation of Palestine, the Arab Liberation Front and the Popular Struggle Front.

Truce set with Arab League aid. The Arab League agreed June 10 to send a symbolic peace-keeping force to Lebanon to oversee a truce arranged the previous day to halt the increased fighting between invading Syrian soldiers and combined units of Lebanese Moslem leftists and Palestinian guerrillas. The force would be composed of troops from Algeria, Libya, Saudi Arabia and Sudan. They would be assisted by Syrian and Palestine Liberation Organization soldiers already in Lebanon.

The fighting eased considerably as both sides accepted the truce, although sporadic clashes continued June 10.

President Suleiman Franjieh denounced the Arab League action, asserting that Lebanon was not legally represented at the Cairo meeting at which the peace-keeping decision was made.

Arab peace force arrives in Lebanon. The vanguard of an Arab League peace-keeping force arrived in Lebanon by truck convoy from Damascus June 21 to implement the league's plan to help end the fighting in the country. A contingent of about 500 troops each from Syria and Libya took up positions around Beirut's battered airport as a new cease-fire mediated by Libyan Premier Abdel Salam Jalloud went into effect.

The truce was part of a seven-point agreement worked out by Jalloud, who had concluded his mediation June 20 after almost two weeks of shuttling between Damascus and Beirut. The truce applied only to the fighting between the Lebanese leftist-Palestinian alliance and the Syrian expeditionary force. It had no effect on the Moslem and Christian combatants, who resumed heavy clashes June 22.

The Lebanese Christian-Moslem fighting that resumed June 22 centered in Beirut around Palestinian refugee camps and the Moslem quarter of Nabaa, with the Christians on the offensive.

Arabs press peace efforts. Arab leaders continued their efforts to end the Lebanese war, focusing their attention on the dispute between Syria and the Palestine Liberation Organization. A PLO delegation conferred with Syrian officials in Damascus July 21–22. Libyan Premier Abdel Salam Jalloud, acting as mediator, participated in most of the discussions. The meetings were the first between the two sides since the Syrian army began to engage the Palestinians in fighting in June.

Syrian President Hafez al-Assad July 20 defended Syrian actions in Lebanon and assailed the Palestinians.

Syria, he disclosed, had provided arms and ammunition to the Palestinians and the Lebanese leftist-Moslem alliance headed by Kamal Jumblat until Jumblat had informed him in March that he was determined to achieve a complete military victory over the Christians.

Syrian troops that had been stationed in Palestinian refugee camps for three years to protect its inhabitants were killed and arrested by the Palestinians themselves, Assad said. The Syrians were about to take over Beirut as a result of clashes with Palestinian forces in the city June 6, but held back at the request of Algeria and Libya, the Syrian president said.

Syria, PLO sign Lebanon peace pact. Syria and the Palestine Liberation Organization signed an agreement in Damascus July 29 providing for a cease-fire in the Lebanese civil war and for measures to pave the way for a political solution to the crisis.

The accord was reached after nine days of talks between Syrian Foreign Minister Abdel Halim Khaddam and Farouk Kaddoumi, head of the PLO's political department. Drafts of the pact were submitted to the rival Lebanese Christian and Moslem factions to the dispute. Libyan Premier Abdel Salam Jalloud was mediator in the Damascus negotiations.

The agreement represented a major concession by the Palestinians, reaffirming the predominant role of Syria in Lebanon, according to the New York Times July 30. The Palestinians and leftist Lebanese Moslems had rejected most of the pact's provisions in the past.

Christians seize Tel Zaatar. Christian forces Aug. 12, 1976 captured the Palestinian refugee camp of Tel Zaatar in eastern Beirut. The Christians Aug. 10 had launched an all-out drive against the stronghold, which had been under siege for 51 days.

About 12,000 refugees fled the camp Aug. 11 and 12. Hassan Sabry el-Kholy, the Arab League's envoy, said they included about 9,000 Palestinians, 3,000 Lebanese and a few others, including 100 Syrians and 12 Egyptians. Kholy said that "there were a lot of civilian losses and casualties," some caused by Moslem leftist shelling during the escape from the camp. Maj. Fouad Malek, Christian commander of rightist forces at Tel Zaatar, said that about 100 Palestinian combatants had been captured and "hundreds" killed in the Aug. 12 fighting.

The Palestinian radio charged that the Christian forces had "used a typical ruse to enter Tel Zaatar," having informed the camp's residents by loudspeaker Aug. 11 that they would be removed the following day. Kholy said that he had arranged with the rightists for the evacuation of the remaining noncombatants Aug. 12. He said he was "surprised and disappointed" upon learning when he awoke Aug. 12 that the rightists had launched their final assault and that thousands of refugees had already fled the camp.

The Palestinians Aug. 12 repeated their charge of Syrian collusion with the Christians. The Palestine Liberation Organization asserted that Syrian Col. Ali al-Madani was in the operations room of the right-wing forces during the Aug. 12 fighting and was seen by Kholy.

Sarkis becomes president. Elias Sarkis was inaugurated as president of Lebanon Sept. 23 in the Syrian-controlled town of Chtaura, 22 miles east of Beirut. Sarkis, regarded as a moderate Christian, replaced hard-line Christian rightist Suleiman Franjieh whose refusal to resign before the end of his six-year term had contributed to the intensification of the Lebanese civil war.

In a message to Sarkis, PLO leader Yasser Arafat promised to order his forces to observe a truce throughout Lebanon to facilitate Sarkis' rule. Arafat did not say when the cease-fire would go into effect and the fighting continued without letup as Sarkis took office.

In his inaugural address, Sarkis promised to seek an end to the civil strife that would preserve "Lebanon's interest" while "saving the Palestinian cause from any harm." He said he would "spare no effort to help the Palestinian commando movement to regain its homeland."

Pro-Palestinians raid Damascus hotel. Four pro-Palestinian guerrillas seized a hotel in Damascus Sept. 26 and fought a seven-hour battle with Syrian troops before being captured. The leader of the gunmen and four of the 90 hostages being held in the Hotel Semiramis were killed. Thirty-four of the hostages and an undisclosed number of Syrian soldiers were wounded. The three captured guerrillas were hanged in public Sept. 27.

The three surviving members of the group had confessed that they were members of Al Fatah, the largest of the Palestinian guerrilla forces, and that the attack had been planned in Iraq to protest Syria's military intervention in Lebanon. They said they took direct orders from Zuheir Abou Hashisha, a Palestinian who was slain in the assault. Syrian sources said that the men had demanded, among other things, the release of about 30 Palestinians who had been arrested for a series of bombings in Damascus and other Syrian cities in July.

A statement issued by Al Fatah in Beirut Sept. 27 denied that the organization was involved in the raid and blamed it on a group in Baghdad, headed by Abou Nidal, who had been expelled from Al Fatah in 1970.

Syrian embassies attacked. Six Palestinian guerrillas Oct. 11, 1976 attacked Syrian embassies in Rome and Islamabad, Pakistan in retaliation for Syria's military intervention in Lebanon.

The Islamabad raid was less successful as Pakistani police prevented three armed men from breaking into the building. In the ensuing shootout, one guerrilla was killed, two were wounded and three policemen were injured.

The Rome attackers, also numbering three men, shot their way into the embassy, took five hostages and then surrendered to police two hours later.

Nabil Hasnen, the leader of the guerrillas, said his group belonged to the Black June Movement, an Iraqi-based faction named after the month in which Syria first intervened in Lebanon. Hasnen said that his men wanted to draw attention "to the betrayal of the Syrian government and the plot of Arab states against the Palestinian people."

A Rome court Nov. 6 convicted and sentenced the three Palestinians to 15 years in prison.

Palestinians assailed at U.N. Edouard Ghorra, Lebanon's chief representative, Oct. 14 denounced the role of the Palestinians in Lebanon in his country's foreign policy report delivered to the United Nations General Assembly. He said that the "Palestinian revolution" and its supporters in the Arab countries were entirely to blame for the civil war. Accusing the Palestinians of abuses, crimes, kidnappings and acts of torture, Ghorra said that "they acted as if they were a state or states within the state of Lebanon and flagrantly defied the laws of the land and the hospitality of its people."

New cease-fire. A new cease-fire was signed in Riyadh Oct. 18 at the conclusion of a two-day meeting attended by President Hafez al-Assad of Syria, President Elias Sarkis of Lebanon, President Anwar Sadat of Egypt, King Khalid of Saudi Arabia, Sheikh Sabah al-Salem al-Sabah, ruler of Kuwait, and Yasir Arafat, head of the Palestine Liberation Organization. The pact also provided for:

■ Expansion of the Arab League peace-keeping force in Lebanon from 2,300 men to 30,000.

■ Withdrawal of all combatants to positions they had held before the civil war erupted in April 1975.

■ Palestinian adherence to the 1969 Cairo agreement that confined Palestinian guerrilla forces in Lebanon to refugee camps and to the Arkub section in the southeast.

The proposals were approved by an Arab League summit conference held in Cairo Oct. 25–26.

The resumption of Syrian-Palestinian ties, in accord with the Riyadh and Cairo summit decisions, paved the way for the return of Palestinian forces to southern Lebanon near the Israeli frontier Oct. 27–28 and for the reopening of the Arafat Trail, the supply route from Syria to Palestinian forces in the south, it was reported Oct. 26.

Relieved of fighting the Syrians, the Palestinians began arriving in large numbers in the south, many of them entering the Moslem-held village of Bint Jbail, three miles from the Israeli border. The reinforcements included men of Al Fatah, the main guerrilla organization, as well as the fighters of the radical Popular Front for the Liberation of Palestine.

Terrorism Continues, Attitudes Remain Unchanged

Hostages rescued in Uganda. Israeli commandos in three transport planes landed at Uganda's Entebbe Airport July 3, 1976 after flying from Tel Aviv and rescued 91 passengers and 12 crew members of an Air France plane that had been hijacked June 27 by seven pro-Palestinian guerrillas. After a clash at the airport in which 31 persons were killed, the three Israeli C-130 Hercules transports flew to Nairobi, Kenya to refuel. They returned to Tel Aviv July 4.

Killed in the fighting were all seven hijackers, 20 of about 100 Ugandan troops guarding the field, three Israeli hostages caught in the crossfire and Lt. Col. Yehonathan Nethanyahu, 30, the U.S.-born commander of the strike force. During the Nairobi stopover, two seriously wounded Israelis were taken to a hospital.

The Israeli attackers landed at Entebbe airport under cover of darkness. Firing machineguns and hurling grenades, they rushed the old passenger terminal where the hostages were being held under guard, gunned down the hijackers, raced into the building and herded the hostages to the waiting planes.

Israeli officials July 4 denied that a ruse had been employed to bring the captives out of Uganda. Briefing the Knesset (Parliament), Premier Yitzhak Rabin said the government had decided on the need for the military operation when it became obvious that international efforts to free all the hostages had failed.

Rabin also accused Amin of "fully cooperating with the hijackers while putting on false pretenses."

Turks thwart hijack attempt. Two Palestinian guerrillas Aug. 11, 1976 shot and killed four passengers and wounded at least 30 others waiting in line at a transit passenger lounge at Yesilkoy Airport in Istanbul, Turkey to board a Tel Aviv-bound El Al Israeli jetliner. Turkish police captured the two terrorists after a one-hour standoff, thwarting an apparent effort to hijack the aircraft.

The fatalities included two Israelis, an American and a Japanese.

Turkish officials Aug. 12 quoted the two gunmen as saying that they had been instructed to kill "as many Israelis as we can" in retaliation for Israel's raid on Entebbe, Uganda July 3–4. They admitted under questioning that they were members of the radical Popular Front for the Liberation of Palestine.

France frees Abu Daoud. A French court in Paris Jan. 11, 1977 released Abu Daoud, a Palestinian militant who had been arrested by police in the French capital Jan. 7 on suspicion of having plotted the terror attack at the 1972 Olympic Games in Munich in which 17 persons, including 11 Israeli athletes, were slain. Daoud was immediately expelled from France and flown to Algeria.

Daoud was a member of the Palestinian Revolutionary Council of Al Fatah, the main guerrilla group in the Palestine Liberation Organization. He was seized in a Paris hotel after he arrived from Beirut with a PLO delegation to attend the funeral Jan. 8 of Mahmoud Saleh, a former PLO representative in Paris who had been shot to death by unknown assailants in his bookstore Jan. 3.

In setting Daoud free, the French court Jan. 11 rejected demands from West Germany and Israel that he be held for extradition hearings. The court upheld the defense argument that Israel, which had requested that Daoud be detained for 60 days pending the hearings, had no right to make this demand since the Munich attack had not been committed on Israeli soil, nor by an Israeli citizen.

The court turned down the West German extradition request on the technical grounds that Bonn had improperly identified the prisoner and that it had not formally confirmed the extradition request through diplomatic channels. The court did not challenge Daoud's contention that he was Youssef Raji Ben Hanna, the alias that appeared on the Iraqi passport with which he had arrived in Paris. Daoud's real name was Mohammed Daoud Audeh.

Several hours after Daoud departed France Jan. 11, the French Interior Ministry officially explained that he had been arrested by agents of the French internal counterintelligence service, the Directorate for the Surveillance of the Territory (DST), after they received telephoned information from the West German police and in response to a warrant issued by Interpol, the international police agency, at Bonn's request. The West German Justice Ministry Jan. 10 denied it was responsible for the Interpol warrant. A French source later acknowledged that the warrant had been sought by Israel.

Palestinians unchanged on Israel. The Palestinian leadership reconfirmed its opposition to the existence of Israel at a meeting of the Palestine National Council (parliament-in-exile) in Cairo March 12-20, 1977.

A 15-point declaration adopted March 20 by a 194-13 vote called for establishment of a Palestinian state on "national soil" and a continuation of the "armed struggle" against Israel—especially in the Israeli-occupied Arab territories. It rejected recognition of Israel or the signing of any complete peace agreement.

The council declaration also affirmed the right of the Palestine Liberation Organization "to participate on an independent, equal footing in all international conferences, forums and efforts concerned with the Palestinian question and with the Arab-Israeli conflict."

The resolution reiterated Palestinian rejection of United Nations Security Council Resolution 242 as the basis for peace negotiations, but implied acceptance of U.N. General Assembly Resolution 3236 adopted after the 1973 war as the foundation for settlement talks. Resolution 242 referred to the Palestinian question as a refugee problem whereas 3236 referred to the Palestinians' national rights.

Adoption of the resolution represented a victory of the so-called moderate wing of the Palestinian movement over the Rejection Front, whose 13 members voted against. The front was opposed to a negotiated settlement in the Middle East.

Khaled Fahoum, a pro-Syrian, had been reelected president of the National Council March 13, defeating Bahjat Abu Gharbiyah by a vote of 172-69. There were 21 abstentions. Abu Gharbiyah was a member of the Popular Struggle Front, one of four groups belonging to the Rejection Front. His candidacy was sponsored by the Popular Front for the Liberation of Palestine, the most radical group in the front.

Exported oranges poisoned. In 1978, some Israeli oranges exported to West Germany and the Netherlands were reported by authorities in those countries Feb. 1 to have been poisoned with mercury. At least six persons were stricken after they ate the oranges, but all recovered.

A group calling itself the Arab Revolutionary Army Palestine Command claimed responsibility for the sabotage in a letter Feb. 1 addressed to 18 European and Arab governments and sent to the Reuters news agency in London.

The message of the terrorists said their aim was not to kill people, "but to sabotage the Israeli economy which is based on suppression, racial discrimination and colonial occupation." The command said the oranges had been injected by "oppressed Palestinian workers" in Israeli-occupied territories.

Israeli authorities denied the terrorists' allegations, saying "investigations had proved that this act was actually committed in Europe," not in the occupied West Bank and Gaza Strip.

Raiders kill 35 Israelis. Eleven Al Fatah guerrillas landed March 11, 1978 on the Israeli coast 20 miles south of Haifa. They killed 35 Israeli civilians in a bloody orgy of shooting that ended several hours later near Tel Aviv. Nine of the raiders were killed and two were captured.

Details of the incident as provided March 12 by Premier Menahem Begin, other Israeli authorities and eyewitnesses:

The gunmen, who had set out from Lebanon, came ashore from two rubber boats north of Maagen Mikhael, a collective settlement. Their first victim was an American woman walking on the beach whom they shot to death after asking her to ascertain their whereabouts.

The Fatah group then moved up to the Haifa-Tel Aviv coastal road where they halted a taxi and killed several passengers. Shortly afterward the guerrillas stopped a Haifa-bound tourist bus, firing from both sides of the road and killing and wounding some passengers.

The terrorists entered the bus and forced the driver to turn around in the direction of Tel Aviv. Further Israeli casualties were inflicted as the gunmen fired at traffic on the highway as they headed south.

Another bus was encountered on the road several minutes later and a number of its passengers were killed and wounded as the gunmen opened fire to stop it. The remaining passengers, including 30 children, were herded into the first bus. Further down the road a taxi was stopped and six more passengers were taken on as hostages.

Police, alerted at this point, established a series of roadblocks in an attempt to stop the speeding bus. The terrorists tossed hand grenades and fired at three policemen at one of the roadblocks, killing one man.

The bus finally stopped near the area of a larger road barrier set up outside the Tel Aviv County Club, seven miles (11 kilometers) north of the city, where soldiers and policemen had been transported by helicopters, trucks and other vehicles. The bus came under heavy fire as it approached the roadblock, and after a 15-minute exchange between the guerrillas and the Israeli forces, the vehicle blew up and caught fire.

At least 25 persons were killed on the bus.

PLO claims Israeli soldiers slain—A PLO version of the attack issued in Beirut March 11 claimed that the guerrilla force killed at least 33 Israeli soldiers in fighting between Tel Aviv and Haifa.

Confirming Al Fatah's involvement, a communique said one of its units seized control of a bridge near Haifa after killing 15 Israeli soldiers, and 18 more soldiers died when their vehicle was destroyed by Palestinian gunmen near the Tel Aviv Country Club. Still another group of Al Fatah men killed an unspecified number of Israeli troops at Kfar Holim, near Haifa, the communique said. The PLO said one of the slain guerrillas was a woman, Dalal Mughrabi, 25, who had commanded the operation.

Salameh slain. A PLO military leader, his four bodyguards and five passersby were killed in Beirut Jan. 22, 1979 when a booby-trapped car exploded as the guerrilla official and his aides drove by in another auto. The PLO official was Ali Hassan Salameh, also known as Abu Hassan, security chief of Al Fatah. He headed Israel's list of most-wanted guerrillas because he allegedly planned the slaying of 11 Israeli athletes at the Munich Olympics in 1972.

Israel-Guerrilla Prisoner Swap. Israel March 14, 1979 exchanged 66 Arab guerrilla prisoners for one Israeli soldier, who had been captured by Palestinian forces in southern Lebanon April 5, 1978.

The trade was carried out at the Geneva airport, with the Red Cross serving as intermediary. The Israelis had released 76 Palestinians, but the other 10 elected to remain in Israeli-occupied territory.

The Palestinians, some of whom had been sentenced to life in prison for terrorist activity against the Israelis, were flown to Geneva in an Israeli passenger plane.

Truce Ends Israel-PLO Clashes. A cease-fire arranged by the United Nations Interim Force in Lebanon (UNIFIL) brought to a near halt April 26, 1979 the fighting that had raged in southern Lebanon since April 22 between Israeli forces and guerrillas of the Palestine Liberation Organization. The latest round of clashes was touched off when Israel launched reprisal attacks for a PLO raid April 22 on the northern Israeli town of Nahariya, in which three Israelis were slain.

According to U.N. sources, the PLO was opposed to accepting a formal cease-fire, but agreed to stop firing rockets into northern Israel if the Israelis ended their offensive. The U.N. source called the truce "a respite until the next round."

In the attack on Nahariya April 22, four PLO guerrillas came ashore and burst into an apartment building, killing a civilian and his four-year-old daughter. In ensuing gun battles, two of the gunmen and an Israeli policeman were killed. The other two guerrillas were wounded and taken prisoner. One of the dead guerrillas had been shot by another civilian in the apartment building.

Communist World

Soviet Union

The refugees from the Soviet Union include famous dancers, musicians, artists, writers and ordinary people who have frequently braved persecution, prison terms and even death in their efforts to escape from the U.S.S.R. Some leave with permission, some without. A few dissidents become involuntary refugees, the Soviet government depriving them of citizenship while they are abroad or (more rarely) sending them into exile arbitrarily.

The most publicized group of would-be emigrants consists of Jews. U.S. Rep. Joshua Eilberg told Congress in a statement March 16, 1976: "Tens of thousands of Soviet Jews have been trying for years to leave Russia in order to live in Israel or other democratic countries. . . . The government reacted by having them fired from their jobs, or expelled from school, evicted from their homes, beaten, and, finally, imprisoned on trumped-up charges and exiled to Siberia." The plight of Soviet Jews, among them "refusniks" (whom the government refused permission to leave), has excited the sympathy and support of many people in the U.S. and other countries. Worldwide protest against persecution of these would-be refugees has persuaded the Soviet government to let several thousand Jews go.

Leningrad plane hijack fails. Ten Soviet Jews and two non-Jews were seized in Leningrad June 15, 1970 in an unsuccessful attempt to flee the Soviet Union by hijacking an airliner.

The official account June 16 in the Leningrad CP newspaper Leningradskaya Pravda said only that "On June 15, in Smolny Airport, a group of criminals, trying to seize a scheduled airplane, was apprehended. An investigation is being carried out."

Apparently the group was arrested while walking from the terminal to board a small Aeroflot AN-2 plane for a flight from Leningrad to Petrozavodsk, in the Soviet Republic of Karelia on the Finnish border. Police said those arrested were carrying two pistols and several knives. Only the following five were identified: Eduard S. Kuznetsov and his wife, Silva Y. Zalmanson, both of Riga, Yuri Tarakandov of Leningrad, Yuri P. Fyodorov of Moscow, and Alexander Murzhenko, from a town near Kharkov.

Following the airport arrests, police June 15 searched the homes of at least 50 Jews in Leningrad, Riga, Moscow and Kharkov

Defendants sentenced, death sentences commuted—Eleven of the hijack defendants were convicted and sentenced by a Leningrad court Dec. 28, 1970, but the death sentences meted out to two of them were commuted by the Supreme Court of the Russian Republic Dec. 31 to 15 years in prison.

The Dec. 31 court action, announced by the Soviet press agency Tass, reduced the sentence of Eduard S. Kuznetsov from death to 15 years in a special labor camp, the severest type of Soviet camp, and that of Mark Y. Dymshits from death to 15 years in a strict camp, a less severe form of detention.

The court reduced the sentences of three other defendants. Iosif M. Mendelevich received 12 instead of 15 years; Leib G. Khnokh was given 10 instead of 13 years and Anatoly Altman received 10 instead of 12 years.

The sentences of the six other accused plotters, also handed down Dec. 28 in Leningrad, were upheld Dec. 31. Those assigned to strict camps and their terms of imprisonment were: Silva Y. Zalmanson, the wife of Kuznetsov, 10 years; Izrail Y. Zalmanson, Silva's brother, eight years and Boris Penson, 10 years. Yuri P. Fyodorov and Alexander Murzhenko, the only non-Jewish members of the group, received 15 years in a special camp. Mendel Bodnya, an invalid, was given four years in an enforced camp, less severe than the strict category. (Volf Zalmanson, a brother of two of the accused and the 12th person arrested at the airport in June, was sentenced Jan. 7, 1971 to 10 years in prison.)

During the trial, which began Dec. 15, Dymshits, a former air force pilot, reportedly admitted helping organize the hijacking plot because of anti-Semitism in the Soviet Union.

2 more hijack trials—In another trial, nine more Soviet Jews were convicted in Leningrad May 20, 1971 of attempted aircraft hijacking. They got labor-camp terms of one to 10 years.

All nine defendants had been charged with anti-Soviet activity and with "participation in anti-Soviet organizations." Five of them had been accused of stealing state property—a duplicating machine with which they were said to have planned to print anti-Soviet literature. Gilya I. Butman and Mikhail L. Korenblit, considered to have had the principal role in planning a previous hijack effort

that was never carried out, were charged with treason.

Nina Isakova, the presiding judge, handed down sentences May 20 which were virtually the same as those requested by the prosecutor. Butman was given a 10-year sentence and Korenblit seven years. The other sentences were: Lassal S. Kaminsky and Lev N. Yagman, five years; Vladimir O. Mogilever, four years; Solomon G. Dreizner, Lev L. Korenblit (Mikhail Korenblit's brother) and Viktor N. Boguslavsky, three years; and Viktor Stilbans, one year. Tass said that Dreizner, Lev Korenblit and Mogilever had been given lesser sentences because of their "sincere repentence and the fact that they helped uncover the crime at the stage of preliminary investigation." Boguslavsky, convicted of distributing anti-Soviet material, had not been implicated in the hijacking plan.

Nine more Soviet Jews were given prison terms by the Moldavian Supreme Court in Kishinev June 30 for their role in plans to hijack a Soviet plane in 1970.

The accused, most of them engineers or skilled technicians, had been charged, according to Tass reports, with trying to hijack a plane, stealing and concealing a photocopying machine and the "spreading of materials aimed at subverting the social and state systems of the U.S.S.R."

Those sentenced were: David Chernoglaz, five years; Anatoly Goldfeld, four years; Alexander Galperin, two and a half years; Arkady Voloshin, Semyon Levit, Lazar Trakhtenberg, Harry Kizhner and Gilel Shur, two years each; and David Rabinovich, one year.

2 planes hijacked to Turkey. Two Soviet planes were hijacked by Soviet nationals in October 1970 and forced to Turkey.

A Soviet Aeroflot AN-24, making a domestic flight between the Black Sea ports of Batumi and Sukhumi in the Georgian Republic, was hijacked by two Lithuanians Oct. 15 and forced to land in Trebizond, Turkey.

The hijackers, identified as Pranas S. Brazinskas, 46, and his son Algirdas, 18, took control of the plane shortly after takeoff and ordered the pilot to fly to Turkey. According to the elder Brazinskas, he and his son accidentally fired their weapons when the pilot "started flipping the plane" in order to throw the hijackers off balance by aerial maneuvers. Nadezhda Kurchenko, the stewardess, was killed and the pilot and navigator were injured.

Passengers later reported that Miss Kurchenko had been shot while trying to block entrance to the pilots' cabin. Both hijackers surrendered to police officials in Turkey and asked for political asylum.

A Soviet Aeroflot plane, on a domestic flight from Kerch to Krasnodar, was forced by two students to land in Sinop, Turkey Oct. 27.

The students, Nikolai Ginlov and Vitaly Pozdeyev, requested political asylum Oct. 28 and said they wanted to live in the U.S. A third passenger, Yuri Derbinov, said he wanted to return to the Soviet Union.

The Turkish Supreme Court ruled March 8, 1971 that the Brazinskases were ordinary criminals and subject to extradition to the Soviet Union. The judgment reversed a lower court decision ordering the release of the hijackers on the ground that the incident had been political.

Ginlov and Pozdeyev were returned by Turkey to the U.S.S.R. at their own request Dec. 20, 1971. Convicted in September 1972, Pozdeyev received a 13-year prison sentence and Ginlov a 10-year term.

Lithuanian hijacker spared. Vitautas Simokaitis was sentenced to death Jan. 14, 1971 by Lithuania's Supreme Court for attempting to hijack a plane November 1970. However, according to a Jan. 31 report, his sentence was commuted by the Supreme Soviet of the Lithuanian Republic to 15 years in a labor camp.

Simokaitis and his wife Grazina, sentenced to three years in a prison camp, had attempted to seize an Aeroflot plane Nov. 9, 1970 while it was flying between the Lithuanian towns of Vilnius and Palanga.

Svetlana loses Soviet citizenship. The Soviet government gazette of laws and decrees said Jan. 21, 1970 that Svetlana Alliluyeva, daughter of the late Joseph Stalin, had been denied Soviet citizen-

ship by an action taken by the Presidium of the Supreme Soviet (parliament) Dec. 19, 1969. A notice said she had been stripped of her citizenship because of her "misconduct defaming the title of citizen of the U.S.S.R." Mrs. Alliluyeva, 45, had defected to the U.S. in April 1967.

In a book published in 1969, "Only One Year," she said she had destroyed her Soviet passport in the summer of 1967. In 1969, Mrs. Alliluyeva's lawyers had written to the Soviet consulate in Washington asking confirmation of her renunciation of Soviet citizenship.

Simas Kudirka's story. Simas Kudirka, a Lithuanian sailor, sprang from a Soviet fishing ship to a U.S. Coast Guard cutter off Martha's Vineyard, Mass. Nov. 23, 1970 in an attempt to defect to the U.S. but was forcibly returned to his ship. (Four years later, after serving in a Soviet prison camp, he was ruled a U.S. citizen and sent back to the U.S.)

Kudirka in 1970 had boarded the U.S. cutter Vigilant Nov. 23 while it was tied to the vessel Sovetskaya Litva as U.S. and Soviet officials discussed fishing rights in the North Atlantic. Kudirka informed the ship's captain, Comdr. Ralph W. Eustis, that he wanted asylum. Several hours of radio contact between the two vessels and between Eustis and Coast Guard and State Department officers produced the order that Kudirka should be returned to the Sovetskaya Litva.

Kudirka was reported May 27, 1971 to have received a 10-year term for treason.

The U.S. State Department ruled in 1974 that Kudirka was a U.S. citizen (reported July 18). In May, U.S. citizenship had been given his mother, Marija Sulsiene, who was born in New York City and taken to Lithuania when she was seven, according to a May 18 report.

Kudirka arrived in New York Nov. 5 with his mother, wife and two children.

Ballerina defects. Natalya Makarova, prominent member of the Leningrad Kirov Ballet, sought and obtained political asylum in Britain Sept. 4, 1970. She had reportedly slipped away from other members of the troupe on the pretext of last-minute shopping.

A Soviet embassy official in London

said Sept. 5 that the embassy's request for an interview with the ballerina had been rejected by British authorities.

Other 1970 emigrants & defectors:

■ Yuli Telesin, reportedly one of 39 Moscow Jews who had protested a Soviet anti-Israel campaign in March, emigrated to Israel May 6, 1970.

■Police in Buenos Aires said July 15 that Naum Fruman, first violinist of the Moscow Philharmonic Orchestra, had asked for political asylum during the group's visit to the Argentine capital.

■Alexander Silippov and Giennadi S. Vostrikov, members of the Moiseyev Ballet, appeared in Mexico City Sept. 10 after leaving the company's rehearsal in Guadalajara. Each was accompanied by a Latin American girl friend and wanted to live in the U.S., expressing disaffection with conditions in the Soviet Union. Vostrikov asked for political asylum.

Fedoseyev defects to Britain.
Soviet scientist Anatoly Fedoseyev defected at the Paris Air Show May 26, 1971 and was given British government permission June 20 to remain in Great Britain.

Mikhail N. Smirnovsky, Soviet ambassador to Britain, requested June 21 that a member of his staff be allowed to speak with Fedoseyev. Smirnovsky's request was made to Sir Denis Greenhill, permanent undersecretary at the Foreign Office, who noted that Fedoseyev was free at any time to contact the Soviet embassy.

Fedoseyev July 10 denied being "a specialist on antiballistic missiles."

Fedoseyev, whose remarks were made in an interview in the Sunday Telegraph, a London newspaper, was referring to a July 7 dispatch from Helsinki, attributed to a Los Angeles Times writer and cited in other Western newspapers. The article had claimed that Fedoseyev was using a cover name to hide his true identity as deputy director of the Soviet space space program in charge of electronics and cybernetics.

Chebotarev defects & redefects.
The U.S. State Department announced Oct. 18, 1971 that Anatoly K. Chebotarev, former Soviet trade mission employe in Brussels who had been missing since early October had been granted U.S. asylum. It said Chebotarev had asked for asylum through the U.S. embassy in Brussels.

Belgian police sources had reported Oct. 17 that they had given the Foreign Ministry a list supplied by Chebotarev naming 30–40 Soviet espionage agents operating in Belgium.

But he redefected and returned to the Soviet Union Dec. 26, according to a State Department announcement the following day. Charles W. Bray 3d, department spokesman, said Cheboratev had disappeared without word after a meeting Dec. 21 at the State Department with a Soviet embassy official who gave him "a number of pieces of correspondence from his family." On Dec. 24 Yuli M. Vorontsev, the Soviet charge d'affaires, requested State Department assistance in transporting Chebotarev to the Soviet Union.

Bray said the Soviet embassy agreed to have Chebotarev submit to an interview to determine if he was returning voluntarily. After a hearing Dec. 26 at Kennedy International Airport in New York, Chebotarev was allowed to board an Aeroflot plane to Moscow.

Some Jews seek return from Israel.
Soviet Premier Alexei N. Kosygin said during a visit to Denmark Dec. 5, 1971 that many of the Soviet Jews who had emigrated to Israel wanted to return to the Soviet Union.

The New York Times had reported Nov. 28 that Israeli officials were blaming local Soviet "agent provocateurs" for a story published Nov. 26 in the newspaper Maariv saying that some 50–200 heads of families of Georgian Jews wanted to return to the U.S.S.R.

More than a year later the Toronto Globe & Mail said (Jan. 5, 1973) that 93 Soviet Jews who had emigrated to Israel had asked to be allowed to return to the U.S.S.R.

Among 1971 Jewish emigrants:

■ Boris Zukerman, a leading advocate of Jewish rights, left the Soviet Union for Israel Jan. 25. Vitaly Svichinsky, who received his exit visa along with Zukerman, left Feb. 1 for Vienna.

■ Maj. Grisha Feigin, a Soviet army officer who had returned medals for valor to authorities in 1970 to protest the government's policies toward Soviet Jews, arrived in Israel Feb. 11 as an immigrant. Feigin, whose exit visa was granted Jan. 31, had been confined for a short time in a mental hospital when he returned the medals.

■ Boris Gaponov, a Soviet Jew from the Georgian Republic who taught himself Hebrew and won an Israeli literary award, arrived in Tel Aviv May 28 as an immigrant. Gaponov's mother said her son, who was suffering from meningitis, was allowed to leave the Soviet Union only after contracting the illness.

■ Mikhail I. Zand, a Jewish scholar who had tried repeatedly to emigrate to Israel, finally succeeded. He arrived June 25 with members of his family. Zand's permission to leave the country, several times revoked, had been once again tendered June 22.

■ Ruth Alexandrovich, sentenced to a year in prison in Riga in May for alleged complicity in a hijack attempt, was released Oct. 7 and arrived in Israel Oct. 28.

Jewish poet emigrates. Iosif A. Brodsky, a Soviet poet who was released from jail in 1964 after serving part of a sentence for "social parasitism," arrived in Vienna and applied for a visa to the U.S. June 8, 1972. He received the visa June 17.

New exit fees for Jews. Jewish spokesmen in Moscow revealed Aug. 15, 1972 that a new system of exit fees for Jews wishing to emigrate to Israel had gone into effect the previous day.

The new regulations, handed down Aug. 3 in a decree signed by Premier Aleksei N. Kosygin, required the payment of anywhere from $4,400 to $37,000, depending on the educational level of the applicant. The fees ostensibly were to reimburse the state for free education given the emigrants.

The Soviet Union was reported Aug. 23 to be advising U.S. Jews on how to insure that relatives could emigrate. David Korn, chairman of the Soviet Jewry Committee in Washington, was said to have been informed in a telephone conversaion Aug. 21 with the deputy head of the visa branch of the Soviet Interior Ministry that "if you want your relatives to leave, transfer through your American bank the necessary amount, and they will leave."

According to the New York Times Oct. 25, some 190 Jewish families had been given visas the previous week without payment of the exit tax.

A Soviet Jewish journalist who had attacked the country's emigration fees was told Dec. 18 he could leave without paying the tax. Viktor Perelman and five other Jews were to be allowed to leave for Israel with their families.

In other developments affecting Soviet Jews, Alexander Yesenin-Volpin, a dissident mathematician, was reported June 6 to have left the Soviet Union the previous week on an exit visa to Israel.

The New York Times March 9, 1973 cited Israeli figures showing that 30,000 Jews had emigrated from the Soviet Union in 1972.

Defectors reach West. The seven-man crew of the Soviet trawler Ishon, mostly from Lithuania and the Ukraine, were given political asylum in Athens, Greece Aug. 19, 1972 after arriving Aug. 14.

Yuri Grodetzky and Alexander Ivanov, trombone players with the Leningrad Music Hall Orchestra, left Mexico City Aug. 25 for New York after obtaining U.S. visas. The men had slipped away from the touring company and obtained political asylum from the Mexican government.

A Danish Foreign Ministry spokesman announced Oct. 2 that the Danish embassador to the Soviet Union had been instructed to lodge a formal protest against Soviet marines who had illegally boarded a Danish fishing boat in the Baltic Sea Sept. 27 and seized a Soviet defector at gunpoint.

2 dissidents lose citizenship. Valery N. Chalidze, a dissident physicist lecturing at U.S. universities, had his passport confiscated by Soviet officials in New York Dec. 13, 1972 and was told he had been deprived of his citizenship.

Chalidze reported that the incident took place in the lobby of his hotel, where the officials requested an interview. Yuri Galishnikov, a consular secretary from Washington, asked for Chalidze's passport "to check my identity" and then gave it to an unidentified associate. The document "ended up in the other man's pocket," Chalidze said.

Chalidze declared that while in the U.S. he had been "occupied with conversations with jurists and with lectures on human rights in the U.S.S.R. and, in particular, speaking about acts of authorities which have discredited the U.S.S.R.—for violations of human rights discredit the state." He had spoken here "the same way I did in the Soviet Union. And if these are the grounds for depriving me of my citizenship, then why was I not deprived of it in the Soviet Union."

Geneticist and liberal activist Zhores A. Medvedev was deprived of Soviet citizenship in London Aug. 7, 1973 and was told not to return to the Soviet Union.

Medvedev, who had been working since January at the National Institute of Medical Research near London, was called to the Soviet embassy and told that the "presidium of the Supreme Soviet took the decision on July 16 to deprive him of his citizenship because of his actions."

Exit fees waived. The Soviet government March 19–20, 1973 waived emigration fees for 40 Soviet Jews in an apparent response to pressure from the U.S. Congress. It revealed indirectly March 21 that the fees had been suspended.

The five persons affected by the March 19 move, who among them had been assessed $34,300 in exit taxes, were Alexander Babchin, Anatoly Gokhshtein, their wives and Valery Korenblit. In a separate action March 20, officials exempted another 35 persons from payment.

According to the Washington Post March 22, the U.S.S.R.'s suspension of its exit fees was revealed the previous day by Victor Louis, the Soviet journalist who had several times leaked information to Western periodicals. In an article appearing in the Israeli newspaper Yediot Aharonot, Louis said the emigration tax "will not be canceled, nor will any changes be made in the law—but it will not be enforced any more. . . . It seems that the Soviet citizens who have decided to emigrate to Israel have won a victory."

U.S. embassy representatives in Moscow emphasized March 22 that there had been no official Soviet confirmation of an indefinite suspension of the exit tax.

Brezhnev asks more U.S. trade; exit tax reported suspended. Soviet Communist party Chairman Leonid I. Brezhnev told a group of seven U.S. senators, during a lengthy unscheduled conversation in Moscow April 23, that the Soviet Union looked forward to a major expansion of its trade with the United States, and would not let the issue of Jewish emigration interfere with trade growth.

Brezhnev assured the senators that the education tax on prospective emigrants from the U.S.S.R. had been suspended. Several of the senators later said Brezhnev's assurances would weaken the chances of passage in Congress of the Jackson amendment, which would deny most-favored-nation tariff treatment to a country that restricted emigration or imposed more than nominal exit fees.

The New York Times reported June 1 that Brezhnev had assured U.S. President Richard M. Nixon's national security adviser, Henry A. Kissinger, that the U.S.S.R. would permit continued Jewish emigration at the current rate of 36,000–40,000 a year. He also said the education tax on emigrants would remain suspended.

Brezhnev reportedly made the pledge in talks with Kissinger in Moscow May 4–8, when he accepted a list of 1,000 "hardship" cases presented to Kissinger by U.S. Jewish leaders May 1. The list included 42 Jews currently imprisoned on various charges related to emigration.

Jewish emigration from the U.S.S.R. had averaged about 2,000 a year up to 1971, when it rose to 13,500. About 30,000 Jews were allowed to leave in 1972.

Brezhnev met U.S. Congressional leaders in Washington June 19 to back most-favored-nation tariff treatment for the Soviet Union.

In response to questions about restrictions on the emigration of Soviet Jews, which had stalled Congressional consideration of the tariff issue, Brezhnev claimed that 97% of all those who had applied had been allowed out. He said 68,-000 Jews had left the Soviet Union through 1971, another 60,200 were given permission to leave in 1972, and 10,100 of 11,400 applicants had been given visas so far in 1973. The figures were higher than Western estimates.

Brezhnev cited a list of 742 Jews who had allegedly been denied permission to leave. He claimed that over 200 either did not live in the Soviet Union or had not requested exit visas. Another 258 had been given permission to leave just before Brezhnev left Moscow, and cases of 149 who had been denied visas for security reasons were being reviewed.

Defections reported. West Germany granted asylum May 30, 1973 to a Soviet air force pilot who had parachuted from his plane after flying from East Germany May 27.

A Russian civil airlines pilot crash-landed in Turkey June 26 and requested political asylum.

Despite a Soviet pact requiring the return of refugees, Finland decided July 26 to grant asylum to a Lithuanian who had tried to row across the Baltic Sea. West Germany had claimed that the youth, whose parents were German, was considered a German under the West German Constitution.

Soviet Air Force Capt. Valery Yanin rowed a raft for 3 days across the Black Sea, reaching the northern shores of Turkey Aug. 16.

Yanin, 26, told Turkish authorities he had jumped overboard with the raft from a Soviet ship, leaving his wife and son aboard. He said he had been planning to get to Turkey for a long time "to escape oppression in Russia."

Dissident writer Andrei Sinyavsky, his wife and two children were reported Aug. 11 to have arrived in Paris, where Sinyavsky was to assume a professorship at the Sorbonne.

Terror curbs Austria refugee transit. Yielding to terrorist action, the Austrian government announced Sept. 29, 1973 that it would no longer allow group transit of Soviet Jewish emigrants through Austria, and would close Israeli-run facilities that housed emigrants awaiting transfer to Israel. The decision was made in return for the release of one Austrian and three Soviet Jewish hostages, whom Arab guerrillas had held under threat of murder at the Vienna airport. Austrian chancellor Bruno Kreisky refused to modify his decision during an Oct. 2 meeting with Israeli Premier Golda Meir.

The three Jewish hostages were seized Sept. 28, along with a woman who later escaped with her infant son, on a Moscow-Vienna train carrying 40 Jewish emigrants in Czechoslovak territory at the Austrian border. The two heavily armed guerrillas, who said they were members of a group called the Eagles of the Palestinian Revolution, left the train at the Austrian customs station, where they seized a customs official, commandeered a car and drove to Vienna's Schwechat airport.

During several hours of negotiations, the Austrian Cabinet offered to fly the guerrillas to the Middle East, but refused their demands to take the hostages with them. The hostages were released early Sept. 29, after Austrian Chancellor Bruno Kreisky agreed to close the Schoenau Castle transit facility outside Vienna, run by the Jewish Agency of Israel, and to bar "group transports" of Jews through Austria, according to Interior Minister Otto Roesch in a radio broadcast Sept. 29.

The guerrillas were given a twin-engine plane with two Austrian pilots, and were allowed to land in Libya only after they had been refused by Tunisia and Algeria and had threatened to blow up the plane.

Austria's government-run television said Sept. 29 that the offer to close Schoenau had been a compromise suggested by Arab governments, "especially Iraq." Kreisky, in several interviews that day, said he had refused demands to bar all future Jewish emigrants from entering Austria, and said "all people with proper papers" would be allowed to pass through. Nearly all the 70,000 Jewish emigrants who had left the European Communist countries since 1971 had passed through Austria in groups, without Austrian visas.

United Nations Secretary General Kurt Waldheim informed Austria Oct. 2 that the Office of High Commissioner for Refugees could not assume responsibility for the Schoenau facility under existing U.N. rules, as Kreisky had suggested in his meeting with Meir. Waldheim said approval for a takeover would have to come from the General Assembly, since the Jews, who had legal Soviet exit visas and assurances of asylum in Israel, did not come under existing U.N. definitions of refugees.

The 17-nation Council of Europe voted unanimously Oct. 2, after hearing Meir, to advise Austria that it considered no government bound by pledges obtained by blackmail. Substantial numbers of Jews continued to enter Austria and be quartered at Schoenau as of Oct. 3. The day before, Kreisky said the closing date was a "technical matter." Moscow sources reported Oct. 1 that a record 3,650 Jews had been permitted to emigrate in September. It was said Nov. 1 that a record 4,200 Jews had been permitted to emigrate during October.

U.S. Rep. Lou Frey (R, Fla.) said in Vienna Oct. 6 that Austrian officials had assured him they would do nothing to curb the movement of emigrants, other than to close down the Schoenau facility within 60 days, which Frey said they "had been looking for an excuse to close" because of security problems.

Jewish emigration falls in '74. The rate of Jewish emigration from the Soviet Union declined from over 5,000 in January–February 1973 to fewer than 4,000 in the first two months of 1974, it was reported March 3.

The drop tended to conflict with reports by Austrian government and Jewish agency officials (according to the New York Times Feb. 24) that the number of Soviet Jews passing through the transit center in Vienna had not fallen off and, in fact, may have increased.

U.S. consular officials in Moscow said Nov. 1 that about 200 of the 790 persons whose names were submitted in April to Soviet officials as wanting to join relatives in the U.S. had been permitted to leave the U.S.S.R.

Emigration to Israel down—The emigration of Jews from the Soviet Union to Israel declined by 37% in the first 10 months of 1974, compared with the same period of 1973, according to figures released by the Geneva-based Intergovern-mental Committee on European Migration, it was reported Nov. 9.

Israeli Immigration Minister Shlomo Rosen said Dec. 11 that Jewish immigration to Israel thus far in 1974 totaled 32,000, compared with a 1973 total of 55,000. He also said that 18% of the Soviet Jews who emigrated in 1974 had decided to settle in the West instead of in Israel.

Soviet authorities quoted in the New York Times May 26 contended that the decline in exits was due to disillusionment with Israel which, they said, accounted for a 50% drop in applications. However, there was reportedly a backlog of 140,000 applicants and Western sources cited increasing bureaucratic restrictions on the application process: police interrogations, extensive documentation and exorbitant exit fees. The often-imposed policy of dismissing emigration applicants from their jobs had also reduced attempts to leave.

Solzhenitsyn forcibly exiled. The Soviet government deported Nobel Prize-winning novelist and historian Alexander Solzhenitsyn to West Germany Feb. 13, 1974 after cancelling his Soviet citizenship. The writer had been arrested by seven policemen the day before at his wife's Moscow apartment.

Solzhenitsyn was believed to be the first Soviet citizen to be forcibly expelled from the country since Leon Trotsky was exiled in 1929.

Upon arrival in West Germany on a Soviet airliner, Solzhenitsyn was taken to the home of fellow Nobel laureate author Heinrich Boell. The Soviet news agency Tass said Feb. 13 that his wife and three children would be allowed to join him.

Tass said Solzhenitsyn had been deprived of citizenship by the Presidium of the Supreme Soviet for "performing systematically actions that are incompatible with being a citizen."

The first indications of the government's intentions came Feb. 8, when a summons from the prosecutor general's office was delivered to Solzhenitsyn's wife, who refused to accept, claiming it was not in proper form. The author himself said Feb. 11 he would not obey a second summons "because of the complete and general illegality ruling in our country for many years."

Soviet sources said Feb. 13 that the government had planned to give the Solzhenitsyn family a few days to pack when they served the summonses, but then decided to "expedite" the case.

Baryshnikov defects. Soviet ballet dancer Mikhail Baryshnikov defected to the West June 29, 1974 while on tour as a guest artist with the Bolshoi Ballet in Toronto, Canada. He had been the leading male dancer with Leningrad's Kirov Ballet.

Canadian immigration officials granted him a special permit July 2 to remain in Canada for a year.

Baryshnikov, 26, was aided in his defection by an American friend, Christina Berlin. Soviet embassy officials in Ottawa charged July 3 that she had abducted him, but allowed the Bolshoi to continue its tour and promised that no reprisals would be taken against Baryshnikov's father in Riga, Latvia.

In an interview with the Toronto Globe and Mail July 4, Baryshnikov asserted that his decision to defect was for personal and artistic, not for political, reasons.

More dissidents get visas for Israel. During 1974 the Soviet government permitted several activist Jews to leave with visas to Israel. Not all actually went to Israel.

Pavel Litvinov, grandson of the late Foreign Minister Maxim Litvinov, left the U.S.S.R. with his family March 18 and applied in Vienna for a U.S. visa, which was granted March 19. The Soviet Union had issued the dissident physicist a visa for Israel.

Jewish ballet dancer Valery Panov and his wife, Galina, also a ballet dancer, arrived in Tel Aviv June 15 after being granted permission June 7 to emigrate to Israel. The couple had struggled for two years in their efforts to leave.

British Prime Minister Harold Wilson had appealed personally to Soviet Premier Alexei Kosygin June 6 on behalf of the Panovs.

Jewish songwriter Alexander Galich was granted permission June 17 to emigrate to Israel with his wife and was given until June 25 to leave the Soviet Union.

Silva Y. Zalmanson, who got a 10-year sentence in 1970 for the attempted hijacking of a Soviet aircraft, was released from jail Aug. 23 and ordered expelled to Israel. She flew to Vienna Sept. 10.

Anatoly Levitin-Krasnov, a religious historian and campaigner for human rights in the Soviet Union, arrived in Vienna Sept. 21 from Moscow. A prominent member of the Russian Orthodox Church, he had reportedly been granted a visa for Israel.

The physicist Victor Polsky, 44, left Moscow for Israel Dec. 22, having received permission to emigrate Nov. 15. He had lost his job at the Moscow Institute nearly four years earlier when he first applied to leave the Soviet Union; he had been repeatedly denied a visa on security grounds.

Polsky was fined 100 rubles (about $140) after having been found guilty Oct. 18 of felonious reckless driving, a charge placed against him in March when his car struck the daughter of an Interior Ministry official in Moscow.

Jewish physicist Alexander Voronel, 43, arrived in Israel Dec. 29. He had been given permission to leave Dec. 11. Voronel, who had left his job at the Institute of Physical-Technical and Radio-Technical Measurements when he first applied to emigrate in April 1972, had in recent months been arrested and otherwise harassed for organizing unauthorized seminars for unemployed Jewish scholars.

Afanasiev a refugee. Pianist Valery Afanasiev got refugee status in Belgium July 2, 1974. He had sought asylum there June 25 while on a concert tour. Officials said the 26-year-old pianist wished to pursue an international career without the restrictions imposed by the Soviet Union.

Yermolenko's double defection. Soviet violinist Georgi Yermolenko, 19, sought to defect in Perth, Australia Aug. 11, 1974 while at an international music conference. When he announced a change of heart the next day, Australian trade unions, alleging that the request had been withdrawn under duress, blocked his departure by refusing to sell him an airline ticket or to allow any aircraft carrying him to leave the airport.

After an interview with Australian immigration officials, the young musician was flown out of the country Aug. 15 on an Australian military aircraft. Foreign Minister Don Willesee said he was convinced of the youth's sincerity in seeking to return to Moscow.

Yermolenko appeared on Soviet television Aug. 23 and reaffirmed his desire to pursue his career in the U.S.S.R.

But Yermolenko came back to Australia March 7, 1975 after the Canberra government gave him and his parents permission to stay as immigrants.

The Yermolenkos' status had been announced by Immigration Minister Clyde Cameron March 4. Cameron said the three had been granted visas by the Soviet Union for a two-month visit to Israel. During a stopover in Vienna the previous week, they applied to the Australian embassy for permission to emigrate to Australia. In a statement he made on his return to Australia March 7, Yermelenko said he had changed his mind about staying in Australia then because he wanted to return to the Soviet Union to rejoin his parents. He said he had left his native country because he believed he could develop his musical talents better in Australia.

Western nations impose refugee curbs.
Belgium Sept. 16, 1974 began enforcing immigration regulations that would bar the entry of Soviet Jews who, after emigrating to Israel, became dissatisfied with life there and wanted to move to other countries, the Washington Post reported Sept. 18.

According to the report, more than 600 such emigres had arrived in Brussels during the preceding weeks and had been assisted by two relief organizations, Caritas Catholica and the Tolstoy Foundation. (A Sept. 10 Reuters report said Jewish welfare groups had not come to the aid of the refugees.)

Italy, France and West Germany had closed their borders to Soviet emigrants from Israel earlier in the year by tightening loopholes in laws pertaining to visitors from Israel.

The West Berlin government announced new regulations Dec. 3 to restrict the "un-

diminished influx" of Jewish refugees from the Soviet Union and Eastern Europe. More than 540 immigrants had settled in West Berlin since August 1973, a spokesman said.

Under the new rules, immigrants must obtain valid entry visas, a regulation applied to the entry of all foreigners. Most Jewish refugees to West Berlin had entered as tourists, who were allowed to stay six months, and then sought to settle. The regulations also provided that those Jews who could prove German ancestry would be allowed to remain under the German resettlement laws.

Moscow bars U.S. trade pact re emigration. The U.S.S.R. informed the U.S. Jan. 10, 1975 that because of restrictions imposed under recently enacted legislation in Washington, it would not put into force the 1972 Trade Agreement "which had called for an unconditional elimination of discriminatory trade restrictions." Secretary of State Henry Kissinger announced the action Jan. 14.

The Soviet Union considered both the limitation placed on the amount of Export-Import Bank credit and the Trade Reform Act amendment linking most-favored-nation status to freer Soviet emigration as "contravening both the 1972 Trade Agreement . . . and the principle of noninterference in domestic affairs."

Jewish emigration declining. In an apparent rejoinder to criticism and fears of reprisals expressed in the West, the Soviet Union asserted that from 1945 to Jan. 1, 1975, 98.5% of all applications by Soviet Jews to emigrate to Israel had been granted. The data appeared in the Jan. 30 issue of the Soviet international affairs weekly Novaya Vremya.

The commentary also documented declining emigration to Israel during the past year, stating that 16,000 had gone there in 1974, half the 1973 figure. Denying that Soviet authorities create any "difficulties for persons who want to go to Israel," Novaya Vremya attributed the decline to a decrease in the number of applications. At present, it said, there were only 1,420 requests pending.

The number of Soviet Jews seeking to emigrate "has been in constant decline since 1973 because of the miserable conditions, unemployment and lack of housing" in Israel, as well as "the hostility with which Soviet Jews are received by the Israelis," the commentary said. Disillusionment with Israel had prompted about 10% of the former Soviet citizens to re-emigrate, while about 4,000 of those who had intended to go to Israel changed their minds and headed instead for other destinations in the West once they reached Vienna, the transit point for the emigrants, according to the journal.

Jewish emigration from the Soviet Union had risen dramatically from 1967–1970 when fewer than 5,000 left the country annually to more than 30,000 in 1972 and 1973; however, emigration had delined to 20,634 in 1974.

Jewish officials in Vienna said March 13 that 3,000 Soviet Jewish emigrants had passed through the transit point since the beginning of the year. This figure was 40% fewer than for the comparable period in 1974. About three-fourths of the emigrants went on to Israel, while most of the others went to the U.S.

Emigres skirting Israel. The U.S. government and refugee organizations in the U.S. had observed an increase in recent months in the number of Soviet Jewish emigres who settled in countries other than Israel (reported May 20, 1975).

More than a third of the 4,499 Jews permitted to leave the U.S.S.R. during the first four months of 1975 had emigrated to the U.S. or other countries in the West and, during the first half of May, the proportion had risen to 45% deciding against going to Israel.

(In 1973, 4% of the total emigre population of 31,082 chose countries other than Israel; most of the 1,429 came to the U.S. In 1974, 3,882, or 19% of the 20,634 emigres, selected destinations other than Israel, with 3,490 settling in the U.S.)

More allowed to go in '75. Dancer Kaleriya Fedicheva, who was dropped from Leningrad's Kirov Ballet after she applied to emigrate in 1974, arrived in Rome Feb. 17, 1975 with her infant son en route to the U.S., after receiving permission from Moscow to leave the Soviet

Union; her application to emigrate had previously been denied. She was joined in Rome by her American husband, ballet dancer Martin Friedman.

In a related development, Alexander Glazer, a promoter of dissident Soviet art, was allowed to emigrate Feb. 16.

The two sons of chemist Benjamin Levich, Alexander and Yevgeny, flew to Vienna April 1 with their families en route to Israel, having been granted, after three years' wait, permission to emigrate from the Soviet Union.

Vladimir Maximov, exiled writer presently living in Paris, was deprived of his Soviet citizenship for "actions harming the prestige of the Soviet Union." The decree had been signed by President Nikolai Podgorny Jan. 30, but was only published in the monthly bulletin of the Supreme Soviet Nov. 12, according to the Financial Times of London Nov. 12.

Natalya Gorbanevskaya, a poet whose book "Red Square at Noon" described her protest in Moscow against the 1968 Soviet invasion of Czechoslovakia, received permission to emigrate and departed the Soviet Union for Vienna Dec. 18, dissident sources in Moscow reported.

Ship technician defects in Hawaii. A Soviet scientist defected May 15, 1975 in Honolulu, Hawaii, where an oceanographic research ship on which he was employed had been conducting experiments with the participation of U.S. scientists. The defector, Vyacheslav Kovalev, 27, was a technician in the ship's laboratory.

Fewer Jews leave in '75. Moscow announced Jan. 22, 1976 that 11,700 Soviet citizens left the U.S.S.R. in 1975 with visas to emigrate to Israel. This was about half of the 1974 figure and one-third of the 1973 figure.

Boris T. Shumlin, deputy minister for internal affairs, attributed the decline in Jewish emigration during 1975 chiefly to letters from emigres to persons remaining in the U.S.S.R., complaining of economic and social conditions in Israel. Shumlin said the main reason given by those seeking to emigrate was a desire to rejoin relatives abroad, most such applications being made by Jews whose families were separated during World War II.

Shumlin also noted that from 1945 to 1976, a total of 122,000 Soviet citizens had departed the U.S.S.R. for Israel. He said permission to leave had been denied to only 1.6% of the Jewish applicants.

Seven Soviet Jews who had returned to the U.S.S.R. after having emigrated to Israel held an officially sponsored press conference in Moscow Feb. 6 and assailed life in Israel as compared with the Soviet Union. The news conference, organized by the Foreign Ministry and the Novosti feature press agency, continued Moscow's efforts to minimize the emigration issue and bolster its image in the area of human rights.

Israel scores U.S. immigration—Israeli officials voiced concern over the number of Soviet Jewish emigres who chose to live in the U.S. instead of Israel once they left the Soviet Union, according to the Dec. 12 New York Times. Israeli officials had said the previous day that the percentage of "dropouts" had averaged 47.4% since Jan. 1, the Times report said.

Israel was concerned not only because of its desire to attract more settlers but also because it feared the Soviet Union might cite the "dropouts" as a pretext for restricting the emigration flow.

The Israeli government and representatives of U.S. Jewish organizations that helped emigres had conducted a series of meetings throughout the year to resolve the problem. Israel reportedly had charged that the U.S. groups were "making it very attractive" for emigres to live in the U.S. Israel had been trying to get U.S. groups that aid emigres to cut off that aid for those who chose not to go to Israel, according to the Nov. 10 Washington Post. The Times report quoted the U.S. organizations as saying they shared Israeli concern over the "dropouts" but felt that their primary obligation was to help all Jews who wished to leave the U.S.S.R., no matter what their destination.

According to figures released Dec. 17 by an international resettlement organization, 13,750 Jews had been permitted to emigrate since Jan. 1. This was 500 more than in 1975 but less than half the 35,000 total permitted in 1973.

Plyushch arrives in Paris. Soviet mathematician Leonid Plyushch arrived in Paris with his family Jan. 12, 1976. The U.S.S.R. had authorized exit permits for the family Dec. 31. He then had been released Jan. 9 from a psychiatric hospital in the Ukraine where he had been interned since 1973 after first being charged with the commission of anti-Soviet acts.

The 36-year-old Plyushch, with his wife and two sons, arrived in Vienna Jan. 11 where he was examined by psychiatrists who reported him free of mental disorders.

Moscow denies psychiatric abuses—In an article published Feb. 4 in the Soviet daily Literaturnaya Gazeta, the U.S.S.R. denied that persons were sent to psychiatric hospitals because of political beliefs and asserted that it was in the West that recourse was made to psychiatry to "control political opponents."

The article characterized a number of emigre dissidents who had been placed in Soviet mental institutions as mental cripples, many of whom were similarly interned upon arriving in the nations to which they had emigrated. The article cited the cases of Alexis Tummerman and Anatoly Yakovson, who, it said, were hospitalized in Israel; Lev Kostantinov, who had been hospitalized in Vienna; and Viktor Fainberg, interned in Great Britain.

(According to the French newspaper Le Monde Feb. 6, Fainberg had never been interned, while the others, having undergone some hospitalization, were presently living "normally and at liberty.")

Neizvestny emigrates. Ernst Neizvestny, the Soviet sculptor who gained notoriety in 1962 for engaging in a public dispute with then Premier Nikita Khrushchev over modern art, left Moscow and arrived in Vienna March 10, 1976 the U.S.S.R. Jan. 27 had granted him permission to emigrate to Israel. The sculptor, whose father was Jewish, had been seeking for over a year to leave the U.S.S.R. Neizvestny reportedly paid 10,000 rubles ($13,200) in customs duties in order to take 17 crates of his own art works with him. The 50-year-old sculptor's wife and children chose to remain in the Soviet Union.

Amalrik emigrates. Andrei Amalrik, the dissident author and historian, renounced his Soviet citizenship and flew to Amsterdam July 15, 1976, accompanied by his wife, Gyusel, a painter.

Amalrik's departure had been scheduled for July 1, but he had postponed it June 30 in a dispute with the Soviet Ministry of Culture over a $5,400 duty placed on his wife's paintings. The Amalriks were permitted July 14 to take the paintings duty-free, but they were required to leave behind antiques and artifacts.

Chess master defects. Viktor Korchnoi, the world's second-ranking chess player, asked for political asylum in Amsterdam July 27, 1976. He had been competing in a tournament in the Dutch capital and was scheduled to return to the Soviet Union that day.

Korchnoi had been in official disfavor since his loss to Anatoly Karpov in December 1974 in a match for the right to challenge then-world champion Bobby Fischer.

Eastern European defections. Six Eastern European athletes—one from the Soviet Union and five from Rumania—defected to Canada during the 1976 Olympic Games.

A Soviet diver, Sergei Nemtsanov, 17, disappeared July 29 after applying to an immigration officer for permanent resident status in Canada.

Rumanian rower Walter Lambertus, 20, requested political refugee status in Canada July 28 and joined relatives in Ontario. Rumanian canoeist Ivan Haralambie, 21, applied for permanent resident status in Toronto July 29 and then disappeared. Two more Rumanians asked for political refugee status Aug. 1 and another was reported Aug. 4 to have defected.

Later, Nemtsanov decided to return to the Soviet Union, the Canadian Federal Department of Immigration announced Aug. 17.

After conferring with his Canadian lawyers and immigration officials, Nemtsanov was taken to a coffee shop where he left with Soviet consular officials.

Pilot defects in Iran. A Soviet pilot Sept. 23, 1976 landed a single-engine mail plane in Ahar in Iran, 63 miles south of the Soviet border, and asked for asylum in the U.S., Iranian sources reported Sept. 25. The U.S. Embassy in Teheran said Sept. 25 that it had received no such request for asylum from the pilot, identified as Lt. Valentin E. Zasimov.

Travelers from Ahar quoted Zasimov as saying he wanted "to describe to the world how the Soviet dissidents are suffering."

The Soviet Embassy in Teheran said Sept. 26 that Moscow had sent a protest to Iran requesting Zasimov's return.

Iran returned Zasimov to the Soviet Union Oct. 25. Tass said he had been extradited under a 1973 anti-hijacking pact.

Prince Sadruddin Agha Khan, U.N. high commissioner for refugees, sent a note to Iran Nov. 1 protesting against its return of Zasmimov. The statement charged that Teheran's action contravened the 1951 convention on the status of refugees to which Iran had subscribed. The convention stipulated that "no contracting state shall expel or return a refugee in any manner whatsoever to ... where his life or freedom would be threatened. . . ."

MiG pilot defects in Japan. The pilot of a Soviet MiG-25 landed the jet fighter at a Japanese air base in Hakodate Sept. 6, 1976 and asked for U.S. asylum.

The pilot, Lieut. Viktor Ivanovich Belenko, swerved off course during a routine training mission over eastern Siberia and landed at the Hokkaido base after evading two Japanese F-4 Phantom fighters sent up to intercept him.

Belenko's plane overshot the 2,000-meter-long runway and landed in an adjacent field.

The police said that during questioning Belenko told them that he had intended to fly to the U.S., but lack of fuel had forced him to land in Japan. The 29-year-old pilot, who left behind a wife and 3-year-old son, was quoted as having said that he had been planning his defection for two years. He wanted "freedom in the U.S." because life in the U.S.S.R. was no different from life in "the days of Czarist Russia."

The White House announced Sept. 7 that President Ford had decided to grant Belenko asylum, but that he had left to Japan the question of the ultimate disposal of the MiG-25. (Japan did not grant political asylum, but it had allowed some people seeking asylum to pass through to other countries.)

Belenko was flown to Tokyo Sept. 7, and he left for the U.S. Sept. 9 after a brief meeting with Soviet officials at the request of the Soviet government.

In the U.S.S.R.'s first public statement on the affair, the news agency Tass charged Sept. 14 that Japan and the U.S. had collaborated in preventing Belenko from returning to the Soviet Union. Tass said that Belenko had lost his bearings during a routine flight and had landed in Hakodate because of a lack of fuel. The news agency accused Japan of keeping Belenko drugged and in isolation and of transporting him to the U.S. with the aid of "American secret agencies."

Belenko's wife and mother, at a Sept. 28 news conference in Moscow, appealed for his return. They denied that he had defected and said that they had received official assurances that he would not be punished.

In response to their plea, the State Department Sept. 28 arranged a meeting between Belenko and Soviet diplomats in Washington. During the 50-minute session, Belenko repeated his refusal to return to the Soviet Union.

U.S.S.R., Chile exchange prisoners. The Soviet Union and Chile Dec. 18, 1976 exchanged two widely known political prisoners, Vladimir Bukovsky and Luis Corvalan. Bukovsky, who had publicized the imprisonment of Soviet dissidents in mental institutions, and Corvalan, who had headed Chile's Communist Party, were exchanged at an airport in Zurich, Switzerland. The exchange was mediated by the U.S. since Moscow and Santiago had no diplomatic relations.

Bukovsky, who had been imprisoned intermittently for 15 years (continuously since 1972), was accompanied to Zurich by his mother, his sister and an ailing nephew. Corvalan, in jail since 1973, was accompanied by his wife.

Bukovsky spoke with reporters Dec. 19 at a press conference arranged by Amnesty International. He said he had been told by a Soviet police official that he had not been deprived of Soviet citizenship but had been given a five-year passport for travel abroad. Some day, Bukovsky said, he hoped to return to the U.S.S.R.

The exchange of political prisoners, thought to be unprecedented, was first proposed by Andrei Sakharov, the Soviet dissident physicist. The Chilean government agreed, but it took more than a month of secret negotiations to obtain Soviet approval, the Associated Press reported Dec. 18.

U.S. eases entry of Soviet Jews. By early 1977 the U.S. was acting to speed the processing of visa applications of thousands of Soviet Jews in Italy who had chosen to go directly to the U.S. instead of to Israel, according to a report Jan. 30 in the New York Times. About 7,000 Jews had arrived in Italy in 1976 and were living in crowded conditions in Ostia, a resort city near Rome, while waiting for U.S. visas. The U.S. Justice Department waived normal visa requirements to admit as many as 4,000 Jews immediately to clear up the backlog of applications, according to the report. There were some 300 Soviet Jews in Ostia who had left Israel for the U.S., but since they held Israeli passports, they were processed as immigrants and not as refugees from racial or political persecution, according to an official cited in the report. (Nationality quotas were waived for persons classified as refugees.)

U.S. to admit more emigres—The U.S. Justice Department Dec. 14 gave approval for 5,000 Jewish emigrants from the U.S.S.R. to enter the U.S. by May 1978. Most of the immigrants were eligible to enter the country but had not been admitted because of limits set by U.S. immigration laws.

Increase in emigrating Soviet Jews noted. Officials aiding Jewish emigrants from the U.S.S.R. noted an increase in the number of Jews permitted to leave during the fall of 1977. According to a report Oct. 14 in the New York Times, welfare officials reported an average of 400 persons arriving weekly in Vienna, the

first stop for emigres outside the U.S.S.R. Previous averages, they said, were 275 a week.

Defection in Uganda. The U.S. State Department Aug. 11, 1977 made public the defection to the U.S. of a Soviet embassy official in Uganda. The man, who was not identified, had been granted political asylum after arriving in the U.S. from Kampala in July. (In an Aug. 10 radio broadcast, Ugandan President Idi Amin said the official was Boris Itaka, "grandson of one of the Soviet heroes." Amin added that the U.S. Central Intelligence Agency had been looking for Itaka for a long time.)

Emigrants leave in '77. More Soviet names were added to the refugee roll in 1977.

Some dissidents were issued visas to emigrate, while others defected to the West while on tours or escaped over the borders.

Rudolf Barshai, a noted Soviet chamber orchestra conductor, arrived in Israel Jan. 30 after having left the Soviet Union earlier in the month. He said he had applied for emigration because the state concert booking agency would not let him arrange his own schedule of foreign performances.

A Soviet sailor who had defected Feb. 8 in New Orleans was granted permission to stay in the U.S. until his application for political asylum in Canada was processed.

In a related development, Ludmila Alexeyeva, a member of an unofficial group monitoring Soviet compliance with the Helsinki accords on human rights, emigrated from the U.S.S.R. with her family, it was reported Feb. 22. Their exit visas were for Israel but they hoped to settle in the U.S., according to friends in Moscow.

Dr. Mikhail Shtern, a Jewish physician imprisoned in 1974 after his sons had emigrated to Israel, arrived in Vienna April 13. He had been released from prison March 14 had been granted an exit visa several days later. In a press conference April 21, Shtern said pressure from foreign sympathizers had led to his release.

Vladimir Solovyov and his wife, Yelena Klepikova, left the Soviet Union June 9, according to dissident sources. In retaliation for an earlier refusal to issue them exit visas, they had set up an unofficial press agency to report on dissident activity and economic problems in the U.S.S.R.

Mark Azbel, a Jewish physicist, arrived in Vienna with his family July 6. He had waited for a visa since 1972.

Avtandil Papiashvili, a Soviet psychiatrist who had defected to the West, Aug. 31 detailed the cases of several dissidents who had been imprisoned in mental institutions in the Soviet Union. In his first press conference since defecting to Austria in May, Papiashvili said he knew of three people in the Tbilisi psychiatric insitute in the Soviet republic of Georgia who had been diagnosed as schizophrenics because they had criticized the Soviet system.

Alexander Melamid, a dissident satirical artist, left the U.S.S.R. for Israel with his family at the beginning of October, according to a report Oct. 31 in the New York Times. He and his partner Vitaly Komar had created a number of satirical works on official Soviet art and ideology that attracted notice in the West after being smuggled out of the Soviet Union. Komar reached Israel Dec. 20.

Tatyana Khodorovich, administrator of a fund to help jailed dissidents and their families, arrived in Vienna Nov. 6 after having been forced to leave the country. She said the fund, financed by exiled author Alexander Solzhenitsyn, would be administered by her brother Sergei and by Irina Ginzburg, the wife of jailed dissident Alexander Ginzburg.

Dina Kaminskaya, a Soviet lawyer, arrived in London Dec. 4 after having been expelled for trying to defend Anatoly Shcharansky.

More Soviet Jews leave for Israel. After a period of declining Soviet Jewish emigration to Israel, Soviet Jews increasingly appeared to be choosing to settle in Israel, it was reported Dec. 21, 1977 in the New York Times. The Times quoted an official working with Soviet Jewish emigres in Vienna, the first stop for emigrants from the Soviet Union.

The official said that before May, more than 50% of the emigrating Soviet Jews had chosen to go to countries other than Israel. After May, he said, slightly more than 50% of the Jewish emigres had chosen to settle in Israel.

A group of 700 Soviet Jews who had emigrated to Israel asked the Kremlin April 28 for permission to return to the U.S.S.R. Spokesmen said the Soviet Jews, who were in Vienna, could not adjust to life in Israel and wanted to return to the Soviet Union or settle in Austria.

Grigorenko & Restropovich lose citizenship. The U.S.S.R. said March 10, 1978 that it had revoked the citizenship of former Gen. Pyotr Grigorenko, who was on a six-month visit in the U.S. The announcement said a decree signed Feb. 13 by Soviet President Leonid Brezhnev had deprived the former general of citizenship because his behavior "damages the prestige of the U.S.S.R."

Grigorenko was the highest-ranking Soviet army officer to protest his country's policies. He had been stripped of his rank of major general in 1961 and had been imprisoned several times since 1964 for his activities.

The U.S. granted Grigorenko asylum April 19, one day after he had applied for it.

In a similar action March 15, the Soviet Union rescinded the citizenships of composer-cellist Mstislav Rostropovich and his wife, soprano Galina Vishnevskaya. The couple had been living abroad on a temporary Soviet travel visa since 1974.

The decree revoking the Rostropoviches' citizenships accused them of having "carried on unpatriotic activity, . . .besmirched the Soviet social system and . . . provided material assistance to subversive anti-Soviet centers. . . ." In particular, Moscow charged, they had given several benefit concerts in 1976–77 for emigre organizations.

■ Oskar Rabin, one of the U.S.S.R.'s best-known nonconformist painters, was stripped of his Soviet citizenship June 30 while living in Paris. He had been permitted to go abroad in January after having served a jail term for parasitism.

Shevchenko defects to U.S. The United Nations announced April 10, 1978 that Arkady Shevchenko, the highest-ranking Soviet official in the U.N., had renounced his Soviet citizenship because of "differences with his government." Shevchenko subsequently announced April 26 that he had left his U.N. post and had applied for asylum in the U.S.

Shevchenko, 47, was believed to be the most important Soviet diplomat to defect to the U.S. He was undersecretary general for political and Security Council affairs, a position that was one rank below that of the U.N. secretary general.

Shevchenko and his family had been scheduled to fly back to Moscow April 9 on a brief visit. However, on April 6 he had ordered new locks and a seal put on the door of his office at the U.N. He then had disappeared until April 10, when he announced his decision to renounce his Soviet citizenship. (Meanwhile, his wife and daughter had flown back to Moscow April 9.)

Shevchenko enlisted the aid of Ernest Gross, a New York lawyer, in arranging his defection. According to Gross, Shevchenko met with Soviet U.N. Ambassador Oleg Troyanovsky and Soviet U.S. Ambassador Anatoly Dobrynin April 9 in Gross's office. Gross said the two men tried unsuccessfully to persuade Shevchenko to change his mind.

The Soviet Union issued a formal statement April 11 charging that Shevchenko was being held "under duress" by U.S. intelligence agents, which the U.S. denied.

Shevchenko met with U.N. Secretary General Kurt Waldheim April 25 to arrange the details of his resignation from the U.N. His contract with the U.N. had been scheduled to end in 1980, and he received more than $76,000 in severance pay. His resignation meant the loss of his international diplomatic status, and he was thus forced to apply for U.S. asylum the next day.

Shevchenko gave no reasons for his action except to cite "serious differences of political philosophy and conviction with the present Soviet system" in his statement April 26.

There were indications that Shevchenko had been in contact with U.S. intelligence since 1976. According to a report April 21 in the New York Times, both the Central Intelligence Agency and the Federal Bureau of Investigation had established links to Shevchenko.

Levich Allowed to Emigrate. Benjamin Levich, the highest-ranking Soviet scientist to seek emigration, left the U.S.S.R. Nov. 30, 1978 with his wife to join their sons in Israel. They had been waiting for more than five years for exit visas, and it was believed that intervention in their behalf by U.S. Sen. Edward Kennedy (D, Mass.) had brought about their release.

In September, Kennedy had held a two-hour meeting with Soviet President Leonid Brezhnev and had given the Soviet leader a list of 18 families, the Leviches among them, who were seeking permission to leave the Soviet Union.

As a result of applying for emigration, Levich had been dismissed from his teaching position at Moscow University and removed from his research post at the Hydrodynamics Institute.

Other Soviet Emigres—Another family on Kennedy's list arrived in Boston Nov. 30 after a three-year wait for visas. The case of Boris and Natalya Kats had attracted much press coverage in the U.S. because of reports that their 13-month-old daughter, Jessica, was suffering from a rare and dangerous disease.

The reports said Jessica suffered from malabsorption syndrome, which in fact was neither rare nor fatal and was easily treated. The disease prevented her from digesting any food except a special formula that was manufactured in the U.S. and had been brought to the family by American tourists.

■ Viktor Bublik, a Soviet laborer, walked 375 miles (630 kilometers) across the U.S.S.R. and Finland to seek asylum in Sweden, it was reported Nov. 1. The journey took about one month, from the end of July to Aug. 22, when he reached the West German Embassy in Stockholm. According to his account of the trip, he had not asked for asylum in Finland because he feared extradition to the U.S.S.R. He was permitted to remain in Sweden.

■ Imant Lesinskis, a Latvian-born Soviet translator at the United Nations, had been granted asylum with his family in the U.S., the State Department reported Sept. 18.

■ Sergei Polikanov and his family arrived in Denmark Oct. 10 after having unexpectedly received exit visas. Polikanov, a physicist, had been expelled from the Communist Party for protesting Soviet travel restrictions, which had prevented him from taking a research post in Switzerland in 1977. Dissident sources believed he had been given a visa because of his rapid emergence as a chief spokesman for the Soviet dissident movement.

■ Kirill Kondrashin, a noted Soviet conductor, defected to the West Dec. 4 after completing a concert engagement in the Netherlands. A Dutch friend of the conductor said he had defected to protest restrictions on artistic freedom in the U.S.S.R.

Jewish emigration rate rising. The number of Jews leaving the U.S.S.R. in 1978 had increased substantially over the totals for the previous two years, according to a report Sept. 28 by Arye Dulzin, chairman of the Jewish Agency. He told a London conference on Soviet Jewry that more Jews were expected to emigrate in 1978 than in any other year except 1973, when more than 30,000 Jews were allowed to leave.

Dulzin added that Jews in the U.S.S.R. already had set a record in 1978 for applications to leave. He said 100,000 Jews had requested exit visas since January, compared with 78,000 in 1977 and 58,000 in 1976. "Attacks on Jews in magazines, television and radio are being stepped up," he explained.

Dulzin said that almost 160,000 Jews had left the U.S.S.R. since 1968, when the Soviet Union first began to let Jews emigrate.

■ A total of 28,864 Jews had left the Soviet Union in 1978, according to figures compiled by Israeli emigration authorities in Vienna and reported March 7, 1979.

5 jailed dissidents traded for 2 convicted Soviet spies. Five imprisoned Soviet dissidents were released and flown to New York April 27, 1979 in exchange for two convicted Soviet spies held in the U.S. One of the freed dissidents was Alexander Ginzburg, whose conviction in July 1978 provoked worldwide protests.

In return, the U.S. released Valdik Enger and Rudolf Chernyayev, two Soviet employees of the United Nations. They had been confined to a Soviet-owned residence in New York since their conviction in October 1978 on charges of espionage.

Besides Ginzburg, the other dissidents who were freed were: Valentin Moroz, Georgi Vins, Mark Dymshits and Eduard Kuznetsov.

The exchange took place at New York's Kennedy International Airport. A regularly scheduled Soviet Aeroflot plane delivered the five dissidents and picked up the two spies.

It was the first time that Soviet dissidents had been exchanged for Soviet espionage agents.

The negotiations for the dramatic exchange had begun in late 1978, according to U.S. officials. They had been conducted in extreme secrecy by U.S. national security adviser Zbigniew Brzezinski, his deputy, David Aaron, Secretary of State Cyrus Vance and Soviet Ambassador Anatoly Dobrynin.

Kuznetsov and Dymshits were made the main attractions at a rally in New York April 29 in support of Soviet Jewry.

Kuznetsov was reunited with his wife, Silva Zalmanson, who had been released from prison in 1974 and permitted to emigrate. She, her husband and Dymshits were part of a group of dissidents convicted in 1970 for plotting to hijack an airplane out of the U.S.S.R.

All three left for Israel after the rally.

Kuznetsov and Dymshits joined five other newly freed Jews who had been convicted with them for the hijacking plot. Volf Zalmanson, Silva Zalmanson's brother, Anatoly Altman, Boris Penson and Leib Khnokh had been sentenced in December 1970. The fifth, Hillel Butman, was sentenced in May 1971.

Bulgaria

Schpeter freed. Henrich Schpeter, a Jewish economist who had been sentenced to death on an espionage charge June 1, 1974, was released from a Soviet prison and flown to Jerusalem Aug. 22, the Israeli Foreign Ministry announced.

Tel Aviv refused to provide details, but said the Israeli government had "made efforts for the release of Schpeter on humanitarian grounds." Bulgaria and Israel had maintained no diplomatic relations since the 1967 Middle East war.

Escapes & defections. The French news agency Agence France-Presse reported April 18, 1974 that 18 Bulgarians had asked Turkish authorities for asylum in March after stopping in Istanbul on tours.

A Bulgarian airliner was hijacked June 28, 1975 and forced to Salonika, Greece, where the hijacker, a Bulgarian building technician, sought political asylum. The plane, with its passengers and crew, returned to Bulgaria that day.

The French regime July 7, 1977 granted political asylum to a Bulgarian journalist and his family. The journalist, Vladimir Borisov Kostov, had been scheduled to return to Bulgaria after his three-year assignment in Paris.

Bulgarian Exile Slain in U.K. The death of Georgi Markov, a Bulgarian defector living in London, was ruled to be murder Sept. 29, 1978 after an autopsy revealed that a metal pellet had injected a poison into his bloodstream. Markov had died Sept. 11, four days after reporting that a man had stabbed him with the tip of an umbrella.

Markov, who worked for the Bulgarian section of the British Broadcasting Corporation (BBC), fell seriously ill shortly after the stabbing incident. He reportedly told friends and relatives before he died that the incident had been deliberate and that he had feared for his life since defecting in 1970.

An autopsy Sept. 12 revealed the presence of poison in Markov's blood, and suspicion of foul play was confirmed Sept. 29 when medical experts found a microscopic metal ball embedded in his skin.

According to Scotland Yard, the ball was identical to a metal pellet found in the back of Vladimir Kostov, another Bulgarian defector, who lived in Paris. Kostov had reported Sept. 14 that he had been stabbed in the back Aug. 26 and had become briefly ill afterward. When news of Markov's death reached him, he said, he underwent a medical examination and doctors found the metal pellet.

In addition to broadcasting BBC reports to Bulgaria, Markov had worked freelance for Radio Free Europe, the U.S.-funded network that broadcast to Eastern Europe, and for Deutsche Welle, a similar station in West Germany.

The Bulgarian Embassy in London issued an official denial Sept. 13 of any involvement in Markov's death. The Bulgarian ambassador was summoned to the Foreign and Commonwealth Office Sept. 29 to receive an official report of Scotland Yard's finding of the poisoned pellet.

Meanwhile, Vladimir Simeonov, another Bulgarian defector who worked for the BBC, was found dead Oct. 2 in his London home.

Another Bulgarian exile who lived in the U.S., Stefan Bankov, had reported Sept. 14 that he had been temporarily paralyzed by a liquid spilled on his shoulder by unidentified foreigners on a plane in 1974.

China

Escape to Hong Kong harder. The Chinese regime was reported Jan. 11, 1971 to have ordered stricter border controls to prevent its citizens from escaping to Hong Kong. The order was contained in a directive issued in Kwangtung Province, adjacent to the British crown colony, and reprinted in Hong Kong newspapers Jan. 9 and 10.

The directive called for prison terms of "more than 10 years" for anyone caught attempting to flee and ordered border guards to "pursue and execute on the spot" persons resisting arrest. It urged close surveillance of Chinese visitors from Hong Kong and the nearby Portuguese colony of Macao, the use of more political agents among the populated Chinese areas adjacent to Hong Kong and Macao and more stringent controls on goods entering and leaving Kwangtung.

An estimated 200 Chinese were said to have escaped to Hong Kong from Kwangtung during November and December 1970. Others were believed drowned while swimming the three to five miles from Kwangtung.

The number of Chinese refugees fleeing to Hong Kong was reported to be increasing in 1971. Hong Kong officials said Sept. 6 that about 2,500 Chinese had been arrested after swimming from the mainland to Hong Kong between January and August. This was almost three times the 1970 figure of 900. Those taken into custody made up only a small percentage of the refugees to reach Hong Kong.

Chinese detained in Paris. An apparently drugged Communist Chinese national was detained April 28, 1971 at Orly Airport by French police, who separated him from a group of Chinese boarding a plane for Shanghai.

Chung Shi-jung, a physician attached to a Chinese medical aid team in Algeria, had reportedly sought political asylum at the French embassy in Algiers. When this was refused, he was placed aboard a plane for Paris with a bodyguard, after first having been heavily drugged.

Those traveling with Chung were joined by staff members of the Communist Chinese embassy in Paris, who argued with police in an effort to prevent Chung's seizure.

Chung later left Paris May 7 on a plane for Canton. Newsweek reported in its May 17 issue that Chung had been made to feel unwelcome in France by Chinese-speaking French police acting on government orders. Newsweek reported that Communist Chinese diplomats had persuaded French President Georges Pompidou that Chung's continued stay in France would prejudice Sino-French relations.

Escapes tried after Lin Piao's death. A Reuters report from Hong Kong Jan. 30, 1972 said that 27 Chinese army officers had been arrested in 1971 during attempts to escape from the mainland to Hong Kong. Twenty officers were said to have been seized in September 1971 when they tried to get past border guards at Shum Chun, another three were stopped there in October and four others were arrested in November when they commandeered a truck in Canton in an attempt to reach Hong Kong.

All 27 were allegedly linked with Defense Minister Lin Piao, who had not been mentioned officially in China since Oct. 8, 1974. In a Peking interview July 28, 1971, a Chinese assistant foreign minister confirmed that Lin had been killed in a plane crash in 1971 while fleeing China after attempting to overthrow Chairman Mao Tsetung and assassinate him.

More escapes to Hong Kong. Opposition of Chinese youths to rural work assignments in Kwangtung Province had led to an upsurge of crime in the provincial capital of Canton and a sharp increase in the number of refugees fleeing to nearby Hong Kong, the New York Times reported Aug. 12, 1973.

According to the Times, an estimated 3,000 Chinese refugees were believed to have made their way to Hong Kong in July, the highest monthly level in 10 years.

Hong Kong seeks cut in refugee influx. The Chinese government was reported Nov. 14, 1973 to be responding to pleas by Hong Kong to reduce the surge of refugees to Hong Kong.

British authorities in London discussed the problem Nov. 14 with Chinese Ambassador Sung Chih-kuang. The British had informed Peking that if the influx continued at the current rate, social services in Hong Kong would be overwhelmed.

More than 7,000 Chinese had entered Hong Kong legally in October, compared with just over 4,000 in May. The 1973 totals thus far were 51,554, contrasted with 20,355 in 1972 and only 2,530 in 1971. The final count for 1973 was 55,658.

Hong Kong announced Nov. 30, 1974 that it would no longer accept refugees found illegally entering from China because of the strain put upon Hong Kong's welfare resources and rising unemployment.

Hong Kong returned five illegal immigrants to China Nov. 30 and another 12 Dec. 1. It was the first such action since 1968 and represented a reversal of the government's policy of permitting ref-ugees from China to remain in the British crown colony.

Pilot defects to Taiwan. A Chinese air force squadron leader July 7, 1977 defected to Taiwan by flying his MiG-19 jet to a Chinese Nationalist air force base at Tainan.

Fan Yuan-yen, who held the rank equivalent to major, broke away from the squadron he was leading on a routine mission after taking off from Tsinkiang air base along the coast of Fukien Province, opposite Taiwan.

Fan told Nationalist officials on landing that he fled China because "life on the mainland is too miserable." He said he came "to seek freedom and human rights."

Fan left his wife and three children behind at their home in Taiho, Kiangsi Province. He expressed hope that the U.S. would get Peking to permit them to join him as part of the Carter Administration's human rights campaign.

As a defector to Taiwan, Fan was eligible to receive a Nationalist government award of about $800,000 worth of gold. He was the fourth Chinese air force pilot known to have defected to Taiwan, but the first since 1965.

Czechoslovakia

Diplomats defect. There was a rash of defections by Czechoslovakian diplomatic personnel during 1970. Jiri Mladek, then Czechoslovakia's third-ranking diplomat at the U.N., was reported Feb. 18 to have sought asylum in the U.S. Mladek, who also asked for asylum for his wife and son, was said to have been reprimanded by the Czech Mission at the U.N. for his failure to show enthusiasm for recent government policies. It was reported Feb. 20 that Mladek had been granted permanent residence status.

Czechoslovak Ambassador to Denmark Anton Vasek requested political asylum for himself and his family June 26 Copenhagen following orders from the Czechoslovak Foreign Ministry to return home.

The U.S. State Department revealed June 30 that Antonin Nenko, the scientific affairs officer at the Czechoslovak embassy, had requested political asylum for himself and his family.

Karel Sachar, serving as the head of the Czechslovak commercial mission in Ecuador, disappeared with his wife and two sons July 7 and was reported to have sought political asylum in the U.S. Sachar had terminated all his functions at the mission June 30.

The first secretary of the Czechoslovak embassy in Kenya was said Aug. 24 to be in London, after resigning his post Aug. 21. A British spokesman declined to reveal whether Vaclav Albert, the diplomat, had sought political asylum.

Vaclav Cihac, second secretary at the Czechoslovak embassy in The Hague, was provisionally granted political asylum in the Netherlands Aug. 26.

Ladislaw Bartos, a Czechoslovak consular official in Sydney, was granted resident status in Australia Sept. 2. Bartos, due to return to Czechoslovakia on leave Sept. 1, had represented Koospol, the Czechoslovak foreign trade corporation.

Other 1970 defections. Among defections reported in 1970:

■Thirty-eight Czechoslovak tourists in a group of 68 sought political asylum in Sweden and Denmark Jan. 4. In late December, 74 of 96 persons in another group had sought asylum in Sweden.

Forty-nine Czechoslovak tourists who had arrived in Stockholm before Christmas were granted political asylum in Sweden Jan. 20.

Dusan Havlicek, former head of the press department of the CP's Central Committee, was granted asylum in Switzerland Jan. 8. Havlicek, 46, had become a correspondent for the CTK press agency in Geneva in February 1969.

■The government announced Jan. 27 that Ota Sik, architect of the 1968 economic reform program, had asked for asylum in Switzerland. He had been living there since 1968.

■ Recent beauty contest winner Kristina Hanzalova, Miss Czechoslovakia of 1969, sought political asylum Aug. 2 in Nuremburg, West Germany.

Hijackings. Four men and four women, all armed, hijacked a Czechoslovak National Airlines plane on a domestic flight from Karlovy Vary to Prague and forced the pilot June 8, 1970 to land it in Nuremburg, West Germany. All asked for political asylum.

Three men hijacked a Czechoslovakian airliner on a flight to Bratislava and forced it to land in Vienna Aug. 8. The men, all Czechoslovaks, requested political asylum.

Two Czechoslovak miners hijacked a domestic airliner on a flight from Prague to Marienbad April 18, 1972 and forced the plane to Nuremberg, West Germany, requesting political asylum. They were identified as Antonin Lerch and Karel Dolezal. Lerch shot and slightly wounded the pilot. A court in Nuremberg July 31 sentenced the hijackers to seven years in prison.

Ten Czechoslovaks forced a Czechoslovakian airliner on a domestic flight to land in Weiden, West Germany June 8, 1972. The hijackers—seven men, three women and a child—seized the plane shortly after takeoff and ordered the pilot to fly to Nuremburg. According to the London Times June 10, the pilot, who refused the order, was shot and killed when a crewman tried to subdue one of the hijackers.

Two uniformed Czechoslovak Airlines employes hijacked an aircraft at gunpoint Oct. 11, 1977 and forced the Prague-bound jetliner to land in Frankfurt, West Germany. After negotiating from the grounded aircraft for two and a half hours, the engaged couple abandoned their plan to fly to Munich and surrendered peacefully.

Ruzena Vlckova, 21 and Vlastimil Toupalik, 29, said the hijacking was politically motivated and requested asylum. It was West German policy not to return political refugees from the East.

Exiles lose citizenship. The Interior Ministry said Feb. 24, 1970 that Jiri Pelikan, Ota Sik, Ivan Svitak and Otakar

Rambousek had been deprived of Czechoslovak citizenship. All four presently were living abroad.

Arthur London, deputy foreign minister under Antonin Novotny, was deprived of citizenship Aug. 28. (Released from prison in 1956 after sentencing in the Slansky trial, London was rehabilitated. In 1968 he published The Confession, a book about the Slansky trial.) He had been living in France since 1956.

In depriving London of his citizenship, the Czechoslovak Interior Ministry said his book "caused damage to the important interests" of Czechoslovakia and London had helped "deepen anti-Soviet and anti-Socialist tendencies."

Eduard Goldstuecker, ex-chairman of the Czechoslovak Writers' Union, was stripped of his citizenship and his Slovak nationality Apr. 12, 1974 for having "lived abroad and conducted alien activities against Czechoslovakia." Goldstuecker had lived in Britain since 1968.

Czechs dun refugees. Czechoslovakian refugees in Western countries were being advised that their presence abroad was illegal and they would have to pay for their legal defense costs, according to a New York Times report Dec. 15, 1970.

Letters sent from "legal advisory centers" in Prague were informing refugees that, under section 109 of the Czechoslovak penal code, they "can be tried in absentia and may be sentenced to prison for terms of six months to five years, to corrective measures and to confiscation of property." In the letters, signed by individual lawyers, recipients were told that "since you have not chosen a defense counsel, I have been nominated to represent you."

The refugees were advised that unless they made a "down payment" in foreign currency within five days for defense costs the amount would be collected from their "nearest relatives" in Czechoslovakia. (An estimated 70,000 refugees were affected by the action.)

Dunning halted—The dunning of refugees for legal expenses was halted Feb. 16, 1971. Gustav Husak, Communist Party first secretary, declared in a speech Feb. 16 that although neither he nor Premier

Lubomir Strougal had known about the practice at first, "the whole matter has been stopped."

Defections continue. Among defections from Czechoslovakia:

Karel Bocek, former director of Czechoslovakia's uranium mines, escaped from detention and traveled to Nuremberg, West Germany, where he asked for asylum Aug. 11, 1971. Bocek had been arrested in September 1970, reportedly for concluding a government-ordered study with the recommendation that Czechoslovakia's nuclear industry be improved by the purchase of British nuclear plants.

Ludek Pachman, the chess grandmaster, crossed the border into Bavaria Nov. 28, 1972 and arrived in Munich the following day. Pachman, who expressed a wish to return one day to Czechoslovakia, said his emigration had been a "stop-go" affair and that he had been turned back at the border three times after previously receiving permission to leave.

Vaclav Nedomansky, captain of the Czechoslovak national hockey team, defected to Canada July 18, 1974. Nedomansky, who signed a contract with the Toronto Toros, indicated he had been attracted by the high salaries paid North American professional hockey players.

Martina Navratilova, 18, Czechoslovakian tennis star, asked for and was granted U.S. asylum Sept. 7, 1975.

Amnesty for refugees. Commemorating the 25th anniversary of Communist rule in Czechoslovakia, President Ludvig Svoboda Feb. 22, 1973 announced an amnesty for the estimated 50,000 Czechoslovaks who had fled the country since the 1968 Soviet invasion.

Czechoslovakia June 30, 1977 announced a general amnesty for persons who had fled the country after the 1968 Soviet invasion. The official news agency said political exiles would be permitted to regain Czechoslovak citizenship without facing charges of having left the country illegally.

Czech defector reveals spy network. A Czechoslovakian agent in West Germany defected to Britain and disclosed the activities of a number of Czechoslovakian intelligence agents working in Bonn.

The defection of Svetozar Simko and his family was confirmed Feb. 24, 1977 in Bonn, and West German counterintelligence said it had been aware of Simko's activities for some time. Simko was described as a military intelligence officer who had worked in Bonn for six years undercover as a foreign correspondent for the official Czechoslovakian news agency CTK.

East Germany

East Germans jump ship. Four East Germans jumped from their Cuba-bound liner and were picked up by a small boat Nov. 27, 1970 off American Shoals, Fla.

The escape was planned by Karl Heinz Bley and his brother Eric, a naturalized American citizen living in Illinois. Eric Bley chartered both the rescue craft and a light airplane which was used to track the liner.

When the airplane passed low across the fantail of the liner as a prearranged signal, Bley jumped into the water near his brother's waiting boat and was joined spontaneously by three medical researchers who had taken the voyage with the idea of planning an escape. The researchers were two brothers, Reinhold and Manfred Kupfer, and Pieter Rost.

All four were taken in the chartered boat to Key West, where they were given temporary asylum.

398 escapes in '71. A report March 3, 1972 by the West German border police disclosed that 398 East Germans escaped to West Germany in 1971, compared with 460 in 1970. The number of desertions of East German soldiers remained at 55—the same as in 1970.

Refugee amnesty approved—The Volkskammer approved a bill Oct. 16 providing that persons who had left the country "without permission" before Jan. 1 would no longer be subject to criminal proceedings. Those who had left "in violation of existing laws" would be deprived of East German citizenship.

Increase in escapes. According to statistics from the West German Interior Ministry Jan. 13, 1973, the number of persons escaping from East to West Germany had increased markedly during the last half of 1972, a period which saw a rise of diplomatic activity between the two states.

The total of those escaping during the year had been 1,245, the highest in six years. Two-thirds of these had fled between June and December.

It was reported Jan. 13 that 96 East Germans had been killed attempting to cross the border in 1972, compared with 153 since the Berlin Wall was constructed in 1961.

Doctors arrested—A West German newspaper reported July 21 that 50 East Berlin doctors had been arrested for conspiring to flee to the West. The arrests were reportedly intended to discourage the upsurge in doctor refugees.

Increase protested—According to an Aug. 2, 1973 report, East Germany had threatened to reimpose tight controls on traffic along the 110-mile land routes between West Germany and West Berlin because of the increasing number of East Germans using the routes to escape the country.

Neues Deutschland, the Communist party daily, charged that "international gangster syndicates" were paid as much as $40,000 to smuggle refugees out in the trunks of cars or in trucks.

Bonn statistics showed that 2,000 of the 3,000 refugees who registered in the first six months of 1973 had arrived via the transit routes. The flow of refugees in the year since the Berlin pact went into effect, facilitating travel to West Berlin, had averaged 500 a month, double the rate before June, 1972.

Refugees in 1973 had included 85 doctors and their families, 11 dentists and six veterinarians.

A total of 1,957 East Germans settled in West Germany or West Berlin without

East German permission in the third quarter of 1973, it was reported Nov. 13. The total included 622 who crossed the border undetected.

Many jailed for aiding escapes—Two West Germans and a West Berliner were sentenced in East Berlin Nov. 5 to terms of 7-11 years in prison after being convicted of smuggling East German escapees out of the country, along East-West transit routes, for money.

Five West Germans and West Berliners were sentenced to 5-15-year terms Jan. 18–21, 1974 for "misusing transit routes" by helping East Germans escape to the West. A West German organization said 133 West Germans or West Berliners had been arrested in the 18 months of free transit on charges connected with escape attempts, it was reported Jan. 21.

Wall shootings protested. The U.S., French and British commandants in West Berlin July 9, 1973 protested the capture under gunfire of refugees trying to flee over the Berlin Wall the day before. About 300 West Berliners also protested the incident, in which one refugee was apparently shot. East Germany reported July 14 it had decorated seven border guards who had opened fire for "special courageous and steadfast conduct in repelling the serious border provocation." Another refugee was reported by witnesses to have been killed by East German border guards July 20.

Earlier in 1973, three East German border guards were killed May 22 by the accidental explosion of mines along the West German border. West German customs officials at Helmstedt said April 27 that two men were killed by East German border guards in an escape attempt.

166 die in escape tries. West Berlin sources said Aug. 12, 1974 that 166 persons had been killed trying to escape to the West from East Germany since the Berlin Wall was erected in 1961. Seventy fugitives had been killed in East Berlin and 96 had been killed attempting to escape across the mined, barbed-wire frontier.

5,324 escapes from East claimed in '74. The West German Frontier Protection Service issued a report on 1974 border crossings, claiming that 5,324 persons had fled from the GDR and East Berlin to West Germany during the year, it was reported Feb. 14, 1975.

U.S. pilot lifts East Germans to West. A civilian U.S. helicopter pilot Aug. 17, 1975 flew into Czechoslovakia, where he picked up three East Germans and brought them to West Germany. Ground fire from Czech border guards forced the pilot, Barry Meeker, of Hartford, Conn., to leave behind an East German woman and a friend of his who had accompanied him on the rescue mission, which had taken off from Munich, West Germany earlier that day.

In remarks Aug. 19, Meeker said he had lifted four other East Germans out of Czechoslovakia in a similar operation Aug. 15.

Czechoslovakia charged Aug. 21 that West German security police and armed forces had been behind the American pilot's actions.

Injured in the elbow and hip by Czech fire during the Aug. 17 escape, Meeker said Aug. 19 that the failure to complete the Aug. 17 mission had resulted from a delay in completing the pickup, which took place on a peninsula on the Vltava River, near the Austrian border.

A Czechoslovakian court Oct. 17 sentenced Meeker in absentia to 10 years in prison after the U.S. pilot had been found guilty of being "a paid employe of an organization professionally engaged in kidnapping." Two persons left behind in the Aug. 17 escape were given three- and six-year prison terms for their roles in the incident.

During the three-day trial, the Cesky Krumlov district court heard evidence that Meeker had conducted three such escape flights—Aug. 24, 1974 and Aug. 15 and 17, 1975—during which a total of 11 East Germans had been brought to West Germany from Czechoslovakia. One of the four flown out in 1974 had since returned, apparently of her own volition, to East Germany and testified for the prosecution at the Czech trial. She stated that a German lawyer, Heinz Heidrich, who had lived in East Germany until 1973, had coordinated the escape plans with Meeker on behalf of "a large organization" that conducted numerous illegal crossings to the West. She had paid Heidrich $5,200 to secure the escape of herself and her daughter, she said.

Reached in Munich, Meeker said he had been paid about $12,000 by Heidrich for the three escape flights.

Bonn reported buying East Germans' exit. Relations conducted in secret between East and West Germany had been responsible for the arrival in the Federal Republic during the course of more than a decade of thousands of East Germans whose release from East German prisons and exit from the Democratic Republic had been purchased for an undisclosed sum by the West German government, according to reports in the French newspaper Le Monde Aug. 17 and in the New York Times Oct. 6, 1975.

Prices as high as $15,000 a head had reportedly been realized in the transactions, which had been taking place since 1961, according to the Times.

Citing an earlier article in the West German magazine Die Welt, the Times noted that since 1969 Bonn had paid $80 million for the release of 5,000 prisoners, many of whom had been jailed in East Germany for trying to flee the country.

The usual channel in the bartering process was between lawyers who apparently acted as private agents for their respective governments. According to the Times, West German lawyer Jurgen Stange and, especially, East German lawyer Wolfgang Vogel were major figures in the activities.

East Germany jails smuggler of refugees. Rainer Schubert, a 29-year-old West Berliner, was sentenced in East Berlin Jan. 26, 1976 to 15 years in prison for having helped 86 East Germans and a Czechoslovakian to flee to the West. Schubert, who was arrested in 1974, had been found guilty after a five-day trial of "organized human trafficking," sabotage, espionage and terrorism. The sabotage charge arose from his having harmed the East German health service by aiding medical personnel to escape.

The West Berliner told the court that he had worked for a profit-making organization, Aramco AG of Zurich, Switzerland, which was reported to have brought hundreds of East Germans to the West during the past few years. According to Schubert, East German refugees were required to sign a contract saying they were fleeing of their own accord. Aramco charged an average of $10,000–$12,00C for each refugee, a fee generally paid by relatives or friends in the West. The profits, Schubert said, were split evenly between members of his own escape cell and the Aramco chief, Hans Lenzlinger. The West Berliner acknowledged having earned the equivalent of $200,000 for his operations over the course of two years.

Dissident poet exiled. Wolf Biermann, dissident poet and songwriter, was deprived of East German citizenship Nov. 16, 1976 while on a concert tour in West Germany. He was barred from returning to East Germany.

Biermann, who had left West Germany for East Germany in 1953, had not been permitted to perform in public since 1965, but he had become one of East Germany's most popular underground poets. He had finally been allowed to perform in October, just before being granted an exit visa for the West German tour.

East German writers Nov. 17 presented a petition to the government asking that Biermann be allowed to return. The protest of his exile grew by Nov. 19 to include more than 70 leading figures in the arts.

East German dissenters leave. Sarah Kirsch, one of East Germany's most popular poets, arrived in West Berlin Aug. 29, 1977 after getting permission to leave.

Five more dissidents were expelled to the West Aug. 29. They were: Karl-Heinz Nitschke, held in detention since 1976 for having signed a petition against the suppression of civil rights in East Germany; Hellmuth Nitsche, who had written to U.S. President Carter for help in emigrating; Juergen Ruchs, a writer, and two members of an East German rock music group that had been suppressed for performing anti-government songs.

Reiner Kunze, an East German writer, and his family were permitted to leave the country April 14 for West Germany. Two young East German men, aged 17 and 20, escaped to West Germany by swimming across a canal to the British sector of West Berlin March 28. A West Berlin spokesman reported Feb. 24 that Eberhard Cohrs, a popular East German comedian, had asked for asylum while working on a film in West Berlin.

Nina Hager, another popular singer, arrived in Hamburg Dec. 10 after authorities ordered her out by Dec. 12 for protesting Biermann's exile. Two more protesters arrived in West Berlin Dec. 12 after having been given permission to leave.

East Germany deports dissidents. East Germany was concentrating on expelling dissidents from the country, according to a New York Times report Sept. 24, 1977. The report said 90 political prisoners had been released from jail and deported to West Germany Sept. 22 and 144 others had been similarly deported during the past weeks.

East German Lawyer Defects. A prominent East German lawyer and economist, Wolfgang Seiffert, said April 21, 1978 he was defecting and would not return to East Germany. Seiffert and his family had arrived in West Germany in autumn 1977 after he had been invited to take a position as a visiting professor at Kiel University in West Berlin.

Seiffert had fled from West to East Germany in 1956 after he had been sentenced in West Germany to four years' imprisonment for his connection with an illegal Communist Party youth group.

Until February, Seiffert had been director of the East Berlin Academy for Political Science and Jurisprudence and a prominent member of the Communist Party.

Hungary

1970 escapes. Several escapes and defections from Hungary were reported during 1970. An Air force pilot flew a MiG-15 April 7 to an unused Italian airport near Udine. The pilot, Sandor Zaboki, 26, was granted political asylum.

Three Hungarians accompanied by a woman and two small children hijacked a Tarom Airlines (Rumanian) plane Sept. 14 and forced it to land in Munich, West Germany. The 89 passengers and crew had been bound from Bucharest for Prague. West German police arrested the hijackers, who asked for political asylum.

Jozsef Guruz, an attache at the Hungarian embassy in Stockholm, defected and sought asylum for himself and his family, it was announced Sept. 25.

The London Times reported Nov. 25 that Joseph Szall, Hungarian ambassador to Italy for eight years, until his resignation in August, had asked Italian authorities for political asylum for himself and his wife.

Mindszenty leaves. Jozsef Cardinal Mindszenty, 79, ended a 15-year exile in the U.S. embassy in Budapest, Hungary Sept. 28, 1971 and went to the Vatican, where he accepted "the heaviest cross of my life," resigned to living out his life in an exile of "prayer and penitence."

The cardinal's departure was announced simultaneously in Rome and Budapest in an official communique which read: "In accordance with an agreement between the Government of the Hungarian People's Republic and the Holy See, Jozsef Cardinal Mindszenty left the territory for good on Tuesday [Sept. 28] and traveled to Rome."

During these years the cardinal had repeatedly refused to leave the U.S. embassy sanctuary unless the Hungarian government agreed to his "rehabilitation"—the rescinding of his 1949 conviction and the life sentence he was given for alleged subversive activities against the Communist regime.

Poland

Katz-Suchy gets asylum. Julius Katz-Suchy, Polish ambassador to the U.N. 1947–52 and to India 1957–62, received political asylum in Denmark, it was reported Jan. 9, 1970. Katz-Suchy, 57, said that he had been persecuted as a Jew in Poland. He had been dismissed as a professor of international affairs at Warsaw University in 1968. Katz-Suchy accepted a professorship at the University of Aarhus (and he died Oct. 28, 1971).

Hijackings. Zbigniew Iawnicki, 29, a Polish butcher, armed with hand grenades, hijacked a Polish jetliner from Warsaw June 5, 1970 and forced it to Denmark.

On arrival in Copenhagen, the man allowed the 23 passengers to leave, then asked for political asylum. Iwanicki was sentenced in Copenhagen Oct. 5 to six years in prison.

The Danish island of Bornholm was the terminal point of Polish hijackings Aug. 19, 25 and 38, 1970. Three men and two women sought asylum Aug. 19 after using hand grenades to commandeer a Polish airliner. Asylum was sought Aug. 25 by five young Poles who hijacked a trawler from Darlowo. Another 10 Poles, including two children, arrived in Bornholm Aug. 31 in a hijacked trawler and asked for asylum.

Other defections. Among other developments involving Polish refugees:

A violinist defected from the Mazowsze Dance Troups March 22, 1971 in New York City. Ryszard Gabryel was given a work permit March 24 and made arrangements to stay in a Detroit suburb with friends and relatives who had aided in his defection. Sen. Philip A. Hart (D, Mich.) said March 31 that the State Department had approved Gabryel's request for asylum.

The Yugoslavian Foreign Ministry July 9, 1971 denied a claim reported July 6 by the Polish news agency PAP that Yugoslavia had expelled 15 vacationing Poles attempting to flee to the West and returned them to their own country.

In a separate case, 28 Poles from the city of Lodz requested asylum June 25 in Gorizia, Italy after spending their vacation in Yugoslavia.

At least 81 vacationing Polish passengers aboard a Polish cruise liner defected in Denmark, West Germany and Norway, it was reported Feb. 1–Feb. 7, 1977. West German authorities said the 64 who left the ship in Hamburg, most of them artisans, would be allowed to settle in West Germany without being granted political asylum status.

The refugees claimed that Polish authorities had excluded 300 of the 700 signed passengers from the cruise a week before it sailed to avoid an exodus.

Dutch police reported March 26 that 21 persons from a Polish cruise ship had failed to return to the ship when it left Rotterdam that day.

Twenty-seven Polish citizens, in Denmark for a World Cup soccer match, asked May 3, 1977 for political asylum in West Germany. Danish authorities assured the Poles, who were in the country on a three-day visa, that they would not be immediately deported to Poland when the visas expired.

Denmark had refused requests from 12 of the defectors for residence and labor permits, citing the nation's high unemployment rate as justification. West Germany granted permission for 15 of the Poles to enter May 4 because 14 had German relatives and one was engaged to a West German woman.

Zaleski dies, Ostroski heads refugee Poles. August Zaleski, 88, president of the Polish Republic in Exile since 1947, died in London April 7, 1972. He was succeeded by Stanislaw Ostrowski.

Rumania

Emigrant flow curbed. The New York Times said July 13, 1970 that Abdullah Zurikat, Jordanian ambassador to Lebanon, had been informed by Rumanian officials that their government was allowing only 30 Jews a year to emigrate to Israel. The number of Rumanians of German origin allowed to emigrate to Austria and West Germany had declined to 125 a month, according to the Washington Post June 13.

Jewish exodus cut—Emigration of Rumanian Jews to Israel had been sharply curtailed, it was reported Jan. 5, 1974. Some emigration had been permitted since 1972, after a halt imposed in 1967.

Hijacking. A Rumanian airliner was hijacked May 27, 1971 and forced to Vienna, where police persuaded the hijackers to release the passengers and give themselves up.

The French newspaper Le Monde reported that shortly after takeoff from Oradea the pilot was overpowered by six persons, including a woman. A weapon was fired but no one was injured and the co-pilot was ordered to fly the plane to Munich.

At a refueling stop in Vienna the front wheel tire burst and police equipped with machine guns surrounded the craft. The hijackers released the 16 passengers and four crewmen and surrendered. The hijackers asked for political asylum.

Defections. Among Rumanian defections: It was reported July 7, 1972 that Constantin Dumitrachescu, first secretary at Rumania's embassy in Tel Aviv, had defected after completing a tour of duty.

Dumitrachescu was believed to have sent his wife and two children to Bucharest and to have flown June 25 to Copenhagen.

An unidentified member of the Rumanian volleyball team at the Olympic games in Munich asked for political asylum in West Germany Sept. 11. An Interior Ministry spokesman confirmed the defection but declined to identify the athlete.

Victor Dimitriu, former Rumanian ambassador to France, asked political asylum for himself and his wife Nov. 10 in Paris.

An officer aboard the Mircea, a Rumanian ship that had participated in the U.S. Bicentennial, asked for political asylum in Philadelphia, according to the New York Times Aug. 7, 1976.

A prominent Rumanian television producer, Dumitru Udrescu, had been granted a 1976 request for asylum in the U.S. (reported Feb. 24, 1977). He had come to the U.S. to work on a special program about Olympic star Nadia Comaneci.

Ion Pacepa, a close adviser to President Nicolae Ceausescu, defected to the West in August 1977.

Emigration visas were granted to some signers of Paul Goma's letter protesting curbs on human rights in Rumania, and many signers left the country in 1977.

The government apparently had succeeded in breaking up the human rights movement by offering most of the dissidents emigration visas.

Amnesty. A June 1976 amnesty pardoned Rumanians who had defected or emigrated illegally, provided that they had not engaged in "hostile" activities and that they returned permanently within two years, the July 7 Financial Times (London) reported.

Yugoslavia

Exiles slay envoy in Sweden. Vladimir Rolovic, Yugoslavia's ambassador to Sweden, died April 15, 1971 in a Stockholm hospital as a result of bullet wounds inflicted April 7 by two Croatian terrorists.

The assailants, later identified as Andjelko Brajkowic and Miro Barzico, entered the embassy on the pretext of obtaining passports and shot Rolovic a number of times.

Two Ustashi members had occupied the Yugoslav consulate at Goteborg for 24 hours Feb. 10 and threatened to kill hostages unless a Croatian militant under death sentence in Belgrade was released. Rolovic had told the men the Yugoslav government rejected their demands. They later released the hostages and were jailed.

The Yugoslav Federal Executive Council protested the attack on Rolovic April 7 in a note transmitted to the Swedish government representative in Belgrade later that day by Mirko Tepavac, Yugoslav foreign minister. The note cited the Goteborg incident as well as previous warnings to the Swedish government about the existence of emigre organizations.

A Stockholm court July 14 sentenced Brajkowic and Barzico to life in prison.

Also sentenced for complicity in the case were Marinko Lemo and Stanislav Milicevic, each given two-year terms. Ante Stojanov, the group's leader, was given four years.

Croatian terrorists killed. An estimated 30 Croatian terrorists, thought to have sneaked into Yugoslavia, were reported killed by security forces by July 28, 1972. The intruders were described as members of the Ustashi, an emigre group which had long urged Croatian independence and which had been linked with violent activities in recent years.

The Croatians were understood to have come from Australia, where as many as 250,000 persons of Yugoslav origin were living, and to have crossed the border from Austria.

Hijackers surrender in Spain. Nine Croatian exiles surrendered to authorities at Madrid airport Sept. 16, 1972, several hours after arriving aboard a DC-9 jetliner they had hijacked from Sweden.

The incident began Sept. 15 when three gunmen believed to be members of the Ustashi terrorist movement, hijacked a Scandanavian Airlines System (SAS) plane bound from Goteborg to Stockholm and forced it to land at Malmo. The hijackers demanded that in exchange for the lives of the plane's 79 passengers and four crewmen the Swedish government release seven Croatian prisoners, including two men convicted for the 1971 murder of the Yugoslav ambassador to Sweden.

After an emergency Cabinet session, Premier Olof Palme ordered the prisoners taken to the Malmo airport, where Justice Minister Lennart Geijer conducted negotiations with the hijackers. When three prisoners had been exchanged for 30 passengers, the terrorists demanded about $200,000 but settled for half that amount before completing the exchange. One of the prisoners refused to join the hijackers.

The hijackers and crew then flew to Madrid. There followed another three hours of negotiations with Spanish officials, much of which reportedly passed with the Croatians arguing among themselves.

Australia to curb Ustashi. Australian Attorney General Lionel Murphy March 27, 1973 released papers as "incontestable evidence" that Croatian terrorist organizations, known as Ustashi, operated out of Australia. Declaring that the "toleration of terrorism in this country is over," he outlined plans to introduce anti-terrorist legislation and said he had already recommended deportation of certain immigrants.

Murphy criticized the former Liberal-Country coalitions for tolerating the Croatian groups and called former Attorney General Ivor Greenwood in the McMahon coalition "an active protector" of right-wing terrorists.

Police raided the homes of about 80 Yugoslavs in Sydney April 1 and charged at least 12 persons with possession of firearms and explosives and assaulting policemen.

Pro-Soviet exile abducted. Vladimir Dapcevic, an emigre leader of pro-Soviet Yugoslav dissidents, had been "arrested on the territory of Yugoslavia while performing hostile activities," the official news agency Tanyug said Dec. 26, 1975. It was the first confirmation by Belgrade regarding Dapcevic's disappearance in early August while on a visit to Rumania.

(Sources in Belgrade indicated that Rumanian authorities had conspired with Yugoslav agents in engineering the emigre's abduction, according to a report in the New York Times Dec. 26.)

Dapcevic had been living in Belgium.

Dapcevic was charged with organizing an illegal Yugoslav Communist Party and seeking to overthrow Tito's government.

Dapcevic was sentenced July 5 to death, but the sentence was immediately commuted to 20 years' imprisonment.

Vice consul slain in West Germany. Edvin Zdovc, a Yugoslav vice consul in Frankfurt, West Germany, was slain outside his residence Feb. 7, 1976 by two assassins believed to be Croatian separatists.

Croatian terrorists hijack TWA jet. Five Croatian nationalists hijacked a New York-to-Chicago Trans World Airlines (TWA) jet Sept. 10, 1976 and forced it on a 30-hour international campaign against "genocidal Yugoslavism." The flight across four countries and the Atlantic Ocean ended in Paris Sept. 12, with the arrest of four men and one woman.

The hijackers were returned to the U.S. and arraigned in U.S. District Court, Brooklyn, Sept. 13 on federal air piracy charges. They also faced state murder charges in the death of a New York City police officer. He was killed Sept. 11 when a bomb that he had been attempting to defuse exploded. The bomb was found in a locker in Grand Central Station.

None of the 81 passengers and seven crew members held hostage was injured during the first successful hijacking of a U.S. domestic airliner since November 1972.

The Boeing 727, TWA flight 355, was hijacked about one hour after taking off from LaGuardia Airport in New York City. The terrorists, brandishing purported bombs that later proved to be harmless fakes, diverted the jet to Montreal.

From Montreal, the Croatians radioed instructions that led police to the Grand Central Terminal locker containing the active bomb and two documents that stated the case for Croatian independence and appealed for American support.

The plane continued on to Gander, Newfoundland, where it was joined by a TWA Boeing 707 equipped to navigate longer-range, trans-Atlantic distances. After the release of 35 passengers, the three-engined hijacked jet and its four-engined "pathfinder" escort left Gander for Keflavik, Iceland. In Iceland, the planes refueled and the 707 was loaded with propaganda leaflets condemning the "oppression and humiliation of which Croats are victims."

As part of their operation to publicize the Croatian cause, the hijackers arranged with TWA to have thousands of these handbills dropped from helicopters over Montreal, Chicago and New York.

At about 9 A.M. (EDT) Sept. 11, the two planes took off for London but were refused permission to land there. The 707 escort conducted leaflet-dropping runs over London and later over Paris, where the aircraft were allowed to land at Charles de Gaulle Airport, but only after authorities had learned that the planes were low on fuel. French sharpshooters punctured the hijacked jet's tires so that it would not take off again.

French Interior Minister Michel Poniatowski and U.S. Ambassador Kenneth Rush directed the ensuing 13-hour negotiations on the ground. A French ultimatum early Sept. 12 gave the hijackers a choice of surrendering and being immediately deported or of facing summary execution for further threats on the hostages' lives. The hijackers turned themselves over to the authorities and were flown to New York aboard a French military transport.

The hijackers were Zvonko Busic, 28; his American-born wife Julienne, 27; Peter Matanic, 31; Frane Pesut, 25, and Mark Vlasic. Matanic was a naturalized U.S. citizen.

Vlasic pleaded guilty March 2, 1977 to reduced New York State charges of kidnapping and was sentenced May 12 to six to 18 years in prison.

The other four were convicted in U.S. District Court in Brooklyn May 5, 1977 on various federal charges of air piracy and conspiracy. The Busics were found guilty on all three counts—air piracy resulting in death, air piracy and conspiracy. Matanic and Pesut were found guilty on the latter two counts.

The Busics were sentenced July 20 to mandatory life sentences for air piracy resulting in death. Their three accomplices were sentenced July 21 to 30-year prison terms for air piracy and conspiracy.

Vlasic, 29, who had faced the same federal charges as the other four defendants, pleaded guilty to air piracy before the others went to trial.

Croatians storm Yugoslav U.N. mission. Three armed Croatian nationalists June 14, 1977 invaded the Yugoslav mission to the United Nations in New York, wounded a chauffeur standing guard, then barricaded themselves on the third floor of the Manhattan building. They surrendered peacefully two hours later, after throwing thousands of leaflets, urging U.N. support of "a free and independent Croatian State," into the street below.

Latin America

Argentina

Argentina, like many Latin American countries, is frequently the host—often reluctantly—of political refugees from other Latin American countries. The overthrow of the Salvador Allende regime in Chile in 1973 and the rise of a rightwing regime in Uruguay led to an influx of leftwing Chilean and Uruguayan refugees in Argentina.

Leftwing exiles under attack. The secret AAA (Argentine Anti-Communist Alliance) and Argentine police elements were accused during 1975 of a terrorist campaign against allegedly leftist Uruguayan and Chilean refugees in Argentina.

The AAA distributed leaflets April 25 threatening to kill 16 prominent newsmen and actors unless they left the country by April 28. The 16, who included the well-known Uruguayan writer Mario Benedetti, went into hiding rather than emigrate, the London Times reported April 29.

Police found six bullet-riddled bodies April 6 on the road from Buenos Aires to Ezeiza International Airport. Next to the victims was a placard, attributed to the AAA, saying: "We were from the ERP, the Montoneros and the FAR." The last group, the Revolutionary Armed Forces, was a leftist guerrilla band. Police said April 8 that four of the victims were Chilean.

Chilean journalist Ernesto Carmona reported in the Venezuelan newspaper El Nacional April 26 that Argentine security forces were carrying out a "pogrom" of Chilean leftists who had taken refuge in Argentina after the 1973 military coup against the late Chilean President Salvador Allende. The persecution and murder of Chileans in Argentina was carried out in collaboration with the Chilean embassy in Buenos Aires and the Chilean military intelligence service, Carmona said.

Pressures against leftwing refugees in Argentina continued during 1976:

The bodies of Zelmar Michelini and Hector Gutierrez Ruiz, both distinguished former legislators, were found by police May 20 in an isolated section of Buenos Aires. Alongside them were the bodies of two more Uruguayans kidnapped a week earlier and identified as William Whitelaw and his wife, Rosario Barreto.

Police said they found a note with the bodies. The note, according to police, said that the exiles had been executed by the People's Revolutionary Army (ERP), Argentina's Marxist guerrilla group, at the request of its Uruguayan counterpart, the National Liberation Movement (Tupamaros). Police quoted the note as saying that the victims were "traitors" to the Tupamaro cause.

The assassinations bore the usual marks of killings by one of Argentina's right-wing death squads, the London newsletter Latin America said May 28.

It was unclear, Latin America noted, whether the murderers had acted on their own or at the behest of the Uruguayan government, which Michelini and Gutierrez repeatedly had denounced for alleged abuse of human rights.

(Miguel Liberoff, an exiled Uruguayan labor leader, was kidnapped in Buenos Aires May 19. Wilson Ferreira Aldunate, exiled leader of Uruguay's Blanco party, took asylum in the Austrian Embassy in Buenos Aires May 24, apparently in fear for his life.)

■ The government assured the United Nations' High Commissioner for Refugees that the 12,000 Chilean and other foreign political refugees in Argentina would not be returned to their native countries, it was reported April 9. At least 35 Chilean refugees were arrested April 3 at U.N.-financed residences in Buenos Aires, but about 20 were freed after questioning.

■ The U.S. affiliate of Amnesty International (A.I.U.S.A.) urged the Organization of American States (OAS) June 4 to take action against the violation of human rights in Argentina. Its statement said:

A.I.U.S.A. notes with deep regret the recent deaths of Uruguayan exiles arrested in Buenos Aires. Their bodies, most bearing marks of torture, were found in the outskirts of Buenos Aires on May 20th. These included two former Uruguayan parliamentarians, Senator Zelmar Michelini and Hector Gutierrez Ruiz, former President of the Uruguayan Chamber of Representatives. Another Uruguayan, Dr. Manuel Liberoff, disappeared at the same time and is still missing.

A.I.U.S.A. is alarmed at the recent tendency toward the abandonment of the traditional right to asylum and lack of tolerance toward political exiles and refugees.

In his inaugural address as President of Argentina in March, General Jorge Rafael Videla promised to respect human rights. Foreign Minister Cesar Augusto Guzetti assured the United Nations High Commissioner

for Refugees April 5th that the thousands of political refugees from other countries living in Argentina will not be persecuted or returned to their countries of origin. There is overwhelming evidence to the contrary.

On April 10, Chilean refugee Edgardo Enriquez Espinosa was abducted from his home in Buenos Aires together with a Brazilian woman, Regina Macondes. In early May it was reported that he had been repatriated and was held in a torture center in Chile. The Argentinian authorities are reported to have denied the repatriation, but they continue missing.

In spite of statements made by the new Argentine authorities that international law would be respected and the rights of refugees protected, reports from Argentina prove otherwise. There are approximately 9,000 de facto refugees who have been declared eligible for U.N. High Commission for Refugees protection but who have not been granted asylum. There are reports of "black lists" that have been circulated to embassies in Argentina naming people who must not be granted asylum.

It is alarming to us that the Argentine government has banned the press to report on arrests, disappearances or killings.

Just as in Chile after the September 1973 coup, Latin American exiles in Argentina are subject to persecution, torture and assassination because, in the eyes of the security forces, exiles are seen as potential "subversive" elements.

■ Amplifying the above accusation, Amnesty International's Committee to Abolish Torture charged that Uruguayan government kidnap, torture and murder squads operated against Uruguayan refugees in Argentina with impunity and with apparent support of the Argentine regime. According to a committee statement:

Convincing evidence that the campaign of terror against refugees in Argentina has increased dramatically since the March 1976 coup there comes from 12 Uruguayan refugees, including three children, who arrived in Paris in mid-July.

Three of the refugees, one woman and two men, had been kidnapped and severely tortured during captivity by unknown assailants, whom the victims believe to have included both Uruguayans and Argentinians. The three torture victims were abducted in Buenos Aires on 6 July by about 30 armed men, who hooded them and bundled them into a car and took them to what they believe to be a private house in the countryside.

The three were released on 13 July, the same day that 23 other Uruguayan refugees, including 11 women and two children, were abducted in Buenos Aires. Amnesty International believes that it is unlikely that many of these 23 are still alive.

The refugees confirmed the substance of the following excerpt from a letter received in August by Amnesty International from other Uruguayan exile sources in Buenos Aires: the Uruguayan security forces, with the tacit support of the Argentinian authorities, are those directly responsible for all that has happened to Uruguayan residents in Buenos Aires. At this moment it would be impossible for their families to negotiate for the life or liberty of these victims because their disappearance forms part of the so-called *Plan Mercurio* destined to eliminate all Uruguayans of leftwing tendencies in both countries. This plan relies on the official support of the police authorities in both countries.

To this information the refugees who arrived in Paris adds that there is a specially selected force of 600 Uruguayan army personnel operating in Argentina under the direction of a certain Colonel RAMIREZ, who, according to the refugees, recently arrived from the United States to direct the campaign. With his second-in-command, Campos HERMIDAS, he operates from private houses without any set headquarters in Argentina.

The particular targets for these semi-clandestine activities are Uruguayan trade unionists in Argentina, who have accounted for a relatively high percentage of the kidnap and murder victims in the last several months.

■ Armed men with presumed government aid kidnapped and then released 25 foreign political refugees in Buenos Aires. The exiles—23 Chileans, a Paraguayan and a Uruguayan—were taken from their hotels June 11. They were released June 12 after strong protests were made to the Argentine government by the office of the United Nations' High Commissioner for Refugees, which looked after thousands of political exiles in Argentina.

All 25 refugees had been beaten and some had been tortured with electric prods. They said that their abductors had given them 48 hours to leave Argentina and had threatened to kill them if they spoke to the press about the kidnapping.

The quick release of the kidnapped refugees was one of several indications that their captors were off-duty policemen.

Officials of the U.N. High Commissioner's office in Geneva said June 14 that they were asking other countries to take Latin American refugees who felt that their lives were endangered in Argentina.

■ About 600–1,000 foreign refugees in Buenos Aires staged a hunger strike July 6-18 to demand that the office of the United Nations High Commissioner for Refugees arrange their transfer to other countries. The refugees, mostly leftists from Chile, feared abduction and assassination by rightist commandos.

The hunger strike ended after Robert Muller, a U.N. official, told strike leaders that the U.N. had sent notes to 34 nations asking them to grant resident visas to refugees in Buenos Aires. Canada had decided to accept 1,000 Chileans currently living in Argentina or jailed in Chile, the London Times reported July 19. Great Britain had agreed to take 75 refugees and their families, Norway was prepared to accept 50, and Sweden and Switzerland were considering harboring others, the Times added.

Twelve Chilean refugees flew to Canada July 15 after staging a sit-in in the Canadian Embassy in Buenos Aires to demand transfer from Argentina. Another 15 Chileans remained in the embassy demanding asylum.

The U.N. refugee office in Buenos Aires reported July 19 that 30 Uruguayan refugees in Buenos Aires had been kidnapped in recent days. The alleged kidnap victims included Margarita Michelini, whose father, former Uruguayan Sen. Zelmar Michelini, had been assassinated in Buenos Aires in May.

Similar charges of atrocities against refugees in Argentina were made by domestic and foreign sources in 1977–79.

Bolivia

Torres exiled to Peru. Deposed Bolivian President Juan Jose Torres flew to exile in Peru Aug. 26, 1971, two days after the new government of Hugo Banzer Suarez decided to give safe-conduct passes to 50 refugees who had earlier sought asylum in embassies in La Paz. Banzer had returned from exile in Argentina to lead in Torres' overthrow.

Before leaving for Lima with 31 other Bolivians on a DC-6 sent by the Peruvian government, Torres issued a statement at the Alto airport calling on the Bolivian people to rise in arms against the new rightist government.

Bolivian escapees reach Cuba. Sixty-seven Bolivian political prisoners, who escaped from the jail on Coati island in Lake Titicaca, were flown to Havana Nov. 6, 1972 after the Peruvian regime refused to grant them political asylum. Six others were returned to Bolivia at their own request, according to the Peruvian Foreign Ministry.

The prisoners, who reportedly included trade unionists, student leaders and members of opposition parties and revolutionary groups, broke out of Coati Nov. 2. According to one escapee, they overpowered prison guards at the end of a soccer match between guards and inmates. Four were recaptured, but the rest crossed the border into Peru, where they were held by police until the government responded to their request for political asylum.

Argentina arrests exiles. A number of prominent Bolivian exiles were seized by Argentine police May 3, 1974 and held until May 7, apparently at the behest of the Bolivian regime.

The detainees, according to the Washington Post May 5, were Juan Lechin Oquendo, former Bolivian vice president and still leader of Bolivia's militant mineworkers; Jorge Gutierrez Mendieta, his political secretary; Edil Sandoval Moron, ex-president of the Bolivian Chamber of Deputies; Col. Samuel Gallardo, former Bolivian army chief of staff, and Ted Cordova-Claure, former press secretary to exiled President Juan Jose Torres and currently foreign editor for the Buenos Aires newspaper La Opinion.

The Argentine government news agency TELAM reported May 7 that Lechin, Cordova-Claure, Sandoval and two other Bolivians not cited in earlier reports—Felipe Malky and Victor Levy—had been freed by police that day, but Gutierrez would remain in jail.

Most press reports alleged the arrests had been made at the request of the Bolivian government, which reportedly had sent a list of exiled enemies to the Argentine government the week before. However, the Bolivian embassy in Buenos Aires denied requesting the arrests, and Argentine Defense Minister Angel Robledo claimed May 9 that the exiles had been detained solely "for trafficking in alkaloids."

Ex-President Juan Jose Torres, in Argentina since May 1973, had been organizing his National Left Alliance (AIN), which consisted of a small group of revolutionary militants.

Other exiled Bolivian leftists had suffered greatly as a result of the Chilean military coup, Latin America reported. Many had been jailed, shot or dispersed to different countries by the Chilean junta, which was aided in this work by the Bolivian police. Simon Reyes, the miners' leader and Communist party official, was in a Santiago prison, and other Bolivians were hiding in foreign embassies, including Maj. Ruben Sanchez in the Honduran embassy. The Bolivians who had gained asylum in the Argentine embassy had generally been transferred to the remote Argentine provinces of Misiones and Corrientes, far from Torres and his organizers in Buenos Aires, according to Latin America.

Torres slain in Argentina. Ex-President Juan Jose Torres, a refugee in Argentina, was kidnapped June 1, 1976.

Torres' blindfolded and bullet-riddled body was found June 2 on a rural road about 60 miles from Buenos Aires.

Ex-refugees arrested despite amnesty. President Hugo Banzer Suarez June 3, 1976 offered amnesty to exiles who feared assassination abroad. Several foes of Banzer, including former Cabinet ministers Ciro Humboldt, Jorge Gallardo and Samuel Gallardo, took advantage of the offer, returned to Bolivia and were promptly arrested, the Associated Press reported June 6. Interior Minister Juan Pereda Asbun later explained that the amnesty did not apply to persons whom the government considered "extremists."

Chile

The overthrow and death of Marxist President Salvador Allende Gossens Sept. 11, 1973 was followed by the installation of a rightwing military junta under which thousands of alleged leftists were arrested and thousands fled.

Refuge sought in embassies. As word of wholesale arrests by the military junta spread, thousands of Chileans sought asylum in foreign embassies in Santiago before going abroad. Mexico withdrew its ambassador from Chile Sept. 14 and said the next day that 332 Chileans were asking asylum in its embassy, and Argentina said Sept. 18 that 300 Chileans had taken refuge in its embassy. Some governments airlifted refugees out of Chile, but the junta informed them Sept. 23 it would no longer give Chileans safe-conduct passes for political asylum abroad.

The Chilean National Committee for Aid to Refugees, under the auspices of the U.N. high commissioner for refugees, had reached an agreement with the junta to establish 15 reception centers in Santiago and 11 in the provinces where foreign refugees would be assisted in putting their identification papers in order, or in leaving the country, it was reported Oct. 2. U.N. officials emphasized they could protect only foreigners, and not Chileans, who under international law were not considered refugees until they left the country. The junta reported Oct. 14 that 1,316 persons had been given safe conduct to leave the country, and 386 were still hiding in foreign embassies. An airplane with 116 refugees aboard had left for Mexico Oct. 13.

The junta said Nov. 22 it had awarded safe-conducts out of the country to 4,342 of the 4,480 Chileans who had taken refuge in European or Latin American embassies in the capital. It added it had expelled 487 other Chileans and had allowed out 182 foreigners hiding in facilities of international organizations.

The Geneva-based Intergovernmental Commission on European Migrations said Nov. 30 that some 1,200 refugees of 28 nationalities had been transferred from Chile to 26 countries since the coup. The majority, about 800, went to Western Europe, and the others to Latin American states. Sweden, the Netherlands and France were the European nations most willing to take refugees from Chile, according to Le Monde Dec. 5.

West German Chancellor Willy Brandt said Bonn would give asylum to more Chilean refugees than any other European nation, it was reported Dec. 11. He said 40 refugees from Chile had arrived in West Germany Dec. 7.

The junta told European embassies in Santiago Dec. 10 that it would not grant courtesy safe-conduct abroad to persons who took political asylum in the embassies after Dec. 11. Military guards were strengthened outside all embassies Dec. 10 to prevent political refugees from gaining entrance.

The Latin embassies with most refugees were those of Argentina, Mexico and Venezuela. Some reports said the refugees remained there because Chile would not grant them safe-conducts, and others asserted the nations in question were reluctant to admit leftists because of their own domestic conditions. The Washington Post reported Dec. 11 that Chileans in the U.S. said the junta had denied safe-conducts to 200–300 Chilean refugees who had been at one time or another leaders of the ousted Popular Unity coalition.

The Bogota newspaper El Tiempo Nov. 29–30 criticized the treatment by the Chilean junta of refugees in the Colombian embassy in Santiago. It also charged Colombian actions to protect refugees had been "weak and irregular."

The wife of Oscar Garreton, leader of the left-wing MAPU party and one of the junta's 10 most wanted persons, had charged Nov. 29 that the junta had offered safe-conducts to a dozen refugees in the Colombian embassy in exchange for Garreton, who was also in the embassy.

The Times of London reported Dec. 12 that more than 2,000 foreign refugees remained in hostels set up by the United Nations High Commissioner for Refugees. Their political background reportedly made them unwelcome in their own countries, and some lacked the official visas necessary to leave Chile.

The U.S. had offered to allow foreign refugees stranded in Chile after the military coup to enter the U.S. under a special "parole" arrangement suspending certain immigration restrictions, it was reported Dec. 1. The offer—initially suggested by Sen. Edward M. Kennedy (D, Mass.)—had been made more than a month before, but fewer than 30 persons had accepted it.

The U.S. Senate had passed an amendment to a foreign aid bill Oct. 2 prohibiting aid to Chile until the new government guaranteed the right to seek political asylum, the right to leave the country for political asylum abroad, and humane treatment in jails and prison camps.

The Geneva-based Intergovernmental Committee on European Migration reported Jan. 2, 1974 that since mid-October 1973, 2,225 refugees, about half Chilean, had left Chile for other countries. Most reportedly went to Western Europe, with the largest number, 442, going to Sweden, and the next largest, 385, to France.

Only three Eastern European countries had taken refugees, with 45 going to East Germany, 17 to Yugoslavia and three to the Soviet Union, the committee reported.

(The Washington Post reported Jan. 5 that only three Communist nations—East Germany, Yugoslavia and Cuba—had responded favorably to an appeal by the U.N. High Commissioner for Refugees, Prince Sadruddin Aga Khan, to take refugees from U.N. posts in Chile.

(Cuba had agreed to take 100 and East Germany 70. The Soviet Union reportedly had been bitterly criticized among Latin American leftists for refusing to accept Chilean refugees, many of whom were loyal members of Chile's Moscow-line Communist Party.)

The junta had extended to Feb. 3 the deadline for refugees in foreign embassies to leave Chile, Le Monde reported Jan. 5.

Mrs. Allende sees Trudeau. Hortensia Bussi de Allende, widow of President Salvador Allende, met with Canadian Prime Minister Pierre Trudeau in Ottawa Nov. 30, 1973. Later, at a press conference, she urged Canada to aid Chilean refugees and cut off loans to and trade with Chile's "fascist" military junta.

Since her husband's ouster and death Sept. 11, Mrs. Allende had visited several Latin American and European cities to seek help for Chilean political refugees and political prisoners.

Swedish envoy expelled. The government Dec. 4, 1973 declared Swedish Ambassador Harald Edelstam "persona non grata" and accused him of exceeding his authority as a foreign diplomat.

Swedish Foreign Minister Sven Andersson Dec. 4 had protested Edelstam's expulsion and commended Edelstam for working "more than any other person [in Chile] to save refugees."

Mrs. Consuelo Alonso Freiria, A Uruguayan woman whose arrest had provoked a clash between Edelstam and Chilean authorities, was allowed to leave Santiago for Stockholm Dec. 3 after authorities determined she had not participated in domestic "subversive" activities. The police had given the press Dec. 1 a sworn statement by Alonso confirming that she was actually Mirta Ercilia Fernandez, widow of a Tupamaro guerrilla leader, and had entered Chile illegally.

Edelstam left Santiago Dec. 9.

Chileans abroad to lose citizenship. A spokesman for the junta told United Press International Dec. 10, 1973 that Chileans abroad who attacked "the essential interests of the state" would lose their citizenship.

The spokesman said there were some 50 persons "directing the campaign against Chile abroad," including Hortensia Bussi de Allende, widow of President Salvador Allende; Volodia Teitelboim, former Communist senator; and Armando Uribe and Carlos Vasallo, former ambassadors to East Germany and Italy, respectively.

France takes 1,000 refugees. The French newspaper Le Monde reported Jan. 3, 1974 that France led all in accepting refugees from Chile, having welcomed some 1,000 persons fleeing the military regime. The figure was confirmed the next day by French Premier Pierre Messmer.

According to Le Monde, the refugees included more than 600 Chileans, some 60 French nationals (many of them priests and nuns) and about 300 other non-Chileans (including leftists from other Latin American countries who had found temporary asylum in posts established by the United Nations High Commissioner for Refugees and the International Red Cross).

The junta had recently granted the French embassy 191 safe-conducts, all requested before the Dec. 11, 1973 deadline, Le Monde reported. This left in question only about 30 so-called "difficult cases," most involving former government officials being investigated by the junta for possible criminal prosecution.

East Germany takes 400 refugees. East Germany had granted asylum to 400 refugees from Chile, identified by the Communist Party newspaper Neues Deutschland as members of the ousted Popular Unity coalition, the New York Times reported Jan. 10.

Canada agreed to accept more than 140 refugees, according to a report Jan. 9, and Sweden raised the number of refugees it had accepted to 600, it was reported Jan. 11. However, some 3,000 Chilean and foreign refugees reportedly remained in Chile—in United Nations sanctuaries, foreign embassies and private homes.

Embassy refugee arrested, others freed. Among developments involving refugees in asylum in embassies in Chile in 1974:

Chilean police entered the Argentine embassy in Santiago and arrested the secretary general of the Revolutionary Radical Youth, Alejandro Montesinos, who had taken asylum there, the Buenos Aires newspaper Noticias reported March 14.

Carmen Lazo, a former Chilean Socialist legislator, had been allowed to fly to Colombia April 29, after living in the Colombian embassy in Santiago for seven months. Miriam Contreras, private secretary to the late President Salvador Allende, was granted safe-conduct to Sweden May 21. Two former Cabinet ministers, Jacques Chonchol and Gonzalo Martner, were granted passes to Venezuela May 24.

Some 72 refugees, including former Transport Undersecretary Jaime Faivovich, were allowed to leave the Mexican embassy in Santiago June 2 and fly to Mexico City.

Among others allowed to leave embassies previously were former Labor Minister Mireya Baltra, who flew to the Netherlands June 3; ex-Agriculture Minister Jacques Chonchol, to Venezuela June 8; and former Allende adviser Mario Palestro, to Norway June 10. The last 16

refugees who had received asylum in the Swedish embassy in Santiago arrived in Stockholm June 19. They included former Labor Minister Luis Figueroa and ex-Agriculture Minister Rolando Calderon.

Two leaders of the outlawed Communist Party, former Sen. Julieta Campusano and ex-Deputy Alejandro Rojas, had left Chile June 10 with safe-conducts for Denmark and France, respectively. Eugenio Massi, former director of the leftist newspaper Puro Chile, had traveled to France June 8.

Ex-Agriculture Minister Jacques Chonchol also had flown to France June 8, after stopping in Caracas, where refugees from the Venezuelan embassy in Santiago, where Chonchol had hidden, received asylum. The Venezuelan embassy, like Sweden's, was now empty of refugees.

More refugees leave in '75. Ex-Foreign Minister Clodomiro Almeyda, former Education Minister Jorge Tapia and three minor officials of the ousted Popular Unity government were freed from prison Jan. 11, 1975 and deported to Rumania.

Almeyda said during a stopover in Frankfurt, West Germany Jan. 12 that he would continue to "fight for Chile" in exile, and he disclosed on arriving in Bucharest that his release had been personally obtained by Rumanian leader Nicolae Ceausescu.

The others deported were Leopoldo Zuljevic, a former customs superintendent, and Maximo Tacchi and Luis Enrique Munoz, whose former positions were not given. The exiles were forced to leave their relatives behind in Chile.

The government freed 27 prominent political prisoners Feb. 13 and deported them to Venezuela. They included Jaime Toha Gonzalez, former agriculture minister and brother of the late ex-defense minister, Jose Toha Gonzalez; Carlos Jorquera, former press secretary to the late President Salvador Allende; and Anselmo Sule, Carlos Morales Abarzua and Hugo Miranda, all ex-presidents of the Radical Party. The majority of the others were Radical Party members.

The government had expelled four other political prisoners earlier. Claudio Huepe, a former deputy from the Christian Democratic Party, was sent to Uruguay Feb. 12 after four months in jail; Angela and Micaela Bachelet, widow and daughter of the late Gen. Alberto Bachelet, had been exiled to Australia Jan. 30 after being held for a month. And Manuel Cabieses, former editor of the magazine Punto Final, had been expelled to Cuba, it was reported Jan. 24.

The Chilean National Committee to Aid Refugees said Feb. 4 that seven European nations—France, West Germany, Italy, Belgium, the Netherlands, Luxembourg and Spain—had agreed to accept 1,000 Chilean political prisoners. Mexican Foreign Minister Emilio Rabasa announced Feb. 17 that Mexico would accept 151 of the 200 prisoners offered it by Chile; the others, he said, had refused to accept exile.

(Sweden had taken some 1,300 refugees from Chile since the September 1973 military coup, including 500 non-Chilean nationals, according to the London Times Jan. 27. The refugees were found jobs after spending three months in special camps to learn Swedish.)

The junta March 21 freed and sent to Mexico 95 political prisoners including Laura Allende de Pascal, the former Socialist deputy and sister of the late President Allende.

The exiles were selected from 200 prisoners whom Chile had offered to send to Mexico in January. Press sources said several dozen prisoners had refused exile and others had been rejected by Mexico.

Meanwhile, political refugees continued to leave Chile under the protection of foreign embassies in which they had taken asylum. The Foreign Ministry March 6 announced the departure the previous week of 44 refugees from the Italian embassy, 25 from the Colombian embassy, 12 from the Venezuelan embassy and two from the Costa Rican embassy. The refugees from the Italian and Venezuelan embassies traveled to Rumania.

The Intergovernmental Committee for European Migration (ICEM) March 11 announced the departure of 16 refugees from the Ecuadorean embassy, 14 of whom went to Ecuador and two to Costa Rica.

(The ICEM, a Geneva-based group founded in 1951 to aid persons displaced because of World War II, had relocated more than 7,000 Chilean political refugees, prisoners and their families since the 1973 military coup, the Miami Herald reported March 3. The group worked in cooperation with the United Nations High Commissioner for Refugees.)

MIR leader exiled. Andres Pascal Allende, leader of the Revolutionary Left Movement (MIR) and nephew of the late President Salvador Allende Gossens, flew to San Jose, Costa Rica Feb. 2, 1976 after getting a safe-conduct to leave the Costa Rican embassy in Santiago, where he had taken political asylum in November 1975.

Chile immediately asked Costa Rica to extradite Pascal and his friend Marie Anne Beausire, who had taken refuge with him in the embassy and accompanied him to San Jose.

Pascal's second-in-command in the MIR, Nelson Gutierrez, was one of nine refugees in the quarters of the Apostolic Nunciature (Vatican embassy) in Santiago who were given safe-conducts to leave the country Jan. 28. Gutierrez, his friend Maria Elena Bachman and the seven others had been offered political asylum by Sweden, according to press reports.

Letelier killed in U.S. Orlando Letelier, a former Cabinet minister and former Chilean ambassador to the U.S., was killed in Washington, D.C. Sept. 21, 1976 when a bomb exploded under his car.

Ronni Karpen Moffitt, an associate of Letelier at the Institute for Policy Studies, also was killed in the blast. Her husband, Michael Moffitt, was in the car but was not injured.

The Chilean Embassy in Washington denied Chilean government complicity in the murder, calling it a "deplorable deed" and an "outrageous act of terrorism."

Richard Barnet and Marcus Raskin, co-directors of the institute, blamed Letelier's assassination on DINA, the Chilean secret police agency. Barnet said at a press conference Sept. 21 that there was "sufficient evidence, based on what has happened in Rome, in Buenos Aires, and now here in Washington, D.C., of a pattern of conduct by Chilean intelligence agencies."

Barnet referred to attacks against Chilean political exiles in the Italian and Argentine capitals. Bernardo Leighton, former leader of the left wing of Chile's Christian Democratic Party, was shot and wounded in Rome in 1975 by presumed agents of DINA. Carlos Prats Gonzalez, a former army general and Cabinet member, had been killed by a bomb that exploded under his car in Buenos Aires in 1974. Chilean exiles in Argentina had been harassed recently by Argentine security forces and right-wing terrorists presumably working in concert with DINA.

Letelier had been defense minister in the Cabinet of the late President Salvador Allende when Allende was overthrown by the Chilean armed forces in September 1973. Letelier was arrested in the military coup and held until September 1974, when he was released and sent into exile through the efforts of both the Venezuelan government and U.S. Secretary of State Henry Kissinger.

After some time in Venezuela, Letelier had moved to Washington, where he had been employed by the Institute for Policy Studies, a privately-funded research organization. He kept silent about Chilean affairs until recently, when he began denouncing the military junta's alleged use of torture and other rights violations. In retaliation, the junta Sept. 10 revoked Letelier's Chilean citizenship.

The week before his death, Letelier had received a letter from a well-placed Chilean who reported a high-level discussion in the military government over whether Letelier should be killed to silence his criticism. Existence of the letter was disclosed to the Washington Post by Eqbal Ahmed, an associate of Letelier at the Institute for Policy Studies.

Letelier had made his last address in New York Sept. 10, at a rally and concert in Madison Square Garden for the benefit of the Chile Human Rights Committee, which was headed by his wife, Isabel.

Chilean refugee situation. U.S. Rep. Richard L. Ottinger (D, N.Y.) inserted a staff report on the Chilean refugee problem in the Congressional Record June 30, 1977. Among excerpts from the report:

... It has been over three-and-three-quarter years since the government of President Salvadore Allende was overthrown. Since that time, nearly 30,000 people have fled Chile. These Chileans, as well as many of their countrymen still inside of Chile, have faced, and continue to face, severe difficulties. Amnesty International reports that over 1,500 Chileans has disappeared since the September, 1973 coup; another 5,000 have been executed. In Argentina, during the past two-and-one-half years, between 3,000 and 30,000 persons have disappeared. Many of these people were Chileans.

... the United States Committee for Refugees reported that, at the beginning of 1977, there were approximately 10,000 Chileans in Argentina and approximately 10,000 in other Latin American countries.

Cuba

Well over a quarter of a million Cubans have fled Cuba for voluntary exile since Fidel Castro came to power in Cuba in 1959. Some refugees have devoted their lives to overturning Castro's Communist regime; they have mounted attempted invasions and have staged acts of terrorism. Other refugees have made new lives for themselves, especially in the U.S., where many former Cubans have become citizens and have prospered.

Infiltration attempts. A group of 15 Cuban exiles tried to infiltrate Cuba Jan. 9, 1970 but failed when one of their two boats capsized off Oriente Province. One of the group drowned and the others sought sanctuary at the U.S. Navy base at Guantanamo, from which they were flown to Miami. After inquiry by U.S. authorities, 13 of the exiles, representatives of the militant anti-Castro group Alpha 66, were released Jan. 14; the other, Jesus Dominguez Benitez, was held in custody for violating bond on a 1968 bombing conviction.

Thirteen Cuban exiles reportedly landed clandestinely in eastern Oriente Province April 17, the ninth anniversary of the Bay of Pigs invasion. After clashes with government forces, during which four exiles and five Cuban soldiers were reported killed, the last four invaders were captured April 24 and 26, according to an April 27 announcement of the Armed Forces Ministry.

The Alpha 66 exile group April 20 took credit for the April 17 landing. Alpha 66's statement said that "various guerrilla groups are at this moment fighting in different parts of Cuba." Explaining that its exile groups were operating on "two basic fronts," Alpha 66 stressed: "Our men are not of the CIA [Central Intelligence Agency], nor of the North American government, nor are they reactionaries or mercenaries." The secretary general of the organization, Andres Nazario Sargen, declined, "for obvious reasons" to disclose the size of the force in Cuba, but he added that the group had made "several" landings in the area.

The U.S. State Department April 15 had told Cuban exile groups that guerrilla raids on Cuba must be stopped.

Suarez defects. Refugees from Cuba occasionally included former leaders of the Castro revolution.

Ismael Suarez de la Paz, friend of Castro and former provisional national coordinator of the 26th of July Movement, defected to the U.S., the Miami Herald reported July 31, 1970. Suarez, who represented the Cuban trading firm Cubalse on the island of Martinique, had fled to Puerto Rico in late June. He and his family were admitted into the U.S. as refugees in late July. Explaining that he had lost faith in the Cuban revolution over the past two years, Suarez said the "present leadership" was unable to meet the economic problems of the country.

Flight by sea. Thirty-three Cuban refugees arrived in Miami Feb. 19, 1970 after being picked up by a U.S. Coast Guard cutter. The group, which had left Cuba 20 days before, had spent 18 days on a small island trying to repair its motor boat.

Fifty-five refugees arrived July 1, 1971 at La Ceiba in Honduras after fleeing Cuba in a fishing boat. The group included 30 men, 13 women and 12 children, all reportedly in good health.

A group of 44 Cubans had hijacked a boat in Cuba and forced it to Mexico, where they asked political asylum, Mexican immigration authorities disclosed Oct. 18, 1972.

A U.S. immigration official had ruled that three Cuban fishermen who had hijacked a Cuban boat to Florida Dec. 6, 1972 and sought asylum in the U.S. had entered the U.S. without proper documentation and were therefore excludable, the State Department announced Dec. 21.

Anti-Castro aid sought. A group of prominent Cuban exiles headed by ex-President Carlos Prio Socarras and former Sen. Eduardo Suarez Rivas asked U.S. President Richard M. Nixon May 10, 1972 to provide them with economic and military aid to overthrow the Castro regime.

The request, presented in writing, was also signed by Andres Rivero Aguero, president-elect at the time Castro seized power, and Juanita Castro, the premier's exiled sister. Eduardo Boza Masdival, former bishop of Havana living in exile in Venezuela, also supported the petition.

The signatories cited a 1966 report by the security commission of the Organization of American States, which claimed meetings of the Organization of Latin American Solidarity in Havana sought to "institutionalize the practice of subversion in the Americas."

Meeting of Castro foes—A meeting of 80 Cuban exiles convened Nov. 23 in San Jose, Costa Rica to plan "the strategy of the first phase of the overthrow of the tyranny of Fidel Castro."

The group, calling itself the Latin American Democratic Left, consisted mainly of Cubans residing in the U.S. Leaders thanked Costa Rican President Jose Figueres for cooperating in the organization of the meeting.

U.S. airlift ends. The Cuba-Miami airlift, which had taken nearly 261,000 Cuban refugees to the U.S. since 1965, ended with two flights April 6, 1973.

Refugee leaders slain in Miami. Jose de Peruyero, 46, a leader of Miami's anti-

Castro Cuban exiles, was shot to death Jan. 7, 1977 by unidentified gunmen. Police described the killing as a "political assassination." Peruyero was a former president of the Bay of Pigs Invasion Brigade Veteran Association.

Peruyero was the seventh Cuban exile leader to die in the last three years. During the same period, about 100 bombs were exploded in the Miami area and a number of reporters, both Cuban and American, had received death threats.

Exiles vow more attacks. Militant Cuban exiles in Miami Aug. 31, 1977 said they would continue "all kinds of actions to fight against the Communist tyranny" in Cuba. The threat was made by Brigade 2506, an organization of veterans of the 1961 Bay of Pigs invasion. The group was under surveillance by the Federal Bureau of Investigation, and its activities were being reported to the Cuban government as part of a joint U.S.-Cuban effort to curb terrorism.

Ex-Political Prisoners Flown to U.S. Forty-six former political prisoners and 33 relatives were flown from Havana to Miami Oct. 21, 1978 as part of Fidel Castro's program to send past and present political offenders to the U.S.

The ex-prisoners, who would be "paroled" in the U.S. under the Federal Immigration Act, included two heroes of the anti-Castro Cuban exile community, Antonio Cuesta Valle (Tony Cuesta) and Eugenio Enrique Zaldivar Cadenas.

Cuesta had led numerous raids on Cuba, including one in 1963 in which a Soviet ship was shelled near Havana. He and Zaldivar were captured in 1966 in an ambush at sea by Cuban authorities. Cuesta blinded himself and lost an arm when he detonated a hand grenade in an attempt to kill himself rather than surrender.

Immediately after arriving in Miami, the former prisoners and their relatives were taken to the Dade County auditorium, where they received an emotional welcome from 2,500 Cuban exiles.

The flight from Havana was arranged by Miami bank executive Bernardo Benes. He led a delegation of six Cuban exiles who flew down to pick up the former prisoners and spoke with Castro about further releases.

The departure of the former prisoners followed Cuba's release of two groups of U.S.-Cuban dual nationals and their relatives in September and October. A third group consisting of 36 Cuban-Americans and 99 dependents arrived in Miami Nov. 14.

The releases were all part of Castro's plan to improve relations with Cuban exiles and, through them, with the U.S. government, whose approval Cuba needed to buy medicine, food and other products from U.S. suppliers.

Castro's chief spokesman in Washington, Ramon Sanchez Parodi, held a press conference Nov. 4 at which he invited Cuban exile leaders to go to Havana and help work out programs for the release of more political prisoners, the reunification of separated families and visits to Cuba by expatriates.

Castro's overtures had, in fact, deeply divided the exile communities in Miami and other American cities, according to the Washington Post Oct. 24.

Many organizations of exiles still opposed any recognition of Castro's government, but other, newer groups favored some contact with the Communist regime, the Post reported. One group of sympathetic exiles, calling themselves the Antonio Maceo Brigade (after a hero of Cuba's war of independence from Spain), visited the island at the end of 1977.

Castro himself had carefully begun referring to exiles as the Cuban "community" in the U.S. rather than *gusanos* (worms), as he used to call them.

Ecuador

An attempted rightwing coup was defeated in 1975, and its leaders went into exile.

Coup fails, rebels exiled. Troops backing President Guillermo Rodriguez Sept. 1 crushed a revolt led by the armed forces chief of staff, Gen. Raul Gonzalez Alvear, and supported by conservative civilian politicans.

The government ordered mass arrests of opposition politicians Sept. 2, effectively disbanding the Civic Junta. The coalition's leader, Jose Joaquin Silva, went into hiding, according to a report that day. Gilberto Contreras, a leader of the party supporting ex-President Jose Maria Velasco Ibarra, took asylum in the Venezuelan embassy in Quito. Velasco had supported the abortive coup attempt from exile in Argentina.

Gen. Gonzalez Alvear sought asylum in the residence of the Chilean ambassador Sept. 1 along with an aide, Maj. Roberto Varas. They then flew to Chile Sept. 5.

Rebel leaders exiled—Nine leaders of the rebellion were exiled to Panama Oct. 12 after the government mishandled and then canceled their court-martial.

The court-martial of 27 alleged leaders of the coup attempt had begun Oct. 5 with a tribunal of senior officers normally attached to Ecuadorean embassies abroad. The defendants immediately protested the court's refusal to let them hire civilian lawyers, and their appointed military defenders—four retired generals—resigned to protest the composition of the tribunal, determined according to a presidential decree issued after the coup attempt. The protests were taken up by the opposition papers and by the Civic Junta, causing the government to suspend the trial Oct. 7. Nine of the defendants and two of their appointed defenders were exiled to Panama Oct. 12 and the other 18 defendants were set free.

Colombia expels opposition leaders. Thirty exiled Ecuadorean opposition leaders were ordered out of Colombia Dec. 15, 1975 for "conspiring against the government of a friendly country [Ecuador]."

The exiles, most of them members of the Civic Junta, a coalition of conservative parties, had planned a summit meeting in Bogota Dec. 16 to organize the overthrow of the government of Gen. Guillermo Rodriguez Lara. They included ex-President Carlos Arosemena, leader of the Revolutionary Nationalist Movement; ex-Defense Minister Jorge Acosta Velasco, nephew of former President Jose Maria Velasco Ibarra; and retired Gen. Raul Gonzalez Alvear, leader of the abortive September coup. Arosemena and Acosta

flew to Panama Dec. 17, and Gonzalez returned to Chile.

The expulsions were denounced Dec. 16 by Velasco Ibarra, who was to have flown to Colombia for the meeting but remained at his residence in Argentina.

The opposition leaders had planned to organize a march to Quito from the Colombian-Ecuadorean frontier to overthrow Rodriguez Lara and replace him as president with retired Gen. Leonidas Plaza, according to opposition sources cited by the Venezuelan newspaper El Nacional Dec. 17. A communique released by the Civic Junta Dec. 28 said most of the exiled leaders had returned secretly to Ecuador after leaving Colombia.

Ecuador doubled its frontier guard Dec. 16 and arrested a number of opposition leaders in Quito including Rodrigo Suarez Morales, deputy director of the Conservative Party, and retired Maj. Cesar Paredes, a participant in the September coup attempt. Authorities also sought Conservative leader Julio Cesar Trujillo, who had returned to Ecuador from exile earlier in the month, it was reported Dec. 17.

Haiti

Rebels flee to U.S. The Haitian government May 4, 1970 demanded that the U.S. agree to return to Haiti 117 Coast Guardsmen who had fled Haiti after shelling the presidential palace April 24. The extradition note accused the men of murder, attempts on the life of President Duvalier and his family, and piracy.

The rebels, who had arrived in Miami May 2, May 4 sent telegrams to the Vatican, the International Committee of the Red Cross, the United Nations, the Organization of American States, the International Jurists Commission, U.S. President Richard M. Nixon and the International Human Rights Commission. They asked international intervention on behalf of their families in Haiti.

The three Coast Guard vessels had arrived May 1 in Puerto Rico with their crews totaling 117 men. One officer, Lt. Fritz Tippenhauer, who did not take part in the Coast Guard revolt, asked to be repatriated; the other 116 persons asked for asylum in the U.S. and were flown to Miami May 2.

3 kidnappers & 12 prisoners win exile.
U.S. Ambassador Clinton E. Knox was seized by three Haitians in Port-au-Prince Jan. 23, 1973 but freed unhurt Jan. 24 in exchange for the release of 12 Haitian prisoners, safe conduct to Mexico and a $70,000 ransom.

Knox's captors, two men and a woman, were not identified but were said to have links with exile groups that had opposed the Haitian government for years. They said the persons released were political prisoners. In New York, a Haitian refugee group called the Coalition of National Liberation Brigades said the released "prisoners have been under constant threat to be eliminated in case of any disorder in the country. And disorder there will be. . . ."

The kidnappers and freed prisoners were refused asylum by Mexico Feb. 1 and flown to Santiago, Chile. The Chilean government gave them transit visas while deciding whether to let them stay in the country.

The Haitian exiles—four men and a woman, most of them teachers—said Jan. 24 that they belonged to the National Antiduvalierist Movement, an organization without ideology or international political affiliations which sought only to free Haiti from the dictatorship of President Jean-Claude Duvalier.

More refugees reach U.S. Fifty-three Haitians reached the coast of Florida in a small sailing boat at the end of September 1974, raising to nearly 1,000 the number of refugees who had illegally fled Haiti for the U.S. in the past two years, it was reported Oct. 25.

The refugees, like their predecessors, were jailed to await deportation. They were supported in their legal fight to stay in the U.S. by local priests and welfare workers who claimed they would be imprisoned, tortured and even killed if they returned to Haiti. The refugees' defenders noted that while poor Haitains were threatened with deportation, thousands of white Cuban exiles from Spain were admitted to the U.S. without work permits and without relatives to support them.

Illegal Haitian immigrants were also under pressure in the Bahamas, where the government ordered them to register for voluntary return to Haiti. Seventy-five refugees were returned to Haiti Aug. 9 in the first flight under the Bahamian repatriation program.

The U.S. Immigration & Naturalization Service announced Nov. 8, 1977 that it would release about 120 Haitians who said they were political refugees and who were being held in detention in Florida. The service added that it would change its procedure for handling applicants for political asylum in the U.S. The applicants now would be able to argue their claim to asylum before an immigration judge. In the past, it had been U.S. policy to return Haitian refugees to Port-au-Prince without a hearing.

Two months earlier the U.S. State Department had said Sept. 6 that it had returned to Haiti 97 of 101 refugees who had sailed into the U.S. naval base at Guantanamo Bay, Cuba, a month earlier.

A spokesman said State Department interviewers had determined that the 97 fled Haiti for economic reasons and thus did not qualify for asylum in the U.S.

The Haitians arrived at Guantanamo Aug. 10 after a five-day journey through shark-infested waters from Haiti's southwestern coast, 200 miles away. They traveled in a small, leaking sailboat that was later determined to be beyond repair.

Spokesmen for the refugees said all 101 had left Haiti to escape political persecution and all would be beaten severely by Haitian authorities if forced to return home. However, State Department specialists sent to interview the Haitians found that almost all had left the island in hope of escaping poverty. After receiving assurances from the Haitian government that the refugees would not be punished, the U.S. flew the 97 to Port-au-Prince.

The incident posed a moral dilemma for the U.S. To have accepted the Haitians as political refugees would have created additional tensions with the Haitian government, which the U.S. was trying to pressure into respecting human rights. But to have accepted them as economic refugees might have encouraged other Haitians to flee to Guantanamo or the U.S. mainland, and might have encouraged the poor of other neighboring countries to do the same.

Mexico

Kidnappings win freedom as refugees for Mexican political prisoners. The Mexican government agreed Nov. 28, 1971 to exchange a group of political prisoners for the life of a kidnap victim, Dr. Jaime Castrejon Diez, rector of the State University of Guerrero who was kidnapped on his way to work Nov. 19.

Castrejon Diez, millionaire owner of the Coca-Cola bottling concession in Guerrero, was released Dec. 1, two days after his family paid a $200,000 ransom and nine political prisoners (eight men and one woman) were flown to Cuba, where they were accepted by the Castro government for "humanitarian reasons," according to a Nov. 30 Havana Radio broadcast.

The kidnapping was believed to be the work of a group of leftist rural guerrillas active in the mountains near Acapulco under command of a former schoolteacher, Genaro Vazquez Rojas. Five of the prisoners exchanged were said to be close associates of Vazquez Rojas and the woman was said to be his sister-in-law.

The U.S. consul general in Guadalajara, Terrance G. Leonhardy, was kidnapped by leftist guerrillas May 4, 1973 but freed unharmed May 7 after the Mexican government agreed to a number of demands, including freedom and safe conduct to Cuba for 30 alleged political prisoners.

The freed prisoners, 26 men and four women, arrived in Havana on a Mexican airliner May 6, and they said that they would return to Mexico to fight the government. Mexican authorities called them "common delinquents," but press sources said most of them belonged to urban guerrilla groups, which had carried out other kidnappings and bank robberies. The best known of those released was José Bracho Campos, an associate of the late guerrilla leader Genaro Vasquez Rojas.

Leonhardy was kidnapped by members of the People's Revolutionary Armed Forces, who demanded May 5 that the government: free the prisoners and transport them to Cuba; order the national press to publish a guerrilla communiqué; suspend the police and military search for Leonhardy; and allow the Cuban ambassador to go on television to confirm the safe arrival in Havana of the prisoners.

President Luis Echeverria Alvarez quickly agreed to meet the demands, saying his government prized human life highly.

Nicaragua

Nicaraguan prisoners freed, flown to Cuba. Eight guerrillas of Nicaragua's Sandanista Liberation Front invaded a party at a Managua businessman's home Dec. 27, 1974 and seized several prominent officials. Through the mediation of the Roman Catholic archbishop of Managua, the guerrillas subsequently negotiated the release of more than a dozen imprisoned comrades, payment of a large ransom and safe-conduct to Cuba.

The hostages were freed Dec. 30 and the guerrillas and released prisoners were flown to Havana accompanied by the archbishop, Msgr. Miguel Ovando y Bravo, the papal nuncio in Managua and the Mexican and Spanish ambassadors to Nicaragua.

Because of strict press censorship, there was some confusion as to how many prisoners were released and how much ransom was paid. Most foreign reports put the freed prisoners at 14 and the ransom at $1 million.

The party invaded by the Sandinistas was at the home of Jose Maria Castillo, a former agriculture minister, who was killed when he apparently tried to resist the guerrillas. Two or three guards at the home (reports varied) were also killed. The Sandinistas took more than 30 hostages—including Foreign Minister Alejandro Montiel Arguello and Ambassador to the U.S. Guillermo Sevilla Sacasa—but they missed Turner Shelton, the U.S. ambassador and guest of honor, who had already left.

The guerrillas demanded the mediation of Archbishop Ovando, release of 18 imprisoned comrades, a $5 million ransom, and wage raises for all maids, workers, employes and National Guardsmen. After Ovando agreed to mediate Dec. 28, they began releasing hostages, retaining only 13 by Dec. 30.

Sandinistas get foreign asylum. Several Sandinistas or persons associated with the guerrilla movement took political asylum in Costa Rica and in foreign embassies in Managua during 1977.

The Costa Rican government announced that it had granted asylum to eight guerrillas who had crossed into Costa Rica after attacking the National Guard barracks in the Nicaraguan border town of San Carlos Oct. 13, it was reported Oct. 27.

Three Nicaraguan students who had sought political asylum in the Mexican Embassy in Managua were flown to Mexico June 8 after receiving safe-conduct assurances from the Nicaraguan government. A fourth refugee remained in the embassy. He was a young lawyer who had been indicted for committing "irregularities" while defending prisoners accused of subversive activities.

Several Sandinistas took refuge in the Mexican Embassy in Managua during a guerrilla offensive Oct. 12–18. National guardsmen tried to enter the embassy Oct. 20 to arrest them, but they were rebuffed by embassy personnel. The Mexican ambassador said Oct. 21 that he would grant asylum to any Sandinista, no matter how much tension this caused in Mexican-Nicaraguan relations. Another guerrilla took refuge in the embassy Oct. 26.

Two Sandinistas took refuge in the French embassy, it was reported Oct. 20. The French ambassador said they would receive political asylum even though France had no asylum agreement with Nicaragua.

There also were two guerrillas in the Venezuelan Embassy, it was reported Oct. 28.

Seizure of Congress wins exile for prisoners. Seventy-five Sandinista guerrillas invaded the National Palace in Managua Aug. 22, 1978. By threatening to execute several hundreds of hostages, the guerrillas obtained a cash ransom, the release of 59 political prisoners and safe conduct to Panama.

The leftist insurgents, wearing uniforms of the Nicaraguan National Guard, entered the building as the Chamber of Deputies (lower house of parliament) was in session. They quickly established control over the palace, killing at least six guards and wounding another 15 persons in the process.

Legislators were tied up with rope in the Chamber, and other government officials and visitors to the palace were rounded up by the guerrillas. The number of hostages at the beginning of the siege was estimated at 1,500, and included two relatives of President Anastasio Somoza—his first cousin, Luis Pallais Debayle, and his nephew, Jose Somoza Obregon.

The Sandinistas demanded a $10-million ransom, release of all Nicaraguan political prisoners (there were thought to be more than 120), broadcast of several revolutionary messages and safe-conduct for the guerrillas and the released prisoners to Venezuela, Mexico or Panama.

The insurgents released more than 100 women and children hostages early Aug. 23, and others escaped from the palace. In the evening, as negotiations continued and the guerrillas' deadline passed, the government granted one of the demands: radio and television stations broadcast three Sandinista communiques, including one that called for the removal of Somoza and the abolition of the National Guard.

The next day the government yielded in part on the other demands. This was sufficient to end the siege. The guerrillas received a ransom of $500,000; 59 political prisoners were released, and the prisoners and the guerrillas were flown safely to Panama on one Panamanian and one Venezuelan airplane.

After all but five prominent hostages were released, the prisoners and the guerrillas were taken to the Managua airport in two buses. Cheering crowds lined the route and massed at the airport itself, shouting anti-government slogans such as, "Down with the dictatorship!"

The prisoners and the guerrillas were put onto the two airplanes, and only then were the last five hostages—including Somoza's two relatives—released.

All the guerrillas wore kerchiefs over their faces except their leader, who was addressed during the palace occupation as Comandante Cero (Commander Zero). The Nicaraguan government identified him as Eden Pastora, a veteran Sandinista leader who had led the occupation of several rural towns in Nicaragua in the past year.

OAS Censures Nicaragua—The Organization of American States censured Nicaragua Oct. 17 for an incident in mid-September in which National Guard fighter planes crossed into Costa Rica in pursuit of fleeing Nicaraguan guerillas.

A resolution accusing the National Guard of "bombing and machine-gunning Costa Rican civilians" was approved by a vote of 19-0, with Honduras and Paraguay abstaining.

Fugitives Enter Foreign Embassies— Dozens of Somoza's opponents had sought political asylum in foreign embassies in Managua and were waiting for safe-conduct passes to leave Nicaragua, according to press reports.

Fifty-two Nicaraguans were in the Mexican Embassy, 40 in the Venezuelan Embassy, 11 in the Panamanian Embassy and nine in the Colombian Embassy, according to the Latin America Political Report Oct. 13.

By Oct. 23 the number in the Venezuelan Embassy reportedly had risen to 100, including Edgardo Pastora, brother of the Sandinistas' military leader, Eden Pastora (Commander Zero).

The guerrillas were thought to be planning a new military offensive against the government, and as rumors of imminent violence spread, refugees streamed out of the cities. Diriamba was half empty, according to the Washington Post, and National Guardsmen had taken up firing positions all over town in case of a guerrilla attack.

Those who could not afford or obtain a plane flight out of the country crossed the borders into Costa Rica, Honduras or El Salvador. Costa Rica alone was reported to have 10,500 refugees in border camps. The United Nations High Commissioner for Refugees pledged Nov. 6 to send $430,000 to help the thousands of Nicaraguans in border camps in Honduras.

Paraguay

800,000 refugees. U.S. Rep. Robert F. Drinan (D, Mass.), discussing alleged rights abuses of President Alfredo Stroessner's regime, said in a March 3, 1976 statement:

Another indication of the low regard in which Paraguayans hold the Stroessner regime is the number of Paraguayans in voluntary or forced exile. Amnesty International determined that 800,000 or one-third of the present population are now in exile. Among these people are many who were involved in protecting human rights in Paraguay.

The freedom of the press in Paraguay remains quite restricted. Any paper that is able to exert any effective opposition to the regime is rapidly closed down. This is reported to have been the reason for the closings of Comunidad and El Radical.

Peru

AP banned, leaders deported. The government of President Juan Velasco Alvarado May 31, 1974 issued a ban on Popular Action (AP), the party of ex-President Fernando Belaunde Terry, and announced the deportation of its secretary general, Javier Alva Orlandini, and its national secretary for political affairs, Javier Arias Stella.

Arias Stella was deported to Argentina May 25. Alva Orlandini was expelled to Bolivia June 2. Both men had served in Belaunde's Cabinet before the armed forces seized power in 1968. The French newspaper Le Monde reported June 4 that two other AP leaders, Francisco Belaunde Terry—the ex-president's brother—and Jose Maria de la Jara, had also been expelled from Peru.

Fernando Belaunde Terry denounced the action against AP from his exile in Washington, D.C. June 1 and 3. In Paris, Belaunde's former finance minister, Manuel Ulloa, asserted AP would "carry on our struggle clandestinely, until we have overthrown the anti-constitutional, personalist and socializing government led by Gen. Velasco."

Belaunde barred—Ex-President Fernando Belaunde Terry was prevented from crossing the Peruvian border from Ecuador Aug. 30. He was deported from Ecuador the next day for making political statements.

Editors & opposition leaders exiled. President Velasco Aug. 5, 1975 banned the magazine Marka and ordered the deportation of 9 Marka editors. Velasco's order exiled 19 other political critics, including opposition politicians, student leaders and labor union officials.

The Aug. 5 decree charged that the Aug. 1 edition of Marka had sought to damage relations between Peru and Chile by making "unacceptable statements against the Chilean government and its main leaders, irresponsibly using offensive words." The article had described Peru's poor treatment of refugees from Chile's right-wing military government, according to the London Times Aug. 8.

The decree ordered the expulsion of the nine Marka editors and of 19 other Peruvians who had allegedly "gone to various places in the country for the purpose of encouraging occupation of lands, lay-offs, strikes and other violent deeds designed to disrupt public order and create situations of insecurity and unrest among the working class."

Among those ordered expelled were APRA leaders Armando Villanueva del Campo, Luis Negreiros Criado and Carlos Enrique Ferreyros, and leaders of the leftist Peruvian Peasant Federation (CCP), The Federation of Peruvian Mine and Metal Workers (FTMMP), and the teachers' union SUTEP.

The measure was not fully carried out—only the nine Marka editors and three members of the opposition APRA party were exiled—but it was widely protested. The newspaper Expreso denounced the decree Aug. 7, and teachers, miners, peasants and students struck in protest Aug. 28. Student demonstrations in Lima late Aug. 28 were broken up by policemen using tear gas.

Velasco ousted, refugees to return. President Velasco was deposed by his military commanders Aug. 29, 1975 and replaced by Gen. Francisco Morales Bermudez, the premier, war minister and army chief.

Leftist military officers expelled. Four radical military officers were expelled from Peru Jan. 8, 1977 for trying to "convince public opinion, and particularly the armed forces, that the revolutionary process has been cut short."

The four, all retired from active duty, were army Gens. Leonidas Rodriguez Figueroa and Arturo Valdez Palacio, navy Capt. Manuel Benza Chacon and Rear Adm. Jorge Dellepiane Ocampo.

More than a dozen leftist military officers and labor leaders had been expelled from Peru in recent months, according to press reports. "Deportations of union leaders and labor lawyers have become an almost weekly occurrence," the London newsletter Latin America reported Jan. 14. Julian Sierra, leader of the metalworkers' union, had been expelled Dec. 28, 1976; Camilo Valqui, lawyer of the Centromin miners' union, had been expelled the next day.

Sierra, Valqui, Rodriguez, Dellepiane and Benza all went to Panama, while Valdez chose exile in Mexico.

The most prominent of the new exiles was Rodriguez, who had headed the social mobilization agency, SINAMOS, under ex-President Juan Velasco Alvarado.

Uruguay

Thousands of leftist or suspected left-wing Uruguayans fled to other countries in the 1970s as increasingly repressive rightwing regimes took control.

Chamber head a refugee. A warrant was issued Sept. 7, 1973 for the arrest of Hector Gutierrez Ruiz, president of the Chamber of Deputies, for alleged collaboration with the Tupamaro guerrilla movement. Gutierrez was in Buenos Aires, Argentina, where he fled immediately after President Bordaberry dissolved the Chamber in late June.

Communist leader deported. Communist Party leader Rodney Arismendi was released from prison Jan. 4, 1975 and deported to an unidentified European country, according to relatives. He had been held since May 1974.

In a related development Jan. 3, Bordaberry ordered the expulsion from Uruguay of Carlos Reverditto, ex-dean of the architecture faculty at the University of the Republic, for "antinational activity."

Flights increase. In the face of increased arrests and charges of torture and murder by Uruguayan authorities in 1976, refugees sought safety abroad or in foreign embassies.

Twenty-four persons were reported March 3 to have taken political asylum in foreign embassies in Montevideo, 20 in Mexico's embassy and the other four in Colombia's. Six of the refugees flew to Mexico March 5, and another eight followed March 12. By then the Mexican embassy had accepted another 70 refugees and the Colombian embassy another four, according to press reports.

The number of Uruguayan political refugees in the Mexican embassy in Montevideo had risen to 100, the Uruguayan government announced April 9. Another 52 Uruguayans had flown to Mexico after taking asylum in the embassy, it was reported the day before.

The refugees were mostly members or sympathizers of the outlawed Uruguayan Communist Party, but they were not being sought for arrest, the government said. They reportedly included students, teachers, professionals, artists and five air force officers.

(The refugees also included Casildo Herreras, the Argentine Peronist labor leader, who fled Argentina before the military coup there March 24. Herreras was granted asylum in the Mexican embassy in Montevideo March 31 and he received safe-conduct to leave Uruguay April 9.)

Of the refugees who had recently flown to Mexico, eight had left Uruguay March

16 and another 14, March 25. Among those departing March 16 was Guillermo Bodner, alleged leader of the Fourth Directorship, described by the government as a Marxist group seeking to infiltrate Uruguay's police and armed forces.

Venezuela charged before the Organization of American States July 8 that Uruguay had committed a "clear violation of the right of asylum and of the sovereignty of states."

According to Julio Ramos, Venezuela's ambassador in Montevideo, a Uruguayan woman had rushed into the embassy's garden June 28 shouting that she wanted asylum. Franklin Becerra, an embassy official, went to her aid. Then three plainclothed Uruguayan security officers entered the yard, struck Becerra and dragged the woman out by her hair. They put her in an automobile and drove her away.

The Venezuelan government said July 6 that a private investigation by Ramos and Becerra had determined that the abducted woman was Elena Quintero de Diaz, 31, a schoolteacher. (The Uruguayan government had no comment other than to say that day that Diaz had left Uruguay in 1975 and had not "returned legally.")

Ramos and Becerra returned to Venezuela July 7. They left the embassy in the hands of Colombian diplomats. The embassy continued to shelter five Uruguayans seeking political asylum in Venezuela, according to press reports.

Meanwhile, 106 Uruguayan political refugees flew from Montevideo to Mexico City June 24-July 2. The refugees, including five airforce officers, had taken asylum in the Mexican embassy in Montevideo in the preceding months.

Mendez sworn in; politicians banned. Aparicio Mendez began a five-year term as president Sept. 1, 1976. Mendez immediately issued a decree suspending for 15 years the political rights of the leaders of all existing parties.

The sanctioned leaders included Wilson Ferreira Aldunate, former presidential candidate of the Blancos; Jorge Batlle, former candidate of the major faction of the Colorado Party; Jorge Pacheco Areco, former president of Uruguay and Colorado leader; and all candidates of the leftist Broad Front coalition who ran on the ticket headed by retired Gen. Liber Seregni in the 1971 general elections.

Ferreira Aldunate, an outspoken critic of the military-civilian government, was living in exile. His arrest was ordered Aug. 5 by the Uruguayan armed forces on unspecified charges of subversion. An unidentified aide of Ferreira later took political asylum in the Mexican embassy in Montevideo, the Mexican newspaper Excelsior said Aug. 21.

Venezuela

Venezuelan plane hijacked to Cuba. Four professed members of the People's Revolutionary Army (Zero Point), a guerrilla group, hijacked a Venezuelan airliner with 42 people aboard May 18, 1973 and flew it to Cuba, where the guerrillas requested political asylum.

The hijackers, led by Zero Point leader Federico Bottini, seized the plane on a domestic flight from Valera to Barquisimeto. They claimed to have a bomb, and threatened to blow up the aircraft unless the government released 79 "political prisoners," including the leading leftist guerrillas in captivity.

The plane was ordered first to Curacao, where it refueled, then to Panama City, where five passengers were allowed to deplane, and then to Merida, on the Yucatan peninsula in Mexico. It continued early May 19 to Mexico City, where an official told the hijackers the Venezuelan government refused to discuss their demands.

The Mexican official, Miguel Nazar, persuaded the guerrillas not to destroy the plane and offered them either political asylum in Mexico or whatever assistance they needed to reach Cuba. They chose the latter, and the plane, with Nazar aboard, proceeded to Havana, where the hijackers were taken into custody by Cuban police. The plane and passengers were returned to Venezuela May 20.

Other Refugees

Burma

Moslems Flee to Bangladesh. About 70,000 Moslems had fled from Burma to neighboring Bangladesh in the previous three weeks, Bangladesh authorities reported April 30, 1978. Burma said the refugees were Bengalis who wanted to escape from officials investigating illegal immigrants from Bangladesh. The Moslems claimed they were driven out by Burmese forces at gunpoint and had been subjected to torture, rape and robbery.

More than 18,000 had entered Bangladesh since April 29 despite efforts by Bangladesh forces to seal the border. Many others had been turned back.

Bangladesh had expressed concern to Burma over the plight of what it termed "Burmese nationals." Dacca contended that the Moslems had been living in what was now Burma for generations.

The Moslem refugee exodus from Burma had risen to about 100,000, according to Bangladesh estimates reported May 10. Meanwhile, Burmese government-owned newspapers that day denied foreign reports that the Burmese army had waged a campaign of extermination against the Moslems.

The U.N. High Commissioner, requesting aid for the refugees, said in early June:

Since March 1978, refugees from the Arakan state of Burma have been crossing the border into Bangladesh. The main influx began in the second half of April. According to recent estimates by the local authorities, there are now some 150,000 arrivals, of whom 113,000 have been given shelter in eight camps. The remainder are awaiting registration for their entry into the camps. The influx of persons crossing the border continues and the Government fears their number is likely soon to reach 200,000. Almost half of the arrivals are under 15 years of age. Living conditions are extremely difficult and urgent action is required, particularly as pre-monsoon rains have already started in the area.

Cyprus

280,000 refugees. The Turkish invasion of Cyprus in July 1974 resulted in the reported "expulsion" of 200,000 Greek Cypriots and 80,000 Turkish Cypriots from more than 142 villages and from Famagusta, Kyrenia and Morphou. It was reported that by June 1977, acceptable accommodations in new settlements had been provided for only 51,666 of the refugees.

Netherlands

A sizable community of South Moluccan refugees has been living in the Netherlands for decades since their formerly Dutch-ruled homeland became part of Indonesia. In the 1970s some members of the community resorted to terrorism to publicize their demands for independence.

2 terrorist strikes in 1975. Two groups of South Moluccans, demanding independence for their homeland from Indonesia, Dec. 2 and Dec. 4, 1975 staged separate terrorist attacks in the Netherlands to dramatize their cause. In the first incident, seven armed South Moluccans Dec. 2 seized a train bound for Amsterdam near the small town of Beilin, killed two people in the takeover and held hostage 50 others. In the second, two days later, another group of seven gunmen Dec. 4 entered the Indonesian consulate in Amsterdam and imprisoned 30, including 16 children.

Both attacks were widely seen to be extensions of recent radical activity among the 35,000 South Moluccans living in the Netherlands. The radicals, for the most part Dutch-born children of natives of the Moluccas, once known as the Spice Islands, asserted that the Dutch had failed to fulfill alleged promises of independence when it allowed Indonesia to take over the territory in 1950.

The Dutch government Dec. 2 dispatched a special tactical force of marines to Beilin.

The South Moluccans on the Beilin train Dec. 3 threatened further violence against the passengers if they were not provided with transportation out of the country to an unspecified destination. One hostage Dec. 3 who had attempted to flee was killed.

In a note released Dec. 3 shortly after the killing, the gunmen, who called themselves the Free South Moluccan Youths, called on the Dutch government to release from prison all South Moluccans held on charges of terrorism.

Moderate leaders of the South Moluccan independence movement Dec. 4 failed in repeated attempts to get the train hijackers to surrender to the authorities.

Mediation attempts in Amsterdam by the Rev. Semuel Metiari, a spiritual leader of the South Moluccan community, Dec. 5 were successful in obtaining the release of all but four children held in the Indonesian consulate. But at Beilin an unexplained explosion ripped through a section of the Beilin train Dec. 5, seriously injuring one of the hijackers. With two other hostages, he was lowered from the train and taken to the hospital.

The five gunmen who held the consulate Dec. 10 issued a set of demands to the Indonesian government. The note, presented to an Indonesian diplomat, called for a Geneva summit between President Suharto of Indonesia and Johannes A. Manusama, the leader of one of the exile groups, to discuss South Moluccan independence.

The Beilin siege Dec. 14 ended when the six South Moluccan hijackers surrendered to police.

Minister of Justice Andreas A. M. van Agt Dec. 14 said at a news conference that the government had conceded nothing to the terrorists.

The consulate siege ended Dec. 19 when the seven South Moluccan gunmen there surrendered to Johannes Manusama.

In the trial of those who had captured the Indonesian consulate, all seven pleaded guilty to charges of illegal possession of weapons and kidnapping.

The seven terrorists who had seized the train were convicted March 26, 1976 of murder and manslaughter. All were sentenced to 14-year prison terms.

During the trial, held March 10–12, the South Moluccans did not contest any of the government's charges, but sought to emphasize that their acts were political, and not criminal, in motivation.

They were sentenced April 8 to six-year prison terms.

2 strikes in '77. Two groups of South Moluccans May 23, 1977 seized fifty persons on a train and 105 children and their six teachers in an elementary school. The coordinated actions took place about the same time near the north Holland town of Groningen.

Six terrorists held the children captive in the school in Bovensmilde while seven others, including two women, held the passengers on a train between Assen and Groningen.

In addition to surrounding the sites where the hostages were held, Dutch security forces were positioned to prevent retaliation against the South Moluccan community by Dutch citizens aroused by the terrorists' actions.

The terrorists were overpowered by Dutch marines who attacked the train and school June 11.

Six of the terrorists and two of the hostages on the train were killed in the assault. Seven passengers were wounded, two seriously, while one hijacker and two marines also were hurt. Two other hijackers on the train were captured.

There were no casualties in the school, where four teachers had been held by four gunmen. The 106 children taken hostage at the school had been released May 27, along with one teacher, after a virus infection swept through the hostages.

The action was taken after mediation efforts had failed and psychiatric advisers had warned the government that the hostages had reached the limit of stress they could safely endure. Prime Minister Joop den Uyl admitted that the government also had been pressured by public opinion. The Dutch public reportedly believed the terrorists had not been dealt with firmly enough and that strong action was needed.

Dutch authorities admitted earlier that the terrorists at the Assen train site were smarter and tougher than those who had made previous attacks in the Netherlands. Psychiatrists had no success with the methods of mental pressure that had caused the gunmen in the 1975 hijacking to surrender. The Moluccan professionalism led Dutch authorities to believe that the terrorists, particularly Max Papilaya, the leader who was killed in the attack, had received training from terrorists outside the country.

The two leaders of the South Moluccan community who had attempted to mediate between the terrorists and the government, were critical of the efforts to negotiate a solution. Hassan Tan and Josine Soumokil said June 9 that their efforts had been "a complete failure." Tan said he had gone to the train with no government concessions and "in the light of the situation, given the stubborn position on both sides, the Netherlands and the South Moluccan people must know how fatal the effects . . . can be."

A Dutch court Sept. 22 sentenced seven of the terrorists to prison terms of six to nine years, and an eighth was given a one-year term for helping plan the operation.

Rioting had broken out Sept. 7 and continued throughout the next day. Gangs of Moluccan youths rampaged through Assen, setting fire to two empty schools and a Red Cross station. They shot at firemen trying to fight the blazes and wounded one policeman.

The youths returned to the Moluccan districts of Assen and Bovensmilde and barricaded the roads that led inside. About 100 riot police attempted to break through the barricades Sept. 9 to search for weapons, but were driven back by machine gun fire.

Police also fought Sept. 9 with Moluccan youths at Krimpen Aan de Ijssel, near Rotterdam, about 100 miles south of Assen.

Dutch police and military units staged a massive raid on Moluccan homes in Assen and Bovensmilde Sept. 10 in another search for weapons. The police used armored cars, dogs and metal detectors in their search, which included the entire community rather than just the homes of known militants. Police found machine guns, pistols, ammunition, clubs and fire-bombs. Thirty-two arrests were made and a plan to seize more hostages reportedly was found by police.

1978 developments. Theo Kuhuwael, a South Moluccan leader who had tried to mediate some of the terrorist incidents involving young Moluccans in the Netherlands, was shot and wounded by two South Moluccans Jan. 29. Kuhuwael was considered the "education minister" in the exiled South Moluccan Republic government headed by Johannes Manusama.

A special anti-terrorist unit of Dutch marines stormed a government building in Assen March 14 to free 70 hostages who had been held by three South Moluccan terrorists since the previous day. Six hostages were wounded in the exchange of fire during the marines' assault.

The incident began March 13 when the three militant South Moluccans entered the building, which housed the Drenthe provincial government offices, and seized 71 employees as hostages. About 200 workers in the building managed to escape by jumping out of windows or fleeing through unguarded doors. The remaining 71 were rounded up by the terrorists and held on the ground floor.

During the Moluccans' attack on the building, one person was killed and five were wounded. The dead man was thrown out the window, but because of gunfire from the South Moluccans, authorities were unable to recover the body until the siege ended.

Two leaders of the South Moluccan community in Holland agreed to act as mediators at the terrorists' request. They entered the building for a two-hour meeting with the gunmen March 14 and managed to secure the release of one of the female hostages, which brought the total held by the Moluccans down to 70.

Justice Minister Jacob de Ruiter said that the decision to attack the Moluccans followed a phone call from the terrorists in which they gave the government 30 minutes to comply with their demands. De Ruiter said the time was too short to accomplish anything through negotiations. The terrorists had threatened to kill two hostages every half hour after the deadline had expired until the government agreed to their demands.

Premier Andreas van Agt reported to parliament March 14 that he regretted that it had proved necessary to use force to end the siege, but that a delay would have endangered the hostages. Van Agt also asked the Dutch public not to judge the rest of the Moluccan community by the acts of a few militants.

India, Pakistan & Bangladesh

The eastern section of Pakistan rebelled in March 1971. By the end of the year, it had achieved independence as the republic of Bangladesh (or Bangla Desh). The bloody fighting uprooted 10 million or more East Pakistanis, many of whom took refuge in India.

India seeks refugee aid. India appealed to the U.N. April 22, 1971 to provide assistance for the thousands of persons who had fled into India to escape the fighting in East Pakistan.

The West Bengal State government reported April 22 that cholera and smallpox had broken out among the refugees.

India warned Pakistan May 14 that the influx of so many refugees could endanger peace in south Asia. According to official Indian estimates, the number totaled 2.6 million.·

A Foreign Ministry note handed the Pakistan High Commission in New Delhi (made public May 15) declared: "This deliberate expulsion of such large numbers of people from their homes has created a human problem of unparalleled magnitude which is capable of producing serious repercussions in the area, leading to a threat to peace in the region."

India charged that the East Pakistanis were "forced to flee from their homes and to take shelter in the adjoining areas of India" because "of a deliberate campaign of terror launched against them by the armed forces of Pakistan."

A spokesman for the Indian Rehabilitation Ministry charged May 15 that the refugee movement was taking on religious overtones. He said that "in recent weeks, more Hindus were being squeezed out of East Pakistan." The Pakistani army's objective, the spokesman claimed, was to rid East Pakistan of its nine million non-Moslems and to reduce the population disparity between the eastern and western wings of the predominantly Moslem country.

Indian Health Minister Uma Shankar Dixit reported to parliament June 7 that as of June 4 the East Pakistani influx totaled 4,738,054 and was growing. He said the cholera death toll had reached 1,250 with another 9,500 East Pakistanis hospitalized. (Informed sources in Calcutta had reported June 5 that about 8,000 refugees had died of the disease. The World Health Organization in Geneva June 7 placed the death toll at 3,000.)

Dixit said 2,722,561 refugees were inhabiting camps in the Indian states of West Bengal, Assam, Bihar and the territories of Meghalaya and Tripura. In addition, 2,015,493 were living outside camps, largely sleeping in the open, he said. Parliament had convened in special session to consider the cholera outbreak.

India had appealed May 31 for international assistance to help it combat the cholera outbreak and to cope with the refugee problem in general. Various governments and private charitable organizations were reported June 8 to have responded by providing or pledging to donate food, medicine, clothing and funds for the millions of East Pakistani refugees. Among the parties involved in the relief mission were Britain, the U.S., West Germany, Denmark, Japan, Canada, Sweden and the Red Cross societies in Belgium, Finland and Norway.

An Indian health official in the Nadia district of West Bengal State said June 5 that "there is growing evidence that the cholera epidemic is raging on the other side of the border" in East Pakistan, where medical facilities were said to be virtually nonexistent. Meanwhile, Indian border security forces June 5 sealed off the frontier in the Nadia district where cholera victims had been crossing into India in the past few days.

Indian police intervened June 8 to prevent a clash between East Pakistani refugees and Indian residents at Barasat, 15 miles north of Calcutta. Moslems reacted violently when some of the 200,000 refugees in the town of 90,000 set up camp in their mosques as well as other public buildings in Barasat.

By mid-October, New Delhi was estimating the number of refugees at 9.4 million.

India gets refugee aid. A 13-nation consortium agreed at an emergency meeting in Paris Oct. 26, 1971 to give to India a "substantial part" of the estimated $700 million for relief of the nearly 10 million East Pakistani refugees in India until March 1972. The meeting was held under the auspices of the World Bank.

A communique issued by the conferees "noted that worldwide contributions pledged to date came to over $200 million."

The consortium consisted of the U.S., Britain, France, West Germany, Canada, the Netherlands, Belgium, Norway, Sweden, Denmark, Italy, Japan and Austria.

(The U.S. Congress March 2, 1972 appropriated another $200 million for the relief of Bangla Desh refugees.)

India sets refugee return. India announced plans Dec. 23, 1971 to repatriate the Pakistani refugees. At a Dec. 20 meeting of Indian and Bangla Desh officials, India agreed to provide all of the transportation and materials needed to transfer the refugees to transit camps in Bangla Desh. Thus far about 130,000 refugees had returned to their homes in Bangla Desh since the war's end.

West Pakistan refugees. International relief officials in Rawalpindi were reported Feb. 5, 1972 to estimate that December 1971 warfare between Pakistan and India had created at least a half million West Pakistani refugees in the fighting. The displaced persons had come from the Punjab region where Indian troops had seized 850 villages. Pakistani officials declined to publicly discuss the problem, but the Rawalpindi government was said to be providing relief to the refugees who had been dispersed over wide areas into the homes of relatives and strangers behind the Indian-Pakistani front lines.

Last refugee camp closes. The last camp in India for Bangla Desh refugees closed March 25, 1972. A train carrying 4,000 Bengalis left the camp for Bangla Desh. Virtually all the 10 million Bengalis who had fled to India in 1971 had returned. According to the Indian Labor and Rehabilitation Ministry, an estimated 60,000 Bengalis remained in India with friends and relatives.

Taiwan

Chiang's son shot at in U.S. Nationalist Chinese Deputy Premier Chiang Ching-kuo returned to Taiwan May 1, 1970 after a visit to the U.S. during which he narrowly escaped assassination by Taiwanese refugees.

Chiang was shot at but missed by a Taiwanese as he entered New York City's Plaza Hotel April 24 to address the Far East-America Council of Commerce and Industry. The gunman, Peter Huang, a member of the World United Formosans for Independence movement, was taken into police custody as was Tzu-tai Cheng, the organization's executive secretary.

Huang and Cheng were convicted of attempted murder but both fled while free on bail. Cheng was ultimately extradited from Britain.

Peng flees. Government sources in Taipei confirmed Jan. 24, 1970 that Peng Ming-min, a leader of the Taiwan independence movement, recently had fled Nationalist China and was living in Sweden. Peng, 46, a former chairman of the Political Science Department at Taiwan University, had been sentenced in 1964 to eight years in jail for allegedly attempting to overthrow the government; he was released after serving 13 months. Since then, he had been under close surveillance. Peng's organization, the World United Formosans for Independence, had advocated that Taiwan be ruled by native-born Taiwanese who constituted 85% of the island's 13.7 million population.

Peng was granted political asylum in Sweden Jan. 30.

Defectors in Peking. Sun Chi-chou, third secretary of Nationalist China's embassy in Senagal, arrived in Peking March 13, 1971 following his defection from his diplomatic post earlier in March. The Chinese news agency Hsinhua said Sun had arrived in Peking by plane after "crossing over to the motherland on March 5 in Geneva on his way from Dakar to Saigon."

Another defector was reported to have reached Peking Sept. 6.

Hsinhua identified the defector as Chang Shuang-chao and said he was a confidential secretary of the Taiwan provincial Department of Finance. Nationalist sources in Hong Kong said Chang was only a minor official and his defection was of no importance.

Index

A

AARON, David—133
ABRAHAM, Eric—62
ABU Gharbiyah, Bahjat—114
ACHEAMPONG, Col. Ignatius Kutu—74–5
ADEMOLA, Sir Adetokunbo—36–7
AFANASIEV, Valery—124
AFRICA—3, 28, 31–75. See also specific
  country
AFRICAN National Council (ANC)—51
AGENCY for International Development
  (AID) (U.S.)—9–13, 31, 60
AHMED, Eqbal—154
AIRCRAFT Hijacking—79, 94–7, 101, 113,
  116–8, 136, 141–5, 164
AKUFFO, Lt. Col. Fred—75
ALAMI, Ragheb el—95
AL ASIFAH (Storm) (PLO guerrilla
  group)—76
ALBERT, Vaclav—136
ALDUNATE, Ferreira—164
ALEXANDROVICH, Ruth—120
ALEXEYEVA, Judmila—130
AL FATAH (PLO guerrilla group)—76–7,
  83–4, 89–92, 99, 109, 112–5
ALGERIA—31, 75, 79
ALLENDE, Hortensia Bussi de—151, 153
ALLENDE Gossens, Salvador—149
ALLILUYEVA, Svetlana—118
ALONSO Freiria, Mrs. Consuelo—151
ALPHA 66 (anti-Castro group)—154–5
AL SAIQAH (Lightning) (PLO guerrilla
  group)—76, 86–8, 90, 109
ALTMAN, Anatoly—117, 133
ALVA Orlandini, Javier—161
AMALRIK, Andrei—128

AMERICAN Council for Nationalities Ser-
  vice—23
AMERICAN Friends Service Committee—9
AMERICAN Fund for Czech Refugees—23
AMERICAN Jewish Committee—34
AMIN, Idi—64–70, 130
AMNESTY International (AI)—147–8, 161
ANDERSSON, Sven—151
ANGOLA—31–2, 61. Map—40
ARABS & Arab States—2, 4, 76–115. See
  also specific individual, group or country
ARAFAT, Yasser—80, 89, 91, 99, 102–5,
  111–2
ARGENTINA—119, 146–8, 150, 163
ARGENTINE Anti-Communist Alliance
  (AAA) (secret police force)—146
ARIAS Stella, Javier—161
ARISMENDI, Rodney—163
ARKANSAS—22
ASSAD, Hafez al-—110, 112
ASSOCIATION of Southeast Asian Na-
  tions—18
AUSTRALIA—15, 30, 66, 124–5, 248
AUSTRIA—2, 122–3, 169
AZBEL, Mar—130

B

BABCHIN, Alexander—121
BACHELET, Angela—153
BACHELET, Micaela—153
BACHMAN, Maria Elena—153
BAGHIR, Mohammed el—99
BAKR, Ibrahim—81
BALIDAWA, Charles—68
BANDA, Hastings—75

BANGLADESH—165, 168–9
BANKOV, Stefan—134
BANTE, Brig. Gen. Teferi—46
BANZER, Hugo—148–9
BAOUD, Abu—99
BARNET, Richard—153–4
BARRE, Mohamed Siad—49
BARRETO, Rosario—147
BARSHAI, Rudolf—130
BARTOS, Ladislaw—136
BARYSHNIKOV, Mikhail—124
BARZICO, Miro—143
BATLLE, Jorge—163
BECERRA, Fran Lin—163
BECKER, Henning—24
BEGIN, Menahem—114
BELAUNDE Terry, Fernando—161–2
BELAUNDE Terry, Francisco—161–2
BELENKO, Lt. Viktor Ivanovich—128–9
BELGIUM—72–3, 125, 153, 169
BELL, Griffin B.—29
BENEDETTI, Mario—146
BENES, Bernardo—156
BENZA Chacon, Manuel—162
BERLIN, Christina—124
BIAFRA—32–7
BIERMANN, Wolf—140
BLACK June Movement—112
BLACK September (PLO guerrilla
    group)—98
BLAKE, Dr. Eugene Carson—33
BOCEK, Karel—137
BODNER, Guillermo—163
BODNYA, Mendel—117
BOELL (or Boll), Heinrich—1, 123
BOGUSLAVSKY, Viktor N.—117
BOLIVIA—148–9, 161
BOLL (or Boell), Heinrich—1, 123
BOLSHEVIK Revolution (1917)—1
BOLSHOI Ballet—124
BONGO, Omar—74
BOTHA, Pieter—39–40, 63
BOTSWANA—31, 61
BOTTINI, Federico—164
BRACHO Campos, Jose—159
BRAJKOWIC, Andjelko—143
BRANDT, Willy—150
BRAY 3d, Charles W.—67, 119
BRAZINSKAS, Algirdas—117–8
BRAZINSKAS, Pranas S.—117–8
BREZHNEV, Leonid I.—121–2, 131–2
BRODSKY, Iosif A.—120
BROWN, L. Dean—18, 21
BROWN Jr., Gov. Edmund G. (Calif.)—20
BRZEZINSKI, Zbigniew—133
BUBLIK, Viktor—132
BUKOVSKY, Vladimir—129
BULGARIA—133–4
BURMA—165

BURUNDI—31–2, 42–5
BUSIA, Kofi A.—75
BUSIC, Julienne—145
BUSIC, Zvonko—145
BUTMAN, Gilya I.—117
BUTMAN, Hillel—133

C

CABIESES, Manuel—153
CALIFORNIA—23
CAMBODIA—3–4, 6–11, 14, 16, 19, 22–6, 28
CAMERON, Clyde—125
CAMEROON—31
CANADA—25, 29–30, 66, 124, 128, 137, 151,
    169
CARDOSO Amaral, Lt. Col. Fernando—38
CARITAS Catholica—125
CARITAS International—43
CARMONA, Ernesto—146
CARR, Robert—65
CARTER, Jimmy—23
CASTILLO, Jose Maria—159
CASTREGON Diez, Dr. Jaime—159
CASTRO, Fidel—2, 154–6
CATHOLIC Church, Roman—20, 23, 34, 43,
    141, 159–60
CATHOLIC Conference, U.S.—20, 23
CATHOLIC Relief Services (U.S.)—34, 43
CENTRAL Intelligence Agency (CIA)—9,
    130, 155
CHALIDZE, Valery N.—120–1
CHATTI, Habib—101–2
CHEBOTAREV, Anatoly K.—119
CHERNE, Leo—31–2
CHERNOGLAZ, David—117
CHERNYAYEV, Rudolf—133
CHIANG Ching-kuo—170
CHIGOWE, Tyupo Shumba—52
CHIKEREMA, James—50
CHILE—129, 146–53, 162
CHINA—2, 28, 134–5, 170
CHITEPO, Herbert—51–2
CHONCHOL, Jacques—152
CHRISTIAN Phalangist Party—107–8
CHUNG Shi-jung—134
CIHAC, Vaclav—136
CIVIL Operations & Rural Development
    Support Organization—9
CLARK, Bronson P.—9
COHRS, Eberhard—141
COLBY, William E.—10
COLOMBIA—150, 157, 160
COLONIALISM—3
COMMUNIST Countries—2, 6–30, 116–45,
    151, 163. See also specific country
CONFESSION, The (book)—137

CONGOLESE National Liberation Front
(FLNC) (Zairian guerrilla group)—70–2
CONNECTICUT—22
CONTRERAS, Miriam—152
CORDOVA-Claure, Ted—149
CORVALAN, Luis—129
COSTA Rica—153, 160–1
CRANSTON, Sen. Alan (D, Calif.)—20
CROATIANS—143–5
CROSLAND, Anthony—54
CUBA—2, 48, 149, 151, 154–6, 159, 164
CUESTA Valle, Antonio—156
CULTURE Preservation (Vietnamese refu-
gee group)—23
CUNNINGHAM, Charles—66
CYPRUS—165–6
CZECHOSLOVAKIA—122, 135–8

D

DABEMEYE, Lt. Col. Thomas—43
DAN, Pham Quang—8, 14
DAOUD, Abu (Mohammed Daoud Au-
deh)—94, 113–4
DAPCEVIC, Vladimir—144
DAVIDSON, Ronald—1–6
DAYAN, Moshe—101
De GUIRINGAUD, Louis—73
DELLEPIANE Ocampo, Jorge—162
DENMARK—24, 120, 142, 169
DERBINOV, Yuri—118
DEUTSCHLAND, Neues—138
De WET, Jennie—62
DIMITRIU, Victor—143
DINA (Chilean secret police agency)—153
DIXIT, Uma Shankar—168–9
DJERMAKOYE, Issoufou—44
DJIBOUTI—31, 45–9. Map—47
DOBRYNIN, Anatoly—131, 133
DOLEZAL, Karel—136
DOUGLAS-Home, Sir Alec—66
DREIZNER, Solomon G.—117
DRINAN, Rep. Robert F. (D, Mass.)—161
DUBE, John—61
DULZIN, Arye—132
DUMITRACHESCU, Constantin—143
DUVALIER, Jean-Claude—158
DYMSHITS, Mark Y.—117, 133

E

EAST African Community (EAC)—68
ECHEVERRIA Alvarez, Luis—159
ECKERT-Schweitzer, Mrs. Rhena—34
ECUADOR—156–7
EDDEN, Mike—54
EDELSTAM, Harald—151

EFFIONG, Maj. Gen. Philip—35
EGYPT—31, 109, 112
EILBERG, Rep. Joshua—116
EL AL (Israeli airlines)—79–80, 94–5, 97
ELIFAS, Philemon—62
EL SALVADOR—161
ENGER, Valdik—133
EQUATORIAL Guinea—31–2
ERCILIA Fernandez, Mirta—151
ERITREAN Liberation Front (ELF) (anti-
Ethiopian guerrilla group)—45, 49
ERITREAN People's Liberation Front
(EPLF) (anti-Ethiopian guerrilla
group)—49
ESPINOSA, Edgardo Enriquez—147
ETHIOPIA—31, 45–9. Map—46
EUROPE—1–4, 31, 80, 123
EUROPE, Council of—123
EUROPEAN Migration, Intergovernmental
Committee on—23, 123, 150–1, 153
EUSTIS, Comdr. Ralph W.—118

F

FAHOUM, Khaled—114
FAINBERG, Viktor—127
FAMINE—32–8
FAN Yuan-yen—135
FEDICHEVA, Kaleriya—126
FEDOSEYEV, Anatoly—119
FEIGIN, Maj. Grisha—119–20
FERREIRA Aldunate, Wilson—147, 163
FERREYROS, Carlos Enrique—162
FIGUEROA, Leonidas Rodriguez—162
FINAL, Punto—153
FINLAND—122
FORBES, James—66
FORD, Gerald R.—11–2, 17, 19
FRANCE—2, 29–30, 71–3, 103, 113–4, 125,
151–3, 160, 169
FRANCO, Francisco—2
FRANJIEY, Suleiman—111
FREY, Rep. Lou (R, Fla.)—123
FRIEDMAN, Martin—126
FRONT for the Liberation of Mozambique
(FRELIMO) (guerrilla group)—41–2
FRONT for the Liberation of Zimbabwe
(Frolizi) (guerrilla group)—50–1
FRUMAN, Naum—119
FYODOROV, Yuri P.—116–7

G

GABON—31
GABRE, Kebede—50
GABRYEL, Ryszard—142
GALER, Noel A. M.—17
GALICH, Alexander—124

GALISHNIKOV, Yuri—120–1
GALLARDO, Jorge—149
GALLARDO, Col. Samuel—149
GALPERIN, Alexander—117
GAPONOV, Boris—120
GARBA, Joseph—59
GARETON, Oscar—150
GAZA Strip—4, 76, 95–6, 99
GEMAYEL, Amin—108
GERMAN Democratic Republic (East Germany)—2, 138–41, 151–2
GERMANY—1–2
GERMANY, Federal Republic of (West Germany)—2, 29–30, 66, 80, 94, 96–8, 101, 113–4, 122–3, 125, 136–42, 150, 153, 169
GHARBIYAH, Bahjat Abu—114
GHORRA, Edouard—112
GINLOV, Nikolai—118
GINZBURG, Alexander—130, 132–3
GINZBURG, Irina—130
GLAZER, Alexander—126
GOKHSHTEIN, Anatoly—121
GOLDFELD, Anatoly—117
GOLDSTUECKER, Eduard—137
GOMA, Paul—143
GOWON, Maj. Gen. Yakubu—35
GREAT Britain—15, 65–7, 94–5, 102–3, 118–9, 124, 134–5, 169
GREECE—79–80
GREENHILL, Sir Denis—119
GREENWOOD, Ivor—144
GRIGORENKO, Gen. Pyotr—131
GRODETZKY, Yuri—120
GROSS, Ernest—131
GUAM—17–8, 22
GULF Oil Corp.—37
GUR, Lt. Gen. Mordechai—101
GURUZ, Jozsef—141
GUTIERREZ, Nelson—153
GUTIERREZ Mendieta, Jorge—149
GUTIERREZ Ruiz, Hector—147, 162

H

HABBASH, George—80
HAGER, Nina—141
HAILSHAM, Lord—66
HAI Hong (Vietnamese refugee boat)—29
HAITI—157–8
HANFERE, Sultan Ali Mirrah—45
HANZALOVA, Kristina—136
HARALAMBIE, Ivan—128
HART, Sen. Philip A. (D, Mich.)—142
HASHISHA, Zuheir Abou—112
HASNEN, Nabil—112
HASSAN, Ali—115
HAVLICEK, Dusan—136
HEIDRICH, Heinz—139–40

HERRERAS, Casildo—163
HILL, Father Mel—56
HINDI, Sharif Hussein al-—75
HITLER, Adolf—1–2
HOAN, Nguyen Cong—25
HOLTZMAN, Rep. Elizabeth (D, N.Y.)—30
HONDURAS—161
HONG Kong (British Crown Colony)—2, 18, 30, 134–5
HORN of Africa—45–5. Map—46–8. See also specific country
HUEY Fong (Vietnamese refugee boat)—30
HUNGARY—141
HUSAK, Gustav—137
HUSSEIN, King—82–4, 86–94

I

IAWNICKI, Zbigniew—142
IMMIGRATION & Naturalization Service (U.S.)—158
INDIA—2, 168–9
INDOCHINESE Refugees—3–4, 6–30. See also specific country
INDONESIA—166
INTERGOVERNMENTAL Committee for European Migration—23, 123, 150–1, 153
INTERNATIONAL Council of Churches—20
INTERNATIONAL Human Rights Commission—157
INTERNATIONAL Jurists Commission—157
INTERNATIONAL Rescue Committee—23, 31–2
IRAN—128
IRAQ—80–1, 86, 112
ISAKOVA, Nina—117
ISHON (Soviet trawler)—120
ISLAMABAD, Pakistan—112
ISRAEL—2, 25, 30, 76, 79–80, 97–8, 100–2, 113–6, 119–27, 130–3, 142–3
ITAKA, Boris—130
ITALY—1–2, 33, 99–100, 112, 125, 153, 169
IVANOV, Alexander—120

J

JALLOUD, Abdel Salam—111
JAPAN—26, 97, 169
JARA, Jose Maria de la—161
JEHOVAH'S Witnesses—75
JERUSALEM—102
JEWISH Agency—122
JEWS—1–2, 76. Soviet Jewry—116–33

JOHNSON, Lyndon B.—34
JORDAN—4, 76, 80, 82–94
JUMBLATT, Kamal—82–3

K

KADDOUMI (or Khaddoumi), Farouk—109, 111
KAFUMUKACHA, Samuel—75
KAMINSKY, Lassal S.—117
KARAMI, Rashid—81–2
KATS, Boris—132
KATS, Natalya—132
KATZ-Suchy, Julius—141–2
KAUNDA, Kenneth—53, 59, 66
KEELEY, Robert V.—22
KEHL, Gustav—101
KENNEDY, Sen. Edward M. (D, Mass.)—4–5, 8–11, 19–22, 34, 43–4, 60, 132, 150
KENNEDY, Robert F.—9
KENYA—28, 31, 65, 113
KENYATTA, Jomo—65
KHADDAM, Abdel Halim—111
KHADDOUMI (or Kaddoumi), Farouk—109, 111
KHALED Ibn Walid (PLO guerrilla group)—76
KHALID, King (Saudi Arabia)—112
KHAMA, Seretse—53, 56
KHNOKH, Leib G.—117, 133
KHODOROVICH, Tatyana—130
KHOLY, Hassan Sabry el- —111
KIRKLEY, Leslie—33
KIROV Ballet—118, 126
KIRSCH, Sarah—140
KISSINGER, Henry A.—17, 121, 125
KIZHNER, Harry—117
KLEINDIENST, Richard G.—67
KNOX, Clinton E.—158
KOMAR, Vitaly—130
KONDRASHIN, Kirill—132
KORCHNOI, Viktor—128
KOREA—2, 18
KORENBLIT, Lev L.—117
KORENBLIT, Mikhail L.—117
KORENBLIT, Valery—121
KORN, David—120
KOSTANTINOV, Lev—127
KOSTOV, Vladimir Borisov—133
KOSYGIN, Alexei N.—119–20, 124
KREISKY, Bruno—122–3
KRUMLOV, Cesky—139
KUDIRKA, Simas—118
KUNDA, Kenneth—52
KUNZE, Reiner—141
KURCHENKO, Nadezhda—118

KUWAIT—100, 112
KUZNETSOV, Eduard S.—116–7, 133
KUZNETSOV, Silva Zalmanson—116–7, 124, 133
KY, Nguyen Cao—8
KYEMBA, Henry—67

L

LEAGUE of Nations—2
LEBANON—4, 76, 81–3, 96, 107–15
LEBER, Georg—97
LECHIN Oquendo, Juan—149
LEIGHTON, Bernardo—154
LEMO, Marinko—143
LENZLINGER, Hans—140
LEONHARDY, Terrance G.—159
LERCH, Antonin—136
LESINSKIS, Imant—132
LETELIER, Isabel—154
LETELIER, Orlando—153–4
LEVICH, Benjamin—132
LEVIT, Semyon—117
LEVITIN-Krasnov, Anatoly—124
LIBEROFF, Miguel—147
LITERATURNAYA Gazeta (Soviet newspaper)—127
LITVINOV, Pavel—124
LONDON, Arthur—137
LOUIS, Victor—121
LUFTHANSA (West German airlines)—96–7, 99–100
LULE, Godfrey—67–8, 70
LUTHERAN Immigration & Refugee Service—23
LUXEMBOURG—153

M

MAARIV (Israeli newspaper)—119
MACAO (Portuguese colony)—134
MACEO Brigade, Antonio (Cuban exile group)—156
MACHEL, Samora M.—53
MACKELLAR, Michael—26
MACONDES, Regina—147
MADEKUROZWA, Edgar—52
MAHDI, Sadik al- —75
MAKAROVA, Natalya—118–9
MALAYSIA—25–6, 29
MALECELA, John—44
MALEK, Maj. Fouad—111
MANUSAMA, Johannes—166
MAPS—27, 40, 46–8
MARIAN, Lt. Col. Mengistu Haile—46

MARKA (Peruvian magazine)—162
MARKOV, Georgi—133-4
MARSTON, Edward—66
MARTIN, Graham A.—14, 19
MASWANYA, Saidi—66
MATANIC, Peter—145
McCLELLAN, Sen. John L. (D, Ark.)—18
McCLOSKEY, Rep. Paul N. (R, Calif.)—10
McGOVERN, Sen. George (D, S.D.)—21
MEDVEDEV, Zhores A.—121
MEEKER, Barry—139
MEKASHA, Getachew—47
MELAMID, Alexander—130
MENDELEVICH, Iosif M.—117
MENDEZ, Aparicio—163
MESSMER, Pierre—151
METIARI, Rev. Semuel—166
MEXICO—150, 153, 159-60, 163
MICHELINI, Margarita—148
MICHELINI, Zelmar—147
MICOMBERO, Col. Michel—42
MIDDLE East Wars—2, 4. See also specific
    country
MIDDLEKOOP, Dr. Herman—33
MILICEVIC, Stanislav—143
MILNER, Aaron—51
MINDSZENTY, Jozsef Cardinal—141
MLADEK, Jiri—135
MOBUTU Sese Seko—70-4
MOFFITT, Michael—153
MOFFITT, Ronni Karpen—153
MOGILEVER, Vladimir O.—117
MOI, Daniel Arap—65
MOISEYEV Ballet—119
MONTIEL Arguello, Alejandro—159
MOOSE, Richard—49
MORMON Church—20
MOROZ, Valentin—133
MOSLEMS—108-12, 165
MOZAMBIQUE—31-2, 41-2, 50-1, 56, 61
MOZAMBIQUE Liberation Front (FRELI-
    MO) (guerrilla group)—51
MUGABE, Robert—54-6, 58
MUGHRABI, Dalal—115
MURPHY, Lionel—144
MURZHENKO, Alexander—116-7
MUSSOLINI, Benito—2
MUTESA, Sir Edward—64
MUZOREWA, Bishop Abel—52-4
MWALE, Deacom Dulani—75

N

NAMBA, Daisuke—97
NANSEN, Fridtjof—2
NATIONAL Council of Churches—20

NATIONAL Front for the Liberation of An-
    gola (FNLA) (guerrilla group)—41, 70
NATIONAL Union for the Total Indepen-
    dence of Angola (Unita) (guerrilla
    group)—41
NAVRATILOVA, Martina—137
NAZAR, Miguel—164
NAZARIO Sargen, Andres—155
NAZIS—1
NDHLOVU, Edward—50
NDIZEYE, Charles—42-3
NEDOMANSKY, Vaclav—137
NEGREIROS Criado, Luis—162
NEIZVESTNY, Ernst—127
NEMTSANOV, Sergei—128
NESSEN, Ron—13
NETHANYAHU, Lt. Col. Yehonathan—113
NETHERLANDS—61-2, 80, 114, 150, 153,
    166-8
NETO, Agostinho—32, 41, 53, 71
NEW Jersey—22
NEWSOM, David—29
NEWSWEEK (magazine)—4-5
NEW York—22
NEW Zealand—25
NGHI, Nguyen Van—23
NGUEMA, Macias—74
NHARI, Thomas—52
NIDAL, Abou—112
NIGERIA—32-7
NIMEIRY, Gaafar el- —75
NITSCHE, Hellmuth—140
NITSCHKE, Karl-Heinz—140
NIXON, Richard M.—35-6, 121
NKOMO, Joshua—52-3, 55, 58
NKRUMAH, Kwame—75
NOOTER, Robert H.—10
NORWAY—169
NOVAYA Vremya (Soviet weekly)—125
NUJOMA, Sam—53, 63
NYANDORO, George—50
NYANZI, Semei—67
NYERERE, Julius K.—53, 65-6

O

OBLEDO, Mario—15
OBOTE, Milton—64, 67, 69
OGON, Michael—36
OJOK, Lt. Col. Oyite—64
OKAMOTO, Kozo—97
OLYMPIC Games—97-8, 113
O'NEILL Jr., Rep. Thomas P.—16
ONN, Hussein Bin Dato—29
ORGANIZATION of American States
    (OAS)—147, 157, 161, 163

P

PACEPA, Ion—143
PACHECO Areco, Jorge—163
PACHMAN, Ludek—137
PAKISTAN—2–3, 112, 168–9
PALESTINE—2
PALESTINE Arab Organization (Arab guerrilla group)—85
PALESTINE National Council—103, 114
PALESTINE Liberation Front (Arab guerrilla group)—76–7
PALESTINE Liberation Organization (PLO) (Arab guerrilla group)—76–7, 79–102, 107–15
PALESTINIAN Revolution (Arab guerrilla group)—76–7
PALESTINIAN Revolution, Eagles of the—122
PALESTINIAN Revolutionary Youth Movement (Arab guerrilla group)—77
PALESTINIANS—76–115
PALLAIS Debayle, Luis—160
PANAMA—160
PANOV, Galina—124
PANOV, Valery—124
PAPIASHVILI, Avtandil—130
PARAGUAY—148, 161
PARKER, Daniel—12–3
PASCAL Allende, Andres—153
PASTORA, Eden—161
PASTORA, Edgardo—161
PAUL VI, Pope—33
PELIKAN, Jiri—136–7
PENG Ming-min—170
PENNSYLVANIA—22
PENSON, Boris—117, 133
PEOPLE'S Revolutionary Army (ERP) (Argentine guerrilla group)—147
PEOPLE'S Revolutionary Army (Zero Point) (Venezuelan guerrilla group)—164
PEREDA Asbun, Juan—149
PERELMAN, Viktor—120
PERKINS, Bernard—66
PERU—149, 161–2
PERUVIAN Mine & Metal Workers (FTMMP)—162
PERUVIAN Peasant Federation (CCP)—162
PERUYERO, Jose de—155–6
PHIEU, Tran Ngoc—8
PHILIPPINES—15, 17–8, 30
PLYUSHCH, Leonid—127
POLAND—141–2
POLIKANOV, Sergei—132
POLISH Republic in Exile—142
POLSKY, Victor—124
POPULAR Democratic Front (Arab guerrilla group)—100–1

POPULAR Front for the Liberation of Palestine (PFLP) (Arab guerrilla group)—77, 79–80, 84–5, 94–7, 104, 110, 112–4. General Command—85, 90, 92–3, 100, 102, 104
POPULAR Movement for the Liberation of Angola (MPLA) (guerrilla group)—37, 39–40
POPULAR Struggle Front (Arab guerrilla group)—114
PORTUGAL—37–41
POZDEYEV, Vitaly—118
PRESS Censorship—159, 161
PRYOR, Gov. David (Ark.)—20

Q

QUINTERO de Diaz, Elena—163

R

RABASA, Emilio—153
RABIN, Oskar—131
RABIN, Yitzhak—113
RABINOVICH, David—117
RAMBOUSEK, Otakar—137
RAMOS, Julio—163
RASKIN, Marcus—153
RED Cross, International—15, 24, 33–5, 41, 44, 55, 60, 115, 157, 169
REFUGEES, High Commissioner for (UNHCR)—3–5, 24–5, 28–31, 34, 36, 40–1, 49, 122, 146–8, 150, 161, 165
REFUGEES, International Office for—2
REJECTION Front (Palestinian)—114
RELIEF & Rehabilitation Administration, United Nations (UNRRA)—2–3
REVERDITTO, Carlos—163
REVOLUTIONARY Armed Forces (FAR) (Argentine guerrilla group)—146
REVOLUTIONARY Left Movement (MIR) (Chilean guerrilla group)—153
REVOLUTIONARY Radical Youth (Chile)—152
REYES, Simon—149
RHODESIA (Zimbabwe)—31–2, 42, 50–61
RIPPON, Geoffrey—65
ROBLEDO, Angel—149
RODINO Jr., Rep. Peter W. (D, N.J.)—20
RODRIGUEZ, Guillermo—156–7
ROESCH, Otto—122
ROGER, William P.—44
ROLOVIC, Vladimir—143
ROSEN, Shlomo—123
ROSTROPOVICH, Galina Vishnevskaya—131

ROSTROPOVICH, Mstislav—131
RUCHS, Juergen—140
RUITER, Jacob de—168
RWANDA—31-2

S

SABAH, Sheikh Sabah al-Salem al-—112
SACH, Pham Nam—23
SACHAR, Karel—136
SADAT, Anwar—112
SADRUDDIN Agha Khan, Prince (Iran)—24, 36, 128, 151
SALAMEH, Ali Hassan—115
SALEH, Mahmoud—113
SANCHEZ, Maj. Ruben—149
SANCHEZ Parodi, Ramon—156
SANDANISTA Liberation Front (Nicaraguan guerrilla group)—159-61
SANDOVAL Moron, Edil—149
SARAKIKYA, Maj. Gen. Sam—67
SARKIS, Elias—109, 111-2
SARTAWI, Dr. Isam—76
SAUDI Arabia—98-9, 112
SCALI, John—15
SCANDANAVIAN Airlines System (SAS)—144
SCHMULEW, Derek Paul—61
SCHPETER, Henrich—133
SCHUBERT, Rainer—140
SCHWEITZER, Dr. Albert—34
SEIFFERT, Wolfgang—141
SELASSIE, Emperor Haile—45, 49
SEMIRAMIS, Hotel (Damascus, Syria)—111
SENEGAL—31
SEVILLE Sacasa, Guillermo—159
SHCHARANSKY, Anatoly—130
SHELTON, Turner—159
SHEVCHENKO, Arkady—131-2
SHIKUKU, Martin—65
SHIPANGA, Andreas—63
SHTERN, Dr. Mikhail—130
SHUMLIN, Boris T.—126-7
SHUR, Gilel—117
SIERRA, Julian—162
SIK, Ota—136-7
SIKES, Rep. Robert L. F. (D, Fla.)—18
SILIPPOV, Alexander—119
SILVA Cardoso, Brig. Gen. Antonio da—38
SIMBANANIYE, Artemon—44
SIMEONOV, Vladimir—134
SIMOKAITIS, Grazina—118
SIMOKAITIS, Vitautas—118
SINGAPORE—2
SINGH, Surendra Pal—65
SINYAVSKY, Andrei—122
SITHOLE, Rev. Ndabaningi—52, 54, 58

SIWELA, Shelton—50
SMIRNOVSKY, Mikhail N.—119
SMITH, Ian—52-5
SOLOVYOV, Vladimir—130
SOLOVYOV, Yelena Klepikova—130
SOLZHENITSYN, Alexander—123-4
SOMALIA—31, 45-9
SOMOZA, Anastasio—160-1
SOMOZA Obregon, Jose—160
SOUMOKIL, Josine—167
SOVIET Union—See UNION of Soviet Socialist Republics
SOUTH Africa—31-2, 39-41, 61-4
SOUTHEAST Asia—3-4, 6-30. See also specific country
SOUTH-West Africa (Namibia)—31, 39-41, 61-4
SOUTH-West Africa People's Organization (SWAPO) (guerrilla group)—62-3
SPAIN—1-2, 144, 153
STANGE, Jurgen—140
STILBANS, Viktor—117
STROESSNER, Alfredo—161
STROUGAL, Lubomir—137
SUAREZ de la Paz, Ismael—155
SUDAN—31, 49, 64, 75, 98-9. Map—48
SUGIZAKI, Jiro—97
SULEIMAN, Maher H.—79-80
SULLIVAN, William H.—10
SULSIENE, Marija—118
SUN Chi-chou—170
SUNG, Vo Van—28
SUN Luck (Vietnamese refugee boat)—30
SUTEP (Peruvian teachers' union)—162
SVICHINSKY, Vitaly—119
SVITAK, Ivan—136-7
SVOBODA, Ludvig—137
SWAZILAND—61
SWEDEN—132, 136, 143, 150-1, 153, 169
SWISSAIR—37, 94-5
SWITZERLAND—136
SYRIA—76, 87-95, 100, 108-10
SZALL, Joseph—141

T

TAFT, Julia Vadala—21-2
TAIWAN—2, 135, 170
TAN, Hassan—167
TANZANIA—31, 44, 64, 67-70
TARAKANDOV, Yuri—116
TAROM Airlines (Rumanian)—141
TELESIN, Yuli—119
TELL, Wasfi—92
TEPAVAC, Mirko—143
TET Offensive (1968)—10
TEXAS—22

THAILAND—3–4, 18, 24–6, 29. Map—27
TINDEMANS, Leo—74
TIRO, Abraham—61
TOLSTOY Foundation—125
TORIO, Ken—97
TORONTO Globe & Mail (newspaper)—119, 124
TORRES, Juan Jose—149
TOUPALIK, Vlastimil—136
TRAKHTENBERG, Lazar—117
TRANS World Airlines (TWA)—94–5, 144–5
TRI, Do Cao—8
TROYANOVSKY, Oleg—131
TRUDEAU, Pierre Elliott—66, 151
TSHOMBE, Daniel—70
TUMMERMAN, Alexis—127
TUNG An (Vietnamese refugee boat)—30
TUNNEY, Sen. John V. (D, Calif.)—20
TURKEY—1, 113, 117–8, 122, 165–6
TY, Pham Huy—8

U

UDRESCU, Dumitru—143
UGANDA—31, 64–70, 113, 130
ULLOA, Manuel—161
UNION of Soviet Socialist Republics (U.S.S.R.)—1, 73, 103, 116–33, 151
UNITED Nations (UN)—26, 28–9, 42, 44, 104–6, 112, 131, 145, 157, 168–9. High Commissioner for Refugees (UNHCR)—3–4, 24–5, 28–31, 34, 36, 40–1, 49, 122, 146–8, 150, 161, 165. Interim Force in Lebanon (UNIFIL)—115. Relief & Rehabilitation Administration (UNRRA)—2–3. Relief & Works Agency for Palestine Refugees (UNRWA)—4, 76, 96
UNITED States (U.S.)—8–11, 13–23, 28–9, 34–7, 42–4, 60, 67, 71, 119, 121, 123, 125–6, 130–1, 136–7, 142, 144–5, 150, 154–8, 161, 169
U.S. NEWS & World Report (magazine)—31
URIBE, Armando—151
URUGUAY—146–8, 151, 162–4

V

VALDEZ Palacio, Arturo—162
VALQUI, Camilo—162
Van AGT, Andreas A. M.—166, 168
Van der BYL, Pierter—56
VANCE, Cyrus—133
VANGUARD for Palestine Liberation (Arab guerrilla group)—77

VANGUARD of the People's War of Liberation (PLO guerrilla group)—77
VASALLO, Carlos—151
VASEK, Anton—135
VAZQUEZ Rojas, Genaro—159
VELASCO Alvarado, Juan—161
VENEZUELA—150, 160, 163–4
VIET Cong—7, 11, 13–4
VIETNAM—3–4, 6–30
VIETNAMESE Alliance Association (refugee group)—23
VIETNAMESE Catholic Committee (refugee group)—23
VIETNAMESE Community Foundation (refugee group)—23
VILLANUEVA del Campo, Armando—162
VINS, Georgi—133
VLCKOVA, Ruzena—136
VOGEL, Wolfgang—140
VOLOSHIN, Arkady—117
Von ROSEN, Count Carl-Gustav—34
VORONEL, Alexander—124
VORONTSEV, Yuli M.—119
VOSTRIKOV, Giennadi S.—119

W

WAKHWEYA, Emmanuel—67
WALDHEIM, Kurt—15, 39, 122–3, 131
WALLS, Lt. Gen. Peter—58
WASHINGTON Post (newspaper)—121
WEINBERGER, Caspar W.—22
WEST Germany (Germany, Federal Republic of)—2, 29–30, 66, 80, 94, 96–8, 101, 113–4, 122–3, 125, 136–42, 150, 153, 169
WILLIAM, Gough—15
WILSON, Harold—124
WOODS, Donald—62
WORLD Conference on Religion in Peace—25
WORLD Council of Churches—33, 58, 63
WORLD Health Organization, The—168–9
WORLD United Formosans for Independence—170
WORLD War I—2
WORLD War II—2
WORRALL, John—31

Y

YAGMAN, Lev N.—117
YAKOVSON, Anatoly—127
YAMANI, Ahmed—104
YANIN, Capt. Valery—122
YERMOLENKO, Georgi—124–5

YESENIN-Volpin, Alexander—120
YUGOSLAVIA—142–5, 151

Z

ZABOKI, Sandor—141
ZAIRE—31–2, 45, 70–4
ZALDIVAR Cadenas, Eugenio Enrique—156
ZALESKI, August—142
ZALMANSON, Izrail Y.—117
ZALMANSON, Sylva Y.—116–7, 124, 133
ZALMANSON, Volf—117, 133
ZAMBIA—50–1, 60–3, 73

ZAND, Mikhail I.—120
ZASIMOV, Valentin E.—128
ZDOVC, Edvin—144
ZIMBABWE African National Union
    (ZANU) (guerrilla group)—50–8
ZIMBABWE African People Union (ZAPU)
    (guerrilla group)—50–9
ZIMBABWE Declaration of Unity (black na-
    tionalist group)—51
ZIMBABWE Liberation Council (ZLC)
    (guerrilla group)—52
ZIMBABWE People Army (ZIPA) (guerrilla
    group)—54
ZIMBABWE Rhodesia—31–2, 42, 50–61
ZUKERMAN, Boris—119
ZURIKAT, Abdulla—142